FIFTEEN POETS

FIFTEEN POETS

CHAUCER SPENSER SHAKESPEARE
MILTON DRYDEN POPE COWPER
COLERIDGE WORDSWORTH SHELLEY
BYRON KEATS BROWNING
TENNYSON ARNOLD

OXFORD
AT THE CLARENDON PRESS
1941

OXFORD UNIVERSITY PRESS

AMEN HOUSE, E.C. 4

London Edinburgh Glasgow New York
Toronto Melbourne Capetown Bombay
Calcutta Madras

HUMPHREY MILFORD

PUBLISHER TO THE UNIVERSITY

PRINTED IN GREAT BRITAIN

PREFACE

Fifteen Poets contains a substantial sample—about 1,000 lines by each poet—of the best work of the great masters of English poetry from Chaucer to Matthew Arnold. The samples are large enough to give the reader a firm and distinct impression of the quality of each of these great writers. The selections are preceded by short essays of appreciation by various hands, and by summaries of the poets' lives.

The selections have not been limited to lyrics, but cover, as far as possible, the whole range of each poet's work. Obscure or obsolete words are explained in footnotes (part of the first piece by Chaucer has been paraphrased), and there is a glossary of proper names at the end.

It is hoped that *Fifteen Poets* will serve as a link between the normal type of anthology, in which a large number of poets are each represented by a small amount of verse, and the 'Complete Works' of the poets. Hitherto this gap has not, to the best of our knowledge, been filled by any single volume.

CONTENTS

GEOFFREY CHAUCER

GEOFFREY CHAUCER (1340?–1400), was son of John Chaucer (d. 1366), vintner, of London. In 1357 he was employed in the service of Lionel, afterwards duke of Clarence. He entered military service in 1359, served in France, was taken prisoner, but shortly ransomed. He married Philippa, probably sister of John of Gaunt's third wife. Chaucer held various positions at court, and was sent on a mission to Genoa and Florence in 1372–3, when he perhaps met Boccaccio and Petrarch. He died in 1400.

Chaucer's writings fall into three periods: (1) The period of French influence (1359–72), in which he uses the octosyllabic couplet. To this period belong *The Book of the Duchesse*, 1369, and the *Romaunt of the Rose*, so far as it was written by Chaucer. (2) The period of Italian influence, especially of Dante and Boccaccio, 1372–86, in which he uses mainly the 'heroic' stanza of seven lines and begins to use the heroic couplet. To this period belong *The Hous of Fame*; *The Parlement of Foules*; *Troilus and Criseyde*; *The Legend of Good Women*; and the first drafts of some of his tales. (3) The period of his maturity, 1386–1400, in which he uses the heroic couplet. To this period belong the *Canterbury Tales*, designed about 1387.

> Thorgh me men gon into that blysful place
> Of hertes hele and dedly woundes cure;
> Thorgh me men gon unto the welle of grace,
> There grene and lusty May shal evere endure.
> This is the wey to al good aventure.
> Be glad, thow redere, and thy sorwe ofcaste;
> Al open am I—passe in, and sped thee faste!

THE above verses, carved in large letters upon the gate leading into the park of *The Parlement of Foules*, are still the best brief summary of that world which we call the works of Geoffrey Chaucer. For once embarked upon a reading of his poems we are transported into another world —different from, yet similar to our own. However different the costumes, the manners, or the civilization that these poems portray on the surface, beneath there pulses a humanity, a knowledge of men and women that we at once recognize as fundamental and timeless.

But Chaucer did not arrive at this happy state of freedom without a great deal of hard work. As a young squire in a royal household he was early familiar with all that achieved wealth of poetry that France had to offer. The alliterative verse, still practised in England, had little attraction for him, and he turned to the more gracious and flowing measures of France, and slowly achieved a mastery of his materials which enabled him to move with such easy assurance in *Troilus and Criseyde* and *The Canterbury Tales*. This early verse is almost entirely lost, but Chaucer's work in this kind is seen at its best in his early *chef d'œuvre—The Book of the Duchesse*. In it the influence of France is everywhere apparent: the dream convention; the imitation of scenes in the *Roman de la Rose*; the personified abstractions; the May-morning *motif*—all these, allied with an absence of any profound emotion or piercing thought, indicate clearly enough where the poet's allegiance lies. Yet, even in so artificial and imitative a poem, Chaucer's management of the dream convention is notable, and still more notable is the sense of real loss which pervades the poem—a sense made the more poignant by reason of the charming background which forms its setting. Chaucer's apprenticeship ended with this poem.

The wider world into which he was introduced by reason of his embassies to France, Flanders, and Italy during the years 1368–79 is rapidly reflected in his work. All these countries contributed to his knowledge of life and letters. Travel and contact with the French only increased his indebtedness to French civilization. In Flanders the flourishing democracies, the busy commercial life, and the highly organized 'shop-work' of *scriptoria* or craftsman's lodge all made a fascinating study for this eager student of the medieval scene, but it was Italy that exercised the greatest influence upon him. He came to Italy first in 1372, and again in 1378—that is in his thirties, while he was still young enough to be open to new ideas and impressions, and yet old enough to know how to control and shape them to his own use. His senses could hardly have failed to thrill as he saw that wealth of architecture, sculpture, and painting which fourteenth-century Italy so proudly displayed in all its glowing originality and pristine beauty. And while the artist in him enjoyed all this, the man of the world absorbed the drama of life which he saw going on all around him. The fierce strife of faction and the harsh assertiveness of tyrants were obvious everywhere, and in his second mission he actually came into contact with one of these tyrants:

> Of Melan grete Barnabo Viscounte,
> God of delyt, and scourge of Lumbardye.

All this was accentuated by his study of the writings of the three great Italians of the 14th century—Dante, Petrarch, and Boccaccio. From them he learnt much, especially from Boccaccio. Dante sounded depths and passed to heights beyond his understanding, but nevertheless taught him much concerning the art of organic structure and of how to present his poetic material. Petrarch's music and humanism were things too refined and remote for Chaucer's full comprehension, but in the pages of Boccaccio he found a writer whom he could fully understand and appreciate, and whose work did not seem beyond his powers of imitation. Of all Boccaccio's work it was the story of Troilus and Cressida (*Il Filostrato*) that most attracted him. The detailed working out of that story, with its episodes and yet its organic movements, was a revelation to him. Yet, as he brooded over this clear-cut narrative of faithless love, with its highly sophisticated and limited characters, there came to him his own wider vision of how it should all be done, and *Troilus and Criseyde* was the result.

Into this poem of some 8,000 lines Chaucer pours all that he had hitherto learnt of men and women. He seems to revel in the fact that his poem is expressed in terms of the chivalric convention, as if determined to show 'a man's a man for a' that'. Troilus is not to be got rid of by calling him 'an undeveloped love-sick youth'. He is a warrior

3

among warriors, 'and, next his brother, holder up of Troy'. It is the measure of his love, and of the God of Love's overwhelming power, that when he loves it is with such abandon and intensity. His complete abasement, his tears, his cries for pity, his swoonings, &c., are all in the right chivalric tradition; yet, despite 'the lover's malady of Hereos' (Eros: Love), Chaucer never allows us to forget that below the conventional attitudinizing a man lies hid.

The other two great characters—Pandarus and Criseyde —are among Chaucer's finest creations. Boccaccio's comparatively shallow light o' love is turned into a lovely, highly complex figure. Chaucer's sojourn at the courts of princes had acquainted him with great ladies and their ways, and in Criseyde he catches their bearing and the tricks of voice and manner so perfectly that we are always convinced that she is a living human being, even at those moments when we least accept her reasons or approve her actions. Criseyde is shown to us at once timid yet proud, a tender, amorous, yielding spirit that clings gladly to the strong prince Troilus and afterwards to the strong man Diomede. The one thing she fears most is having to stand alone, and her consciousness of her own lack of strength is most pathetic. This lovely figure almost subdues Chaucer's judgement: he puts off and off the fatal moment when he must speak of her desertion of Troilus, and not till the final book does he do so, when he is forced to show 'this sely woman, slyding of courage,' unable to stand up to the force of circumstances which indeed were powerful enough to test a much stronger character. For she is no Juliet, no Cordelia, and the poet shows how her timid, dependent nature is worked upon until she yields, to become a byword for all time—'as false as Cressida'. Yet in the creation of this character he far transcends his original, as the sensual easily-persuaded Cressida is refashioned in the highly motivated many-sided Criseyde of his poem.

Pandarus, also, is no simple character. He is not the

young roué of Boccaccio, but is represented as Criseyde's uncle, a man of some years, whose garrulous, easy-going nature makes him everywhere welcome. He has a wealth of worldly-wise experience, and places it fully at the disposal of his niece and his friend. The service of love is peculiarly dear to him, and once he is convinced that Troilus is serious he does everything in his power to bring the lovers together. His resourcefulness, cunning, and *savoir faire* are too much for Criseyde, just as his comfort, encouragement, and action are the main agents in keeping Troilus from despair. Well may Criseyde cry on the morrow after the consummation of her love for Troilus

> For that ye ben! God yeve youre herte kare
> God help me so, ye caused al this fare.

This is not entirely true, however. The 'double sorwe of Troilus . . . how his aventures fallen Fro wo to wele, and after out of joye', is in part bound up inextricably with the fate of Troy, and Chaucer shows with the finest skill how the ineluctable pressure of the events of the Trojan war plays its part, and how helpless the lovers are against such forces. The 'star-crossed' lovers cannot control their fate, which seems the more moving as Chaucer's skill weaves about them those serene and lovely settings in which the nightingale sings, or maidens play at ball or listen to a Trojan song in sheltered gardens.

While *Troilus* was being written Chaucer was much occupied by divers official duties which all helped to increase his knowledge of humanity and of affairs, and gave him that intimate, sympathetic acquaintance with men and women which was the raw stuff of his final accomplishment—*The Canterbury Tales*. Whatever suggested the idea to him, a pilgrimage provided just the framework he needed—a method by which he could exhibit all his contemporaries in carefree action. The result is the drama of *The Canterbury Tales*.

Nowhere is this more apparent than in the 'links' which join the several tales one to the other. One tale leads inevitably to the next as the Host, or an incensed hearer, makes his comment on what has gone before and hastens to introduce his own subject. A man's character is made clear in his interjections, or his demands to tell the next tale, and the docile submission of some is well contrasted with the overbearing boisterousness of others. The Prologue needs no praise: it is a set piece, a glowing tapestry on which are brilliantly depicted the characters who spring into a more vivid life in the 'links' and in the tales. As for the tales themselves, Dryden has said the last word: 'Here is God's plenty!' Chaucer has given us something of every variety of medieval story—romances, lives of saints, the working of miracles are intermingled with more earthy tales told by churls for churls. There is also room for a number of stories dealing with various aspects of contemporary life, or others like the *Nun's Priest's Tale* or the *Pardoner's Tale* which instructed while they amused. So throughout, grave and gay, worldly, supernatural, or elemental—all have their turn and mingle together to make up the world of *The Canterbury Tales*.

This great body of stories is given exuberant life by the variety and richness of observation which Chaucer exercised in the making of his characters. The selective revealing detail that went to the description of 'hende Nicholas', or of Alison is only one of Chaucer's ways of creating character, just as his pregnant condensations—'and fro the bench he droof awey the cat', or 'she was proud, and pert as is a pye' are another. And with this eye for characterization goes an eye for constructive detail, and for the dramatic possibilities of a scene.

When we review all these qualities, and the range of Chaucer's work, we may well claim a high place for him. Arnold has accused him of a lack of 'high seriousness' and we may well admit that much of his work moves along with a controlled and easy tempo which is indicative of the equable and balanced mind that created the poetry.

Only now and then does any strong internal emotion give that pressure to his writing that we discern in 'Pray you undo this button', or 'O dark, dark, dark, amid the blaze of noon', or 'The world is too much with us, late and soon'.

We must not ask for this from Chaucer. Rather must we be grateful for the panorama of men and women which his tolerant inquiring eye constantly beheld and understood. Chaucer is great because of the 'wise passiveness' with which he viewed what Langland calls 'the faire feld ful of folk', and for the clarity, charm, and liveliness with which he reproduced it. As we read his verses we are conscious that we are being led by a wise and tolerant guide—one who knows the transitory nature of man's ardours and strivings, and yet one whose vision is as humane and compassionate as it is far-ranging and clear.

H. S. Bennett.

[Note. In the following extracts from Chaucer every final *e* is to be scanned as a separate syllable, except where it falls before an initial vowel or *h*. Inflexional *-es*, *-ed* are also separate syllables.]

7

CANTERBURY TALES
PROLOGUE
Here biginneth the Book of the Tales of Caunterbury.

Whan that Aprille with his shoures sote
The droghte of Marche hath perced to the rote,
And bathed every veyne in swich licour,
Of which vertu engendred is the flour;
Whan Zephirus eek with his swete breeth
Inspired hath in every holt and heeth
The tendre croppes, and the yonge sonne
Hath in the Ram his halfe cours y-ronne,
And smale fowles maken melodye,
That slepen al the night with open yë,
(So priketh hem nature in hir corages):
Than longen folk to goon on pilgrimages
(And palmers for to seken straunge strondes)
To ferne halwes, couthe in sondry londes;
And specially, from every shires ende
Of Engelond, to Caunterbury they wende,
The holy blisful martir for to seke,
That hem hath holpen, whan that they were seke.

Bifel that, in that seson on a day,
In Southwerk at the Tabard as I lay
Redy to wenden on my pilgrimage
To Caunterbury with ful devout corage,
At night was come in-to that hostelrye
Wel nyne and twenty in a companye,
Of sondry folk, by aventure y-falle

Prose paraphrase of ll. 1–22.

When April with its sweet showers has penetrated the dry earth of March down to the roots, and bathed their every vein in moisture such that from its vital power the flowers are born; when the west wind too has breathed with its sweet breath upon the tender shoots in every wood and field, and the spring sun has run the (April) half of its course through the Ram; and little birds that sleep all night with eyes open (for the dawn) make their music, because Nature so thrills their hearts: then men long to go on pilgrimage, and palmers to seek strange shores, (visiting the shrines of) distant saints famous in many lands; and above all, from the ends of every shire in England, they go to Canterbury to seek the holy, blessed martyr (St. Thomas) who has helped them when they were sick.

In felawshipe, and pilgrims were they alle,
That toward Caunterbury wolden ryde;
The chambres and the stables weren wyde,
And wel we weren esed atte beste.
And shortly, whan the sonne was to reste,
So hadde I spoken with hem everichon,
That I was of hir felawshipe anon,
And made forward erly for to ryse,
To take our wey, ther as I yow devyse.

A-morwe, whan that day bigan to springe,
Up roos our host, and was our aller[1] cok,
And gadrede us togidre, alle in a flok,
And forth we riden, a litel more than pas,[2]
Un-to the watering of seint Thomas.
And there our host bigan his hors areste,
And seyde; 'Lordinges, herkneth, if yow leste.[3]
Ye woot your forward,[4] and I it yow recorde.[5]
If even-song and morwe-song acorde,
Lat see now who shal telle the firste tale.
As ever mote I drinke wyn or ale,
Who-so be rebel to my jugement
Shal paye for al that by the weye is spent.
Now draweth cut,[6] er that we ferrer[7] twinne;[8]
He which that hath the shortest shal biginne.
'Sire knight,' quod he, 'my maister and my lord,
Now draweth cut, for that is myn acord.
Cometh neer,' quod he, 'my lady prioresse;
And ye, sir clerk, lat be your shamfastnesse,[9]
Ne studieth[10] noght; ley hond to, every man.'

One day in that season as I lay at the Tabard Inn in Southwark, ready to go with very devout heart on my pilgrimage to Canterbury, in the evening there happened to come to the inn as many as twenty-nine in a party, a mixed lot whom chance had brought together, and they were all pilgrims who intended to ride to Canterbury. Rooms and stables were ample, and we were comfortably entertained in the best style. And, in short, by sunset I had spoken with every one of them so that I became forthwith one of their party, and we agreed to rise early to start our journey to Canterbury, as I describe it to you.

[1] our aller] of us all　　[2] pas] walking pace　　[3] leste] list　　[4] forward] compact　　[5] recorde] remind of　　[6] cut] lot　　[7] ferrer] further
[8] twinne] separate　　[9] shamfastnesse] shyness　　[10] studieth] meditate

Anon to drawen every wight bigan,
And shortly for to tellen, as it was,
Were it by aventure, or sort,[1] or cas,[2]
The sothe is this, the cut fil to the knight,
Of which full blythe and glad was every wight;
And telle he moste his tale, as was resoun,
By forward and by composicioun,[3]
As ye han herd; what nedeth wordes mo?
And whan this gode man saugh it was so,
As he that wys was and obedient
To kepe his forward by his free assent,
He seyde: 'Sin I shal beginne the game,
What, welcome be the cut, a Goddes name!
Now lat us ryde, and herkneth what I seye.'
And with that word we riden forth our weye.

(Prologue, 1–34, 822–58).

INTRODUCTION TO THE MAN OF LAW'S PROLOGUE

The wordes of the Hoost to the companye

Our Hoste sey[4] wel that the brighte sonne
Th' ark[5] of his artificial day[6] had ronne
The fourthe part, and half an houre, and more;
And though he were not depe expert in lore,
He wiste[7] it was the eightetethe day
Of April, that is messager to May;
And sey wel that the shadwe of every tree
Was as in lengthe[8] the same quantitee
That was the body erect that caused it.
And therefor by the shadwe he took his wit[9]
That Phebus, which that shoon so clere and brighte,
Degrees was fyve and fourty clombe on highte;
And for that day, as in that latitude,
It was ten of the clokke, he gan[10] conclude,
And sodeynly he plighte[11] his hors aboute.

---

[1] sort] fate   [2] cas] chance   [3] composicioun] agreement
[4] sey] saw   [5] ark] arc of the horizon   [6] artificial day] the time
from sunrise to sunset   [7] wiste] knew   [8] as in lengthe] with respect
to its length   [9] wit] knowledge   [10] gan] did   [11]plighte] pulled

'Lordinges,' quod he, 'I warne yow, al this route,
The fourthe party[1] of this day is goon;
Now, for the love of god and of seint John,
Leseth[2] no tyme, as ferforth as ye may;[3]
Lordinges, the tyme wasteth night and day,
And steleth from us, what[4] prively slepinge,
And what thurgh necligence in our wakinge,
As dooth the streem, that turneth never agayn,
Descending fro the montaigne in-to playn.
Wel can Senek, and many a philosophre
Biwailen tyme, more than gold in cofre.
"For los of catel[5] may recovered be,
But los of tyme shendeth[6] us," quod he.
It wol nat come agayn, withouten drede,[7]
Na more than wol Malkins[8] maydenhede,
Whan she hath lost it in hir wantownesse;
Lat us nat moulen[9] thus in ydelnesse.
Sir man of lawe,' quod he, 'so have ye blis,[10]
Tel us a tale anon,[11] as forward is;[12]
Ye been submitted[13] thurgh your free assent
To stonde in this cas[14] at my jugement.[15]
Acquiteth yow,[16] and holdeth your biheste,[17]
Than have ye doon your devoir[18] atte leste.'[19]
'Hoste,' quod he, '*depardieux*[20] ich assente,
To breke forward is not myn entente.
Biheste is dette, and I wol holde fayn[21]
Al my biheste; I can no better seyn.
For swich lawe as man yeveth another wight,
He sholde him-selven usen it by right;
Thus wol our text;[22] but natheles certeyn
I can right now no thrifty[23] tale seyn,

[1] party] part   [2] leseth] lose   [3] as ferforth as ye may] as far as
you can   [4] what] what with   [5] catel] goods   [6] shendeth] ruins
[7] withouten drede] there is no doubt   [8] Malkin] (the name for a
wanton woman)   [9] moulen] grow mouldy, rot   [10] so have ye blis]
as you hope to reach the joy of heaven   [11] anon] forthwith   [12] as
forward is] according to the agreement   [13] ye been submitted] you
have agreed   [14] cas] affair   [15] jugement] decree   [16] acquiteth
yow] absolve yourself   [17] biheste] promise   [18] devoir] duty   [19] atte
leste] at least   [20] *depardieux*] in God's name   [21] holde fayn] gladly
perform   [22] thus wol our text] that is what the phrase implies
[23] thrifty] profitable

But Chaucer, though he can but lewedly[1]
On metres and on ryming craftily,
Hath seyd hem in swich English as he can
Of olde tyme, as knoweth many a man.
And if he have not seyd hem, leve[2] brother,
In o book, he hath seyd hem in another.
For he hath told of loveres up and doun[3]
Mo than Ovyde made of mencioun
In his Epistelles, that been ful olde.
What[4] sholde I tellen hem, sin they ben tolde?
In youthe he made of Ceys and Alcion,
And sithen[5] hath he spoke of everichon,
Thise noble wyves and thise loveres eke.
Who-so that wol his large volume seke
Cleped the Seintes Legende of Cupyde,
Ther may he seen the large woundes wyde
Of Lucresse, and of Babilan Tisbee;
The swerd of Dido for the false Enee;
The tree of Phillis for hir Demophon;
The pleinte of Dianire and Hermion,
Of Adriane and of Isiphilee;
The bareyne yle stonding in the see;
The dreynte[6] Leander for his Erro;
The teres of Eleyne, and eek the wo
Of Brixseyde, and of thee, Ladomëa;
The crueltee of thee, queen Medëa,
Thy litel children hanging by the hals[7]
For thy Jason, that was of love so fals!
O Ypermistra, Penelopee, Alceste,
Your wyfhod[8] he comendeth with the beste!
        But certeinly no word ne wryteth he
Of thilke wikke[9] ensample of Canacee,
That lovede hir owne brother sinfully;
Of swiche cursed stories I sey 'fy';
Or elles of Tyro Apollonius,
How that the cursed king Antiochus

---

[1] can but lewedly on] has but little skill in   [2] leve] dear   [3] up
and doun] in various places (in his books)   [4] what] why   [5] sithen]
afterwards   [6] dreynte] drowned   [7] hals] neck   [8] wyfhod]
womanhood   [9] wikke] wicked

Birafte his doghter of hir maydenhede,
That is so horrible a tale for to rede,
Whan he hir threw up-on the pavement.
And therefor he, of ful avysement,[1]
Nolde never[2] wryte in none of his sermouns[3]
Of swiche unkinde[4] abhominaciouns,
Ne I wol noon reherse,[5] if that I may.[6]
But of[7] my tale how shal I doon this day?
Me were looth[8] be lykned, doutelees,
To Muses that men clepe[9] Pierides—
Metamorphoseos[10] wot what I mene:—
But nathelees, I recche noght a bene[11]
Though I come after him with hawe-bake;[12]
I speke in prose, and lat him rymes make.'
And with that word he, with a sobre chere,[13]
Bigan his tale, as ye shal after here.

The Prologe of the Mannes Tale of Lawe

O hateful harm! condicion of poverte!
With thurst, with cold, with hunger so confounded!
To asken help thee shameth in thyn herte;
If thou noon aske, with nede artow[14] so wounded,
That verray nede unwrappeth al thy wounde hid!
Maugree thyn heed,[15] thou most for indigence
Or stele, or begge, or borwe thy despence![16]

Thou blamest Crist, and seyst ful bitterly,
He misdeparteth[17] richesse temporal;
Thy neighebour thou wytest[18] sinfully,
And seyst thou hast to lyte,[19] and he hath al.
'Parfay,' seistow, 'somtyme he rekne[20] shal,
Whan that his tayl shal brennen in the glede,[21]
For[22] he noght helpeth needfulle in hir nede.'

---

[1] offul avysement] quite deliberately   [2] nolde never] always refused to
[3] sermouns] discourses, writings   [4] unkinde] unnatural   [5] reherse]
recount   [6] if that I may] as far as in me lies   [7] of] in regard to   [8] me
were looth] it would be displeasing to me   [9] clepe] call   [10] Ovid's *Meta-
morphoses*   [11] recche] care   [12] hawe-bake] baked haws, i.e. plain fare
[13] chere] countenance   [14] artow [art thou   [15] maugree thyn heed] in
spite of all you can do   [16] despence] money for expenses   [17] misdepar-
teth] divides amiss   [18] wytest] blamest, reproachest   [19] to lyte] too little
[20] rekne] give an account   [21] glede] glowing coal   [22] for] because

Herkne what is the sentence[1] of the wyse:—
'Bet is to dyën than have indigence;'
'Thy selve[2] neighebour wol thee despyse;'
If thou be povre, farwel thy reverence![3]
Yet of the wyse man tak his sentence:—
'Alle the dayes of povre men ben wikke;'
Be war therfor, er thou come in that prikke![4]

'If thou be povre, thy brother hateth thee,
And alle thy freendes fleen fro thee, alas!'
O riche marchaunts, ful of wele[5] ben ye,
O noble, o prudent folk, as in this cas!
Your bagges been nat filled with *ambes as*,[6]
But with *sis cink*,[7] that renneth for[8] your chaunce;
At Cristemasse merie may ye daunce!

Ye seken lond and see for your winninges,
As wyse folk ye knowen al th'estaat
Of regnes;[9] ye ben fadres of tydinges
And tales, bothe of pees and of debat.[10]
I were right now of tales desolat,[11]
Nere that[12] a marchaunt, goon is many a yere,
Me taughte a tale, which that ye shal here.

THE PARDONERS TALE

Here biginneth the Pardoners Tale

In Flaundres whylom[13] was a companye
Of yonge folk, that haunteden[14] folye,
As ryot,[15] hasard,[16] stewes,[17] and tavernes,
Wher-as,[18] with harpes, lutes, and giternes,[19]
They daunce and pleye at dees[20] bothe day and night,
And ete also and drinken over hir might,[21]

---

[1] sentence] opinion   [2] selve] very   [3] thy reverence] the respect shown to you   [4] in that prikke] to that point   [5] wele] wealth
[6] *ambes as*] double aces   [7] *sis cink*] six-five, i.e. a throw with two dice
[8] renneth for] runs in favour of   [9] estaat of regnes] condition of king-doms   [10] debat] war   [11] desolat] destitute   [12] nere that] were it not that   [13] whylom] once   [14] haunteden] practised   [15] ryot] riotous living   [16] hasard] a game of dice   [17] stewes] brothels
[18] wher-as] where   [19] giternes] guitars   [20] dees] dice   [21] over hir might] beyond their capacity

Thurgh which they doon the devel sacrifyse[1]
With-in that develes temple, in cursed wyse,
By superfluitee[2] abhominable;
Hir othes been so grete and so dampnable,
That it is grisly[3] for to here hem swere;
Our blissed lordes body they to-tere;[4]
Hem thoughte[5] Jewes rente him noght y-nough;
And ech of hem at otheres sinne lough.[6]
And right anon than comen tombesteres[7]
Fetys and smale,[8] and yonge fruytesteres,[9]
Singers with harpes, baudes, wafereres,[10]
Whiche been the verray develes officeres
To kindle and blowe the fyr of lecherye,
That is annexed[11] un-to glotonye;
The holy writ take I to my witnesse,
That luxurie[12] is in wyn and dronkenesse.

Lo, how that drunken Loth, unkindely,[13]
Lay by his doghtres two, unwitingly;
So dronke he was, he niste[14] what he wroghte.

Herodes, (who-so wel the stories soghte),[15]
Whan he of wyn was replet at his feste,
Right at his owene table he yaf his heste[16]
To sleen the Baptist John ful giltelees.

Senek seith eek a good word douteless;
He seith, he can no difference finde
Bitwix a man that is out of his minde
And a man which that is dronkelewe,[17]
But that woodnesse,[18] y-fallen in a shrewe,[19]
Perservereth lenger than doth dronkenesse.
O glotonye, ful of cursednesse,
O cause first of our confusioun,

---

[1] they doon the devel sacrifyse] they do sacrifice to the devil   [2] superfluitee] excess   [3] grisly] horrible   [4] to-tere] tear in pieces   [5] hem thoughte] it seemed to them   [6] lough] laughed   [7] tombesteres] dancing-girls   [8] fetys and smale] graceful and slender   [9] fruytesteres] fruit-sellers   [10] wafereres] sellers of cakes   [11] annexed] attached   [12] luxurie] lust   [13] unkindely] in a way contrary to nature   [14] niste] knew not   [15] who-so wel the stories soghte] as any who would consult the 'Stories' may see   [16] yaf his heste] gave his command   [17] dronkelewe] drunk   [18] But that woodnesse, &c.] Except that madness, when it has come upon a man of evil nature, lasts longer   [19] shrewe] rascal

O original of our dampnacioun,
Til Crist had boght us with his blood agayn!
Lo, how dere, shortly for to sayn,
Aboght was thilke cursed vileinye;
Corrupt was al this world for glotonye!

Adam our fader, and his wyf also,
Fro Paradys to labour and to wo
Were driven for that vyce, it is no drede;[1]
For whyl that Adam fasted, as I rede,
He was in Paradys; and whan that he
Eet of the fruyt defended[2] on the tree,
Anon he was out-cast to wo and peyne.
O glotonye, on thee wel oghte us pleyne!
O, wiste a man[3] how many maladyes
Folwen of excesse and of glotonyes,
He wolde been the more mesurable
Of his diete, sittinge at his table.
Allas! the shorte throte, the tendre mouth,
Maketh that, Est and West, and North and South,
In erthe, in eir, in water men to-swinke[4]
To get a glotoun deyntee mete and drinke!
Of this matere, o Paul, wel canstow trete,
'Mete un-to wombe,[5] and wombe eek un-to mete,
Shal god destroyen bothe,' as Paulus seith.
Allas! a foul thing it is, by my feith,
To seye this word, and fouler is the dede,
Whan man so drinketh of the whyte and rede,[6]
That of his throte he maketh his privee,
Thurgh thilke cursed superfluitee.

The apostel weping seith ful pitously,
'Ther walken many of whiche yow told have I,
I seye it now weping with pitous voys,
[That] they been enemys of Cristes croys,
Of whiche the ende is deeth, wombe is her god.'
O wombe! O bely! O stinking cod,[7]
Fulfild[8] of donge and of corrupcioun!

---

[1] it is no drede] there is no doubt   [2] defended] forbidden   [3] wiste
a man] if a man knew   [4] to-swinke] toil hard   [5] wombe] belly
[6] whyte and rede] white wine and red wine   [7] cod] belly, stomach
[8] fulfild] filled full

At either ende of thee foul is the soun.[1]
How greet labour and cost is thee to finde![2]
Thise cokes, how they stampe, and streyne, and grinde,
And turnen substaunce in-to accident,[3]
To fulfille al thy likerous talent![4]
Out of the harde bones knokke they
The mary,[5] for they caste noght a-wey
That may go thurgh the golet softe and swote;
Of spicerye,[6] of leef, and bark, and rote
Shal been his sauce y-maked by delyt,
To make him yet a newer appetyt.
But certes, he that haunteth swich delyces[7]
Is deed, whyl that he liveth in tho vyces.

  A lecherous thing is wyn, and dronkenesse
Is ful of stryving and of wrecchednesse.
O dronke man, disfigured is thy face,
Sour is thy breeth, foul artow to embrace,
And thurgh thy dronke nose semeth the soun
As though thou seydest ay 'Sampsoun, Sampsoun';
And yet, god wot, Sampsoun drank never no wyn.
Thou fallest, as it were a stiked swyn;
Thy tonge is lost, and al thyn honest cure;[8]
For dronkenesse is verray sepulture
Of mannes wit and his discrecioun.
In whom that drinke hath dominacioun,
He can no conseil kepe, it is no drede.
Now kepe yow fro the whyte and fro the rede,
And namely[9] fro the whyte wyn of Lepe,
That is to selle[10] in Fish-strete or in Chepe.
This wyn of Spayne crepeth subtilly
In othere wynes, growing faste by,
Of which ther ryseth swich fumositee,[11]
That whan a man hath dronken draughtes three,
And weneth[12] that he be at hoom in Chepe,
He is in Spayne, right at the toune of Lepe,

---

[1] soun] sound   [2] is thee to finde] (it) is to provide for thee   [3] substaunce in-to accident] essence into appearance   [4] likerous talent] greedy appetite   [5] mary] marrow   [6] spicerye] mixture of spices   [7] delyces] pleasures   [8] honest cure] care for honourable things   [9] namely] especially   [10] to selle] for sale   [11] fumositee] vapour   [12] weneth] imagines

Nat at the Rochel, ne at Burdeux toun;
And thanne wol he seye, 'Sampsoun, Sampsoun.'
   But herkneth, lordings, o word, I yow preye,
That alle the sovereyn actes, dar I seye,
Of victories in th'olde testament,
Thurgh verray god, that is omnipotent,
Were doon in abstinence and in preyere;
Loketh the Bible, and ther ye may it lere.[1]

   Loke, Attila, the grete conqueror,
Deyde in his sleep, with shame and dishonour,
Bledinge ay at his nose in dronkenesse;
A capitayn shoulde live in sobrenesse.
And over al this, avyseth[2] yow right wel
What was comaunded un-to Lamuel—
Nat Samuel, but Lamuel, seye I—
Redeth the Bible, and finde it expresly
Of wyn-yeving to hem that han justyse.[3]
Na-more of this, for it may wel suffyse.

   And now that I have spoke of glotonye,
Now wol I yow defenden[4] hasardrye.[5]
Hasard is verray moder of lesinges,
And of deceite, and cursed forsweringes,
Blaspheme of Crist, manslaughtre, and wast also
Of catel and of tyme; and forthermo,
It is repreve[6] and contrarie of honour
For to ben holde a commune hasardour.
And ever the hyër he is of estaat,
The more is he holden desolaat.[7]
If that a prince useth hasardrye,
In all governaunce and policye
He is, as by commune opinioun,
Y-holde the lasse in reputacioun.

   Stilbon, that was a wys embassadour,
Was sent to Corinthe, in ful greet honour,
Fro Lacidomie, to make hir alliaunce.
And whan he cam, him happede,[8] par chaunce,

---

[1] lere] learn   [2] avyseth] consider   [3] of wyn-yeving to hem that
han justyse] about giving wine to those who dispense justice   [4] de-
fenden] forbid   [5] hasardrye] playing at hazard   [6] repreve] shame
[7] holden desolaat] shunned   [8] him happede] it befell him

That alle the grettest that were of that lond,
Pleyinge atte hasard he hem fond.[1]
For which,[2] as sone as it mighte be,
He stal him[3] hoom agayn to his contree,
And seyde, 'ther wol I nat lese my name,[4]
N' I wol nat take on me so greet defame,[5]
Yow for to allye un-to none hasardours.
Sendeth othere wyse embassadours;
For, by my trouthe, me were lever dye,
Than I yow sholde to hasardours allye.
For ye that been so glorious in honours
Shul nat allyen yow with hasardours
As by my wil,[6] ne as by my tretee.'
This wyse philosophre thus seyde he.

Loke eek[7] that, to the king Demetrius
The king of Parthes, as the book seith us,
Sente him a paire of dees of gold in scorn,
For he hadde used hasard ther-biforn;
For which he heeld his glorie or his renoun
At no value or reputacioun.
Lordes may finden other maner pley
Honeste y-nough to dryve the day awey.[8]

Now wol I speke of othes false and grete
A word or two, as olde bokes trete.
Gret swering is a thing abhominable,
And false swering is yet more reprevable.
The heighe god forbad swering at al,
Witnesse on Mathew; but in special
Of swering seith the holy Jeremye,
'Thou shalt seye sooth thyn othes, and nat lye,
And swere in dome,[9] and eek in rightwisnesse;'
But ydel swering is a cursednesse.
Bihold and see, that in the firste table
Of heighe goddes hestes honurable,
How that the seconde heste of him is this—

---

[1] fond] found   [2] for which] on account of which   [3] stal him]
stole, went stealthily   [4] lese my name] lose my reputation   [5] defame]
dishonour   [6] as by my wil] with my consent   [7] loke eek] consider also   [8] dryve the day awey] pass the time   [9] dome]
judgement

'Tak nat my name in ydel[1] or amis.'
Lo, rather[2] he forbedeth swich swering
Than homicyde or many a cursed thing;
I seye that, as by ordre, thus it stondeth;
This knowen,[3] that his hestes understondeth,
How that the second heste of god is that.
And forther over,[4] I wol thee telle al plat,[5]
That vengeance shal nat parten[6] from his hous,
That of his othes is to outrageous.[7]
'By goddes precious herte, and by his nayles,
And by the blode of Crist, that is in Hayles,[8]
Seven is my chaunce,[9] and thyn is cink and treye;[10]
By goddes armes, if thou falsly pleye,
This dagger shal thurgh-out thyn herte go'—
This fruyt cometh of the bicched[11] bones two,
Forswering, ire, falsnesse, homicyde.
Now, for the love of Crist that for us dyde,
Leveth your othes, bothe grete and smale;
But, sirs, now wol I telle forth my tale.

THISE ryotoures three, of whiche I telle,
Longe erst er pryme[12] rong of any belle,
Were set hem in a taverne for to drinke;
And as they satte, they herde a belle clinke
Biforn[13] a cors, was carried to his grave;
That oon of hem gan callen to his knave,[14]
'Go bet,'[15] quod he, 'and axe redily,
What cors is this that passeth heer forby;
And look that thou reporte his name wel.'

'Sir,' quod this boy, 'it nedeth never-a-del.[16]
It was me told, er ye cam heer, two houres;
He was, pardee, an old felawe[17] of youres;
And sodenly he was y-slayn to-night,[18]

[1] in ydel] in vain   [2] rather] sooner, earlier   [3] this knowen, &c.]
they that understand his commandments know this   [4] forther over]
moreover   [5] plat] plainly   [6] parten] depart   [7] outrageous]
violent   [8] Hayles] Abbey of Hailes, in Gloucestershire. Portion of
Christ's blood supposed to be preserved there   [9] chaunce] i.e. number
[10] cink and treye] five and three   [11] bicched] cursed   [12] pryme] *c.*
nine a.m.   [13] cors] body (that)   [14] knave] boy   [15] go bet] go
better, i.e. quickly   [16] it nedeth never-a-del] there is no need at all
[17] felawe] companion   [18] to-night] last night

For-dronke,[1] as he sat on his bench upright;
Ther cam a privee theef, men clepeth[2] Deeth,
That in this contree al the peple sleeth,
And with his spere he smoot his herte a-two,
And wente his wey with-outen wordes mo.
He hath a thousand slayn this pestilence:
And, maister, er ye come in his presence,
Me thinketh that it were necessarie
For to be war of swich an adversarie:
Beth redy for to mete him evermore.
Thus taughte me my dame,[3] I sey na-more.'
'By seinte Marie,' seyde this taverner,
'The child seith sooth, for he hath slayn this yeer,
Henne over a myle,[4] with-in a greet village,
Both man and womman, child and hyne,[5] and page.
I trowe his habitacioun be there;
To been avysed[6] greet wisdom it were,
Er that he dide a man a dishonour.'
'Ye, goddes armes,' quod this ryotour,
'Is it swich peril with him for to mete?
I shal him seke by wey and eek by strete,
I make avow to goddes digne[7] bones!
Herkneth, felawes, we three been al ones;[8]
Lat ech of us holde up his hond til other,
And ech of us bicomen otheres brother,[9]
And we wol sleen this false traytour Deeth;
He shal be slayn, which that so many sleeth,
By goddes dignitee, er it be night.'
   Togidres han thise three her trouthes plight,
To live and dyen ech of hem for other,
As though he were his owene y-boren brother.
And up they sterte al dronken, in this rage,
And forth they goon towardes that village,
Of which the taverner had spoke biforn,
And many a grisly ooth than han they sworn,
And Cristes blessed body they to-rente—

---

[1] for-dronke] very drunk   [2] clepeth] call   [3] dame] mother
[4] henne over a myle] over a mile from here   [5] hyne] servant
[6] to been avysed] to consider, reflect   [7] digne] honoured   [8] al
ones] all of one mind   [9] brother] i.e. sworn friend

Deeth shal be deed, if that they may him hente.[1]
   Whan they han goon nat fully half a myle,
Right as they wolde han troden over a style,
An old man and a povre with hem mette.
This olde man ful mekely hem grette,
And seyde thus, 'now, lordes, god yew see!'[2]
   The proudest of this ryotoures three
Answerde agayn, 'what? carl, with sory grace,[3]
Why artow al forwrapped[4] save thy face?
Why livestow so longe in so greet age?'
   This olde man gan loke in his visage,
And seyde thus, 'for I ne can nat finde
A man, though that I walked in-to Inde,
Neither in citee nor in no village,
That wolde chaunge his youthe for myn age;
And therfore moot[5] I han myn age stille,
As longe time as it is goddes wille.
   Ne deeth, allas! ne wol nat han my lyf;
Thus walke I, lyk a restelees caityf,
And on the ground, which is my modres gate,
I knokke with my staf, bothe erly and late,
And seye, "leve[6] moder, leet me in!
Lo, how I vanish, flesh, and blood, and skin!
Allas! whan shul my bones been at reste?
Moder, with yow wolde I chaunge my cheste,
That in my chambre longe tyme hath be,
Ye! for an heyre clout to wrappe me!"
But yet to me she wol nat do that grace,[7]
For which ful pale and welked[8] is my face.
   But, sirs, to yow it is no curteisye
To speken to an old man vileinye,
But[9] he trespasse in worde, or elles in dede.
In holy writ y e may your-self wel rede,
"Agayns[10] an old man, hoor upon his heed,
Ye sholde aryse;" wherfor I yeve yow reed,[11]

---

[1] hente] seize   [2] god yew see] may God preserve you   [3] carl, with sory grace] ill-favoured churl   [4] forwrapped] wrapped up   [5] moot] must   [6] leve] dear   [7] grace] favour   [8] welked] withered   [9] but] unless   [10] agayns] in the presence of   [11] yeve reed] give counsel, advise

Ne dooth un-to an old man noon harm now,
Na-more than ye wolde men dide to yow
In age, if that ye so longe abyde;
And god be with yow, wher ye go or ryde.
I moot go thider as I have to go.'
   'Nay, olde cherl, by god, thou shalt nat so,'
Seyde this other hasardour anon;
'Thou partest nat so lightly, by seint John!
Thou spak right now of thilke traitour Deeth,
That in this contree alle our frendes sleeth.
Have heer my trouthe, as thou art his aspye,
Tel wher he is, or thou shalt it abye,[1]
By god, and by the holy sacrament!
For soothly thou art oon of his assent,[2]
To sleen us yonge folk, thou false theef!'
   'Now, sirs,' quod he, 'if that yow be so leef[3]
To finde Deeth, turne up this croked wey,
For in that grove I lafte him, by my fey,
Under a tree, and ther he wol abyde;
Nat for your boost he wol him no-thing hyde.
See ye that ook?[4] right ther ye shul him finde.
God save yow, that boghte agayn mankinde,
And yow amende!'—thus seyde this olde man.
And everich of thise ryotoures ran,
Til he cam to that tree, and ther they founde
Of florins fyne of golde y-coyned rounde
Wel ny an eighte busshels, as hem thoughte.
No lenger thanne after Deeth they soughte,
But ech of hem so glad was of that sighte,
For that the florins been so faire and brighte,
That doun they sette hem by this precious hord.
The worste of hem he spake the firste word.
   'Brethren,' quod he, 'tak kepe[5] what I seye;
My wit is greet, though I bourde[6] and pleye.
This tresor hath fortune un-to us yiven,
In mirthe and jolitee our lyf to liven,
And lightly as it comth, so wol we spende.

---

[1] it abye] pay for, suffer for, it   [2] assent] opinion   [3] leef]
desirous   [4] ook] oak   [5] kepe] heed   [6] bourde] jest

Ey! goddes precious dignitee! who wende[1]
To-day, that we sholde han so fair a grace?[2]
But mighte this gold be caried fro this place
Hoom to myn hous, or elles un-to youres—
For wel ye woot[3] that al this gold is oures—
Than were we in heigh felicitee.
But trewely, by daye it may nat be;
Men wolde seyn that we were theves stronge,
And for our owene tresor doon us honge.[4]
This tresor moste y-caried be by nighte
As wysly and as slyly as it mighte.
Wherfore I rede that cut[5] among us alle
Be drawe, and lat see wher the cut wol falle;
And he that hath the cut with herte blythe
Shal renne to the toune, and that ful swythe,[6]
And bringe us breed and wyn ful prively.
And two of us shul kepen subtilly
This tresor wel; and, if he wol nat tarie,
Whan it is night, we wol this tresor carie
By oon assent, wher-as us thinketh best.'
That oon of hem the cut broughte in his fest,[7]
And bad hem drawe, and loke wher it wol falle;
And it fil on the yongeste of hem alle;
And forth toward the toun he wente anon.
And al-so sone as that he was gon,
That oon of hem spak thus un-to that other,
'Thou knowest wel thou art my sworne brother,
Thy profit wol I telle thee anon.
Thou woost wel that our felawe is agon;
And heer is gold, and that ful greet plentee,
That shal departed[8] been among us three.
But natheles, if I can shape it so
That it departed were among us two
Hadde I nat doon a freendes torn to thee?'
  That other answerde, 'I noot how that may be;
He woot how that the gold is with us tweye,
What shal we doon, what shal we to him seye?'

[1] wende] would have thought   [2] so fair a grace] such good fortune
[3] woot] know   [4] doon us honge] have us hanged   [5] cut] lot
[6] swythe] quickly   [7] fest] fist   [8] departed] shared

'Shal it be conseil?'[1] seyde the first shrewe,[2]
'And I shal tellen thee, in wordes fewe,
What we shal doon, and bringe it wel aboute.'
  'I graunte,'[3] quod that other, 'out of doute,'[4]
That, by my trouthe, I wol thee nat biwreye.'[5]
  'Now,' quod the firste, 'thou woost wel we be tweye,
And two of us shul strenger be than oon.
Look whan that he is set,[6] and right anoon
Arys, as though thou woldest with him pleye;
And I shal ryve him thurgh the sydes tweye
Whyl that thou strogelest with him as in game,
And with thy dagger look thou do the same;
And than shal al this gold departed be,
My dere freend, bitwixen me and thee;
Than may we bothe our lustes al fulfille,
And pleye at dees right at our owene wille.'
And thus acorded been thise shrewes tweye
To sleen the thridde, as ye han herd me seye.
This yongest, which that wente un-to the toun,
Ful ofte in herte he rolleth up and doun[7]
The beautee of thise florins newe and brighte.
'O lord!' quod he, 'if so were that I mighte
Have al this tresor to my-self allone,
Ther is no man that liveth under the trone
Of god, that sholde live so mery as I!'
And atte laste the feend, our enemy,
Putte in his thought that he shold poyson beye,[8]
With which he mighte sleen his felawes tweye;
For-why[9] the feend fond him in swich lyvinge,[10]
That he had leve him to sorwe bringe,
For this was outrely[11] his fulle entente
To sleen hem bothe, and never to repente.
And forth he gooth, no lenger wolde he tarie,
Into the toun, un-to a pothecarie,
And preyed him, that he him wolde selle
Som poyson, that he mighte his rattes quelle;[12]

---

[1] conseil] a secret   [2] shrewe] scoundrel   [3] graunte] agree   [4] out of doute] without doubt   [5] biwreye] betray   [6] set] seated [7] rolleth up and doun] revolves, considers   [8] beye] buy   [9] for-why] because   [10] lyvinge] way of life   [11] outrely] utterly   [12] quelle] kill

And eek ther was a polcat in his hawe,[1]
That, as he seyde, his capouns[2] hadde y-slawe,[3]
And fayn he wolde wreke[4] him, if he mighte,
On vermin, that destroyed him by nighte.
  The pothecarie answerde, 'and thou shalt have
A thing that, al-so god my soule save,[5]
In al this world ther nis no creature,
That ete or dronke hath of this confiture[6]
Noght but the mountance[7] of a corn of whete,
That he ne shal his lyf anon forlete;[8]
Ye, sterve he shal, and that in lasse whyle
Than thou wolt goon a paas nat but a myle;[9]
This poyson is so strong and violent.'
  This cursed man hath in his hond y-hent
This poyson in a box, and sith[10] he ran
In-to the nexte strete, un-to a man,
And borwed [of] him large botels three;
And in the two his poyson poured he;
The thridde he kepte clene for his drinke.
For al the night he shoop him[11] for to swinke[12]
In caryinge of the gold out of that place.
And whan this ryotour, with sory grace,
Had filled with wyn his grete botels three,
To his felawes agayn repaireth he.
  What nedeth it to sermone[13] of it more?
For right as they had cast[14] his deeth bifore,
Right so they han him slayn, and that anon.
And whan that this was doon, thus spak that oon,
'Now lat us sitte and drinke, and make us merie,
And afterward we wol his body berie.'
And with that word it happed him, par acas,[15]
To take the botel ther the poyson was,
And drank, and yaf his felawe drinke also,
For which anon they storven[16] bothe two.

---

[1] hawe] yard   [2] capouns] capons   [3] y-slawe] slain   [4] wreke him] avenge himself   [5] al-so god, &c.] as (I hope) God may save my soul   [6] confiture] mixture   [7] mountance] amount   [8] forlete] give up   [9] goon a paas nat but a myle] walk no more than a mile   [10] sith] then   [11] shoop him] intended   [12] swinke] labour   [13] sermone] speak   [14] cast] planned   [15] par acas] by chance   [16] storven] died

But, certes, I suppose that Avicen
Wroot never in no canon, ne in no fen,[1]
Mo wonder[2] signes of empoisoning
Than hadde thise wrecches two, er hir ending.
Thus ended been thise homicydes two,
And eek the false empoysoner also.

From THE NONNE PREESTES TALE

THIS Chauntecleer stood hye up-on his toos,
Strecching his nekke, and heeld his eyen cloos,[3]
And gan to crowe loude for the nones;
And daun[4] Russel the fox sterte up at ones,
And by the gargat[5] hente[6] Chauntecleer,
And on his bak toward the wode him beer,
For yet ne was ther no man that him sewed.[7]
O destinee, that mayst nat been eschewed!
Allas, that Chauntecleer fleigh[8] fro the bemes!
Allas, his wyf ne roghte[9] nat of dremes!
And on a Friday fil[10] al this meschaunce.
O Venus, that art goddesse of plesaunce,[11]
Sin[12] that thy servant was this Chauntecleer,
And in thy service dide al his poweer,
More for delyt, than world to multiplye,[13]
Why woldestow suffre him on thy day to dye?
O Gaufred, dere mayster soverayn,
That, whan thy worthy king Richard was slayn
With shot, compleynedest[14] his deth so sore,
Why ne hadde I now thy sentence[15] and thy lore,[16]
The Friday for to chyde, as diden ye?
(For on a Friday soothly slayn was he.)
Than wolde I shewe yow how that I coude pleyne
For Chauntecleres drede, and for his peyne.
Certes, swich cry ne lamentacioun
Was never of ladies maad, whan Ilioun

[1] fen] chapter   [2] wonder] wondrous   [3] cloos] shut   [4] daun]
Master   [5] gargat] throat   [6] hente] seized   [7] sewed] pursued
[8] fleigh] flew   [9] roghte] heeded   [10] fil] fell   [11] plesaunce] pleasure
[12] sin] since   [13] world to multiplye] to make the world populous
[14] compleynedest] lamented   [15] sentence] noble sentiments   [16] lore]
learning, wisdom

Was wonne, and Pirrus with his streite swerd,
Whan he hadde hent king Priam by the berd,
And slayn him (as saith us *Eneydos*),
As maden alle the hennes in the clos,[1]
Whan they had seyn of Chauntecleer the sighte.
But sovereynly[2] dame Pertelote shrighte,[3]
Ful louder than dide Hasdrubales wyf,
Whan that hir housbond hadde lost his lyf,
And that the Romayns hadde brend[4] Cartage;
She was so ful of torment and of rage,
That wilfully into the fyr she sterte,[5]
And brende hir-selven with a stedfast herte.
O woful hennes, right so cryden ye,
As, whan that Nero brende the citee
Of Rome, cryden senatoures wyves,
For that[6] hir housbondes losten alle hir lyves;
Withouten gilt this Nero hath hem slayn.
Now wol I torne to my tale agayn:—

This sely widwe,[7] and eek hir doghtres two,
Herden thise hennes crye and maken wo,
And out at dores sterten they anoon,
And syen[8] the fox toward the grove goon,
And bar upon his bak the cok away;
And cryden, 'Out! harrow! and weylaway![9]
Ha, ha, the fox!' and after him they ran,
And eek with staves many another man;
Ran Colle our dogge, and Talbot, and Gerland,
And Malkin, with a distaf in hir hand;
Ran cow and calf, and eek the verray hogges
So were they fered for berking of the dogges
And shouting of the men and wimmen eke,
They ronne so, hem thoughte hir herte breke.[10]
They yelleden as feendes doon in helle;
The dokes cryden as men wolde hem quelle;[11]
The gees for fere flowen over the trees;

---

[1] clos] yard   [2] sovereynly] above all others   [3] shrighte] shrieked
[4] brend] burnt   [5] sterte] leapt   [6] for that] because   [7] sely
widwe] simple widow   [8] syen] saw   [9] harrow! and weylaway]
help alas!   [10] hem thoughte hir herte breke] it seemed to them that
their hearts would break   [11] as men wolde hem quelle] as if they were
being killed

Out of the hyve cam the swarm of bees;
So hidous was the noyse, a! *benedicite*![1]
Certes, he Jakke Straw, and his meynee,[2]
Ne made never shoutes half so shrille,
Whan that they wolden any Fleming kille,
As thilke day was maad upon the fox.
Of bras thay broghten bemes, and of box,[3]
Of horn, of boon,[4] in whiche they blewe and pouped,[5]
And therwithal thay shryked and they houped;
It semed as that heven sholde falle.
Now, gode men, I pray yow herkneth alle!
   Lo, how fortune turneth sodeinly
The hope and pryde eek of hir enemy!
This cok, that lay upon the foxes bak,
In al his drede, un-to the fox he spak,
And seyde, 'sire, if that I were as ye,[6]
Yet sholde I seyn (as wis god helpe me),
Turneth agayn, ye proude cherles alle!
A verray pestilence up-on yow falle!
Now am I come un-to this wodes syde,
Maugree your heed,[7] the cok shal heer abyde;
I wol him ete in feith, and that anon.'—
The fox answerde, 'in feith, it shal be don,'—
And as he spak that word, al sodeinly
This cok brak from his mouth deliverly,[8]
And heighe up-on a tree he fleigh anon.
And whan the fox saugh that he was y-gon,
'Allas!' quod he, 'O Chauntecleer, allas!
I have to yow,' quod he, 'y-doon trespas,
In-as-muche as I maked yow aferd,
Whan I yow hente, and broghte out of the yerd;
But, sire, I dide it in no wikke entente;
Com doun, and I shal telle yow what I mente.
I shal seye sooth to yow, god help me so.'
'Nay than,'[9] quod he, 'I shrewe[10] us bothe two,
And first I shrewe my-self, bothe blood and bones,

---

[1] *benedicite*] pronounced *bensitee* [2] meynee] following [3] box]
wood of the box-tree [4] boon] bone [5] pouped] tooted [6] were
as ye] were in your place [7] maugree your heed] in spite of all you
can do [8] deliverly] deftly [9] than] then [10] shrewe] curse

If thou bigyle me ofter than ones.
Thou shalt na-more, thurgh thy flaterye,
Do[1] me to singe and winke with myn yë.
For he that winketh, whan he sholde see,
Al wilfully, god lat him never thee!'[2]
'Nay,' quod the fox, 'but god yeve him meschaunce,
That is so undiscreet of governaunce,
That jangleth whan he sholde holde his pees.'

Lo, swich it is for to be recchelees,
And necligent, and truste on flaterye.
But ye that holden this tale a folye,
As of a fox, or of a cok and hen,
Taketh the moralitee, good men.
For seint Paul seith, that al that writen is,
To our doctryne it is y-write, y-wis.
Taketh the fruyt, and lat the chaf be stille.

Now, gode god, if that it be thy wille,
As seith my lord, so make us alle good men;
And bringe us to his heighe blisse. Amen.

From THE WIFE OF BATH'S PROLOGUE

My fifthe housbonde, god his soule blesse!
Which that I took for love and no richesse,
He som-tyme was a clerk of Oxenford,
And had left scole, and wente at hoom to bord
With my gossib,[3] dwellinge in oure toun,
God have hir soule! hir name was Alisoun.
. . . This joly clerk Jankin, that was so hende,[4]
Hath wedded me with greet solempnitee,
And to him yaf I al the lond and fee[5]
That ever was me yeven ther-bifore;
But afterward repented me ful sore.
He nolde suffre nothing of my list.[6]
By god, he smoot me ones on the list,
For that[7] I rente out of his book a leef,
That of the strook myn ere wex al deef.

---

[1] do] cause   [2] thee] thrive   [3] gossib] woman friend   [4] hende] courteous   [5] fee] property   [6] list] (1) will (2) ear   [7] for that because

. . . Now wol I seye yow sooth, by seint Thomas,
Why that I rente out of his book a leef,
For which he smoot me so that I was deef.
  He hadde a book that gladly, night and day,
For his desport he wolde rede alway.
He cleped it Valerie and Theofraste,
At whiche book he lough alwey ful faste.
And eek ther was som-tyme a clerk at Rome,
A cardinal, that highte[1] Seint Jerome,
That made a book agayn Jovinian;
In whiche book eek ther was Tertulan,
Crisippus, Trotula, and Helowys,
That was abbesse nat fer fro Parys;
And eek the Parables of Salomon,
Ovydes Art, and bokes many on,
And alle thise were bounden in o volume.
And every night and day was his custume,
Whan he had leyser and vacacioun
From other worldly occupacioun,
To reden on this book of wikked wyves.
He knew of hem mo legendes and lyves
Than been of gode wyves in the Bible.
For trusteth wel, it is an impossible
That any clerk wol speke good of wyves,
But-if[2] it be of holy seintes lyves,
Ne of noon other womman never the mo.
Who peyntede the leoun,[3] tel me who?
By god, if wommen hadde writen stories,
As clerkes han with-inne hir oratories,
They wolde han writen of men more wikkednesse
Than all the mark[4] of Adam may redresse.

  . . . But now to purpos, why I tolde thee
That I was beten for a book, pardee.
Up-on a night Jankin, that was our syre,[5]
Redde on his book, as he sat by the fyre,
Of Eva first, that, for hir wikkednesse,[6]

---

[1] highte] was called   [2] but-if] unless   [3] leoun] lion   [4] mark]
race   [5] syre] husband   [6] that, for hir wikkednesse] for whose
wickedness

Was al mankinde broght to wrecchednesse,
For which that Jesu Crist him-self was slayn,
That boghte us with his herte-blood agayn,
Lo, here expres[1] of womman may ye finde,
That womman was the los of al mankinde.
Tho redde he me how Sampson loste his heres,
Slepinge, his lemman[2] kitte hem with hir sheres;
Thurgh whiche tresoun loste he bothe his yën.
Tho redde he me, if that I shal nat lyen,
Of Hercules and of his Dianyre,
That caused him to sette himself a-fyre.

. . . And whan I saugh he wolde never fyne[3]
To reden on this cursed book al night,
Al sodeynly three leves have I plight[4]
Out of his book, right as he radde, and eke,
I with my fist so took him on the cheke,
That in our fyr he fil bakward adoun.
And he up-stirte[5] as dooth a wood[6] leoun,
And with his fist he smoot me on the heed,
That in the floor I lay as I were deed.
And when he saugh how stille that I lay,
He was agast, and wolde han fled his way,
Til atte laste out of my swogh[7] I breyde:[8]
"O! hastow slayn me, false theef?" I seyde,
"And for my land thus hastow mordred me?
Er I be deed, yet wol I kisse thee."
    And neer he cam, and kneled faire adoun,
And seyde, "dere suster Alisoun,
As help me god, I shal thee never smyte;
That I have doon,[9] it is thy-selfe to wyte.
Foryeve it me, and that I thee biseke"—
And yet eft-sones I hitte him on the cheke,
And seyde, "theef, thus muchel am I wreke,[10]
Now wol I dye, I may no lenger speke."

[1] expres] expressly   [2] lemman] lover   [3] fyne] cease   [4] plight]
plucked, torn   [5] up-stirte] rose up   [6] wood] raging   [7] swogh]
swoon   [8] breyde] awoke   [9] that I have doon, &c.] you are yourself
to blame for what I have done   [10] wreke] avenged

But atte laste, with muchel care and wo,
We fille accorded,[1] by us selven two.
He yaf me al the brydel in myn hond
To han the governance of hous and lond,
And of his tonge and of his hond also,
And made him brenne[2] his book anon right tho.
And whan that I hadde geten un-to me,
By maistrie,[3] al the soveraynetee,
And that he seyde, "myn owene trewe wyf,
Do as thee lust[4] the terme of al thy lyf,
Keep thyn honour, and keep eek myn estaat"—
After that day we hadden never debaat.[5]
God help me so, I was to him as kinde
As any wyf from Denmark un-to Inde,
And also trewe, and so was he to me.
I prey to god that sit in magestee,
So blesse his soule, for his mercy dere!
Now wol I seye my tale, if ye wol here.'

THE BOOK OF THE DUCHESSE

THE DREAM

ME thoughte[6] thus:—that hit was May,
And in the dawning ther[7] I lay,
Me mette[8] thus, in my bed al naked:—
I loked forth, for I was waked
With smale foules a gret hepe,
That had affrayed[9] me out of slepe
Through noyse and swetnesse of hir song;
And, as me mette, they sate among,[10]
Upon my chambre-roof withoute,
Upon the tyles, al a-boute,
And songen, everich[11] in his wyse,
The moste solempne servyse[12]

---

[1] fille accorded] fell into agreement   [2] brenne] burn   [3] maistrie]
superiority   [4] as thee lust] as pleases thee   [5] debaat] quarrel
[6] me thoughte] it seemed to me   [7] ther] where   [8] me mette]
I dreamed   [9] affrayed] roused   [10] among] all the while
[11] everich] each   [12] solempne servyse] festive performance

By note, that ever man, I trowe,
Had herd; for som of hem song lowe,
Som hye, and al of oon acorde.
To telle shortly, at oo worde,[1]
Was never y-herd so swete a steven,[2]
But[3] hit had be a thing of heven;—
So mery a soun, so swete entunes,[4]
That certes, for the toune of Tewnes,
I nolde but I had herd hem singe;[5]
For al my chambre gan to ringe
Through singing of hir armonye.
For instrument nor melodye
Was nowher herd yet half so swete,
Nor of acorde half so mete;[6]
For ther was noon of hem that feyned
To singe, for ech of hem him peyned[7]
To finde out mery crafty[8] notes;
They ne spared not hir throtes.
And, sooth to seyn, my chambre was
Ful wel depeynted, and with glas
Were al the windowes wel y-glased,
Ful clere, and nat an hole y-crased,[9]
That to beholde hit was gret joye.
For hoolly al the storie of Troye
Was in the glasing y-wroght thus,
Of Ector and king Priamus,
Of Achilles and Lamedon,
Of Medea and of Jason,
Of Paris, Eleyne, and Lavyne.
And alle the walles with colours fyne
Were peynted, bothe text and glose,[10]
Of al the Romaunce of the Rose.
My windowes weren shet[11] echon,
And through the glas the sunne shon
Upon my bed with brighte bemes,

---

[1] at oo worde] in a word   [2] steven] sound   [3] but] unless
[4] entunes] tunes   [5] I nolde but, &c.] I would not have given up
hearing them sing (even for the town of Tunis)   [6] acorde half so
mete] harmony half as perfect   [7] him peyned] strove   [8] crafty] skilful
[9] y-crased] broken   [10] glose] comment   [11] shet] shut

With many glade gilden[1] stremes;
And eek the welken was so fair,
Blew, bright, clere was the air,
And ful atempre,[2] for sothe, hit was;
For nother cold nor hoot hit nas,[3]
Ne in al the welkin was a cloude.

PROEM TO THE PARLEMENT OF FOULES

THE lyf so short, the craft so long to lerne,
Th'assay so hard, so sharp the conquering,
The dredful joye, that alwey slit[4] so yerne,[5]
Al this mene I by[6] love, that my feling
Astonyeth with his wonderful worching
So sore y-wis, that whan I on him thinke,
Nat wot[7] I wel wher[8] that I wake or winke.[9]

For al be that[10] I knowe not love in dede,
Ne wot how that he quyteth[11] folk hir hyre,
Yet happeth me ful ofte[12] in bokes rede
Of his miracles, and his cruel yre;
Ther rede I wel he wol be lord and syre,
I dar not seyn, his strokes been so sore,
But god save swich a lord! I can[13] no more.

Of usage,[14] what for luste what for lore,[15]
On bokes rede I ofte, as I yow tolde.
But wherfor that I speke al this? not yore
Agon, hit happed me for to beholde
Upon a boke, was write with lettres olde;
And ther-upon, a certeyn thing to lerne,
The longe day ful faste I radde[16] and yerne.

---

[1] gilden] golden   [2] atempre] mild   [3] nas] was not   [4] slit] passes away   [5] yerne] quickly   [6] mene I by] I say in respect of   [7] wot] know   [8] wher] whether   [9] winke] sleep   [10] al be that] although   [11] quyteth folk hir hyre] rewards people   [12] happeth me ful ofte] it often happens (that I read)   [13] can] am able to say   [14] of usage] as a habit, regularly   [15] what for luste what for lore] partly for pleasure, partly for profit   [16] radde] read

For out of olde feldes, as men seith,[1]
Cometh al this newe corn fro yeer to yere;
And out of olde bokes, in good feith,
Cometh al this newe science that men lere.[2]

TROILUS AND CRISEYDE

THE ENVOY

Go, litel book, go litel myn tregedie,
Ther god thy maker yet,[3] er that he dye,
So sende might to make in som comedie!
But litel book, no making thou n'envye,
But subgit be to alle poesye;
And kis the steppes, wher-as[4] thou seest pace
Virgile, Ovyde, Omer, Lucan, and Stace.

And for ther is so greet diversitee
In English and in wryting of our tonge,
So preye I god that noon miswryte thee,
Ne thee mismetre[5] for defaute of tonge.
And red wher-so thou be, or elles songe,
That thou be understonde I god beseche!
But yet to purpos of my rather speche.[6]—

The wraththe, as I began yow for to seye,
Of Troilus, the Grekes boughten dere;
For thousandes his hondes maden deye,
As he that was with-outen any pere,[7]
Save Ector, in his tyme, as I can here.
But weylaway,[8] save only goddes wille,
Dispitously[9] him slough the fiers Achille.

---

[1] men seith] one says   [2] lere] teach   [3] ther god thy maker yet,
&c.] may God send power to him that wrote thee to compose a happy
tale   [4] wher-as] where   [5] mismetre] scan wrongly   [6] to
purpose of my rather speche] to return to the subject of my previous
discourse   [7] as he that was, &c.] since he was without an equal
[8] weylaway] alas   [9] dispitously] spite-fully

And whan that he was slayn in this manere,
His lighte goost ful blisfully is went
Up to the holownesse of the seventh spere,[1]
In convers letinge[2] every element;
And ther he saugh, with ful avysement,[3]
The erratik sterres,[4] herkeninge armonye
With sownes fulle of hevenish melodye.

And doun from thennes faste[5] he gan[6] avyse[7]
This litel spot of erthe, that with the see
Enbraced is, and fully gan despyse
This wrecched world, and held al vanitee
To respect of[8] the pleyn[9] felicitee
That is in hevene above; and at the laste,
Ther[10] he was slayn, his loking doun he caste;

And in him-self he lough[11] right at the wo
Of hem that wepten for his deeth so faste;[12]
And dampned[13] al our werk that folweth so
The blinde lust,[14] the which that may not laste,
And sholden[15] al our herte on hevene caste.
And forth he wente, shortly for to telle,
Ther as Mercurie sorted[16] him to dwelle.—

Swich fyn[17] hath, lo, this Troilus for love,
Swich fyn hath al his grete worthinesse;
Swich fyn hath his estat real above,[18]
Swich fyn his lust, swich fyn hath his noblesse;
Swich fyn hath false worldes brotelnesse.[19]
And thus bigan his lovinge of Criseyde,
As I have told, and in this wyse he deyde.

O yonge fresshe folkes, he or she,
In which that love up groweth with your age,
Repeyreth hoom[20] from worldly vanitee,

[1] spere] sphere   [2] in convers letinge] leaving on the other side   [3] avysement] view, consideration   [4] erratik sterres] wandering stars (the planets)   [5] faste] intently   [6] gan] did   [7] avyse] consider   [8] to respect of] in comparison with   [9] pleyn] full, complete   [10] ther] (to) where   [11] lough] laughed   [12] faste] much   [13] dampned] condemned   [14] lust] desire   [15] sholden] we ought   [16] sorted] allotted   [17] swich fyn] such an end, death   [18] estat real above] high and royal rank   [19] brotelnesse] brittleness, frailty   [20] repeyreth hoom] turn back (imp.)

37

And of your herte up-casteth the visage
To thilke[1] god that after his image
Yow made, and thinketh al nis but a fayre
This world, that passeth sone as floures fayre.

And loveth him, the which that right for love
Upon a cros, our soules for to beye,
First starf,[2] and roos, and sit[3] in hevene a-bove;
For he nil falsen[4] no wight, dar I seye,
That wol his herte al hoolly on him leye.
And sin[5] he best to love is, and most meke,
What nedeth feyned loves for to seke?

Lo here, of Payens corsed[6] olde rytes,
Lo here, what alle hir goddes may availle;
Lo here, these wrecched worldes appetytes;
Lo here, the fyn and guerdon for travaille
Of Jove, Appollo, of Mars, of swich rascaille!
Lo here, the forme of olde clerkes speche
In poetrye, if ye hir bokes seche.—

O moral Gower, this book I directe
To thee, and to the philosophical Strode,
To vouchen sauf,[7] ther nede is, to corecte,
Of your benignitees and zeles gode.
And to that sothfast Crist, that starf on rode,
With al myn herte of mercy ever I preye;
And to the lord right thus I speke and seye:

Thou oon, and two, and three, eterne on-lyve,[8]
That regnest ay in three and two and oon,
Uncircumscript, and al mayst circumscryve,
Us from visible and invisible foon
Defende; and to thy mercy, everychoon,
So make us, Jesus, for thy grace, digne,[9]
For love of mayde and moder thyn benigne! Amen.

---

[1] thilke] that (same)   [2] starf] died   [3] sit] sits   [4] falsen] betray
[5] sin] since   [6] corsed] cursed   [7] vouchen sauf] vouchsafe, deign
[8] on-lyve] alive   [9] digne] worthy, suitable

LEGEND OF GOOD WOMEN

BALADE

HYD, Absolon, thy gilte tresses clere;[1]
Ester, ley thou thy meknesse al a-doun;
Hyd, Jonathas, al thy frendly manere;
Penalopee, and Marcia Catoun,
Mak of your wyfhod[2] no comparisoun;
Hyde ye your beautes, Isoude and Eleyne,
Alceste is here, that al that may desteyne.[3]

Thy faire bodye, lat hit nat appere,
Lavyne; and thou, Lucresse of Rome toun,
And Polixene, that boghte love so dere,
Eek Cleopatre, with al thy passioun,
Hyde ye your trouthe in love and your renoun;
And thou, Tisbe, that hast for love swich peyne:
Alceste is here, that al that may desteyne.

Herro, Dido, Laudomia, alle in-fere,[4]
Eek Phyllis, hanging for thy Demophoun,
And Canace, espyed by thy chere,[5]
Ysiphile, betrayed with[6] Jasoun,
Mak of your trouthe in love no bost ne soun;[7]
Nor Ypermistre or Adriane, ne pleyne;[8]
Alceste is here, that al that may desteyne.

---

[1] clere] bright, beautiful   [2] wyfhood] wife-hood   [3] desteyne]
bedim   [4] in-fere] together   [5] chere] appearance   [6] with] by
[7] soun] vaunt   [8] ne pleyne] do not lament

EDMUND SPENSER

EDMUND SPENSER (1552?–99), was educated at Merchant Taylors' School and Pembroke Hall, Cambridge. He obtained in 1578 a place in Leicester's household, and became acquainted with Sir Philip Sidney. In 1579 he began the *Faerie Queene* and published his *Shepheards Calendar*, which was enthusiastically received. In 1580 he settled in Ireland and occupied himself with literary work, preparing the *Faerie Queene* for the press, three books of this work being entrusted to the printer on the poet's visit to London in 1589. The reputation of the *Faerie Queene* led the printer, Ponsonby, to issue in 1591 his minor verse, in part rewritten. In 1594 Spenser married Elizabeth Boyle, whom he had wooed in his *Amoretti*, and possibly celebrated the marriage in his splendid *Epithalamion* (the two were printed together in 1595). He published the second instalment of three books of the *Faerie Queene* in 1596. He died in destitution in London, and was buried near Chaucer in Westminster Abbey.

BEYOND all doubt it is best to have made one's first acquaintance with Spenser in a very large—and, preferably, illustrated—edition of the *Faerie Queene*, on a wet day, between the ages of twelve and sixteen; and if, even at that age, certain of the names aroused unidentified memories of some still earlier, some almost prehistoric, commerce with a selection of 'Stories from Spenser', heard before we could read, so much the better. But those who have had this good fortune are not likely to be reading the following extracts. They will never have lost touch with the poet. His great book will have accompanied them year by year and grown up with them as books do: to the youthful appreciation of mere wonder-tale they will have added a critically sensuous enjoyment of the melodious stanza, to both these a historical understanding of its significance in English poetry as a whole, and an ever-increasing perception of its wisdom. To them I need not speak; the problem is rather how to find substitutes for their slowly ripened habit of mind which may enable a mature reader to enter the Spenserian world for the first time: to do for him, in a few minutes, what they have done for themselves in many years.

It must be admitted that this is impossible, but on the

following lines an effort may be made. Our imaginary child began with *The Faerie Queene*, and the mature reader must do the same. Passages from Spenser's other works appear, quite rightly, in the following pages, and it would certainly be a pity not to know the *Epithalamion*: but it must never be forgotten that he stands or falls by his great poetic romance, and if you do not like it and yet believe that you like Spenser you are probably deceiving yourself. Secondly, there is that large edition and that wet day. It is not, perhaps, absolutely necessary to have a large edition *in fact*; but it is imperative that you should think of *The Faerie Queene* as a book suitable for reading in a heavy volume, at a table—a book to which limp leather is insulting—a massy, antique story with a blackletter flavour about it—a book for devout, prolonged, and leisurely perusal. The illustrations (real or imagined) raise a problem. There are fantastic palaces and voluptuous nudes in Spenser which seem to ask for Tintoretto or Correggio or Claude: but there are also, and more abundantly, wicket-gates and ugly fiends and stiffly bearded elders which we would rather see in woodcuts—such violent, unforgettable little cuts as Wordsworth mentions in *The Excursion*. This double need for two quite different kinds of picture is characteristic. There is a renaissance element in the *Faerie Queene*—a gorgeous, luxurious, Italianate, and florid element: but this is not the basis of it. All this new growth sprouts out of an old, gnarled wood, and, as in very early spring, mists it over in places without concealing it. The cloth of gold is an occasional decoration: most of the coat is homespun. And it is best to begin with a taste for homespun, accepting the cloth of gold when it comes but by no means depending on it for your pleasure, or you will be disappointed—to keep your *Faerie Queene* on the same shelf with Bunyan and Malory and *The Seven Champions* and even with *Jack the Giant Killer*, rather than with *Hero and Leander* or *Venus and Adonis*. For this is the paradox of Spenser's poem; it is not really medieval—no medieval romance is very like it—yet everyone who has really enjoyed it, from the Wartons down, has enjoyed it as the very consummation of the Middle Ages, the quintessence of 'the blackletter flavour'.

It came about in this way. Spenser's friends wanted him to be in the Movement, to be an extreme Puritan and a servile classicist, which were the two fashionable things at Cambridge in his day. Under their tutelage he produced the pretentious, and (to tell the truth) nearly worthless, *Shepheards Calendar*. But even in it he was straining at the tether, and his friend E. K. had to write pretty sharp cautionary notes on 'Ladies of the Lake' and 'friendly fairies', hinting that the poet had approached much too nearly to the medieval and the papistical—things as shocking to the fierce young intellectuals of that day as the bourgeois and the Victorian are to their descendants in our own. But Spenser, in his great work, went back to what he had always liked, and took all his renaissance accomplishments with him. What he had always liked was the Middle Ages as he imagined them to have been and as they survived in his time in the pageant, the morality play, and the metrical romance. They were real survivals, yet they smelled already a little archaic: they had already, for Spenser himself, a touch of the blackletter flavour. He thus became something between the last of the medieval poets and the first of the romantic medievalists; he was enabled to produce a tale more solemn, more redolent of the past, more venerable, than any real medieval romance—to deny, in his own person, the breach between the Middle Ages and the Renaissance and to hand on to succeeding generations a poetic symbol of the former whose charms have proved inexhaustible.

It will be remembered that we attributed to our ideal reader—along with the wet day, the large volume, and the unjaded appetite of boyhood—a haunting memory that he has met all these knights and ladies, all these monsters and enchanters, somewhere before. What corresponds to this in the experience of the mature reader is the consciousness of Spenser's moral allegory. Critics differ as regards the degree of attention which we must pay to it. It may not be necessary for all readers at all stages of the narrative to know exactly what the poet means, but it is emphatically necessary that they should surrender themselves to the sense of some dim significance in the background—that they should feel themselves to be moving in regions 'where more is meant than meets the ear'. Even if this feeling were only an illusion, it would be an essential part of the whole poetic illusion intended. The present writer, however, thinks that it is nothing of the sort: that Spenser's beautiful or alarming visions do truly embody, in forms as unsophisticated as those of our pantomime fairies and devils, though incomparably more potent, moral and psychological realities of the utmost simplicity and profundity. Certainly they are, at their best, as Mr. Yeats says of the figures in Spenser's House of Busirane, 'so visionary, so full of ghostly midnight animation, that one is persuaded that they had some strange purpose and did truly appear in just that way'.

C. S. LEWIS.

JANUARY ECLOGUE

A SHEPEHEARDS boye (no better doe him call)
When Winters wastful spight was almost spent,
All in a sunneshine day, as did befall,
Led forth his flock, that had bene long ypent.[1]
So faynt they woxe,[2] and feeble in the folde,
That now vnnethes[3] their feete could them vphold.

All as the Sheepe, such was the shepeheards looke,
For pale and wanne he was, (alas the while),
May seeme[4] he lovd, or els some care he tooke:
Well couth[5] he tune his pipe, and frame his stile.
Tho[6] to a hill his faynting flocke he ledde,
And thus him playnd,[7] the while his shepe there fedde.

'Ye Gods of loue, that pitie louers payne,
(If any gods the paine of louers pitie:)
Looke from aboue, where you in ioyes remaine,
And bowe your eares vnto my dolefull dittie.
And *Pan* thou shepheards God, that once didst loue,
Pitie the paines, that thou thy selfe didst proue.[8]

Thou barrein ground, whome winters wrath hath wasted,
Art made a myrrhour, to behold my plight:
Whilome[9] thy fresh spring flowrd, and after hasted
Thy sommer prowde with Daffadillies dight.[10]
And now is come thy wynters stormy state,
Thy mantle mard, wherein thou maskedst late.[11]

Such rage as winters, reigneth in my heart,
My life bloud friesing with vnkindly cold:
Such stormy stoures[12] do breede my balefull smart,[13]
As if my yeare were wast, and woxen old.
And yet alas, but now my spring begonne,
And yet alas, yt is already donne.

---

[1] ypent] pent up   [2] woxe] grew   [3] vnnethes] scarcely   [4] may seeme] it seemed as if   [5] couth] could, knew how to   [6] tho] then   [7] him playnd] bemoaned   [8] didst proue] did suffer   [9] whilome] once, formerly   [10] dight] clothed, attired   [11] Thy mantle, wherein thou didst sport until lately, is ruined   [12] stoures] fits, storms   [13] balefull smart] harmful pain

You naked trees, whose shady leaues are lost,
Wherein the byrds were wont to build their bowre,
And now are clothd with mosse and hoary frost,
Instede of bloosmes, wherwith your buds did flowre:
I see your teares, that from your boughes doe raine,
Whose drops in drery ysicles remaine.

All so my lustfull leafe is drye and sere,
My timely buds with wayling all are wasted:
The blossome, which my braunch of youth did beare,
With breathed sighes is blowne away, and blasted:
And from mine eyes the drizling teares descend,
As on your boughes the ysicles depend.

Thou feeble flocke, whose fleece is rough and rent,
Whose knees are weake through fast[1] and euill fare:
Mayst witnesse well by thy ill gouernement,
Thy maysters mind is ouercome with care.
Thou weake, I wanne: thou leane, I quite forlorne:
With mourning pyne I, you with pyning mourne.

A thousand sithes[2] I curse that carefull hower,
Wherein I longd the neighbour towne to see:
And eke tenne thousand sithes I blesse the stoure,
Wherein I sawe so fayre a sight, as shee.
Yet all for naught: such sight hath bred my bane.
Ah God, that loue should breede both ioy and payne.

It is not *Hobbinol*, wherefore I plaine,
Albee my loue he seeke with dayly suit:
His clownish gifts and curtsies I disdaine,
His kiddes, his cracknelles, and his early fruit.
Ah foolish *Hobbinol*, thy gyfts bene vayne:
Colin them giues to *Rosalind* againe.

I loue thilke[3] lasse, (alas why doe I loue?)
And am forlorne, (alas why am I lorne?)[4]
Shee deignes not my good will, but doth reproue,
And of my rurall musick holdeth scorne.
Shepheards deuise[5] she hateth as the snake,
And laughes[6] the songes, that *Colin Clout* doth make.

---

[1] fast] fasting   [2] sithes] times   [3] thilke] that   [4] lorne] lost
[5] shepheards deuise] shepherd's skill   [6] laughes] laughs at

45

Wherefore my pype, albee[1] rude *Pan* thou please,
Yet for thou pleasest not, where most I would:
And thou vnlucky Muse, that wontst to ease
My musing mynd, yet canst not, when thou should:
Both pype and Muse, shall sore the while abye.
So broke his oaten pype, and downe dyd lye.

By that, the welked[2] *Phœbus* gan availe,[3]
His weary waine,[4] and nowe the frosty *Night*
Her mantle black through heauen gan ouerhaile.[5]
Which seene, the pensife boy halfe in despight
Arose, and homeward droue his sonned[6] sheepe,
Whose hanging heads did seeme his carefull[7] case to weepe.

Colins Embleme.

Anchôra speme.

EPITHALAMION

Now al is done; bring home the bride againe,
Bring home the triumph of our victory,
Bring home with you the glory of her gaine,
With ioyance bring her and with iollity.
Neuer had man more ioyfull day then this,
Whom heauen would heape with blis.
Make feast therefore now all this liue long day,
This day for euer to me holy is,
Poure out the wine without restraint or stay,
Poure not by cups, but by the belly full,
Poure out to all that wull,
And sprinkle all the postes and wals with wine,
That they may sweat, and drunken be withall.
Crowne ye God Bacchus with a coronall,
And Hymen also crowne with wreathes of vine,
And let the Graces daunce vnto the rest;
For they can doo it best:

[1] albee] although   [2] welked] faded   [3] availe] bring down
[4] waine] wagon   [5] ouerhaile] draw over   [6] sonned] sunned?
[7] carefull] sorrowful

The whiles the maydens doe theyr carroll sing,
To which the woods shal answer and theyr eccho ring.

Ring ye the bels, ye yong men of the towne,
And leaue your wonted labors for this day:
This day is holy; doe ye write it downe,
That ye for euer it remember may.
This day the sunne is in his chiefest hight,
With Barnaby the bright,
From whence declining daily by degrees,
He somewhat loseth of his heat and light,
When once the Crab behind his back he sees.
But for this time it ill ordained was,
To chose the longest day in all the yeare,
And shortest night, when longest fitter weare:
Yet neuer day so long, but late would passe.
Ring ye the bels, to make it weare away,
And bonefiers make all day,
And daunce about them, and about them sing,
That all the woods may answer, and your eccho ring.

Ah when will this long weary day haue end,
And lende me leaue to come vnto my loue?
How slowly do the houres theyr numbers spend?
How slowly does sad Time his feathers moue?
Hast thee O fayrest Planet to thy home
Within the Westerne fome:
Thy tyred steedes long since haue need of rest.
Long though it be, at last I see it gloome,
And the bright euening star with golden creast
Appeare out of the East.
Fayre childe of beauty, glorious lampe of loue
That all the host of heauen in rankes doost lead,
And guydest louers through the nightes dread,
How chearefully thou lookest from aboue,
And seemst to laugh atweene thy twinkling light
As ioying in the sight
Of these glad many which for ioy doe sing,
That all the woods them answer and their echo ring.

Now ceasse ye damsels your delights forepast;
Enough is it, that all the day was youres:
Now day is doen, and night is nighing fast:
Now bring the Bryde into the brydall boures.
Now night is come, now soone her disaray,
And in her bed her lay;
Lay her in lillies and in violets,
And silken courteins ouer her display,
And odourd sheetes, and Arras couerlets.
Behold how goodly my faire loue does ly
In proud humility;
Like vnto Maia, when as Ioue her tooke,
In Tempe, lying on the flowry gras,
Twixte sleepe and wake, after she weary was,
With bathing in the Acidalian brooke.
Now it is night, ye damsels may be gon,
And leaue my loue alone,
And leaue likewise your former lay to sing:
The woods no more shal answere, nor your echo
    ring.

Now welcome night, thou night so long expected,
That long daies labour doest at last defray,
And all my cares, which cruell loue collected,
Hast sumd in one, and cancelled for aye:
Spread thy broad wing ouer my loue and me,
That no man may vs see,
And in thy sable mantle vs enwrap,
From feare of perrill and foule horror free.
Let no false treason seeke vs to entrap,
Nor any dread disquiet once annoy
The safety of our ioy:
But let the night be calme and quietsome,
Without tempestuous storms or sad afray:
Lyke as when Ioue with fayre Alcmena lay,
When he begot the great Tirynthian groome:
Or lyke as when he with thy selfe did lie,
And begot Maiesty.
And let the mayds and yongmen cease to sing:
Ne let the woods them answer, nor theyr eccho ring.

Let no lamenting cryes, nor dolefull teares,
Be heard all night within nor yet without:
Ne let false whispers, breeding hidden feares,
Breake gentle sleepe with misconceiued dout.
Let no deluding dreames, nor dreadful sights
Make sudden sad affrights;
Ne let housefyres, nor lightnings helplesse harmes,
Ne let the Pouke, nor other euill sprights,
Ne let mischiuous witches with theyr charmes,
Ne let hob Goblins, names whose sence we see not,
Fray vs with things that be not.
Let not the shriech Oule nor the Storke be heard:
Nor the night Rauen that still deadly yels,
Nor damned ghosts cald vp with mighty spels,
Nor griesly vultures make vs once affeard:
Ne let th'unpleasant Quyre of Frogs still croking
Make vs to wish theyr choking.
Let none of these theyr drery accents sing;
Ne let the woods them answer, nor theyr eccho ring.

But let stil Silence trew night watches keepe,
That sacred peace may in assurance rayne,
And tymely sleep, when it is tyme to sleepe,
May poure his limbs forth on your pleasant playne,
The whiles an hundred little winged loues,
Like diuers fethered doues,
Shall fly and flutter round about your bed,
And in the secret darke, that none reproues,
Their prety stealthes shal worke, and snares shal spread
To filch away sweet snatches of delight,
Conceald through couert night.
Ye sonnes of Venus, play your sports at will,
For greedy pleasure, carelesse of your toyes,
Thinks more vpon her paradise of ioyes,
Then what ye do, albe it good or ill.
All night therefore attend your merry play,
For it will soone be day:
Now none doth hinder you, that say or sing,
Ne will the woods now answer, nor your Eccho ring.

Who is the same, which at my window peepes?
Or whose is that faire face, that shines so bright?
Is it not Cinthia, she that neuer sleepes,
But walkes about high heauen al the night?
O fayrest goddesse, do thou not enuy
My loue with me to spy:
For thou likewise didst loue, though now vnthought,
And for a fleece of woll, which priuily
The Latmian shephard once vnto thee brought,
His pleasures with thee wrought.
Therefore to vs be fauorable now;
And sith[1] of wemens labours thou hast charge,
And generation goodly dost enlarge,
Encline thy will t'effect our wishfull vow,
And the chast wombe informe with timely seed,
That may our comfort breed:
Till when we cease our hopefull hap to sing,
Ne let the woods vs answere, nor our Eccho ring.

And thou great Iuno, which with awful might
The lawes of wedlock still dost patronize,
And the religion of the faith first plight
With sacred rites hast taught to solemnize:
And eeke for comfort often called art
Of women in their smart,
Eternally bind thou this louely band,
And all thy blessings vnto vs impart.
And thou glad Genius, in whose gentle hand,
The bridale bowre and geniall bed remaine,
Without blemish or staine,
And the sweet pleasures of theyr loues delight
With secret ayde doest succour and supply,
Till they bring forth the fruitfull progeny,
Send vs the timely fruit of this same night.
And thou fayre Hebe, and thou Hymen free,
Grant that it may so be.
Til which we cease your further prayse to sing,
Ne any woods shal answer, nor your Eccho ring.

[1] sith] since

And ye high heauens, the temple of the gods,
In which a thousand torches flaming bright
Doe burne, that to vs wretched earthly clods,
In dreadful darknesse lend desired light;
And all ye powers which in the same remayne,
More then we men can fayne,
Poure out your blessing on vs plentiously,
And happy influence vpon vs raine,
That we may raise a large posterity,
Which from the earth, which they may long possesse
With lasting happinesse,
Vp to your haughty pallaces may mount,
And for the guerdon of theyr glorious merit
May heauenly tabernacles there inherit,
Of blessed Saints for to increase the count.
So let vs rest, sweet loue, in hope of this,
And cease till then our tymely ioyes to sing,
The woods no more vs answer, nor our eccho ring.

LAMENT FOR DAPHNAIDA

SHE is the Rose, the glorie of the day,
And mine the Primrose in the lowly shade,
Mine, ah not mine; amisse I mine did say:
Not mine but his, which mine awhile her made:
Mine to be his, with him to liue for ay:
O that so faire a flower so soone should fade,
And through vntimely tempest fall away.

She fell away in her first ages spring,
Whil'st yet her leafe was greene, and fresh her rinde,[1]
And whil'st her braunch faire blossomes foorth did bring,
She fell away against all course of kinde:[2]
For age to dye is right, but youth is wrong;
She fel away like fruit blowne downe with winde:
Weepe Shepheard weepe to make my vndersong.

What hart so stony hard, but that would weepe,
And poure foorth fountaines of incessant teares?
What *Timon*, but would let compassion creepe
Into his brest, and pierce his frosen eares?

[1] rinde] bark   [2] kinde] nature

In stead of teares, whose brackish bitter well
I wasted haue, my heart blood dropping weares,
To thinke to ground how that faire blossome fell.

Yet fell she not, as one enforst to dye,
Ne dyde with dread and grudging discontent,
But as one toyld with trauaile downe doth lye,
So lay she downe, as if to sleepe she went,
And closde her eyes with carelesse quietnesse;
The whiles soft death away her spirit hent,
And soule assoyld[1] from sinfull fleshlinesse.

Yet ere that life her lodging did forsake,
She all resolu'd and ready to remoue,
Calling to me (ay me) this wise bespake;
Alcyon, ah my first and latest loue,
Ah why does my *Alcyon* weepe and mourne,
And grieue my ghost, that ill mote him behoue,
As if to me had chanst some euill tourne?

I, since the messenger is come for mee,
That summons soules vnto the bridale feast
Of his great Lord, must needes depart from thee,
And straight obay his soueraine beheast:
Why should *Alcyon* then so sore lament,
That I from miserie shall be releast,
And freed from wretched long imprisonment?

Our daies are full of dolor and disease,
Our life afflicted with incessant paine,
That nought on earth may lessen or appease.
Why then should I desire here to remaine?
Or why should he that loues me, sorie bee
For my deliuerance, or at all complaine
My good to heare, and toward ioyes to see?

I goe, and long desired haue to goe,
I goe with gladnesse to my wished rest,
Whereas no worlds sad care, nor wasting woe
May come their happie quiet to molest,
But Saints and Angels in celestiall thrones
Eternally him praise, that hath them blest;
There shall I be amongst those blessed ones.

[1] assoyld] absolved

52

Yet ere I goe, a pledge I leaue with thee
Of the late loue, the which betwixt vs past,
My yong *Ambrosia*, in lieu of mee
Loue her: so shall our loue for euer last.
Thus deare adieu, whom I expect ere long:
So hauing said, away she softly past:
Weep Shepheard weep, to make mine vndersong.

SONNET

ONE day I wrote her name vpon the strand,
    but came the waues and washed it away:
    agayne I wrote it with a second hand,
    but came the tyde, and made my paynes his pray.
Vayne man, sayd she, that doest in vaine assay
    a mortall thing so to immortalize,
    for I my selue shall lyke to this decay,
    and eek my name bee wyped out lykewize.
Not so, (quod I) let baser things deuize
    to dy in dust, but you shall liue by fame:
    my verse your vertues rare shall eternize,
    and in the heuens wryte your glorious name.
Where whenas death shall all the world subdew,
    our loue shall liue, and later life renew.

INVOCATION TO THE FAERIE QUEENE

Lo I the man, whose Muse whilome[1] did maske,
    As time her taught, in lowly Shepheards weeds;
Am now enforst a far vnfitter taske,
    For trumpets sterne to chaunge mine Oaten reeds,
    And sing of Knights and Ladies gentle deeds;
Whose prayses hauing slept in silence long,
Me, all too meane, the sacred Muse areeds[2]
To blazon broad emongst her learned throng:
Fierce warres and faithfull loues shall moralize[3] my song.

Helpe then, O holy Virgin chiefe of nine,[4]
    Thy weaker Nouice to performe thy will,
    Lay forth out of thine euerlasting scryne[5]
    The antique rolles, which there lye hidden still,

---

[1] whilome] formerly   [2] areeds] counsels   [3] moralize] give a moral
meaning to   [4] i.e. the Nine muses   [5] scryne] shrine

Of Faerie knights and fairest *Tanaquill*,
Whom that most noble Briton Prince so long
Sought through the world, and suffered so much ill,
That I must rue his vndeserued wrong:
O helpe thou my weake wit, and sharpen my dull tong.

And thou most dreaded impe of highest *Ioue*,
    Faire *Venus* sonne, that with thy cruell dart
At that good knight so cunningly didst roue,
    That glorious fire it kindled in his hart,
    Lay now thy deadly Heben[1] bow apart,
    And with thy mother milde come to mine ayde:
    Come both, and with you bring triumphant *Mart*,
    In loues and gentle iollities arrayd,
After his murdrous spoiles and bloudy rage allayd.

And with them eke, O Goddesse heauenly bright,
    Mirrour of grace and Maiestie diuine,
Great Lady of the greatest Isle,[2] whose light
    Like *Phœbus* lampe throughout the world doth shine,
    Shed thy faire beames into my feeble eyne,[3]
    And raise my thoughts too humble and too vile,
    To thinke of that true glorious type of thine,
    The argument of mine afflicted stile:
The which to heare, vouchsafe, O dearest dred a-while.

THE FIGHT OF THE RED CROSS KNIGHT AND THE HEATHEN SANSJOY

THE noble hart, that harbours vertuous thought,
And is with child of glorious great intent,
Can neuer rest, vntil it forth haue brought
Th'eternall brood of glorie excellent:
Such restless passion did all night torment
The flaming corage of that Faery knight,
Deuizing, how that doughtie turnament
With greatest honour he atchieuen might;
Still did he wake, and still did watch for dawning light.

[1] Heben] of ebony   [2] i.e. Elizabeth   [3] eyne] eyes

At last the golden Orientall gate
Of greatest heauen gan to open faire,
And *Phœbus* fresh, as bridegrome to his mate,
Came dauncing forth, shaking his deawie haire:
And hurld his glistring beames through gloomy aire.
Which when the wakeful Elfe[1] perceiu'd, streight way
He started vp, and did him selfe prepaire,
In sun-bright armes, and battailous[2] array:
For with that Pagan proud he combat will that day.

And forth he comes into the commune hall,
Where earely waite him many a gazing eye,
To weet[3] what end to straunger knights may fall.
There many Minstrales maken melody,
To driue away the dull melancholy,
And many Bardes, that to the trembling chord
Can tune their timely[4] voyces cunningly,
And many Chroniclers, that can record
Old loues, and warres for Ladies doen by many a Lord.

Soone after comes the cruell Sarazin,[5]
In wouen maile all armed warily,
And sternly lookes at him, who not a pin
Does care for looke of liuing creatures eye.
They bring them wines of *Greece* and *Araby*,
And daintie spices fetcht from furthest *Ynd*,
To kindle heat of corage priuily:
And in the wine a solemne oth they bynd
T'obserue the sacred lawes of armes, that are assynd.

At last forth comes that far renowmed Queene,
With royall pomp and Princely maiestie;
She is ybrought vnto a paled greene,[6]
And placed vnder stately canapee,
The warlike feates of both those knights to see.
On th'other side in all mens open view
Duessa placed is, and on a tree
Sans-foy his shield is hangd with bloudy hew:
Both those the lawrell girlonds to the victor dew.

---

[1] i.e. the Red Cross Knight.   [2] battailous] martial   [3] weet] know
[4] timely] keeping time or measure   [5] Sansjoy   [6] paled greene]
lawn surrounded with a palisade

A shrilling trompet sownded from on hye,
And vnto battaill bad them selues addresse:
Their shining shieldes about their wrestes they tye,
And burning blades about their heads do blesse,[1]
The instruments of wrath and heauinesse:
With greedy force each other doth assayle,
And strike so fiercely, that they do impresse
Deepe dinted furrowes in the battred mayle;
The yron walles to ward their blowes are weake and fraile.

The Sarazin was stout, and wondrous strong,
And heaped blowes like yron hammers great:
For after bloud and vengeance he did long.
The knight was fiers, and full of youthly heat:
And doubled strokes, like dreaded thunders threat;
For all for prayse and honour he did fight.
Both stricken strike, and beaten both do beat,
That from their shields forth flyeth firie light,
And helmets hewen deepe shew marks of eithers might.

So th'one for wrong, the other striues for right:
As when a Gryfon seized of his pray,
A Dragon fiers encountreth in his flight,
Through widest ayre making his ydle way,
That would his rightfull rauine[2] rend away:
With hideous horrour both together smight,
And souce[3] so sore, that they the heauens affray:[4]
The wise Southsayer seeing so sad sight,
Th'amazed vulgar[5] tels of warres and mortall fight.

So th'one for wrong, the other striues for right,
And each to deadly shame would driue his foe:
The cruell steele so greedily doth bight
In tender flesh, that streames of bloud down flow,
With which the armes, that earst so bright did show,
Into a pure vermillion now are dyde:
Great ruth in all the gazers harts did grow,
Seeing the gored woundes to gape so wyde,
That victory they dare not wish to either side.

[1] blesse] wave, brandish   [2] ravine] spoil, prey   [3] souce] clash?
[4] affray] frighten   [5] vulgar] common people

At last the Paynim chaunst to cast his eye,
His suddein eye, flaming with wrathfull fyre,
Vpon his brothers shield, which hong thereby:
Therewith redoubled was his raging yre,
And said, Ah wretched sonne of wofull syre,
Doest thou sit wayling by black *Stygian* lake,
Whilest here thy shield is hangd for victors hyre,
And sluggish german[1] doest thy forces slake,[2]
To after-send his foe, that him may ouertake?

Goe caytiue Elfe, him quickly ouertake,
And soone redeeme from his long wandring woe;
Goe guiltie ghost, to him my message make,
That I his shield haue quit from dying foe.
Therewith vpon his crest he stroke him so,
That twise he reeled, readie twise to fall;
End of the doubtfull battell deemed tho[3]
The lookers on, and lowd to him gan call
The false *Duessa*, Thine the shield, and I, and all.

Soone as the Faerie heard his Ladie speake,
Out of his swowning dreame he gan awake,
And quickning faith, that earst[4] was woxen weake,
The creeping deadly cold away did shake:
Tho[3] mou'd with wrath, and shame, and Ladies sake,
Of all attonce he cast auengd to bee,
And with so'exceeding furie at him strake,
That forced him to stoupe vpon his knee;
Had he not stouped so, he should haue clouen bee,

And to him said, Goe now proud Miscreant,
Thy selfe thy message doe to german deare,
Alone he wandring thee too long doth want:
Goe say, his foe thy shield with his doth beare.
Therewith his heauie hand he high gan reare,
Him to haue slaine; when loe a darkesome clowd
Vpon him fell: he no where doth appeare,
But vanisht is. The Elfe him cals alowd,
But answer none receiues: the darknes him does shrowd.

---

[1] german] twin brother   [2] slake] slacken   tho] then   [4] earst]
formerly

In haste *Duessa* from her place arose,
And to him running said, O prowest knight,
That euer Ladie to her loue did chose,
Let now abate the terror of your might,
And quench the flame of furious despight,
And bloudie vengeance; lo th' infernall powres
Couering your foe with cloud of deadly night,
Haue borne him hence to *Plutoes* balefull bowres.
The conquest yours, I yours, the shield, and glory yours.

Not all so satisfide, with greedie eye
He sought all round about, his thirstie blade
To bath in bloud of faithlesse enemy;
Who all that while lay hid in secret shade:
He standes amazed, how he thence should fade.
At last the trumpets Triumph sound on hie,
And running Heralds humble homage made,
Greeting him goodly with new victorie,
And to him brought the shield, the cause of enmitie.

Wherwith he goeth to that soueraine Queene,
And falling her before on lowly knee,
To her makes present of his seruice seene:
Which she accepts, with thankes, and goodly gree,[1]
Greatly aduancing his gay cheualree.
So marcheth home, and by her takes the knight,
Whom all the people follow with great glee,
Shouting, and clapping all their hands on hight,
That all the aire it fils, and flyes to heauen bright.

Home is he brought, and laid in sumptuous bed:
Where many skilfull leaches him abide,
To salue his hurts, that yet still freshly bled.
In wine and oyle they wash his woundes wide,
And softly can[2] embalme on euery side.
And all the while, most heauenly melody
About the bed sweet musicke did diuide,
Him to beguile of griefe and agony:
And all the while *Duessa* wept full bitterly.

(*Faerie Queene* I. v. 1–17)

[1] gree] favour goodwill   [2] can] began to: did

EDMUND SPENSER

THE CAUE OF MAMMON

At length they came into a larger space,
That stretcht it selfe into an ample plaine,
Through which a beaten broad high way did trace,
That streight did lead to *Plutoes* griesly raine:[1]
By that wayes side, there sate infernall Payne,
And fast beside him sat tumultuous Strife:
The one in hand an yron whip did straine,
The other brandished a bloudy knife,
And both did gnash their teeth, and both did threaten life.

On thother side in one consort there sate,
Cruell Reuenge, and rancorous Despight,
Disloyall Treason, and hart-burning Hate,
But gnawing Gealosie out of their sight
Sitting alone, his bitter lips did bight,
And trembling Feare still to and fro did fly,
And found no place, where safe he shroud him might,
Lamenting Sorrow did in darknesse lye,
And Shame his vgly face did hide from liuing eye.

And ouer them sad Horrour with grim hew,
Did alwayes sore, beating his yron wings;
And after him Owles and Night-rauens flew:
The hatefull messengers of heauy things,
Of death and dolour telling sad tidings;
Whiles sad *Celeno*,[2] sitting on a clift,
A song of bale and bitter sorrow sings,
That hart of flint asunder could haue rift:
Which hauing ended, after him she flyeth swift.

All these before the gates of *Pluto* lay,
By whom they passing, spake vnto them nought.
But th'Elfin knight with wonder all the way
Did feed his eyes, and fild his inner thought.
At last him to a litle dore he brought,

---

[1] griesly raine] grim kingdom   [2] *Celeno*] one of the Harpies

59

That to the gate of Hell, which gaped wide,
Was next adioyning, ne them parted ought:
Betwixt them both was but a litle stride,
That did the house of Richesse from hell-mouth diuide.

Before the dore sat selfe-consuming Care,
Day and night keeping wary watch and ward,
For feare lest Force or Fraud should vnaware
Breake in, and spoile the treasure there in gard:
Ne would he suffer Sleepe once thither-ward
Approch, albe his drowsie den were next;
For next to death is Sleepe to be compard:
Therefore his house is vnto his annext;
Here Sleep, there Richesse, and Hel-gate them both be-
    twext.[1]

So soone as *Mammon* there arriu'd, the dore
To him did open, and affoorded way;
Him followed eke Sir *Guyon* euermore,
Ne darkenesse him, ne daunger might dismay.
Soone as he entred was, the dore streight way
Did shut, and from behind it forth there lept
An vgly feend, more fowle then dismall day,
The which with monstrous stalke behind him stept,
And euer as he went, dew watch vpon him kept.

Well hoped he, ere long that hardy guest,
If euer couetous hand, or lustfull eye,
Or lips he layd on thing, that likt him best,
Or euer sleepe his eye-strings did vntye,
Should be his pray. And therefore still on hye
He ouer him did hold his cruell clawes,
Threatning with greedy gripe to do him dye
And rend in peeces with his rauenous pawes,
If euer he transgrest the fatall *Stygian* lawes.

That houses forme within was rude and strong,
Like an huge caue, hewne out of rocky clift,
From whose rough vaut the ragged breaches hong,
Embost with massy gold of glorious gift,
And with rich metall loaded euery rift,

[1] both betwext] between them both

That heuy ruine they did seeme to threat;
And ouer them *Arachne* high did lift
Her cunning web, and spred her subtile net,
Enwrapped in fowle smoke and clouds more blacke then
    iet.

Both roofe, and floore, and wals were all of gold,
But ouergrowne with dust and old decay,
And hid in darknesse, that none could behold
The hew thereof: for vew of chearefull day
Did neuer in that house it selfe display,
But a fainte shadow of vncertain light;
Such as a lamp, whose life does fade away:
Or as the Moone cloathed with clowdy night,
Does shew to him, that walkes in feare and sad affright.

In all that rowme was nothing to be seene,
But huge great yron chests and coffers strong,
All bard with double bends, that none could weene[1]
Them to efforce[2] by violence or wrong;
On euery side they placed were along.
But all the ground with sculs was scattered,
And dead mens bones, which round about were flong,
Whose liues, it seemed, whilome there were shed,
And their vile carcases now left vnburied.

They forward passe, ne *Guyon* yet spoke word,
Till that they came vnto an yron dore,
Which to them opened of his owne accord,
And shewd of richesse such exceeding store,
As eye of man did neuer see before;
Ne euer could within one place be found,
Though all the wealth, which is, or was of yore,
Could gathered be through all the world around,
And that aboue were added to that vnder ground.

The charge thereof vnto a couetous Spright
Commaunded was, who thereby did attend,
And warily awaited day and night,
From other couetous feends it to defend,
Who it to rob and ransacke did intend.

---

[1] weene] think   [2] efforce] break open

Then *Mammon* turning to that warriour, said;
Loe here the worldes blis, loe here the end,
To which all men do ayme, rich to be made:
Such grace now to be happy, is before thee laid.

(*Faerie Queene*, II. vii. 21–32.)

THE BOWER OF BLISS

THENCE passing forth, they shortly do arriue,
Whereas the Bowre of *Blisse* was situate;
A place pickt out by choice of best aliue,
That natures worke by art can imitate:
In which what euer in this worldly state
Is sweet, and pleasing vnto liuing sense,
Or that may dayntiest fantasie aggrate,[1]
Was poured forth with plentifull dispence,
And made there to abound with lauish affluence.

Goodly it was enclosed round about,
Aswell their entred guestes to keepe within,
As those vnruly beasts to hold without;
Yet was the fence thereof but weake and thin;
Nought feard their force, that fortilage to win,
But wisedomes powre, and temperaunces might,
By which the mightiest things efforced bin:
And eke the gate was wrought of substaunce light,
Rather for pleasure, then for battery or fight.

Yt framed was of precious yuory,
That seemd a worke of admirable wit;
And therein all the famous history
Of *Iason* and *Medaea* was ywrit;
Her mighty charmes, her furious louing fit,
His goodly conquest of the golden fleece,
His falsed faith, and loue too lightly flit,
The wondred *Argo*, which in venturous peece
First through the *Euxine* seas bore all the flowr of *Greece*.

Ye might haue seene the frothy billowes fry[2]
Vnder the ship, as thorough them she went,
That seemd the waues were into yuory,
Or yuory into the waues were sent;

---

[1] aggrate] gratify [2] fry] boil, seethe

62

And other where the snowy substaunce sprent[1]
With vermell, like the boyes bloud therein shed,
A piteous spectacle did represent,
And otherwhiles with gold besprinkeled;
Yt seemd th'enchaunted flame, which did *Creusa* wed.

All this, and more might in that goodly gate
Be red; that euer open stood to all,
Which thither came: but in the Porch there sate
A comely personage of stature tall,
And semblaunce pleasing, more then naturall,
That trauellers to him seemd to entize;
His looser garment to the ground did fall,
And flew about his heeles in wanton wize,
Not fit for speedy pace, or manly exercize.

They in that place him *Genius* did call:
Not that celestiall powre, to whom the care
Of life, and generation of all
That liues, pertaines in charge particulare,
Who wondrous things concerning our welfare,
And straunge phantomes doth let vs oft forsee,
And oft of secret ill bids vs beware:
That is our Selfe, whom though we do not see,
Yet each doth in him selfe it well perceiue to bee.

Therefore a God him sage Antiquity
Did wisely make, and good *Agdistes* call:
But this same was to that quite contrary,
The foe of life, that good enuyes to all,
That secretly doth vs procure to fall,
Through guilefull semblaunts, which he makes vs see.
He of this Gardin had the gouernall,[2]
And Pleasures porter was deuized to bee,
Holding a staffe in hand for more formalitee.

With diuerse flowres he daintily was deckt,
And strowed round about, and by his side
A mighty Mazer bowle[3] of wine was set,
As if it had to him bene sacrifide;

---

[1] sprent] sprinkled   [2] gouernall] governance   [3] Mazer bowel]
wooden drinking-cup

Wherewith all new-come guests he gratifide:
So did he eke Sir *Guyon* passing by:
But he his idle curtesie defide,
And ouerthrew his bowle disdainfully;
And broke his staffe, with which he charmed semblants sly.

Thus being entred, they behold around
A large and spacious plaine, on every side
Strowed with pleasauns, whose faire grassy ground
Mantled with greene, and goodly beautifide
With all the ornaments of *Floraes* pride,
Wherewith her mother Art, as halfe in scorne
Of niggard Nature, like a pompous bride
Did decke her, and too lauishly adorne,
When forth from virgin bowre she comes in th' early morne.

Thereto the Heauens alwayes Iouiall,
Lookt on them louely, still in stedfast state,
Ne suffred storme nor frost on them to fall,
Their tender buds or leaues to violate,
Nor scorching heat, nor cold intemperate
T'afflict the creatures, which therein did dwell,
But the milde aire with season moderate
Gently attempred, and disposed so well,
That still it breathed forth sweet spirit and holesome smell.

More sweet and holesome, then the pleasaunt hill
Of *Rhodope*, on which the Nimphe, that bore
A gyaunt babe, her selfe for griefe did kill;
Or the Thessalian *Tempe*, where of yore
Faire *Daphne Phoebus* hart with loue did gore;
Or *Ida*, where the Gods lou'd to repaire,
When euer they their heauenly bowres forlore;
Or sweet *Parnasse*, the haunt of Muses faire;
Or *Eden* selfe, if ought with *Eden* mote[1] compaire.

(*Faerie Queene*, II. xii. 42–52.)

BRITOMART IN THE HOUSE OF BUSIRANE

THERE they dismounting, drew their weapons bold
And stoutly came vnto the Castle gate;
Whereas no gate they found, them to withhold,

[1] mote] may

Nor ward to wait at morne and euening late,
But in the Porch, that did them sore amate,[1]
A flaming fire, ymixt with smouldry smoke,
And stinking Sulphure, that with griesly hate
And dreadfull horrour did all entraunce choke,
Enforced them their forward footing to reuoke.

Greatly thereat was *Britomart* dismayd,
Ne in that stownd[2] wist, how her selfe to beare;
For daunger vaine it were, to haue assayd
That cruell element, which all things feare,
Ne none can suffer to approchen neare:
And turning backe to *Scudamour*, thus sayd;
What monstrous enmity prouoke we heare?
Foolhardy as th'Earthes children, the which made
Battell against the Gods, so we a God inuade.

* * * * *

Therewith resolu'd to proue her vtmost might,
Her ample shield she threw before her face,
And her swords point directing forward right,
Assayld the flame, the which eftsoones gaue place,
And did it selfe diuide with equall space,
That through she passed; as a thunder bolt
Perceth the yielding ayre, and doth displace
The soring clouds into sad showres ymolt;[3]
So to her yold[4] the flames, and did their force reuolt.[5]

Whom whenas *Scudamour* saw past the fire,
Safe and vntoucht, he likewise gan assay,
With greedy will, and enuious desire,
And bad the stubborne flames to yield him way:
But cruell *Mulciber* would not obay
His threatfull pride, but did the more augment
His mighty rage, and with imperious sway
Him forst (maulgre)[6] his fiercenesse to relent,
And backe retire, all scorcht and pitifully brent.

---

[1] amate] dismay   [2] stownd] bewilderment   [3] ymolt] melted
[4] yold] yielded   [5] reuolt] turn back   [6] maulgre] reluctantly

With huge impatience he inly swelt,[1]
More for great sorrow, that he could not pas,
Then for the burning torment, which he felt,
That with fell woodnesse[2] he effierced was,
And wilfully him throwing on the gras,
Did beat and bounse his head and brest full sore;
The whiles the Championesse now entred has
The vtmost rowme, and past the formest dore,
The vtmost rowme, abounding with all precious store.

For round about, the wals yclothed were
With goodly arras[3] of great maiesty,
Wouen with gold and silke so close and nere,
That the rich metall lurked priuily,
As faining to be hid from enuious eye;
Yet here, and there, and euery where vnwares
It shewd it selfe, and shone vnwillingly;
Like a discoulourd Snake, whose hidden snares   [declares.
Through the greene gras his long bright burnisht backe

And in those Tapets[4] weren fashioned
Many faire pourtraicts, and many a faire feate,
And all of loue, and all of lusty-hed,
As seemed by their semblaunt did entreat;
And eke all *Cupids* warres they did repeate,
And cruell battels, which he whilome fought
Gainst all the Gods, to make his empire great;
Besides the huge massacres, which he wrought
On mighty kings and kesars, into thraldome brought.

* * * * *

The warlike Mayde beholding earnestly
The goodly ordinance of this rich place,
Did greatly wonder, ne could satisfie
Her greedy eyes with gazing a long space,
But more she meruaild that no footings trace,
Nor wight appear'd, but wastefull[5] emptinesse,
And solemne silence ouer all that place:
Straunge thing it seem'd, that none was to possesse
So rich purueyance,[6] ne them keepe with carefulnesse.

[1] swelt] swelled   [2] fell woodnesse] dire madness   [3] arras] tapestry
[4] tapet] tapestry   [5] wastefull] desolate   [6] purueyance] equipment

And as she lookt about, she did behold,
How ouer that same dore was likewise writ,
Be bold, be bold, and euery where *Be bold*,
That much she muz'd, yet could not construe it
By any ridling skill, or commune wit.[1]
At last she spyde at that roomes vpper end,
Another yron dore, on which was writ,
Be not too bold; wherto though she did bend
Her earnest mind, yet wist not what it might intend.

Thus she there waited vntill euentyde,
Yet liuing creature none she saw appeare:
And now sad[2] shadowes gan the world to hyde,
From mortall vew, and wrap in darkeness dreare;
Yet nould she doff her weary armes, for feare
Of secret daunger, ne let sleepe oppresse
Her heauy eyes with natures burdein deare,
But drew her selfe aside in sickernesse,[3]
And her welpointed weapons did about her dresse.[4]

Tho[5] when as chearelesse Night ycouered had
Faire heauen with an vniuersall cloud,
That euery wight dismayd with darknesse sad,
In silence and in sleepe themselues did shroud,
She heard a shrilling Trompet sound aloud,
Signe of nigh battell, or got victory;
Nought therewith daunted was her courage proud,
But rather stird to cruell enmity,
Expecting euer, when some foe she might descry.

With that, an hideous storme of winde arose,
With dreadfull thunder and lightning atwixt,
And an earth-quake, as if it streight would lose
The worlds foundations from his centre fixt;
A direfull stench of smoke and sulphure mixt
Ensewd, whose noyance fild the fearefull sted,[6]
From the fourth houre of night vntill the sixt;
Yet the bold *Britonesse* was nought ydred,[7]
Though much emmou'd, but stedfast still perseuered.

[1] commune wit] common sense   [2] sad] heavy   [3] sickernesse] safety
[4] dresse] prepare   [5] Tho] then   [6] sted] place   [7] ydred] afraid

All suddenly a stormy whirlwind blew
Throughout the house, that clapped euery dore,
With which that yron wicket open flew,
As it with mightie leuers had bene tore:
And forth issewd, as on the ready flore
Of some Theatre, a graue personage,
That in his hand a branch of laurell bore,
With comely haueour[1] and count'nance sage,
Yclad in costly garments, fit for tragicke Stage

Proceeding to the midst, he still did stand,
As if in mind he somewhat had to say,
And to the vulgar beckning with his hand,
In signe of silence, as to heare a play,
By liuely actions he gan bewray[2]
Some argument of matter passioned;
Which doen, he backe retyred soft away,
And passing by, his name discouered,
Ease, on his robe in golden letters cyphered.

The noble Mayd, still standing all this vewd,
And merueild at his strange intendiment,[3]
With that a ioyous fellowship issewd
Of Minstrals, making goodly meriment,
With wanton Bardes, and Rymers impudent,
All which together sung full chearefully
A lay of loues delight, with sweet concent:
After whom marcht a iolly company,
In manner of a maske, enranged orderly.

The whiles a most delitious harmony,
In full straunge notes was sweetly heard to sound,
That the rare sweetnesse of the melody
The feeble senses wholly did confound,
And the fraile soule in deepe delight nigh dround:
And when it ceast, shrill trompets loud did bray,
That their report did farre away rebound,
And when they ceast, it gan againe to play,
The whiles the maskers marched forth in trim array.

(*Faerie Queene*, III, from xi & xii.)

[1] haueour] bearing   [2] bewray] reveal   [3] intendiment] intention

WILLIAM SHAKESPEARE

WILLIAM SHAKESPEARE (1564–1616), was born at Stratford-on-Avon, and baptized on 26 April 1564. He was educated at the free grammar school at Stratford. He married in 1582 Anne, probably daughter of Richard Hathaway of Shottery. He left Stratford about 1585 and arrived in London about 1586, where perhaps he became acquainted with Lord Southampton. He was probably engaged in some subordinate capacity at one of the two theatres (The Theatre or The Curtain) then existing in London, and afterwards became a member of the Lord Chamberlain's (after the accession of James I, the King's) company of players. His earliest work as a dramatist probably dates from 1591, and is to be found in the three parts of *Henry VI*. *Henry VI* was followed by *Richard III* and *The Comedy of Errors* in 1592–3, and by *Titus Andronicus* and *The Taming of the Shrew* in 1593–4. Shakespeare published the poems *Venus and Adonis* and *Lucrece* respectively in 1593 and 1594. The *Sonnets* were printed in 1609, but the bulk of them appear to have been written between 1593 and 1596. *Two Gentlemen of Verona, Love's Labour's Lost*, and *Romeo and Juliet* (Shakespeare's first tragedy) are assigned to 1594–5; *Richard II* and *A Midsummer Night's Dream* to 1595–6. *King John* and *The Merchant of Venice* are assigned to 1596–7, the two parts of *Henry IV* to 1597–8. Shakespeare's most perfect essays in comedy, *Much Ado about Nothing, As You Like It*, and *Twelfth Night* belong to the years 1598–1600, together with *Henry V* and *Julius Caesar*. *Hamlet* and *The Merry Wives of Windsor* are assigned to 1600–1, *Troilus and Cressida* and *All's Well that Ends Well* to the next two theatrical seasons. The probable order and dates of the plays which followed is *Measure for Measure* and *Othello*, 1604–5; *King Lear* and *Macbeth*, 1605–6; *Antony and Cleopatra*, 1606–7; *Coriolanus* and *Timon of Athens*, 1607–8, *Pericles, Cymbeline*, and *The Winter's Tale* are assigned to the next three seasons; and *The Tempest*, probably the last drama that Shakespeare completed, to 1611–12. *Henry VIII*, of which only some half-dozen scenes are thought to be by Shakespeare, was produced in 1613.

He spent the concluding years of his life (1611–16) mainly at Stratford.

SHAKESPEARE'S style has a wider range than that of any other writer ancient or modern. It includes within its compass the comic and the tragic, and can give perfect expression to the humours of Falstaff, no less than to the heart-searchings of Hamlet or the tragic passion of Lear. And with this range goes as remarkable a flexibility; for the poet may pass from one key to another by an almost imperceptible subtlety of modulation or by one of those startling changes in the music that give so dynamic an expression to the dramatic content. Yet though Shakespeare's style is instantly recognizable and felt as masterly in whatever register it moves, he is seldom proclaimed as among the supreme masters of style, and is indeed in this respect often compared unfavourably with poets who are admitted by common consent to be his inferiors in range and vitality.

Such judgements rest on a classification of styles which is altogether inadequate, and whose shortcomings are never so clearly revealed as in the absurdities to which critics are reduced when they rigorously apply such categories to Shakespeare. When Arnold talked of the grand style there was in his words an echo of the old rhetorical division of styles into the high, the middle, and the low. Shakespeare, Arnold thought, was not for all his virtuosity an assured master of the grand style, the style that was highest and best. And the critic obviously had in mind some form such as the epic in Milton's hands, or the drama of Aeschylus or Sophocles, forms in which many of Shakespeare's most admired turns of expression would be completely out of keeping. But this is to think of artistic form as a jelly mould instead of as a vital force,[1] as something into which is poured an appropriate content instead of as a shaping spirit informing matter with life and meaning.

We may say, if we choose, that such phrases as 'Hell is murky' and 'The Thane of Fife had a wife' do not seem to us at first sight to be in the grand style. But it is as unprofitable to judge words or expressions in isolation as it would be to take some collocation of notes or rhythmical phrase from a great musical composition and say that they are not in themselves beautiful or interesting; for what matters is the significance they take on in composition, where the composer may achieve a miracle with four drum taps.

[1] See Sir Donald Tovey's observations on the ridiculous criticism of Beethoven's forms, in his *Companion to the Pianoforte Sonatas*, p. 301, and elsewhere.

And Shakespeare can give the simple and only half-coherent phrases that fall from the lips of the sleep-walking Lady Macbeth a weight of magic fear and pity that oppresses the very soul of the listener. This great scene is technically in prose, and like so many other of Shakespeare's finest scenes cannot be included in this selection; but its hushed and broken utterance is as truly great poetry as the murder-scene itself (*see* p. 88) whose depths we should never be able to sound but for the art with which Shakespeare contrives this amazing return of its main theme, but in how changed a key and rhythm.

It is the large and all-pervading design in Shakespeare's masterpieces that the reader of extracts is in danger of forgetting. The short passages that follow are not a selection from the 'beauties of Shakespeare'; and what is admirable in them is not the brief perfection of an isolated moment, but a revelation made possible by his art as a whole, and to be understood fully only in its context.

The late Professor Housman, in a provocative mood, once quoted[1] with approval Dr. Johnson's assertion that Shakespeare had nowhere written more than six consecutive lines of good poetry. In such a sally the speaker is not to be taken as on oath, yet the remark but carries to an extreme the attitude to Shakespeare's work, common in the eighteenth century, which saw great beauties amidst much it took to be unpoetical matter, and which admired his inspiration and lamented his lack of art. Against Johnson's verdict may be put that of one whose task compelled him to consider the style of one of the tragedies not merely for its adequacy in one scene or another but as expressive, on the various planes of dramatic intensity into which Shakespeare had divided the action, of the central idea. And this is the judgement which the laborious examination demanded by a translation that shall be faithful not merely to the meaning of any passage, but to its

[1] Introductory Lecture, 1892.

significance for the whole play, forced on Maeterlinck's poetic mind:

Il est le plus sage, le plus savant, le plus conscient et le plus harmonieux des poètes. Pas un vers dans *Macbeth* qui ne soit musical et ne paraisse modelé, si l'on peut hasarder cette image, sur le rythme intérieur et profond de la passion qu'il exprime.[1]

Maeterlinck is here considering the play as a composition, judging whether the parts are expressed in language fitted to their respective importance in the work as a whole, not picking out the passages that seem to his casual ear good tunes or good lines.

As Shakespeare built his plays on a scheme of contrasts and oppositions much sharper and more violent than those acceptable in the classical forms, we must not look in his style for the more uniform and sustained organ tone of Milton's mighty harmonies. What we must ask is whether the contrasting parts of the drama are in a style fitted to their respective importance; and, if the answer is, Yes, then no style could be greater, for the total effect is unsurpassed in grandeur.

To those who read the plays as plays, and not to pick out good lines, Shakespeare's art is visible in many of the less elevated passages and scenes, in his transitions, and often in the management of what might seem the mechanical features of his form, no less than in the passages here selected.

Though the critical world has been slow to acknowledge the perfection of what may be described as the larger rhythms in Shakespeare's style, it has always acclaimed the perfection with which his phrasing is moulded on what Maeterlinck has called 'the inner rhythm' of the objects or feelings described. This must not of course be confused with the simple onomatopoetic effects with which Pope illustrates the dictum that

The sound must seem an Echo to the sense.

[1] Introduction to Maeterlinck's translation of *Macbeth*, p. xxiv.

Shakespeare does sometimes achieve a singular beauty in this kind of effect as with

> The singing masons building roofs of gold,[1]

a line which Keats defended against Wordsworth's criticism that there was too much uniformity in the vowel-sound by observing that Shakespeare did not wish to vary them. But obvious and merely external imitation, especially imitation that is too insistent on its mimicry, is not what Maeterlinck admires, but rather the realization of the unheard melody in such lines as Hamlet's

> Absent thee from felicity awhile,
> And in this harsh world draw thy breath in pain,

where, as a critic observes, 'The breast actually labours to get through this last line'.

Though Shakespeare could never have acquired by study his power of phrasing, he did not achieve such masterly effects without prolonged and intense application to his art. As an index of this effort may stand the modifications in his verse form that appear from period to period of his development. His early verse is in an unbroken form, with the line falling into two parts, divided by the caesura near the middle, and claused by the pause at the end:

> The current that with gentle murmur glides,
> Thou know'st, being stopp'd, impatiently doth rage;
> But when his fair course is not hindered,
> He makes sweet music with th'enamell'd stones,
> Giving a gentle kiss to every sedge
> He overtaketh in his pilgrimage;
> And so by many winding nooks he strays
> With willing sport to the wild ocean.[2]

But verse built of such more or less similar or symmetrical units does not admit of the emphasis, contrast, and climax Shakespeare's growing powers demanded. He therefore breaks up the symmetrical arrangement by reducing or eliminating the strong pause at the end of the line, and

[1] *Henry V*, I. ii. 198.   [2] *The Two Gentlemen of Verona*, II. vii. 24–32.

draws out the sense from line to line, so that the paragraph, not the line, becomes the unit of the verse. In this paragraph what is to be emphasized can be given a form that will mark it off from the rest, so that every part receives its appropriate and different treatment. As an illustration of this later and more broken style may stand some lines from *The Tempest.*[1]

> Full many a lady
> I have ey'd with best regard, and many a time
> The harmony of their tongues hath into bondage
> Brought my too diligent ear: for several virtues
> Have I lik'd several women; never any
> With so full soul but some defect in her
> Did quarrel with the noblest grace she ow'd,
> And put it to the foil: but you, O you!
> So perfect and so peerless are created
> Of every creature's best.

And Daniel Webbe's comment[2] may stand as a summary of these features of Shakespeare's style: 'In this passage, the rising from the feeble and prosaic movement of the first lines, to the even tenor of harmony in the last, is entirely Miltonic.'

In rhythmical artistry Shakespeare stands among English poets with Milton, as supreme in the dramatic form as the latter in the slower planetary wheelings of his epic verse; in his command of metaphor Shakespeare is alone. His language, as his thought, is like a discharge leaping between the poles of Heaven and Earth, bridging the material and the spiritual with the intensest form of illumination. At its simplest this combination of concrete and abstract is found in such familiar phrases as 'the shot and danger of desire', 'the whips and scorns of time', 'some sweet oblivious antidote', while, in such a phrase as 'the dark backward and abysm of time', Shakespeare's metaphor like his rhythm seems to catch from the object the very essence of its otherwise impalpable reality.

---

[1] III. i. 39–48. [2] In *Remarks on the Beauties of Poetry.*

Sometimes Shakespeare sustains his metaphor to a con-clusion:

> the seeded pride
> That hath to this maturity blown up
> In rank Achilles must or now be cropp'd,
> Or, shedding, breed a nursery of like evil,
> To overbulk us all.[1]

Of a type where the metaphors are parallels a very beautiful example is Macbeth's speech beginning

> Canst thou not minister to a mind diseased[2]

and this should be compared with his next speech (see p. 90) where the changes are abrupter and the metaphors climb on each other's backs to the assault on heaven itself.

By the tragic period metaphor has completely dropped any ornamental role it sometimes assumes in the earlier plays; it is now strictly functional. By this means Shake-speare gives to each play its appropriate atmosphere and often to the characters their peculiar mode of expression. Every commentator on *Macbeth* has noted the ominous imagery in which Shakespeare paints the thought and fears of the characters, and how it is throughout modified by a central idea, which the imagery in turn almost makes visible to the senses. For the human situation as displayed by Shakespeare is not 'done wholly for the *understanding*; bald and naked—nature divested of her chiaroscuro' as Constable complained of some paintings, 'which she never is under any circumstances, for we never see her but through a medium'. Shakespeare studies the emotional light and shade of his actions as passionately as Constable studied the light and shade that plays over the cornfield or the foliage of his trees. And taking up Constable's definition of chiaroscuro, this play of light and shade in nature, as the power which creates space and which enables us to judge what is distant and what near, Shakespeare's imagery,

---

[1] *Troilus and Cressida*, i. iii. 316–20.   [2] *Macbeth*, v. iii. 40.

which is the chiaroscuro of his moral world, contributes to the dramas their space, that sense of infinite issues with which Shakespeare has invested the actions of men.

PETER ALEXANDER.

JOHN OF GAUNT'S DYING SPEECH

METHINKS I am a prophet new inspir'd,
And thus expiring do foretell of him:
His rash fierce blaze of riot cannot last,
For violent fires soon burn out themselves;
Small showers last long, but sudden storms are short;
He tires betimes that spurs too fast betimes;
With eager feeding food doth choke the feeder:
Light vanity, insatiate cormorant,
Consuming means, soon preys upon itself.
This royal throne of kings, this scepter'd isle,
This earth of majesty, this seat of Mars,
This other Eden, demi-paradise,
This fortress built by Nature for herself
Against infection and the hand of war,
This happy breed of men, this little world,
This precious stone set in the silver sea,
Which serves it in the office of a wall,
Or as a moat defensive to a house,
Against the envy of less happier lands,
This blessed plot, this earth, this realm, this England,
This nurse, this teeming womb of royal kings,
Fear'd by their breed and famous by their birth,
Renowned for their deeds as far from home,—
For Christian service and true chivalry,—
As is the sepulchre in stubborn Jewry
Of the world's ransom, blessed Mary's Son:
This land of such dear souls, this dear, dear land,
Dear for her reputation through the world,
Is now leas'd out,—I die pronouncing it,—
Like to a tenement, or pelting[1] farm:
England, bound in with the triumphant sea,

[1] pelting] paltry.

76

Whose rocky shore beats back the envious siege
Of watery Neptune, is now bound in with shame,
With inky blots, and rotten parchment bonds:
That England, that was wont to conquer others,
Hath made a shameful conquest of itself.
Ah! would the scandal vanish with my life,
How happy then were my ensuing death.

(Richard II, II. i.)

SOLILOQUY ON SLEEP

How many thousand of my poorest subjects
Are at this hour asleep! O sleep! O gentle sleep!
Nature's soft nurse, how have I frighted thee,
That thou no more wilt weigh my eyelids down
And steep my senses in forgetfulness?
Why rather, sleep, liest thou in smoky cribs,
Upon uneasy pallets stretching thee,
And hush'd with buzzing night-flies to thy slumber,
Than in the perfum'd chambers of the great,
Under the canopies of costly state,
And lull'd with sound of sweetest melody?
O thou dull god! why liest thou with the vile
In loathsome beds, and leav'st the kingly couch
A watch-case or a common 'larum bell?
Wilt thou upon the high and giddy mast
Seal up the ship-boy's eyes, and rock his brains
In cradle of the rude imperious surge,
And in the visitation of the winds,
Who take the ruffian billows by the top,
Curling their monstrous heads, and hanging them
With deaf'ning clamour in the slippery clouds,
That with the hurly death itself awakes?
Canst thou, O partial sleep! give thy repose
To the wet sea-boy in an hour so rude,
And in the calmest and most stillest night,
With all appliances and means to boot,
Deny it to a king? Then, happy low, lie down!
Uneasy lies the head that wears a crown.

(2 Henry IV, iii. i.)

QUEEN MAB

Mercutio. O! then, I see, Queen Mab hath been with
you.
Benvolio. Queen Mab! What's she?
Mercutio. She is the fairies' midwife, and she comes
In shape no bigger than an agate-stone
On the fore-finger of an alderman,
Drawn with a team of little atomies
Athwart men's noses as they lie asleep:
Her waggon-spokes made of long spinners' legs;
The cover, of the wings of grasshoppers;
The traces, of the smallest spider's web;
The collars, of the moonshine's watery beams;
Her whip, of cricket's bone; the lash, of film;
Her waggoner, a small grey-coated gnat,
Not half so big as a round little worm
Prick'd from the lazy finger of a maid;
Her chariot is an empty hazel-nut,
Made by the joiner squirrel or old grub,
Time out o' mind the fairies' coach-makers.
And in this state she gallops night by night
Through lovers' brains, and then they dream of love;
O'er courtiers' knees, that dream on curtsies straight;
O'er lawyers' fingers, who straight dream on fees;
O'er ladies' lips, who straight on kisses dream;
Which oft the angry Mab with blisters plagues,
Because their breaths with sweetmeats tainted are.
Sometimes she gallops o'er a courtier's nose,
And then dreams he of smelling out a suit;
And sometimes comes she with a tithe-pig's tail,
Tickling a parson's nose as a' lies asleep,
Then dreams he of another benefice;
Sometimes she driveth o'er a soldier's neck,
And then dreams he of cutting foreign throats,
Of breaches, ambuscadoes, Spanish blades,
Of healths five fathom deep; and then anon
Drums in his ear, at which he starts and wakes;
And, being thus frighted, swears a prayer or two,
And sleeps again. This is that very Mab

That plats the manes of horses in the night;
And bakes the elf-locks in foul sluttish hairs,
Which once untangled much misfortune bodes;
This is the hag, when maids lie on their backs,
That presses them and learns them first to bear,
Making them women of good carriage.

(Romeo and Juliet, 1. iv.)

ROMEO'S LAST WORDS

How oft when men are at the point of death
Have they been merry! which their keepers call
A lightning before death: O! how may I
Call this a lightning? O my love! my wife!
Death, that hath suck'd the honey of thy breath,
Hath had no power yet upon thy beauty:
Thou art not conquer'd; beauty's ensign yet
Is crimson in thy lips and in thy cheeks,
And death's pale flag is not advanced there.
Tybalt, liest thou there in thy bloody sheet?
O! what more favour can I do to thee,
Than with that hand that cut thy youth in twain
To sunder his that was thine enemy?
Forgive me, cousin! Ah! dear Juliet,
Why art thou yet so fair? Shall I believe
That unsubstantial Death is amorous,
And that the lean abhorred monster keeps
Thee here in dark to be his paramour?
For fear of that I still will stay with thee,
And never from this palace of dim night
Depart again: here, here will I remain
With worms that are thy chambermaids; O! here
Will I set up my everlasting rest,
And shake the yoke of inauspicious stars
From this world-wearied flesh. Eyes, look your last!
Arms, take your last embrace! and, lips, O you
The doors of breath, seal with a righteous kiss
A dateless bargain to engrossing death!

79

Come, bitter conduct, come, unsavoury guide!
Thou desperate pilot, now at once run on
The dashing rocks thy sea-sick weary bark!
Here's to my love! [*Drinks.*] O true apothecary!
Thy drugs are quick. Thus with a kiss I die.   [*Dies.*
                        (*Romeo and Juliet*, v. iii.)

'ALL THE WORLD'S A STAGE'

                                All the world's a stage,
And all the men and women merely players:
They have their exits and their entrances;
And one man in his time plays many parts,
His acts being seven ages. At first the infant,
Mewling and puking in the nurse's arms.
And then the whining school-boy, with his satchel,
And shining morning face, creeping like snail
Unwillingly to school. And then the lover,
Sighing like a furnace, with a woful ballad
Made to his mistress' eyebrow. Then a soldier,
Full of strange oaths, and bearded like the pard,
Jealous in honour, sudden and quick in quarrel,
Seeking the bubble reputation
Even in the cannon's mouth. And then the justice,
In fair round belly with good capon lin'd,
With eyes severe, and beard of formal cut,
Full of wise saws and modern instances;
And so he plays his part. The sixth age shifts
Into the lean and slipper'd pantaloon,
With spectacles on nose and pouch on side,
His youthful hose well sav'd, a world too wide
For his shrunk shank; and his big manly voice,
Turning again toward childish treble, pipes
And whistles in his sound. Last scene of all,
That ends this strange eventful history,
Is second childishness and mere oblivion,
Sans teeth, sans eyes, sans taste, sans everything.
                            (*As you Like It*, ii. vii.)

'IN SUCH A NIGHT'

Lorenzo. The moon shines bright: in such a night as this,
When the sweet wind did gently kiss the trees
And they did make no noise, in such a night
Troilus methinks mounted the Troyan walls,
And sigh'd his soul toward the Grecian tents,
Where Cressid lay that night.

Jessica.   In such a night
Did Thisbe fearfully o'ertrip the dew,
And saw the lion's shadow ere himself,
And ran dismay'd away.

Lorenzo.   In such a night
Stood Dido with a willow in her hand
Upon the wild sea-banks, and waft her love
To come again to Carthage.

Jessica.   In such a night
Medea gather'd the enchanted herbs
That did renew old Æson.

Lorenzo.   In such a night
Did Jessica steal from the wealthy Jew,
And with an unthrift love did run from Venice,
As far as Belmont.

Jessica.   In such a night
Did young Lorenzo swear he lov'd her well,
Stealing her soul with many vows of faith,
And ne'er a true one.

Lorenzo.   In such a night
Did pretty Jessica, like a little shrew,
Slander her love, and he forgave it her.

*   *   *   *   *

How sweet the moonlight sleeps upon this bank!
Here will we sit, and let the sounds of music
Creep in our ears: soft stillness and the night
Become the touches of sweet harmony.
Sit, Jessica: look, how the floor of heaven
Is thick inlaid with patines of bright gold:
There's not the smallest orb which thou behold'st

But in his motion like an angel sings,
Still quiring to the young-eyed cherubins;

Such harmony is in immortal souls;
But whilst this muddy vesture of decay
Doth grossly close it in, we cannot hear it.
Come, ho! and wake Diana with a hymn:
With sweetest touches pierce your mistress' ear,
And draw her home with music.

(Merchant of Venice, v. i.)

THE LUNATIC, THE LOVER, AND THE POET

Lovers and madmen have such seething brains,
Such shaping fantasies, that apprehend
More than cool reason ever comprehends.
The lunatic, the lover, and the poet,
Are of imagination all compact:
One sees more devils than vast hell can hold,
That is, the madman; the lover, all as frantic,
See Helen's beauty in a brow of Egypt:
The poet's eye, in a fine frenzy rolling,
Doth glance from heaven to earth, from earth to heaven;
And, as imagination bodies forth
The forms of things unknown, the poet's pen
Turns them to shapes, and gives to airy nothings
A local habitation and a name.
Such tricks hath strong imagination,
That, if it would but apprehend some joy,
It comprehends some bringer of that joy;
Or in the night, imagining some fear,
How easy is a bush suppos'd a bear!

(Midsummer Night's Dream, v. i.)

ON DEATH

Isabella. What says my brother?
Claudio.   Death is a fearful thing.
Isabella. And shamed life a hateful.
Claudio. Ay, but to die, and go we know not where;
To lie in cold obstruction and to rot;
This sensible warm motion to become

A kneaded clod; and the delighted spirit
To bathe in fiery floods, or to reside
In thrilling[1] region of thick-ribbed ice;
To be imprison'd in the viewless winds,
And blown with restless violence round about
The pendant world; or to be worse than worst
Of those that lawless and incertain thoughts
Imagine howling: 'tis too horrible!
The weariest and most loathed worldly life
That age, ache, penury and imprisonment
Can lay on nature is a paradise
To what we fear of death.

(Measure for Measure, III. i.)

TO BE OR NOT TO BE

Hamlet. To be, or not to be: that is the question:
Whether 'tis nobler in the mind to suffer
The slings and arrows of outrageous fortune,
Or to take arms against a sea of troubles,
And by opposing end them? To die: to sleep;
No more; and, by a sleep, to say we end
The heart-ache and the thousand natural shocks
That flesh is heir to, 'tis a consummation
Devoutly to be wish'd. To die, to sleep;
To sleep: perchance to dream: ay, there's the rub;
For in that sleep of death what dreams may come
When we have shuffled off this mortal coil,
Must give us pause. There's the respect
That makes calamity of so long life;
For who would bear the whips and scorns of time,
The oppressor's wrong, the proud man's contumely,
The pangs of dispriz'd love, the law's delay,
The insolence of office, and the spurns
That patient merit of the unworthy takes,
When he himself might his quietus make
With a bare bodkin? who would fardels bear,
To grunt and sweat under a weary life,

[1] thrilling] piercing

But that the dread of something after death,
The undiscover'd country from whose bourn
No traveller returns, puzzles the will,
And makes us rather bear those ills we have
Than fly to others that we know not of?
Thus conscience does make cowards of us all;
And thus the native hue of resolution
Is sicklied o'er with the pale cast of thought,
And enterprises of great pith and moment
With this regard their currents turn awry,
And lose the name of action.

(Hamlet, III. i.)

DEATH OF HAMLET

Hamlet. I am dead, Horatio. Wretched queen, adieu!
You that look pale and tremble at this chance,
That are but mutes or audience to this act,
Had I but time,—as this fell sergeant, death,
Is strict in his arrest,—O! I could tell you—
But let it be. Horatio, I am dead;
Thou liv'st; report me and my cause aright
To the unsatisfied.
    Horatio.   Never believe it;
I am more an antique Roman than a Dane:
Here's yet some liquor left.
    Hamlet.   As thou'rt a man,
Give me the cup: let go; by heaven, I'll have 't.
O God! Horatio, what a wounded name,
Things standing thus unknown, shall live behind me!
If thou didst ever hold me in thy heart,
Absent thee from felicity awhile,
And in this harsh world draw thy breath in pain,
To tell my story.

[March afar off, and shot within.

                    What war-like noise is this?
    Osric. Young Fortinbras, with conquest come from Po-
land,
To the ambassadors of England gives
This war-like volley.

Hamlet.   O! I die, Horatio;
The potent poison quite o'er-crows my spirit:
I cannot live to hear the news from England,
But I do prophesy the election lights
On Fortinbras: he has my dying voice;
So tell him, with the occurrents, more and less,
Which have solicited—The rest is silence.   [*Dies.*

    Horatio. Now cracks a noble heart. Good-night, sweet
        prince,
And flights of angels sing thee to thy rest!

                                        (*Hamlet*, v. ii.)

DEATH OF ANTONY

    Antony. I am dying, Egypt, dying:
Give me some wine, and let me speak a little.
    Cleopatra. No, let me speak; and let me rail so high,
That the false housewife Fortune break her wheel,
Provok'd by my offence.

    *   *   *

    Antony. The miserable change now at my end
Lament nor sorrow at; but please your thoughts
In feeding them with those my former fortunes
Wherein I liv'd, the greatest prince o' the world,
The noblest; and do now not basely die,
Not cowardly put off my helmet to
My countryman; a Roman by a Roman
Valiantly vanquish'd. Now my spirit is going;
I can no more.
    Cleopatra.   Noblest of men, woo 't die?
Hast thou no care of me? shall I abide
In this dull world, which in thy absence is
No better than a sty? O! see my women,   [ANTONY *dies.*
The crown o' the earth doth melt. My lord!
O! wither'd is the garland of the war,
The soldier's pole is fall'n; young boys and girls
Are level now with men; the odds is gone,
And there is nothing left remarkable
Beneath the visiting moon.   [*Swoons.*
                        (*Antony and Cleopatra*, IV. xiii.)

DEATH OF CLEOPATRA

Cleopatra. Give me my robe, put on my crown; I have
Immortal longings in me; now no more
The juice of Egypt's grape shall moist this lip.
Yare, yare, good Iras; quick. Methinks I hear
Antony call; I see him rouse himself
To praise my noble act; I hear him mock
The luck of Caesar, which the gods give men
To excuse their after wrath: husband, I come:
Now to that name my courage prove my title!
I am fire, and air; my other elements
I give to baser life. So; have you done?
Come then, and take the last warmth of my lips.
Farewell, kind Charmian; Iras, long farewell.

       [*Kisses them.* IRAS *falls and dies.*

Have I the aspic in my lips? Dost fall?
If thou and nature can so gently part,
The stroke of death is as a lover's pinch,
Which hurts, and is desir'd. Dost thou lie still?
If thus thou vanishest, thou tell'st the world
It is not worth leave-taking.

Charmian. Dissolve, thick cloud, and rain; that I may say,
The gods themselves do weep.

Cleopatra.   This proves me base:
If she first meet the curled Antony,
He'll make demand of her, and spend that kiss
Which is my heaven to have. Come, thou mortal wretch,

    [*To the asp, which she applies to her breast.*

With thy sharp teeth this knot intrinsicate
Of life at once untie; poor venomous fool,
Be angry, and dispatch. O! couldst thou speak,
That I might hear thee call great Caesar ass
Unpolicied.

Charmian. O eastern star!

Cleopatra.   Peace, peace!
Dost thou not see my baby at my breast,
That sucks the nurse asleep?

Charmian.   O, break! O, break!

Cleopatra. As sweet as balm, as soft as air, as gentle,—

O Antony!—Nay, I will take thee too.

[Applying another asp to her arm.

What should I stay—   *[Dies.*

    Charmian. In this vile world? So, fare thee well.
Now boast thee, death, in thy possession lies
A lass unparallel'd. Downy windows, close;
And golden Phœbus never be beheld
Of eyes again so royal! Your crown's awry;
I'll mend it, and then play.   (*Antony and Cleopatra*, v. ii.)

VAULTING AMBITION

    Macbeth. If it were done when 'tis done, then 'twere well
It were done quickly; if the assassination
Could trammel up the consequence, and catch
With his surcease success; that but this blow
Might be the be-all and the end-all here,
But here, upon this bank and shoal of time,
We'd jump the life to come. But in these cases
We still have judgment here; that we but teach
Bloody instructions, which, being taught, return
To plague the inventor; this even-handed justice
Commends the ingredients of our poison'd chalice
To our own lips. He's here in double trust:
First, as I am his kinsman and his subject,
Strong both against the deed; then, as his host,
Who should against his murderer shut the door,
Not bear the knife myself. Besides, this Duncan
Hath borne his faculties so meek, hath been
So clear in his great office, that his virtues
Will plead like angels trumpet-tongu'd against
The deep damnation of his taking-off;
And pity, like a naked new-born babe,
Striding the blast, or heaven's cherubin, hors'd
Upon the sightless couriers of the air,
Shall blow the horrid deed in every eye,
That tears shall drown the wind. I have no spur
To prick the sides of my intent, but only
Vaulting ambition, which o'er-leaps itself
And falls on the other.—   (*Macbeth*, I. vii.)

'MACBETH DOES MURDER SLEEP'

Macbeth. I have done the deed. Didst thou not hear a
noise?

Lady Macbeth. I heard the owl scream and the crickets cry.
Did not you speak?

Macbeth.　　　　　　　When?

Lady Macbeth.　　　　　　　Now.

Macbeth.　　　　　　　　　　　　As I descended?

Lady Macbeth. Ay.

Macbeth. Hark!

Who lies i' the second chamber?

Lady Macbeth.　　　　　　　Donalbain.

Macbeth. [*Looking on his hands.*] This is a sorry sight.

Lady Macbeth. A foolish thought to say a sorry sight.

Macbeth. There's one did laugh in 's sleep, and one cried
'Murder!'

That they did wake each other: I stood and heard them;
But they did say their prayers, and address'd them
Again to sleep.

Lady Macbeth. There are two lodg'd together.

Macbeth. One cried 'God bless us!' and 'Amen' the other:
As they had seen me with these hangman's hands.
Listening their fear, I could not say 'Amen,'
When they did say 'God bless us!'

Lady Macbeth.　　　　　　　Consider it not so deeply.

Macbeth. But wherefore could not I pronounce 'Amen'?
I had most need of blessing, and 'Amen'
Stuck in my throat.

Lady Macbeth.　　　These deeds must not be thought
After these ways; so, it will make us mad.

Macbeth. Methought I heard a voice cry 'Sleep no more!
Macbeth does murder sleep,' the innocent sleep,
Sleep that knits up the ravell'd sleave of care,
The death of each day's life, sore labour's bath,
Balm of hurt minds, great nature's second course,
Chief nourisher in life's feast,—

Lady Macbeth.　　　　　　　What do you mean?

Macbeth. Still it cried, 'Sleep no more!' to all the house:
'Glamis hath murder'd sleep, and therefore Cawdor
Shall sleep no more, Macbeth shall sleep no more!'

Lady Macbeth. Who was it that thus cried? Why, worthy
    thane,
You do unbend your noble strength to think
So brainsickly of things. Go get some water,
And wash this filthy witness from your hand.
Why did you bring these daggers from the place?
They must lie there: go carry them, and smear
The sleepy grooms with blood.
    Macbeth.   I'll go no more:
I am afraid to think what I have done;
Look on 't again I dare not.
    Lady Macbeth.   Infirm of purpose!
Give me the daggers. The sleeping and the dead
Are but as pictures; 'tis the eye of childhood
That fears a painted devil. If he do bleed,
I'll gild the faces of the grooms withal;
For it must seem their guilt.   [*Exit. Knocking within.*
    Macbeth.   Whence is that knocking?
How is 't with me, when every noise appals me?
What hands are here! Ha! they pluck out mine eyes.
Will all great Neptune's ocean wash this blood
Clean from my hand? No, this my hand will rather
The multitudinous seas incarnadine,
Making the green one red.

                                   (*Macbeth*, II. ii.)

'O! FULL OF SCORPIONS'

Macbeth. O! full of scorpions is my mind, dear wife;
Thou know'st that Banquo and his Fleance lives.
    Lady Macbeth. But in them nature's copy's not eterne.
    Macbeth. There's comfort yet; they are assailable;
Then be thou jocund. Ere the bat hath flown
His cloister'd flight, ere, to black Hecate's summons
The shard-borne beetle with his drowsy hums
Hath rung night's yawning peal, there shall be done
A deed of dreadful note.
    Lady Macbeth.   What's to be done?
    Macbeth. Be innocent of the knowledge, dearest chuck,
Till thou applaud the deed. Come, seeling night,

Scarf up the tender eye of pitiful day,
And with thy bloody and invisible hand
Cancel and tear to pieces that great bond
Which keeps me pale! Light thickens, and the crow
Makes wing to the rooky wood;
Good things of day begin to droop and drowse,
Whiles night's black agents to their preys do rouse.
Thou marvell'st at my words: but hold thee still;
Things bad begun make strong themselves by ill:
So, prithee, go with me.   [*Exeunt.*

(*Macbeth*, III. ii.)

'SHE SHOULD HAVE DIED HEREAFTER'

Macbeth. Wherefore was that cry?
Seyton. The queen, my lord, is dead.
Macbeth. She should have died hereafter;
There would have been a time for such a word.
To-morrow, and to-morrow, and to-morrow,
Creeps in this petty pace from day to day,
To the last syllable of recorded time;
And all our yesterdays have lighted fools
The way to dusty death. Out, out, brief candle!
Life's but a walking shadow, a poor player
That struts and frets his hour upon the stage,
And then is heard no more; it is a tale
Told by an idiot, full of sound and fury,
Signifying nothing.

(*Macbeth*, v. v.)

OTHELLO AND DESDEMONA

Othello. It is the cause, it is the cause, my soul;
Let me not name it to you, you chaste stars!
It is the cause. Yet I'll not shed her blood,
Nor scar that whiter skin of hers than snow,
And smooth as monumental alabaster.
Yet she must die, else she'll betray more men.
Put out the light, and then put out the light:
If I quench thee, thou flaming minister,

90

I can again thy former light restore,
Should I repent me; but once put out thy light,
Thou cunning'st pattern of excelling nature,
I know not where is that Promethean heat
That can thy light relume.

(Othello, v. ii.)

DEATH OF OTHELLO

Othello. Soft you; a word or two before you go.
I have done the state some service, and they know 't;
No more of that. I pray you, in your letters,
When you shall these unlucky deeds relate,
Speak of me as I am; nothing extenuate,
Nor set down aught in malice: then, must you speak
Of one that lov'd not wisely but too well;
Of one not easily jealous, but, being wrought,
Perplex'd in the extreme; of one whose hand,
Like the base Indian, threw a pearl away
Richer than all his tribe; of one whose subdu'd eyes,
Albeit unused to the melting mood,
Drop tears as fast as the Arabian trees
Their med'cinable gum. Set you down this;
And say besides, that in Aleppo once,
Where a malignant and a turban'd Turk
Beat a Venetian and traduc'd the state,
I took by the throat the circumcised dog,
And smote him thus.   [*Stabs himself.*

(Othello, v. ii.)

LEAR AND CORDELIA

Enter, in conquest, with drum and colours, EDMUND; LEAR *and*
CORDELIA, *prisoners*; Officers, Soldiers, *&c.*

Edmund. Some officers take them away: good guard,
Until their greater pleasures first be known
That are to censure them.
Cordelia.   We are not the first
Who, with best meaning, have incurr'd the worst.
For thee, oppressed king, am I cast down;
Myself could else out-frown false Fortune's frown.
Shall we not see these daughters and these sisters?

Lear. No, no, no, no! Come, let's away to prison;
We two alone will sing like birds i' the cage:
When thou dost ask me blessing, I'll kneel down,
And ask of thee forgiveness: so we'll live,
And pray, and sing, and tell old tales, and laugh
At gilded butterflies, and hear poor rogues
Talk of court news; and we'll talk with them too,
Who loses and who wins; who's in, who's out;
And take upon 's the mystery of things,
As if we were God's spies: and we'll wear out,
In a wall'd prison, packs and sets of great ones
That ebb and flow by the moon.
  Edmund.   Take them away.

*   *   *   *   *

Enter LEAR, *with* CORDELIA *dead in his arms.*

 Lear. Howl, howl, howl, howl! O! you are men of stones:
Had I your tongues and eyes, I'd use them so
That heaven's vaults should crack. She's gone for ever.
I know when one is dead, and when one lives;
She's dead as earth. Lend me a looking-glass;
If that her breath will mist or stain the stone,
Why, then she lives.
  Kent.   Is this the promis'd end?
  Edgar. Or image of that horror?
  Albany.   Fall, and cease!
  Lear. This feather stirs; she lives! if it be so,
It is a chance which does redeem all sorrows
That ever I have felt.
  Kent. [*Kneeling.*] O, my good master!
  Lear. Prithee, away.
  Edgar.   'Tis noble Kent, your friend.
  Lear. A plague upon you, murderers, traitors all!
I might have sav'd her; now, she's gone for ever!
Cordelia, Cordelia! stay a little. Ha!
What is 't thou sayst? Her voice was ever soft,
Gentle and low, an excellent thing in woman.
             (*King Lear*, v. iii.)

DEATH OF LEAR

Lear. And my poor fool is hang'd! No, no, no life!
Why should a dog, a horse, a rat, have life,
And thou no breath at all? Thou'lt come no more,
Never, never, never, never, never!
Pray you, undo this button: thank you, sir.
Do you see this? Look on her, look, her lips,
Look there, look there!   [*Dies.*
  Edgar.   He faints!—my lord, my lord!
  Kent. Break, heart; I prithee, break.
  Edgar.   Look up, my lord.
  Kent. Vex not his ghost: O! let him pass; he hates him
That would upon the rack of this tough world
Stretch him out longer.

                              (*King Lear*, v. iii.)

THE FLOWERS OF PERDITA

HERE's flowers for you;
Hot lavender, mints, savory, marjoram;
The marigold, that goes to bed wi' the sun,
And with him rises weeping: these are flowers
Of middle summer, and I think they are given
To men of middle age. You 're very welcome.
  Camillo. I should leave grazing, were I of your flock,
And only live by gazing.
  Perdita.   Out, alas!
You'd be so lean, that blasts of January
Would blow you through and through. Now, my fair'st
    friend,
I would I had some flowers o' the spring that might
Become your time of day; and yours, and yours,
That wear upon your virgin branches yet
Your maidenheads growing: O Proserpina!
For the flowers now that frighted thou let'st fall
From Dis's waggon! daffodils,
That come before the swallow dares, and take
The winds of March with beauty; violets dim,
But sweeter than the lids of Juno's eyes

93

Or Cytherea's breath; pale prime-roses,
That die unmarried, ere they can behold
Bright Phœbus in his strength, a malady
Most incident to maids; bold oxlips and
The crown imperial; lilies of all kinds,
The flower-de-luce being one. O! these I lack
To make you garlands of, and my sweet friend,
To strew him o'er and o'er!

(The Winter's Tale, IV. iii.)

CALIBAN

BE not afeard: the isle is full of noises,
Sounds and sweet airs, that give delight, and hurt not.
Sometimes a thousand twangling instruments
Will hum about my ears; and sometime voices,
That, if I then had wak'd after long sleep,
Will make me sleep again: and then, in dreaming,
The clouds methought would open and show riches
Ready to drop upon me; that, when I wak'd,
I cried to dream again.

(The Tempest, III. ii.)

PROSPERO

YOU do look, my son, in a mov'd sort,
As if you were dismay'd: be cheerful, sir:
Our revels now are ended. These our actors,
As I foretold you, were all spirits and
Are melted into air, into thin air:
And, like the baseless fabric of this vision,
The cloud-capp'd towers, the gorgeous palaces,
The solemn temples, the great globe itself,
Yea, all which it inherit, shall dissolve
And, like this insubstantial pageant faded,
Leave not a rack behind. We are such stuff
As dreams are made on, and our little life
Is rounded with a sleep.

(The Tempest, IV. i.)

SONNETS

XVIII

SHALL I compare thee to a summer's day?
Thou art more lovely and more temperate:
Rough winds do shake the darling buds of May,
And summer's lease hath all too short a date:
Sometime too hot the eye of heaven shines,
And often is his gold complexion dimm'd;
And every fair from fair sometime declines,
By chance, or nature's changing course untrimm'd;
But thy eternal summer shall not fade,
Nor lose possession of that fair thou ow'st,
Nor shall death brag thou wander'st in his shade,
When in eternal lines to time thou grow'st;
  So long as men can breathe, or eyes can see,
  So long lives this, and this gives life to thee.

LXV

SINCE brass, nor stone, nor earth, nor boundless sea,
But sad mortality o'ersways their power,
How with this rage shall beauty hold a plea,
Whose action is no stronger than a flower?
O! how shall summer's honey breath hold out
Against the wrackful siege of battering days,
When rocks impregnable are not so stout,
Nor gates of steel so strong, but Time decays?
O fearful meditation! where, alack,
Shall Time's best jewel from Time's chest lie hid?
Or what strong hand can hold his swift foot back?
Or who his spoil of beauty can forbid?
  O! none, unless this miracle have might,
  That in black ink my love may still shine bright.

LXXIII

THAT time of year thou mayst in me behold
When yellow leaves, or none, or few, do hang
Upon those boughs which shake against the cold,
Bare ruin'd choirs, where late the sweet birds sang.
In me thou see'st the twilight of such day
As after sunset fadeth in the west;

Which by and by black night doth take away,
Death's second self, that seals up all in rest.
In me thou see'st the glowing of such fire,
That on the ashes of his youth doth lie,
As the death-bed whereon it must expire,
Consum'd with that which it was nourish'd by.
  This thou perceiv'st, which makes thy love more strong,
  To love that well which thou must leave ere long.

CVI

When in the chronicle of wasted time
I see descriptions of the fairest wights,
And beauty making beautiful old rime,
In praise of ladies dead and lovely knights,
Then, in the blazon of sweet beauty's best,
Of hand, of foot, of lip, of eye, of brow,
I see their antique pen would have express'd
Even such a beauty as you master now.
So all their praises are but prophecies
Of this our time, all you prefiguring;
And, for they look'd but with divining eyes,
They had not skill enough your worth to sing:
  For we, which now behold these present days,
  Have eyes to wonder, but lack tongues to praise.

CVII

Not mine own fears, nor the prophetic soul
Of the wide world dreaming on things to come,
Can yet the lease of my true love control,
Suppos'd as forfeit to a confin'd doom.
The mortal moon hath her eclipse endur'd,
And the sad augurs mock their own presage;
Incertainties now crown themselves assur'd,
And peace proclaims olives of endless age.
Now with the drops of this most balmy time
My love looks fresh, and Death to me subscribes,
Since, spite of him, I'll live in this poor rime,
While he insults o'er dull and speechless tribes:
  And thou in this shalt find thy monument,
  When tyrants' crests and tombs of brass are spent.

SONGS

When daisies pied and violets blue
   And lady-smocks all silver-white
And cuckoo-buds of yellow hue
   Do paint the meadows with delight,
The cuckoo then, on every tree,
Mocks married men; for thus sings he,
                    Cuckoo;
Cuckoo, cuckoo: O, word of fear,
Unpleasing to a married ear!

When shepherds pipe on oaten straws,
   And merry larks are ploughmen's clocks,
When turtles tread, and rooks, and daws,
   And maidens bleach their summer smocks,
The cuckoo then, on every tree,
Mocks married men; for thus sings he,
                    Cuckoo;
Cuckoo, cuckoo: O, word of fear,
Unpleasing to a married ear!

                        (*Love's Labour's Lost.*)

When icicles hang by the wall,
   And Dick the shepherd blows his nail,
And Tom bears logs into the hall,
   And milk comes frozen home in pail,
When blood is nipp'd, and ways be foul,
Then nightly sings the staring owl,
                    Tu-who;
Tu-whit, tu-who—a merry note,
While greasy Joan doth keel the pot.

When all aloud the wind doth blow,
   And coughing drowns the parson's saw,
And birds sit brooding in the snow,
   And Marian's nose looks red and raw,

When roasted crabs hiss in the bowl,
Then nightly sings the staring owl,
     Tu-who;
Tu-whit, tu-who—a merry note,
While greasy Joan doth keel the pot.

        (*Love's Labour's Lost.*)

You spotted snakes with double tongue,
 Thorny hedge-hogs, be not seen;
Newts, and blind-worms, do no wrong;
  Come not near our fairy queen.
   Philomel, with melody,
    Sing in our sweet lullaby;
Lulla, lulla, lullaby; lulla, lulla, lullaby:
   Never harm,
   Nor spell, nor charm,
   Come our lovely lady nigh;
   So, good night, with lullaby.

   Weaving spiders come not here;
    Hence, you long-legg'd spinners, hence!
   Beetles black, approach not near;
    Worm nor snail, do no offence.

    Philomel, with melody, &c.

       (*Midsummer-Night's Dream.*)

Sigh no more, ladies, sigh no more,
 Men were deceivers ever;
One foot in sea, one foot on shore,
 To one thing constant never.
   Then sigh not so,
   But let them go,
 And be you blithe and bonny,
Converting all your sounds of woe
 Into Hey nonny, nonny.

Sing no more ditties, sing no mo
  Of dumps so dull and heavy;
The fraud of men was ever so,
  Since summer first was leavy.
    Then sigh not so,
    But let them go,
  And be you blithe and bonny,
Converting all your sounds of woe
  Into Hey nonny, nonny. (*Much Ado about Nothing.*)

IT was a lover and his lass,
  With a hey, and a ho, and a hey nonino,
That o'er the green corn-field did pass,
  In the spring time, the only pretty ring time,
When birds do sing, hey ding a ding, ding;
Sweet lovers love the spring.

Between the acres of the rye,
  With a hey, and a ho, and a hey nonino,
These pretty country folks would lie,
  In the spring time, &c.

This carol they began that hour,
  With a hey, and a ho, and a hey nonino,
How that a life was but a flower
  In the spring time, &c.

And therefore take the present time,
  With a hey, and a ho, and a hey nonino;
For love is crowned with the prime
  In the spring time, &c.   (*As You Like It.*)

        BLOW, blow, thou winter wind,
        Thou art not so unkind
            As man's ingratitude;
        Thy tooth is not so keen,
        Because thou art not seen,
            Although thy breath be rude.
Heigh-ho! sing, heigh-ho! unto the green holly:
Most friendship is feigning, most loving mere folly.
        Then heigh-ho! the holly!
            This life is most jolly.

99

Freeze, freeze, thou bitter sky,
That dost not bite so nigh
  As benefits forgot:
Though thou the waters warp,
Thy sting is not so sharp
  As friend remember'd not.
Heigh-ho! sing, heigh-ho! unto the green holly:
Most friendship is feigning, most loving mere folly.
    Then heigh-ho! the holly!
      This life is most jolly.

(As You Like It.)

UNDER the greenwood tree
Who loves to lie with me,
And turn his merry note
Unto the sweet bird's throat,
Come hither, come hither, come hither:
    Here shall he see
      No enemy
But winter and rough weather.

Who doth ambition shun,
And loves to live i' the sun,
Seeking the food he eats,
And pleas'd with what he gets,
Come hither, come hither, come hither:
    Here shall he see
      No enemy
But winter and rough weather.

(As You Like It.)

O MISTRESS mine! where are you roaming?
O! stay and hear; your true love's coming,
  That can sing both high and low.
Trip no further, pretty sweeting;
Journeys end in lovers meeting,
  Every wise man's son doth know.

What is love? 'tis not hereafter;
Present mirth hath present laughter;
  What's to come is still unsure:
In delay there lies no plenty;
Then come kiss me, sweet and twenty,
  Youth's a stuff will not endure.

(Twelfth Night.)

COME away, come away, death,
  And in sad cypress let me be laid;
Fly away, fly away, breath;
  I am slain by a fair cruel maid.

My shroud of white, stuck all with yew,
  O! prepare it.
My part of death, no one so true
  Did share it.

Not a flower, not a flower sweet,
  On my black coffin let there be strown;
Not a friend, not a friend greet
  My poor corse, where my bones shall be thrown.
A thousand thousand sighs to save,
  Lay me, O! where
Sad true lover never find my grave,
  To weep there.

(Twelfth Night.)

WHEN that I was and a little tiny boy,
  With hey, ho, the wind and the rain;
A foolish thing was but a toy,
  For the rain it raineth every day.

But when I came to man's estate,
  With hey, ho, the wind and the rain;
'Gainst knaves and thieves men shut their gate,
  For the rain it raineth every day.

But when I came, alas! to wive,
  With hey, ho, the wind and the rain;
By swaggering could I never thrive,
  For the rain it raineth every day.

But when I came unto my beds,
  With hey, ho, the wind and the rain;
With toss-pots still had drunken heads,
  For the rain it raineth every day.

A great while ago the world begun,
  With hey, ho, the wind and the rain;
But that's all one, our play is done,
  And we'll strive to please you every day.
                              (*Twelfth Night.*)

TAKE, O take those lips away,
  That so sweetly were forsworn;
And those eyes, the break of day,
  Lights that do mislead the morn:
But my kisses bring again,
                        bring again,
Seals of love, but seal'd in vain,
                        seal'd in vain.
                      (*Measure for Measure.*)

HARK! hark! the lark at heaven's gate sings,
  And Phœbus 'gins arise,
His steeds to water at those springs
  On chalic'd flowers that lies;
And winking Mary-buds begin
  To ope their golden eyes:
With every thing that pretty is,
  My lady sweet, arise:
Arise, arise!   (*Cymbeline.*)

FEAR no more the heat o' the sun,
  Nor the furious winter's rages;
Thou thy worldly task hast done,
  Home art gone, and ta'en thy wages;
Golden lads and girls all must,
As chimney-sweepers, come to dust.

Fear no more the frown o' the great,
   Thou art past the tyrant's stroke:
Care no more to clothe and eat;
   To thee the reed is as the oak:
The sceptre, learning, physic, must
All follow this, and come to dust.

Fear no more the lightning-flash,
   Nor the all-dreaded thunder-stone;
Fear not slander, censure rash;
   Thou hast finish'd joy and moan:
All lovers young, all lovers must
Consign to thee, and come to dust.

No exorciser harm thee!
   Nor no witchcraft charm thee!
Ghost unlaid forbear thee!
   Nothing ill come near thee!
Quiet consummation have;
And renowned be thy grave!

                (Cymbeline.)

WHEN daffodils begin to peer,
   With heigh! the doxy, over the dale,
Why, then comes in the sweet o' the year;
   For the red blood reigns in the winter's pale.

The white sheet bleaching on the hedge,
   With heigh! the sweet birds, O, how they sing!
Doth set my pugging tooth on edge;
   For a quart of ale is a dish for a king.

The lark, that tirra-lirra chants,
   With, heigh! with, heigh! the thrush and the jay,
Are summer songs for me and my aunts,
   While we lie tumbling in the hay.

                (Winter's Tale.)

JOHN MILTON

JOHN MILTON (1608–74), son of John Milton the elder (a scrivener and composer of music), was educated at St. Paul's School and Christ's College, Cambridge. While at Cambridge he wrote the poems *On the Death of a Fair Infant, On the morning of Christ's Nativity* (1629), and the poem on Shakespeare (1630). After leaving Cambridge, Milton lived at Horton in Bucks. with his father, reading the classics and preparing himself for his vocation as a poet, from 1632 to 1637. Here he composed *L'Allegro* and *Il Penseroso* in 1632, the *Arcades* (part of a masque, 1633?) and the masque *Comus* (1634, published 1637). In 1637 he wrote *Lycidas*. During the twenty years that elapsed between this and his composition of *Paradise Lost,* Milton wrote no poetry but the sonnets and some Latin and Italian pieces. From 1641 to the Restoration he was engaged in political work and pamphleteering. At the Restoration he was arrested and fined, but released. He returned to poetry and set about the composition of *Paradise Lost,* published in 1667. His last poems, *Paradise Regained* and *Samson Agonistes,* were published together in 1671.

UNTIL quite recent times it was the habit to express the greatness of Milton through the word sublime. But to-day we are weary of mere size and of crude superlatives, and we shall be fairer to him if we seek another form for the same thought. If our fathers called Milton sublime, it was because of his vitality; and it is the sheer abundance and thrust of the life within him that make the first claim for his poetic greatness. Nor is this vitality any less obvious in his biography. From the time when, as a boy of twelve, he insisted on working at his books up to midnight till his old age when he was in the habit of fighting the pains of gout with song, his life is the story of arduous, sustained, and often joyous activity. The mood of his sonnet on his blindness 'When I consider . . . ' with its passiveness and resignation is a miraculous triumph of will over this side of his own natural temper; it is far from expressing the permanent bent of his nature.

The true Miltonic vitality takes various literary forms. It shows itself in the heat and turbulence of his prose, in the youthful exuberances of the *Nativity Ode,* and in such sheer outbursts of fierceness as the denunciation of the clergy in *Lycidas* and Satan's defiance of the Almighty in *Paradise Lost*. On the side of doctrine we can detect it in Milton's defence of the will's freedom, in his passionate denial of asceticism, in his belief in the goodness of the flesh, and in his sympathy with the productive forces of nature. He speaks of the *enormous bliss* of nature's wanton exuberance in the Garden of Eden, and with Comus's enthusiasm for her prodigality ('Wherefore did Nature poure her bounties forth . . . ') he is in fundamental accord. And on the side of prosody Milton's vitality shows itself in some of the hugely prolonged verse-paragraphs of *Paradise Lost*.

Why, it may be asked, if Milton had such vitality, did he write, comparatively, so little verse? If, as is probable, Milton's vitality resembles that of another seventeenth-century exuberant, Rubens, why did the poet write so little and the painter paint so much? It is because Milton owned, some might even say was obsessed by, another quality which, according to taste, can be labelled idealism, conscience, fastidiousness, pride, or a perfection-complex. There is evidence that at the age of twenty-one Milton dedicated himself, before God, to poetry. Certainly he took the poetic profession with extreme seriousness, and he refused to allow any work to see the light that he did not consider to be the best he was good for, at the age when he wrote it. Not that he seems to have destroyed any poetry. With his abnormally retentive memory he could conduct his experiments in his head and commit to paper only those things about whose right to survive he had no qualms. A painter, dependent on constant manual practice, cannot make his experiments so inconspicuous. He must be ever producing. Rubens, to have resembled Milton in fastidiousness as well as in vitality, would have had to destroy quite nine-tenths of his pictorial output.

There are those who, seeing this fastidiousness of Milton, accuse him of a crime which is not easily forgiven to-day, that of taking himself and his poetry too seriously. It is an unjust charge. First, it must be remembered how seriously Milton's age took certain kinds of poetry. Tragedy and still more the epic had then a high moral function. It was really believed that a true epic, so rare an achievement in human history, could sway through its didactic virtues the destiny of a whole nation. It would have been alien to the opinion of his age for Milton to attempt *Paradise Lost* in any mood but one of high solemnity. Secondly, the doctrine of poetic inspiration was still powerful in Milton's day. In part the poet was but a passive vehicle; it was not the poet but what Milton calls the Muse who was ultimately responsible and to whom the credit is due. And to take your Muse seriously is a different thing from taking yourself seriously. But the most revealing evidence for the way Milton took himself and his poetry is *Lycidas*. *Lycidas* is a great poem; and all great poetry is complex; you do it a violence if you try to simplify it to a single motive. But a principal motive in *Lycidas* is the status of Milton's own poetry in the general scheme of things. The poet is reduced almost to despair when he considers simultaneously the seriousness with which he takes his poetic task and the cool way in which blind fate can cut off the good work. If a man stakes everything on some great object, how can he bear to live in a world which is quite likely to fool him? Milton does not state the answer in *Lycidas* but he implies it, through the resurrection of Lycidas at the end of the poem. But he did make his statement later when, in the sonnet on his blindness, he said that God did not need man's works. Man must be ready to act as if God needed them, he must proceed to the fresh woods and pastures new; but he must know at the same time that his work is a detail and subordinate to life as a whole. Milton was indeed tempted, as not many artists have been, to take his art too seriously; the way he completely defeated that temptation is one of the greatest things about him.

One of the commonplaces about Milton is that from first to last his work bears the unmistakable stamp of his own personality. It is indeed true that what Wotton called the 'Doric delicacy' of his verse appears early and remains to the end. There is an accent of grave sweetness that appears faintly in the paraphrases of the Psalms he wrote at the age of fifteen and which is not extinguished in *Samson Agonistes*. But there is a right and a wrong interpretation of this fact. This constant command of a certain kind of music argues some kind of native endowment, something Milton was born with and which he always retained. In one sense it is that general gift of music which, as Coleridge remarked, is one of the two poetic gifts which talent can never reach and which belong to genius alone. But Milton's gift of music is also his own, and the quality of it, its constancy and its certainty, seem to me to express above all an extraordinary strength and serenity in Milton's instincts. Beneath an imperfect knowledge of men that hampered him in his early years, beneath pride and a temptation to excessive ambition, beneath a superficial hastiness of judgement, lay this deep instinctive wisdom which found its poetic embodiment in that strong and sweet verbal music that has always been the prime fascination of Milton's verse. This wisdom never failed him. It solved his dilemma at the time of *Lycidas*, it reconciled him to his blindness, and it preserved for him a sense of proportion when the political ideals of which he had expected so much failed him completely.

But the strong, unmistakable quality of the Miltonic music and its constant presence have borne another interpretation: that Milton never changed from first to last, that his nature was excessively rigid and austere. It is true indeed that Milton had his share of austerity, though the *Nativity Ode*, *L'Allegro*, and *Il Penseroso* should clear him of the charge of excess. But that he did not develop is entirely false. It is equally false that his development was a steady hardening from the joyousness of the *Nativity Ode* to the grimness of *Samson Agonistes*. Far more than is recognized, Milton's later poems catch up and include with much else those apparently lighter and more amiable qualities that mark the early poems—as the feeling for nature's exuberance in *Comus* reappears in the description of Eden in *Paradise Lost*. The real development of Milton's poetry is in his experience, in his contact with the world of real men. Throughout the whole of his poetry Milton mixed the personal and the bookish in his imagery and in his allusions; and none of his contemporaries would have felt the slightest qualm in passing abruptly from one kind to another. The Elder Brother in *Comus*, benighted, begs for the light of a rush candle sending from a cottage window its 'long levell'd rule of streaming light' to be his 'star of *Arcady* or *Tyrian* cynosure'. The vision is acutely personal. It is even possible that the common sight of a shaft of light from a cottage in a wood on a dark night had on some one occasion made a lasting impression on him, and that like Wordsworth he now recollects it in tranquillity. But this personal experience leads to a pair of generalized classical commonplaces. Similarly at the end of *Paradise Lost* Milton introduces the homely picture—again perhaps recollected from some one occasion—of the labourer returning home as the mist rises into the gigantic artificial picture of the angels driving Adam and Eve from Paradise. This blend recurs throughout Milton's work and is one of the things that make it so rich and varied. But when we pass from the strictly personal experience to the knowledge of men and of contemporary affairs, we find an immense enrichment in *Paradise Lost* over the early poems. The process had indeed begun with *Lycidas* and its denunciation of the corrupt clergy of the day, but it reaches its full in some of the sonnets and in *Paradise Lost*. Milton depicts Eve with a subtlety and sympathy that show how much he had learnt about the other sex since the beginning of his first venture in matrimony.

Along with the classical allusions come a whole host of allusions to contemporary science and contemporary travel. The debate in Pandemonium shows not only how much Milton had learnt of general political psychology, but how close he was to the contemporary House of Commons. *Samson Agonistes* can be read simultaneously as a political tract and as the purest dramatization of an episode in the Old Testament.

It is only when this enrichment of content is understood, when Milton is read on more than one level, that his true poetic stature can be justly appraised.

E. M. W. TILLYARD.

ON THE MORNING OF CHRIST'S NATIVITY

It was the winter wild,
While the heav'n-born child
    All meanly wrapt in the rude manger lies;
Nature in awe to him
Had doffed her gaudy trim,
    With her great Master so to sympathize:
It was no season then for her
To wanton with the sun, her lusty paramour.

Only with speeches fair
She wooes the gentle air
    To hide her guilty front with innocent snow,
And on her naked shame,
Pollute with sinfull blame,
    The saintly vail of maiden white to throw,
Confounded that her Maker's eyes
Should look so near upon her foul deformities.

But he, her fears to cease,
Sent down the meek-eyed Peace,
    She, crown'd with olive green, came softly sliding
Down through the turning sphere
His ready harbinger,
    With turtle wing the amorous clouds dividing,
And waving wide her myrtle wand,
She strikes a universal peace through sea and land.

No war or battles sound
Was heard the world around,
   The idle spear and shield were high up hung;
The hookèd chariot stood
Unstain'd with hostile blood,
   The trumpet spake not to the arméd throng,
And kings sat still with awful eye,
As if they surely knew their sovereign Lord was by.

But peaceful was the night
Wherein the Prince of light
   His reign of peace upon the earth began:
The winds with wonder whist,[1]
Smoothly the waters kissed,
   Whispering new joys to the mild ocean,
Who now hath quite forgot to rave,
While birds of calm sit brooding on the charmèd wave.

The stars with deep amaze
Stand fixed in steadfast gaze,
   Bending one way their precious influence,
And will not take their flight,
For all the morning light,
   Or Lucifer that often warn'd them thence;
But in their glimmering orbs did glow,
Until their Lord himself bespake, and bid them go.

And though the shady gloom
Had given day her room,
   The sun himself withheld his wonted speed,
And hid his head for shame,
As his inferior flame
   The new-enlightened world no more should need;
He saw a greater sun appear
Then his bright throne or burning axle-tree[2] could bear.

The shepherds on the lawn,
Or ere the point of dawn,
   Sat simply chatting in a rustic row;
Full little thought they than[3]

---

[1] whist] hushed to silence   [2] axle-tree] i.e. the axle of the sun's
chariot   [3] than] other than

That the mighty Pan
   Was kindly come to live with them below;
Perhaps their loves, or else their sheep,
Was all that did their silly[1] thoughts so busy keep.

When such music sweet
Their hearts and ears did greet,
   As never was by mortal finger strook,[2]
Divinely warbled voice
Answering the stringéd noise,
   As all their souls in blissful rapture took:
The air such pleasure loath to lose,
With thousand echoes still prolongs each heav'nly close.

Nature that heard such sound
Beneath the hollow round
   Of Cynthia's seat, the airy region thrilling,
Now was almost won
To think her part was done,
   And that her reign had here its last fulfilling;
She knew such harmony alone
Could hold all heav'n and earth in happier union.

At last surrounds their sight
A globe of circular light,
   That with long beams the shame-faced night array'd,
The helmed Cherubim
And sworded Seraphim
   Are seen in glittering ranks with wings displayed,
Harping in loud and solemn quire,
With unexpressive[3] notes to heav'ns new-born heir.

Such music (as 'tis said)
Before was never made,
   But when of old the sons of morning sung,
While the Creator great
His constellations set,
   And the well-balanced world on hinges hung,
And cast the dark foundations deep,
And bid the weltering waves their oozy channel keep.

[1] silly] simple, artless   [2] strook] struck   [3] unexpressive] inexpressible

Ring out, ye crystal spheres,
Once bless our human ears,
   (If ye have power to touch our senses so)
And let your silver chime
Move in melodious time;
   And let the base of heaven's deep organ blow,
And with your ninefold harmony
Make up your consort to th'angelic symphony.

For if such holy song
Enwrap our fancy long,
   Time will run back, and fetch the age of gold,
And speckled vanity
Will sicken soon and die,
   And leprous sin will melt from earthly mould,
And Hell itself will pass away,
And leave her dolorous mansions to the peering[1] day.

Yea Truth and Justice then
Will down return to men,
   Th'enamelled arras of the rainbow wearing,
And Mercy set between,
Throned in celestial sheen,
   With radiant feet the tissued clouds down steering,
And heaven, as at some festival,
Will open wide the gates of her high palace hall.

But wisest Fate says no,
This must not yet be so,
   The babe lies yet in smiling infancy,
That on the bitter cross
Must redeem our loss;
   So both himself and us to glorify:
Yet first to those ychain'd[2] in sleep,
The wakeful trump of doom must thunder through the
     deep,

With such a horrid clang
As on mount Sinai rang
   While the red fire and smouldering clouds out brake.
The aged Earth aghast

---

   [1] peering] peeping out, i.e. day breaking   [2] ychain'd] chained

With terror of that blast,
  Shall from the surface to the centre shake,
When at the world's last session,
The dreadful Judge in middle air shall spread his throne,

And then at last our bliss
Full and perfect is,
  But now begins; for from this happy day
Th'old dragon under ground
In straiter[1] limits bound,
  Not half so far casts his usurpéd sway,
And wroth to see his kingdom fail,
Swinges[2] the scaly horror of his folded tail.

The oracles are dumb,
No voice or hideous hum
  Runs through the archéd roof in words deceiving.
Apollo from his shrine
Can no more divine,
  With hollow shriek the steep of Delphos leaving.
No nightly trance, or breathéd spell,
Inspires the pale-eyed Priest from the prophetic cell.

The lonely mountains o'er,
And the resounding shore,
  A voice of weeping heard, and loud lament;
From haunted spring, and dale
Edged with poplar pale,
  The parting genius is with sighing sent,
With flower-inwoven tresses torn
The Nymphs in twilight shade of tangled thickets mourn.

In consecrated earth,
And on the holy hearth,
  The Lars and Lemures moan with midnight plaint,
In urns, and altars round,
A drear and dying sound
  Affrights the flamens at their service quaint;
And the chill marble seems to sweat,
While each peculiar power forgoes his wonted seat.

---

[1] straiter] narrower   [2] swinges] lashes violently

Peor, and Baalim,
Forsake their Temples dim,
  With that twice-batter'd god of Palestine,
And moonéd Ashtaroth,
Heaven's queen and mother both,
  Now sits not girt with tapers' holy shine,
The Libyc Hammon shrinks his horn,
In vain the Tyrian maids their wounded Thamuz mourn.

And sullen Moloch, fled,
Hath left in shadows dred,
  His burning idol all of blackest hue,
In vain with cymbals' ring,
They call the grisly king,
  In dismal dance about the furnace blue;
The brutish gods of Nile as fast,
Isis and Orus, and the dog Anubis haste.

Nor is Osiris seen
In Memphian grove, or green,
  Trampling the unshowr'd grass with lowings loud:
Nor can he be at rest
Within his sacred chest,
  Naught but profoundest hell can be his shroud;
In vain with timbrel'd anthems dark
The sable-stoled[1] sorcerers bear his worshipped ark.

He feels from Juda's land
The dreaded infant's hand,
  The rays of Bethlehem blind his dusky eyn;[2]
Nor all the gods beside,
Longer dare abide,
  Not Typhon huge, ending in snaky twine:
Our Babe to shew his godhead true,
Can in his swaddling bands control the damnéd crew.

So when the sun in bed,
Curtain'd with cloudy red,
  Pillows his chin upon an orient wave,
The flocking shadows pale,

---

[1] sable-stoled] dressed in black   [2] eyn] eyes

Troop to th'infernal jail,
    Each fetter'd ghost slips to his several[1] grave,
And the yellow-skirted fays,
Fly after the night-steeds, leaving their moon-lov'd maze.

But see! The virgin blest
Hath laid her babe to rest.
    Time is our tedious song should here have ending,
Heav'ns youngest teeméd[2] star
Hath fixed her polished car,
    Her sleeping lord with handmaid lamp attending:
And all about the courtly stable,
Bright-harnessed Angels sit in order serviceáble.[3]

ON HIS TWENTY-THIRD BIRTHDAY

How soon hath Time, the subtle thief of youth,
    Stolen on his wing my three and twentieth year!
    My hasting days fly on with full career,
    But my late spring no bud or blossom shew'th.
Perhaps my semblance might deceive the truth,
    That I to manhood am arriv'd so near,
    And inward ripeness doth much less appear,
    That some more timely-happy spirits endu'th.
Yet be it less or more, or soon or slow,
    It shall be still in strictest measure even,
    To that same lot, however mean, or high,
Toward which Time leads me, and the will of Heav'n;
    All is, if I have grace to use it so,
    As ever in my great Task-Master's eye.

A MASK (From 'Comus')

THE star that bids the shepherd fold,[4]
Now the top of Heav'n doth hold,
And the gilded car of day,
His glowing axle doth allay
In the steep Atlantic stream,
And the slope[5] sun his upward beam

[1] several] separate   [2] youngest teeméd] latest born   [3] serviceáble]
ready to serve   [4] fold] put his sheep into the fold   [5] slope] sloping,
sinking

Shoots against the dusky pole,
Pacing toward the other goal
Of his chamber in the east.
Meanwhile welcome joy, and feast,
Midnight shout, and revelry,
Tipsy dance, and jollity.
Braid your locks with rosy twine
Dropping odours, dropping wine.
Rigour now is gone to bed,
And advice with scrupulous head,
Strict Age, and sour Severity,
With their grave saws in slumber lie,
We that are of purer fire
Imitate the starry choir,
Who in their nightly watchful spheres,
Lead in swift round the months and years.
The sounds, and seas with all their finny drove
Now to the moon in wavering morris move,
And on the tawny sands and shelves,
Trip the pert fairies and the dapper elves;
By dimpled brook, and fountain brim,
The wood-nymphs, decked with daisies trim,
Their merry wakes and pastimes keep:
What hath night to do with sleep?
Night hath better sweets to prove;
Venus now wakes, and wakens love.

L'ALLEGRO

HENCE loathéd Melancholy,
   Of Cerberus and blackest midnight born,
In Stygian cave forlorn
   'Mongst horrid shapes, and shrieks, and sights unholy,
Find out some uncouth[1] cell,
   Where brooding darkness spreads his jealous wings,
And the night-raven sings;
   There under ebon shades, and low-brow'd rocks,
As ragged as thy locks,
   In dark Cimmerian desert ever dwell.

               [1] uncouth] unknown

But come thou goddess fair and free,
In Heav'n yclept[1] Euphrosyne,
And by men heart-easing mirth,
Whom lovely Venus at a birth
With two sister graces more
To ivy-crowned Bacchus bore;
Or whether (as some sager sing)
The frolic wind that breathes the spring,
Zephyr with Aurora playing,
As he met her once a-Maying,
There on beds of violets blue
And fresh-blown roses washed in dew,
Fill'd her with thee a daughter fair,
So buxom, blithe, and debonair.
Haste thee nymph, and bring with thee
Jest and youthful jollity,
Quips and cranks, and wanton wiles,
Nods, and becks, and wreathéd smiles,
Such as hang on Hebe's cheek,
And love to live in dimple sleek;
Sport that wrinkled care derides,
And laughter holding both his sides.
Come, and trip it as ye go
On the light fantastic toe,
And in thy right hand lead with thee,
The mountain nymph, sweet Liberty;
And if I give thee honour due,
Mirth, admit me to thy crew
To live with her, and live with thee,
In unreprovéd pleasures free;
To hear the lark begin his flight,
And singing startle the dull night,
From his watch-tower in the skies,
Till the dappled dawn doth rise;
Then to come in spite of sorrow,
And at my window bid good-morrow,
Through the sweet-briar, or the vine,
Or the twisted eglantine;

---

[1] yclept] named

While the cock with lively din,
Scatters the rear of darkness thin,
And to the stack, or the barn-door,
Stoutly struts his dames before:
Oft list'ning how the hounds and horn
Chearly rouse the slumbering morn,
From the side of some hoar hill,
Through the high wood echoing shrill.
Some time walking not unseen
By hedge-row elms, on hillocks green,
Right against the eastern gate,
Where the great sun begins his state,
Robed in flames, and amber light,
The clouds in thousand liveries dight;
While the plowman near at hand,
Whistles o'er the furrow'd land,
And the milkmaid singeth blithe,
And the mower whets his scythe,
And every shepherd tells his tale
Under the hawthorn in the dale.
Straight mine eye hath caught new pleasures
Whilst the landscape round it measures,
Russet lawns, and fallows gray,
Where the nibbling flocks do stray,
Mountains on whose barren breast
The labouring clouds do often rest:
Meadows trim with daisies pied,
Shallow brooks, and rivers wide.
Towers and battlements it sees
Bosom'd high in tufted trees,
Where perhaps some beauty lies,
The cynosure of neighbouring eyes.
Hard by, a cottage chimney smokes,
From betwixt two aged oaks,
Where Corydon and Thyrsis met,
Are at their savoury dinner set
Of herbs, and other country messes,
Which the neat-handed Phyllis dresses;
And then in haste her bower she leaves,
With Thestylis to bind the sheaves;

Or if the earlier season lead
To the tann'd haycock in the mead,[1]
Sometimes with secure delight
The up-land hamlets will invite,
When the merry bells ring round,
And the jocund rebecks[2] sound
To many a youth, and many a maid,
Dancing in the chequer'd shade;
And young and old come forth to play
On a sunshine holiday,
Till the live-long day-light fail;
Then to the spicy nut-brown ale,
With stories told of many a feat,
How Faery Mab the junkets eat,
She was pinched, and pull'd she said,
And he by friar's lanthorn led
Tells how the drudging Goblin sweat,
To earn his cream-bowl duly set,
When in one night, ere glimpse of morn,
His shadowy flail hath thresh'd the corn
That ten day-labourers could not end,
Then lies him down the lubber[3] fiend.
And stretch'd out all the chimney's length,
Basks at the fire his hairy strength;
And crop-full out of doors he flings,
Ere the first cock his matin rings.
Thus done the tales, to bed they creep,
By whispering winds soon lull'd asleep.
Towred cities please us then,
And the busy hum of men,
Where throngs of knights and barons bold,
In weeds of peace high triumphs hold,
With store of ladies, whose bright eyes
Rain influence, and judge the prize
Of wit, or arms, while both contend
To win her grace, whom all commend.
Then let Hymen oft appear
In saffron robe, with taper clear,
And pomp, and feast, and revelry,

[1] mead] meadow   [2] rebecks] fiddle   [3] lubber] awkward

With mask, and antique pageantry,
Such sights as youthful poets dream
On summer eves by haunted stream.
Then to the well-trod stage anon,
If Jonson's learned sock be on,
Or sweetest Shakespeare, fancy's child,
Warble his native wood-notes wild,
And ever against eating cares,
Lap me in soft Lydian airs,
Married to immortal verse
Such as the meeting soul may pierce
In notes, with many a winding bout
Of linkéd sweetness long drawn out,
With wanton heed, and giddy cunning,
The melting voice through mazes running,
Untwisting all the chains that tie
The hidden soul of harmony.
That Orpheus' self may heave his head
From golden slumber on a bed
Of heaped Elysian flowers, and hear
Such strains as would have won the ear
Of Pluto, to have quite set free
His half regain'd Eurydice.
These delights, if thou canst give,
Mirth, with thee, I mean to live.

IL PENSEROSO

HENCE vain deluding joys,
 The brood of folly without father bred!
How little you bested,[1]
 Or fill the fixéd mind with all your toys;
Dwell in some idle brain,
 And fancies fond with gaudy shapes possess,
As thick and numberless
 As the gay motes that people the sun-beams,
Or likest hovering dreams,
 The fickle pensioners of Morpheus' train.
But hail thou Goddess, sage and holy,
Hail divinest Melancholy,

---

[1] bested] help

Whose saintly visage is too bright
To hit the sense of human sight;
And therefore to our weaker view,
O'erlaid with black, staid Wisdom's hue.
Black, but such as in esteem,
Prince Memnon's sister might beseem,
Or that starr'd Ethiop queen that strove
To set her beauty's praise above
The Sea-Nymphs, and their powers offended.
Yet thou art higher far descended;
Thee bright-hair'd Vesta long of yore
To solitary Saturn bore;
His daughter she (in Saturn's reign,
Such mixture was not held a stain)
Oft in glimmering bowers and glades
He met her, and in secret shades
Of woody Ida's inmost grove,
While yet there was no fear of Jove.
Come pensive Nun, devout and pure,
Sober, steadfast, and demure,
All in a robe of darkest grain,[1]
Flowing with majestic train,
And sable stole of cypress lawn,[2]
Over thy decent shoulders drawn.
Come, but keep thy wonted state,
With even step, and musing gait,
And looks commercing with the skies,
Thy rapt soul sitting in thine eyes:
There held in holy passion still,
Forget thy self to marble, till
With a sad leaden downward cast,
Thou fix them on the earth as fast.
And join with thee calm Peace, and Quiet,
Spare Fast, that oft with gods doth diet,
And hears the Muses in a ring,
Ay round about Jove's altar sing.
And add to these retired Leisure,
That in trim gardens takes his pleasure;
But first, and chiefest, with thee bring,

<hr />

[1] grain] colour   [2] lawn] linen

Him that yon soars on golden wing,
Guiding the fiery-wheeléd throne,
The Cherub Contemplation,
And the mute Silence hist along,
'Less Philomel will deign a song,
In her sweetest, saddest plight,
Smoothing the rugged brow of night,
While Cynthia checks her dragon yoke,
Gently o'er th'accustom'd oak;
Sweet bird that shunn'st the noise of folly,
Most musical, most melancholy!
Thee, chauntress, oft the woods among,
I woo to hear thy even-Song;
And missing thee, I walk unseen
On the dry smooth-shaven green,
To behold the wandering moon,
Riding near her highest noon,
Like one that had been led astray
Through the heav'ns wide pathless way;
And oft, as if her head she bow'd,
Stooping through a fleecy cloud.
Oft on a plat of rising ground,
I hear the far-off curfew sound,
Over some wide-water'd shore,
Swinging slow with sullen roar;
Or if the air will not permit,
Some still removed place will fit,
Where glowing embers through the room
Teach light to counterfeit a gloom,
Far from all resort of mirth,
Save the cricket on the hearth,
Or the bellman's drowsy charm
To bless the doors from nightly harm:
Or let my lamp at midnight hour,
Be seen in some high lonely Tower,
Where I may oft out-watch the Bear,
With thrice great Hermes, or unsphere
The spirit of Plato to unfold
What worlds, or what vast regions hold
The immortal mind that hath forsook

Her mansion in this fleshly nook:
And of those demons that are found
In fire, air, flood, or under ground,
Whose power hath a true consent
With planet, or with element.
Sometime let gorgeous tragedy
In scepter'd pall come sweeping by,
Presenting Thebes, or Pelops line,
Or the tale of Troy divine.
Or what (though rare) of later age,
Ennobled hath the buskined stage.
But, O sad Virgin, that thy power
Might raise Musaeus from his bower,
Or bid the soul of Orpheus sing
Such notes as warbled to the string,
Drew iron tears down Pluto's cheek,
And made Hell grant what love did seek.
Or call up him that left half told
The story of Cambuscan bold,
Of Camball, and of Algarsife,
And who had Canace to wife,
That own'd the vertuous ring and glass,
And of the wondrous horse of brass,
On which the Tartar king did ride;
And if ought else great Bards beside,
In sage and solemn tunes have sung,
Of tourneys and of trophies hung;
Of forests, and enchantments drear,
Where more is meant then meets the ear.
Thus, Night, oft see me in thy pale career,
Till civil-suited Morn appear,
Not tricked and frounced as she was wont,
With the Attic boy to hunt,
But kerchiefed in a comely cloud,
While rocking winds are piping loud,
Or usher'd with a shower still,
When the gust hath blown his fill,
Ending on the rustling leaves,
With minute drops from off the eaves.
And when the sun begins to fling

His flaring beams, me Goddess bring
To archéd walks of twilight groves,
And shadows brown that Sylvan loves
Of pine, or monumental oak,
Where the rude axe with heavéd stroke,
Was never heard the Nymphs to daunt,
Or fright them from their hallow'd haunt.
There in close covert by some brook,
Where no profaner eye may look,
Hide me from day's garish eye,
While the bee with honied thigh,
That at her flowery work doth sing,
And the waters murmuring
With such consort as they keep,
Entice the dewy-feather'd sleep;
And let some strange mysterious dream,
Wave at his wings in airy stream,
Of lively portraiture display'd,
Softly on my eye-lids laid.
And as I wake, sweet music breathe
Above, about, or underneath,
Sent by some spirit to mortals good,
Or th' unseen Genius of the wood.
But let my due feet never fail,
To walk the studious cloisters pale,
And love the high embowéd roof,
With antique pillars massy proof,
And storied windows richly dight,
Casting a dim religious light.
There let the pealing organ blow,
To the full voic'd choir below,
In service high, and anthems clear,
As may with sweetness, through mine ear,
Dissolve me into ecstasies,
And bring all Heav'n before mine eyes.
And may at last my weary age
Find out the peaceful hermitage,
The hairy gown and mossy cell,
Where I may sit and rightly spell
Of every star that Heav'n doth shew,

And every herb that sips the dew;
Till old experience do attain
To something like prophetic strain.
These pleasures Melancholy give,
And I with thee will choose to live.

SONG FROM ARCADES

Nymphs and shepherds dance no more
        By sandy Ladon's lillied banks.
On old Lycæus or Cyllene hoar,
        Trip no more in twilight ranks,
Though Erymanth your loss deplore,
        A better soil shall give ye thanks.
From the stony Mænalus,
Bring your Flocks, and live with us,
Here ye shall have greater grace,
To serve the Lady of this place.
        Though Syrinx your Pan's Mistress were,
        Yet Syrinx well might wait on her.
            Such a rural Queen
        All Arcadia hath not seen.

LYCIDAS

In this Monody the Author bewails a learned Friend, unfortunately
drown'd in his passage from Chester on the Irish Seas, 1637. And by
occasion foretells the ruin of our corrupted Clergy, then in their height.

Yet once more, O ye laurels, and once more
Ye myrtles brown, with ivy never sere,
I come to pluck your berries harsh and crude,
And with forc'd fingers rude,
Shatter your leaves before the mellowing year.
Bitter constraint, and sad occasion dear,
Compels me to disturb your season due:
For Lycidas is dead, dead ere his prime,
Young Lycidas, and hath not left his peer:
Who would not sing for Lycidas? he knew
Himself to sing, and build the lofty rhyme.
He must not float upon his watery bier
Unwept, and welter to the parching wind,
Without the meed of some melodious tear.

125

Begin then, Sisters of the sacred well,
That from beneath the seat of Jove doth spring,
Begin, and somewhat loudly sweep the string.
Hence with denial vain, and coy excuse,
So may some gentle Muse
With lucky words favour my destin'd Urn,
And as he passes turn,
And bid fair peace be to my sable shroud.
For we were nursed upon the self-same hill,
Fed the same flock, by fountain, shade, and rill.

Together both, ere the high lawns appear'd
Under the opening eye-lids of the morn,
We drove a-field, and both together heard
What time the gray-fly winds her sultry horn,
Batt'ning our flocks with the fresh dews of night,
Oft till the star that rose, at ev'ning, bright
Toward Heav'ns descent had slop'd his westering wheel.
Meanwhile the rural ditties were not mute,
Temper'd to th'oaten flute;
Rough Satyrs danc'd, and Fauns with cloven heel,
From the glad sound would not be absent long,
And old Damætas lov'd to hear our song.

But O the heavy change, now thou art gone,
Now thou art gone, and never must return!
Thee Shepherd, thee, the woods, and desert caves,
With wild thyme and the gadding vine o'ergrown,
And all their echoes mourn.
The willows, and the hazel copses green
Shall now no more be seen,
Fanning their joyous leaves to thy soft lays.
As killing as the canker to the rose,
Or taint-worm to the weanling herds that graze,
Or frost to flowers, that their gay wardrobe wear,
When first the white thorn blows;
Such, Lycidas, thy loss to shepherd's ear.

Where were ye Nymphs when the remorseless deep
Clos'd o'er the head of your lov'd Lycidas?
For neither were ye playing on the steep,
Where your old Bards, the famous Druids lie,
Nor on the shaggy top of Mona high,

Nor yet where Deva spreads her wizard stream:
Ay me, I fondly dream!
Had ye been there—for what could that have done?
What could the muse herself that Orpheus bore,
   The muse herself, for her enchanting son
Whom universal nature did lament,
When, by the rout that made the hideous roar,
His goary visage down the stream was sent,
Down the swift Hebrus to the Lesbian shore.
   Alas! What boots it with incessant care
To tend the homely slighted shepherd's trade,
And strictly meditate the thankless muse?
Were it not better done as others use,
To sport with Amaryllis in the shade,
Or with the tangles of Neæra's hair?
Fame is the spur that the clear spirit doth raise
(That last infirmity of noble mind)
To scorn delights, and live laborious days;
But the fair guerdon when we hope to find,
And think to burst out into sudden blaze,
Comes the blind Fury with th'abhorréd shears,
And slits the thin-spun life. But not the praise,
Phœbus replied, and touch'd my trembling ears;
Fame is no plant that grows on mortal soil,
Nor in the glistering foil
Set off to th'world, nor in broad rumour lies,
But lives and spreads aloft by those pure eyes,
And perfect witness of all judging Jove;
As he pronounces lastly on each deed,
Of so much fame in Heav'n expect thy meed.
   O Fountain Arethuse, and thou honour'd flood,
Smooth-sliding Mincius, crown'd with vocal reeds,
That strain I heard was of a higher mood:
But now my oat proceeds,
And listens to the Herald of the sea
That came in Neptune's plea.
He ask'd the waves, and ask'd the felon winds,
What hard mishap hath doom'd this gentle swain?
And question'd every gust of rugged wings
That blows from off each beaked promontory.

They knew not of his story,
And sage Hippotades their answer brings,
That not a blast was from his dungeon stray'd,
The air was calm, and on the level brine,
Sleek Panope with all her sisters play'd.
It was that fatal and perfidious Bark
Built in th'eclipse, and rigg'd with curses dark,
That sunk so low that sacred head of thine.

Next Camus, reverend sire, went footing slow,
His mantle hairy, and his bonnet sedge,
Inwrought with figures dim, and on the edge
Like to that sanguine flower inscrib'd with woe.
'Ah, who hath reft,' quoth he, 'my dearest pledge?'
Last came, and last did go,
The Pilot of the Galilean lake;
Two massy keys he bore of metals twain,
(The golden opes, the iron shuts amain)
He shook his mitre'd locks, and stern bespake,
How well could I have spar'd for thee, young swain,
Enow[1] of such as for their bellies sake,
Creep and intrude, and climb into the fold?
Of other care they little reckoning make,
Then how to scramble at the shearers' feast,
And shove away the worthy bidden guest.
Blind mouths! that scarce themselves know how to hold
A sheep-hook, or have learn'd ought else the least
That to the faithful herdman's art belongs!
What recks it them? What need they? They are sped;
And when they list, their lean and flashy songs
Grate on their scrannel pipes of wretched straw;
The hungry sheep look up, and are not fed,
But, swoln with wind and the rank mist they draw,
Rot inwardly, and foul contagion spread:
Besides what the grim wolf with privy paw
Daily devours apace, and nothing said.
But that two-handed engine at the door,
Stands ready to smite once, and smite no more.
Return Alpheus, the dread voice is past,
That shrunk thy streams; return Sicilian Muse,

[1] enow] enough

128

And call the vales, and bid them hither cast
Their bells, and flowerets of a thousand hues.
Ye valleys low, where the mild whispers use
Of shades, and wanton winds, and gushing brooks,
On whose fresh lap the swart star sparely looks,
Throw hither all your quaint enamelled eyes,
That on the green turf suck the honeyed showers,
And purple all the ground with vernal flowers.
Bring the rathe primrose that forsaken dies,
The tufted crow-toe, and pale jessamine,
The white pink, and the pansy freaked with jet,
The glowing violet,
The musk-rose, and the well-attir'd woodbine,
With cowslips wan that hang the pensive head,
And every flower that sad embroidery wears:
Bid Amaranthus all his beauty shed,
And daffodillies fill their cups with tears,
To strew the laureat hearse where Lycid lies.
For so to interpose a little ease,
Let our frail thoughts dally with false surmise.
Ay me! Whilst thee the shores, and sounding seas
Wash far away, where'er thy bones are hurled,
Whether beyond the stormy Hebrides,
Where thou perhaps under the whelming tide
Visit'st the bottom of the monstrous world;
Or whether thou to our moist vows deny'd,
Sleep'st by the fable of Bellerus old,
Where the great vision of the guarded mount
Looks toward Namancos and Bayona's hold;
Look homeward, Angel, now, and melt with ruth:
And, O ye dolphins, waft the hapless youth.
　　Weep no more, woeful shepherds, weep no more,
For Lycidas your sorrow is not dead,
Sunk though he be beneath the watery floor.
So sinks the day-star in the ocean bed,
And yet anon repairs his drooping head,
And tricks his beams, and with new spangled ore,
Flames in the forehead of the morning sky:
So Lycidas sunk low, but mounted high,
Through the dear might of Him that walk'd the waves,

Where other groves and other streams along,
With nectar pure his oozy locks he laves,
And hears the unexpressive nuptial Song,
In the blest kingdoms meek of joy and love.
There entertain him all the saints above,
In solemn troops and sweet societies,
That sing, and singing in their glory move,
And wipe the tears for ever from his eyes.
Now, Lycidas, the shepherds weep no more;
Henceforth thou art the genius of the shore,
In thy large recompense, and shalt be good
To all that wander in that perilous flood.

    Thus sang the uncouth[1] swain to the oaks and rills,
While the still morn went out with sandals gray,
He touch'd the tender stops of various quills,
With eager thought warbling his Doric lay:
And now the sun had stretch'd out all the hills,
And now was dropt into the western bay;
At last he rose, and twitch'd his mantle blue:
To-morrow to fresh woods, and pastures new.

ON HIS BLINDNESS

WHEN I consider how my light is spent,
    Ere half my days in this dark world and wide,
    And that one talent which is death to hide,
    Lodg'd with me useless, though my soul more bent
To serve therewith my Maker, and present
    My true account, lest he returning chide;
    'Doth God exact day-labour, light deny'd?'
    I fondly ask; but Patience to prevent
That murmur, soon replies, 'God doth not need
    Either man's work or his own gifts. Who best
    Bear his mild yoke, they serve him best. His state
Is kingly: thousands at his bidding speed,
    And post o'er land and ocean without rest:
    They also serve who only stand and wait.'

[1] uncouth] simple

OF MAN'S FIRST DISOBEDIENCE

OF Man's first disobedience, and the fruit
Of that forbidden tree, whose mortal taste
Brought death into the world, and all our woe,
With loss of Eden, till one greater Man
Restore us, and regain the blissful seat,
Sing heav'nly Muse, that on the secret top
Of Oreb, or of Sinai, didst inspire
That shepherd, who first taught the chosen seed,
In the beginning how the heav'ns and earth
Rose out of chaos: or if Sion hill
Delight thee more, and Siloa's brook that flow'd
Fast by the oracle of God; I thence
Invoke thy aid to my adventurous song,
That with no middle flight intends to soar
Above th' Aonian Mount, while it pursues
Things unattempted yet in prose or rhyme.
And chiefly thou, O Spirit, that dost prefer
Before all temples th' upright heart and pure,
Instruct me, for thou know'st.   Thou from the first
Wast present, and with mighty wings outspread
Dove-like satst brooding on the vast abyss
And mad'st it pregnant. What in me is dark
Illumine, what is low raise and support;
That to the highth of this great argument
I may assert eternal providence,
And justify the ways of God to men.
                                    (*Paradise Lost*, Bk. I, ll. 1–26.)

THE FALL OF THE ANGELS

'Is this the region, this the soil, the clime,'
Said then the lost archangel, 'this the seat
That we must change for heav'n, this mournful gloom
For that celestial light? Be it so, since he
Who now is Sovereign can dispose and bid
What shall be right: farthest from him is best

Whom reason hath equalled, force hath made supreme
Above his equals. Farewell happy fields
Where joy for ever dwells! Hail, horrors, hail
Infernal world, and thou profoundest hell
Receive thy new possessor, one who brings
A mind not to be chang'd by place or time.
The mind is its own place, and in itself
Can make a heav'n of hell, a hell of heav'n.
What matter where, if I be still the same,
And what I should be, all but less than he
Whom thunder hath made greater? Here at least
We shall be free; th'Almighty hath not built
Here for his envy, will not drive us hence:
Here we may reign secure, and in my choice
To reign is worth ambition though in hell:
Better to reign in hell, than serve in heav'n.
But wherefore let we then our faithful friends,
Th' associates and co-partners of our loss
Lie thus astonished on th' oblivious pool,
And call them not to share with us their part
In this unhappy mansion, or once more
With rallied arms to try what may be yet
Regained in heav'n, or what more lost in hell?'
   So Satan spake, and him Beëlzebub
Thus answer'd: 'Leader of those armies bright,
Which but th' Omnipotent none could have foiled,
If once they hear that voice, their liveliest pledge
Of hope in fears and dangers, heard so oft
In worst extremes, and on the perilous edge
Of battle when it rag'd, in all assaults
Their surest signal, they will soon resume
New courage and revive, though now they lie
Grovelling and prostrate on yon lake of fire,
As we erewhile, astounded and amaz'd,
No wonder, fall'n such a pernicious highth!'
   He scarce had ceased when the superior fiend
Was moving toward the shore; his ponderous shield,
Ethereal temper, massy, large and round,
Behind him cast; the broad circumference
Hung on his shoulders like the moon, whose orb

Through optic glass the Tuscan artist views
At ev'ning from the top of Fesole,
Or in Valdarno, to descry new lands,
Rivers or mountains in her spotty globe.
His spear, to equal which the tallest pine
Hewn on Norwegian hills, to be the mast
Of some great ammiral,[1] were but a wand,
He walked with to support uneasy steps
Over the burning marl,[2] not like those steps
On heaven's azure, and the torrid clime
Smote on him sore besides, vaulted with fire;
Nathless he so endur'd, till on the beach
Of that inflamed sea, he stood and call'd
His legions, angel forms, who lay entranced
Thick as autumnal leaves that strow the brooks
In Vallombrosa, where th' Etrurian shades
High overarched embower; or scattered sedge
Afloat, when with fierce winds Orion arm'd
Hath vexed the Red-Sea coast, whose waves o'erthrew
Busiris and his Memphian chivalry,
While with perfidious hatred they pursued
The sojourners of Goshen, who beheld
From the safe shore their floating carcases
And broken chariot wheels. So thick bestrewn
Abject and lost lay these, covering the flood,
Under amazement of their hideous change.
He call'd so loud, that all the hollow deep
Of hell resounded: 'Princes, Potentates,
Warriors, the flower of heav'n, once yours, now lost,
If such astonishment as this can seize
Eternal spirits; or have ye chos'n this place
After the toil of battle to repose
Your wearied virtue, for the ease you find
To slumber here, as in the vales of heav'n?
Or in this abject posture have ye sworn
To adore the conqueror? who now beholds
Cherub and seraph rolling in the flood
With scatter'd arms and ensigns, till anon
His swift pursuers from heav'n gates discern

---

[1] ammiral] ship   [2] marl] soil of clay and lime

Th' advantage, and descending tread us down
Thus drooping, or with linked thunderbolts
Transfix us to the bottom of this gulf.
Awake, arise, or be for ever fall'n.'
   They heard, and were abashed, and up they sprung
Upon the wing, as when men wont to watch
On duty, sleeping found by whom they dread,
Rouse and bestir themselves ere well awake.
Nor did they not perceive the evil plight
In which they were, or the fierce pains not feel;
Yet to their general's voice they soon obeyed
Innumerable. As when the potent rod
Of Amram's son in Egypt's evil day
Wav'd round the coast, up call'd a pitchy cloud
Of locusts, warping on the eastern wind,
That o'er the realm of impious Pharaoh hung
Like night, and darken'd all the land of Nile:
So numberless were those bad angels seen
Hovering on wing under the cope of hell
'Twixt upper, nether, and surrounding fires;
Till, as a signal giv'n, th' uplifted spear
Of their great Sultan waving to direct
Their course, in even balance down they light
On the firm brimstone, and fill all the plain;
A multitude, like which the populous north
Pour'd never from her frozen loins, to pass
Rhine or the Danube, when her barbarous sons
Came like a deluge on the south, and spread
Beneath Gibraltar to the Lybian sands.
Forthwith from every squadron and each band
The heads and leaders thither haste where stood
Their great commander; godlike shapes and forms
Excelling human, princely dignities,
And powers that erst in heaven sat on thrones;
Though of their names in heav'nly records now
Be no memorial, blotted out and rased
By their rebellion, from the Books of Life.

                  (*Paradise Lost*, Bk. I, ll. 242–363.)

HAIL, HOLY LIGHT

HAIL, holy light, offspring of heav'n, first-born,
Or of th' eternal coeternal beam
May I express thee unblam'd? since God is light,
And never but in unapproached light
Dwelt from eternity, dwelt then in thee,
Bright effluence of bright essence increate.
Or hear'st thou rather pure ethereal stream,
Whose fountain who shall tell? Before the sun,
Before the heavens thou wert, and at the voice
Of God, as with a mantle didst invest
The rising world of waters dark and deep,
Won from the void and formless infinite.
Thee I revisit now with bolder wing,
Escap't the Stygian pool, though long detain'd
In that obscure sojourn, while in my flight
Through utter and through middle darkness borne,
With other notes than to th' Orphean lyre
I sung of chaos and eternal night,
Taught by the heav'nly Muse to venture down
The dark descent, and up to reascend,
Though hard and rare: thee I revisit safe,
And feel thy sovereign vital lamp; but thou
Revisit'st not these eyes, that roll in vain
To find thy piercing ray, and find no dawn;
So thick a drop serene hath quenched their orbs,
Or dim suffusion veiled. Yet not the more
Cease I to wander where the Muses haunt
Clear spring, or shady grove, or sunny hill,
Smit with the love of sacred song; but chief
Thee, Sion, and the flowery brooks beneath
That wash thy hallowed feet, and warbling flow,
Nightly I visit: nor sometimes forget
Those other two equalled with me in Fate,
So were I equalled with them in renown,
Blind Thamyris and blind Maeonides,
And Tiresias and Phineus, prophets old.
Then feed on thoughts, that voluntary move
Harmonious numbers; as the wakeful bird

Sings darkling, and in shadiest covert hid
Tunes her nocturnal note. Thus with the year
Seasons return, but not to me returns
Day, or the sweet approach of ev'n or morn,
Or sight of vernal bloom, or summer's rose,
Or flocks, or herds, or human face divine;
But cloud instead, and ever-during dark
Surrounds me, from the cheerful ways of men
Cut off, and for the book of knowledge fair
Presented with a universal blank
Of nature's works to me expunged and rased,
And wisdom at one entrance quite shut out.
So much the rather thou, Celestial Light,
Shine inward, and the mind through all her powers
Irradiate, there plant eyes, all mist from thence
Purge and disperse, that I may see and tell
Of things invisible to mortal sight.

(*Paradise Lost*, Bk. III, ll. 1–55.)

INVOCATION TO URANIA

DESCEND from heav'n Urania, by that name
If rightly thou art call'd, whose voice divine
Following, above th' Olympian hill I soar,
Above the flight of Pegasean wing.
The meaning, not the name I call: for thou
Nor of the Muses nine, nor on the top
Of old Olympus dwell'st, but heav'nly born,
Before the hills appeared, or fountain flow'd,
Thou with eternal wisdom didst converse,
Wisdom thy sister, and with her didst play
In presence of th' Almighty Father, pleas'd
With thy celestial song. Up led by thee
Into the heav'n of heav'ns I have presum'd,
An earthly guest, and drawn empyreal air,
Thy tempering; with like safety guided down
Return me to my native element:
Lest from this flying steed unrein'd, (as once
Bellerophon, though from a lower clime)
Dismounted, on th' Aleian field I fall

Erroneous, there to wander and forlorn.
Half yet remains unsung, but narrower bound
Within the visible diurnal sphere;
Standing on earth, not rapt above the pole,
More safe I sing with mortal voice, unchang'd
To hoarse or mute, though fallen on evil days,
On evil days though fallen, and evil tongues;
In darkness, and with dangers compassed round,
And solitude; yet not alone, while thou
Visit'st my slumbers nightly, or when morn
Purples the east: still govern thou my song,
Urania, and fit audience find, though few.
But drive far off the barbarous dissonance
Of Bacchus and his revellers, the race
Of that wild rout that tore the Thracian bard
In Rhodope, where woods and rocks had ears
To rapture, till the savage clamor drowned
Both harp and voice; nor could the Muse defend
Her son. So fail not thou, who thee implores:
For thou art heav'nly, she an empty dream.

                  (*Paradise Lost*, Bk. VII, ll. 1–39.)

PARADISE LOST

To whom thus also th' angel last replied:
'This having learnt, thou hast attained the sum
Of wisdom; hope no higher, though all the stars
Thou knew'st by name, and all th' ethereal powers,
All secrets of the deep, all Nature's works,
Or works of God in heav'n, air, earth, or sea,
And all the riches of this world enjoyed'st,
And all the rule, one empire; only add
Deeds to thy knowledge answerable, add faith,
Add virtue, patience, temperance, add love,
By name to come call'd Charity, the soul
Of all the rest: then wilt thou not be loath
To leave this Paradise, but shalt possess
A Paradise within thee, happier far.
Let us descend now therefore from this top
Of speculation; for the hour precise

Exacts our parting hence; and see the guards,
By me encamped on yonder hill, expect
Their motion, at whose front a flaming sword,
In signal of remove, waves fiercely round.
We may no longer stay: go, waken Eve;
Her also I with gentle dreams have calm'd
Portending good, and all her spirits compos'd
To meek submission: thou at season fit
Let her with thee partake what thou hast heard,
Chiefly what may concern her faith to know,
The great deliverance by her seed to come
(For by the woman's seed) on all mankind.
That ye may live, which will be many days,
Both in one faith unanimous, though sad
With cause for evils past, yet much more cheer'd
With meditation on the happy end.'
    He ended, and they both descend the hill;
Descended, Adam to the bower where Eve
Lay sleeping ran before, but found her waked;
And thus with words not sad she him received.
    'Whence thou return'st, and whither went'st, I know;
For God is also in sleep, and dreams advise,
Which he hath sent propitious, some great good
Presaging, since with sorrow and heart's distress
Wearied I fell asleep: but now lead on;
In me is no delay; with thee to go,
Is to stay here; without thee here to stay,
Is to go hence unwilling; thou to me
Art all things under Heav'n, all places thou,
Who for my wilful crime art banished hence.
This further consolation yet secure
I carry hence; though all by me is lost,
Such favour I unworthy am vouchsafed,
By me the promis'd seed shall all restore.'
    So spake our mother Eve, and Adam heard
Well pleas'd, but answer'd not; for now too nigh
Th' archangel stood, and from the other hill
To their fixed station, all in bright array
The cherubim descended; on the ground
Gliding meteorous, as ev'ning mist

Ris'n from a river o'er the marish[1] glides,
And gathers ground fast at the labourer's heel
Homeward returning. High in front advanced,
The brandished sword of God before them blaz'd
Fierce as a comet; which with torrid heat,
And vapour as the Libyan air adust,
Began to parch that temperate clime; whereat
In either hand the hastening angel caught
Our lingering parents, and to th' eastern gate
Led them direct, and down the cliff as fast
To the subjected plain; then disappear'd.
They looking back, all th' eastern side beheld
Of Paradise, so late their happy seat,
Wav'd over by that flaming brand, the gate
With dreadful faces throng'd and fiery arms.
Some natural tears they dropped, but wiped them soon.
The world was all before them, where to choose
Their place of rest, and Providence their guide:
They, hand in hand, with wandering steps and slow,
Through Eden took their solitary way.

(Paradise Lost, Bk. XII, ll. 574–649.)

SAMSON AGONISTES

Manoa. Come, come, no time for lamentation now,
Nor much more cause, Samson hath quit himself
Like Samson, and heroicly hath finish'd
A life heroic, on his enemies
Fully reveng'd, hath left them years of mourning,
And lamentation to the sons of Caphtor
Through all Philistian bounds. To Israel
Honour hath left, and freedom, let but them
Find courage to lay hold on this occasion,
To himself and father's house eternal fame;
And which is best and happiest yet, all this
With God not parted from him, as was feared,
But favouring and assisting to the end.
Nothing is here for tears, nothing to wail
Or knock the breast, no weakness, no contempt,
Dispraise, or blame, nothing but well and fair,

<hr>

[1] marish] marsh

And what may quiet us in a death so noble.
Let us go find the body where it lies
Soaked in his enemies' blood, and from the stream
With lavers[1] pure and cleansing herbs wash off
The clotted gore. I with what speed the while
(Gaza is not in plight to say us nay)
Will send for all my kindred, all my friends
To fetch him hence and solemnly attend
With silent obsequy, and funeral train
Home to his father's house. There will I build him
A monument, and plant it round with shade
Of laurel ever green, and branching palm,
With all his trophies hung, and acts enroll'd
In copious legend, or sweet lyric song.
Thither shall all the valiant youth resort,
And from his memory inflame their breasts
To matchless valour, and adventures high:
The virgins also shall on feastful days
Visit his tomb with flowers, only bewailing
His lot unfortunate in nuptial choice,
From whence captivity and loss of eyes.

   Chorus. All is best, though we oft doubt,
What th' unsearchable dispose
Of highest wisdom brings about,
And ever best found in the close.
Oft he seems to hide his face,
But unexpectedly returns
And to his faithful Champion hath in place
Bore witness gloriously; whence Gaza mourns
And all that band them to resist
His uncontrollable intent.
His servants he with new acquist[2]
Of true experience from this great event
With peace and consolation hath dismissed,
And calm of mind, all passion spent.

    [1] lavers] basins   [2] acquist] acquisition

JOHN DRYDEN

JOHN DRYDEN (1631–1700) was educated at Westminster and at
Trinity College, Cambridge. In 1658 he wrote his remarkable *Heroic
Stanzas* (quatrains) on the death of Cromwell, *Astraea Redux* in 1660, on
the return of Charles II, in which he first showed his mastery of the
heroic couplet. His early plays are not of great importance, but *The
Indian Emperor* (1665) was very popular and is one of the best of its kind.
In 1667 Dryden published his *Annus Mirabilis*. He was appointed poet
laureate in 1668 and historiographer in 1670, and wrote some fourteen
plays between 1668 and 1681.

In 1680 began the period of Dryden's satirical and didactic poems.
Absalom and Achitophel appeared in 1681; *The Medal* in 1682; *Mac
Flecknoe* (probably written *c.* 1679) and *Religio Laici* also in 1682; *The Hind
and the Panther* in 1687, after his conversion to Roman Catholicism in
1686. Dryden refused to take the oaths at the Revolution and was
deprived of the laureateship. The last part of his life was occupied
largely with translations.

EVERY poet is to be enjoyed for, and to be judged by,
his own particular qualities; and Dryden, as other
poets, will yield no delight if you go to him for qualities he
does not possess. It is no use expecting from him the high
colours of Milton, the semi-mystic nature love of Wordsworth, the idealism of Shelley, for he lacked these things,
as they in their turn wanted other qualities. If you go to
him with an idea, conceived from reading the metaphysical
or the romantic poets, of what 'poetry' should do for you,
you will meet with disappointment. But for fine vigour,
for complete mastery of his instrument, for making words
do exactly what he wanted them to do, he is almost un-
matchable. 'Posterity will at least say', he remarked, 'that
I was a good versifier.'

His claim was modest: he is the greatest of our satirists,
and the only outstanding ratiocinative poet that we have.
And there is more than that to be said for him: he was the
almost perfect exponent of the precise in poetry. Pope, it
may be, was more exquisitely precise; he, even more perfectly than Dryden, perhaps, could make words express
exactly what he wanted to say; but in Dryden we find a

robustness and a largeness which from one point of view make him a more important figure. His breadth and variety never cease to astonish; and if his thoughts are not very profound, if he deals with the commonplaces of emotion, they are the commonplaces upon which men base their actions, and towards which their thoughts everlastingly turn.

Yet the business of the poet, as he was never tired of saying, is to delight, and mere prose precision of statement alone will never attract the average reader in any medium, certainly not the reader of verse; for the kind of imagination required for precision is not the kind of imagination the reader of poetry justly demands. What he asks is to be stimulated, even moved, by imagery, which is in the main of two kinds, the visual and the aural. Dryden is not very strong in visual imagery as compared with most great poets, though he can describe with the best, and give the actuality of an object with a graceful vividness that makes it memorable. He can focus the outward eye, though he gives the inward eye little to do. His pleasure, however, and his strength, lay in aural imagery: 'By the harmony of sounds we allure the soul', he declared; and Purcell was right in declining to set to notes *Alexander's Feast* on the ground that it was already its own music.

The music was often consciously constructed, on the then current theory of what was called 'imitative harmony', where 'The sound must be an echo to the sense'; the aim being to produce a kind of poetic onomatopoeia, which was not always very successful but could sometimes be effective, as in *A Song for St. Cecilia's Day*. But this sort of artificer's work, though it may provide the pleasure we gain from any display of skill, is not essentially poetic, for poetry rises from deeper wells than the immediately conscious. Where Dryden is magnificent is in the fitting of the sound to the sense in a way far more subtle than that of the St. Cecilia song, a way that raises his work from the level of aural imagery to that of aural imagination. Take, for instance, the opening of *Religio Laici*, and note how the play of vowel sounds and the modulating effect of the consonants produce the desired, the essential atmosphere. Or take again the famous lines from *Aureng-Zebe*, in which Dryden paraphrases the end of Lucretius' passage on the fear of death, which he was later to render more directly in a frank translation, with a different emotional stress. Take, from the play, the line

> I'm tired with waiting for this chymic gold,

and try to substitute some other word for 'chymic', say 'wondrous', or even 'magic', and see how the effect is weakened, since the hard beginning and end of the word, and the sharp 'i' sounds, give just that touch of sad scepticism and faint contempt which the sentiment needs to save it from flatness. There may be few overtones in Dryden, few connotations; but he relied on being able to denote, and was justified in his reliance.

His great skill, however, lay in—or should we say his poetic sensibility resided in and expressed itself by—his grasp of movement: his tempo is always exactly right, so that under his hand there springs up gaiety, melancholy, derision, or philosophic doubt. Look at his songs alone, a side of his art too much neglected. He has twenty different kinds. He can rattle you along joyfully in *Farewell ungrateful Traitor*, introduce a note of poignant regret in that earliest of Jacobite laments, *The Lady's Song*, or he can vary it as in the enchanting 'Ah Fading Joy'. Again and again he repeats the feat, often conquering stubborn metres to do it, not as a *tour de force*, but to get his emotional effect. You are forced to take his pace, you cannot avoid it, and so are bound to absorb his feeling too. By his command over prosody, a command later to become more subtly applied but more surely, he compels you to his mood, provided that you cultivate the ear; for unless you *listen* to Dryden you had better not read him at all; you lose half his force, and a large proportion of his fun.

His power over tempo gave him yet another advantage, perfect control over rise and fall. This is difficult to illustrate in extracts as it applies mainly in the longer pieces, especially in the various parts of *The Hind and the Panther*; but the well-known memorial verses on Oldham will serve to make the point. Its tone is exactly right; just so much, but no more, emotion is expressed as is needed for the purpose in hand: less would have been ineffective, more would have been sham. He does not try to wring a tear from the reader, nor pretend himself to wet the paper he writes on; he tells you why he regrets Oldham, and makes you also feel the loss. Or take again that piece of 'immortal ragtime', *Alexander's Feast*, and observe the modulations there; or better still, the *Secular Masque*, the last thing he wrote, in which he reviewed the past century with the privileged disillusion of his seventy years. The power there is superb and final; he never for a moment falters.

A poet is in the last resort judged by what he imparts; virtuosity is not enough. And it must be confessed that here Dryden will seem to many to have failed to achieve a very high place. He does not unlock the mysteries of the soul, nor provide a key to the universe, nor legislate (unacknowledged) for the world: he is not profound. Yet he has something very valuable to give; a sense of the fascinating variety of life, and a faith in life, sharpened by a healthy scepticism. If he partakes little of the divine, he is rich in humanity, and his hatreds are redeemed by generosity. Above all, what one gets from Dryden, not always and everywhere, but so often as to make one regard it as his distinguishing characteristic, is a sense of exhilaration, of living on equal terms with an athlete, of scaling, not mountains where the air is rarefied, but high hills, where to walk is cleansing and tonic.

BONAMY DOBRÉE.

JOHN DRYDEN

ANNUS MIRABILIS

I. THE SEA BATTLE

ALREADY batter'd, by his lee they lay;
In vain upon the passing winds they call:
The passing winds through their torn canvas play,
And flagging sails on heartless[1] sailors fall.

Their open'd sides receive a gloomy light,
Dreadful as day let in to shades below:
Without, grim death rides bare-fac'd in their sight,
And urges ent'ring billows as they flow.

When one dire shot, the last they could supply,
Close by the board the Prince's main-mast bore:
All three now, helpless, by each other lie,
And this offends not, and those fear no more.

So have I seen some fearful hare maintain
A course, till tir'd before the dog she lay,
Who, stretch'd behind her, pants upon the plain,
Past power to kill as she to get away.

With his loll'd tongue he faintly licks his prey,
His warm breath blows her flix[2] up as she lies;
She, trembling, creeps upon the ground away,
And looks back to him with beseeching eyes.

(Stanzas 128–32.)

II. THE GREAT FIRE

AND now four days the sun had seen our woes;
Four nights the moon beheld th' incessant fire;
It seem'd as if the stars more sickly rose,
And farther from the feverish north retire.

In th' empyrean heav'n (the Bless'd abode,)
The Thrones and the Dominions prostrate lie,
Not daring to behold their angry God:
And an hush'd silence damps the tuneful sky.

[1] heartless] spiritless, lacking in courage   [2] flix] fur

At length th' Almighty cast a pitying eye,
And mercy softly touch'd his melting breast:
He saw the town's one half in rubbish lie,
And eager flames drive on to storm the rest.

An hollow crystal pyramid he takes,
In firmamental waters dipt above;
Of it a broad extinguisher he makes
And hoods the flames that to their quarry strove.

(Stanzas 278–81.)

THE FALSE ACHITOPHEL[1]

OF these the false Achitophel was first,
A name to all succeeding ages cursed.
For close designs and crooked counsels fit,
Sagacious, bold, and turbulent of wit,
Restless, unfixed in principles and place,
In power unpleased, impatient of disgrace;
A fiery soul, which working out its way,
Fretted the pigmy body to decay:
And o'er-informed[2] the tenement of clay.
A daring pilot in extremity,
Pleased with the danger, when the waves went high
He sought the storms; but, for a calm unfit,
Would steer too nigh the sands to boast his wit.
Great wits are sure to madness near allied
And thin partitions do their bounds divide;
Else, why should he, with wealth and honour blest,
Refuse his age the needful hours of rest?
Punish a body which he could not please,
Bankrupt of life, yet prodigal of ease?
And all to leave what with his toil he won
To that unfeather'd two-legg'd thing, a son:
Got, while his soul did huddled notions try;
And born a shapeless lump, like anarchy.
In friendship false, implacable in hate,
Resolv'd to ruin or to rule the state;
To compass this the triple bond he broke,
The pillars of the public safety shook,
And fitted Israel for a foreign yoke;

[1] Achitopel] Shaftesbury   [2] o'er-informed] over-moulded

Then, seized with fear, yet still affecting fame,
Usurp'd a patriot's all-atoning name.
So easy still it proves in factious times
With public zeal to cancel private crimes:
How safe is treason and how sacred ill,
Where none can sin against the people's will,
Where crowds can wink, and no offence be known,
Since in another's guilt they find their own.
Yet, fame deserv'd, no enemy can grudge;
The statesman we abhor, but praise the judge.
In Israel's courts ne'er sat an Abbethdin[1]
With more discerning eyes or hands more clean,
Unbrib'd, unsought, the wretched to redress;
Swift of dispatch and easy of access.
Oh, had he been content to serve the crown
With virtues only proper to the gown,
Or had the rankness of the soil been freed
From cockle,[2] that oppressed the noble seed,
David for him his tuneful harp had strung,
And heav'n had wanted one immortal song.

(*Absalom and Achitophel*, ll. 150–97.)

OG[3] AND DOEG[4]

Now stop your noses, readers, all and some,
For here's a tun of midnight work to come,
Og from a treason tavern rolling home.
Round as a globe, and liquored ev'ry chink,
Goodly and great he sails behind his link;
With all this bulk there's nothing lost in Og,
For ev'ry inch that is not fool is rogue:
A monstrous mass of foul corrupted matter,
As all the devils had spew'd to make the batter.
When wine has given him courage to blaspheme,
He curses God, but God before cursed him;
And if man could have reason, none has more,
That made his paunch so rich and him so poor.
With wealth he was not trusted, for Heav'n knew
What 'twas of old to pamper up a Jew;

[1] Abbethdin] magistrate   [2] cockle] corncockle, a weed   [3] Og] Shadwell   [4] Doeg] Settle

To what would he on quail and pheasant swell,
That ev'n on tripe and carrion could rebel?
But though Heaven made him poor, (with reverence speak-
      ing,)
He never was a poet of God's making;
The midwife laid her hand on his thick skull,
With this prophetic blessing—*Be thou Dull*;
Drink, swear, and roar, forbear no lewd delight
Fit for thy bulk, do anything but write.
Thou art of lasting make, like thoughtless men,
A strong nativity—but for the pen;
Eat opium, mingle arsenic in thy drink,
Still thou mayst live, avoiding pen and ink.
I see, I see, 'tis counsel given in vain,
For treason botched in rhyme will be thy bane;
Rhyme is the rock on which thou art to wreck,
'Tis fatal to thy fame and to thy neck.
Why should thy metre good King David blast?
A psalm of his will surely be thy last.
Darest thou presume in verse to meet thy foes,
Thou whom the penny pamphlet foil'd in prose?
Doeg, whom God for mankind's mirth has made,
O'er-tops thy talent in thy very trade;
Doeg to thee, thy paintings are so coarse,
A poet is, though he's the poet's horse.
A double noose thou on thy neck dost pull
For writing treason and for writing dull;
To die for faction is a common evil,
But to be hang'd for nonsense is the devil.
Hadst thou the glories of thy King expressed,
Thy praises had been satire at the best;
But thou in clumsy verse, unlicked, unpointed,
Hast shamefully defied the Lord's anointed:
I will not rake the dunghill of thy crimes,
For who would read thy life that reads thy rhymes?
But of King David's foes be this the doom,
May all be like the young man Absalom;
And for my foes may this their blessing be,
To talk like Doeg and to write like thee.

                    (*Absalom and Achitophel*, pt. ii, ll. 457–509.)

THE POET SHADWELL

ALL human things are subject to decay,
And, when fate summons, monarchs must obey;
This Flecknoe found, who, like Augustus, young
Was called to empire and had govern'd long:
In prose and verse was own'd, without dispute
Through all the realms of Nonsense, absolute.
This aged prince now flourishing in peace,
And blest with issue of a large increase,
Worn out with business, did at length debate
To settle the succession of the state;
And pondering which of all his sons was fit
To reign, and wage immortal war with wit,
Cried, "Tis resolved; for Nature pleads that he
Should only rule, who most resembles me:
Shadwell alone my perfect image bears,
Mature in dullness from his tender years;
Shadwell alone of all my sons is he
Who stands confirmed in full stupidity.
The rest to some faint meaning make pretence,
But Shadwell never deviates into sense.
Some beams of wit on other souls may fall,
Strike through and make a lucid interval;
But Shadwell's genuine night admits no ray,
His rising fogs prevail upon the day:
Besides, his goodly fabric fills the eye
And seems design'd for thoughtless majesty:
Thoughtless as monarch oaks that shade the plain,
And, spread in solemn state, supinely reign.
Heywood and Shirley were but types of thee,
Thou last great prophet of tautology.

                              (*Mac Flecknoe*, ll. 1–30.)

REASON AND RELIGION

DIM, as the borrowed beams of moon and stars
To lonely, weary, wandering travellers
Is Reason to the soul: and as on high
Those rolling fires discover but the sky,
Not light us here, so Reason's glimmering ray

149

Was lent, not to assure our doubtful way,
But guide us upward to a better day.
And as those nightly tapers disappear
When day's bright lord ascends our hemisphere;
So pale grows Reason at Religion's sight;
So dies, and so dissolves in supernatural light.

(*Religio Laici*, ll. 1-11.)

A PRAYER

WHAT weight of ancient witness can prevail,
If private reason hold the public scale?
But, gracious God, how well dost Thou provide
For erring judgments an unerring guide!
Thy throne is darkness in th' abyss of light,
A blaze of glory that forbids the sight;
O teach me to believe Thee thus concealed,
And search no farther than Thyself revealed;
But her alone for my director take
Whom Thou hast promis'd never to forsake!
My thoughtless youth was winged with vain desires,
My manhood, long misled by wandering fires,
Followed false lights; and when their glimpse was gone,
My pride struck out new sparkles of her own.
Such was I, such by nature still I am,
Be Thine the glory and be mine the shame.

(*The Hind and the Panther*, i, ll. 62-77.)

WORLDLY VANITY

BE vengeance wholly left to powers divine,
And let Heaven judge betwixt your sons and mine:
If joys hereafter must be purchas'd here
With loss of all that mortals hold so dear,
Then welcome infamy and public shame,
And, last, a long farewell to worldly fame.
'Tis said with ease, but oh, how hardly tried
By haughty souls to human honour tied!
O sharp convulsive pangs of agonizing pride!
Down then, thou rebel, never more to rise,
And what thou didst and dost so dearly prize,
That fame, that darling fame, make that thy sacrifice.

'Tis nothing thou hast given; then add thy tears
For a long race of unrepenting years:
'Tis nothing yet; yet all thou hast to give:
Then add those *may-be* years thou hast to live.
Yet nothing still: then poor and naked come,
Thy father will receive his unthrift home,
And thy blest Saviour's blood discharge the mighty sum.

(*The Hind and the Panther*, iii, ll. 279–97.)

PROLOGUE TO 'AURENG-ZEBE'

Our Author by experience finds it true,
'Tis much more hard to please himself than you;
And out of no feign'd modesty, this day,
Damns his laborious trifle of a play;
Not that it's worse than what before he writ,
But he has now another taste of wit;
And, to confess a truth, (though out of time),
Grows weary of his long-loved mistress rhyme.
Passion's too fierce to be in fetters bound,
And nature flies him like enchanted ground:
What verse can do he has perform'd in this,
Which he presumes the most correct of his;
But spite of all his pride, a secret shame
Invades his breast at Shakespeare's sacred name:
Awed when he hears his godlike Romans rage,
He in a just despair would quit the stage;
And to an age less polish'd, more unskill'd,
Does with disdain the foremost honours yield.
As with the greater dead he dares not strive,
He would not match his verse with those who live:
Let him retire, betwixt two ages cast,
The first of this, and hindmost of the last.
A losing gamester, let him sneak away;
He bears no ready money from the play.
The fate, which governs poets, thought it fit
He should not raise his fortunes by his wit.
The clergy thrive, and the litigious bar;
Dull heroes fatten with the spoils of war:

All southern vices, Heav'n be prais'd, are here;
But wit's a luxury you think too dear.
When you to cultivate the plant are loath,
'Tis a shrewd sign 'twas never of your growth:
And wit in northern climates will not blow,
Except, like orange-trees, 'tis housed from snow.
There needs no care to put a play-house down,
'Tis the most desert place of all the town:
We and our neighbours, to speak proudly, are
Like monarchs, ruined with expensive war;
While, like wise English, unconcerned you sit,
And see us play the tragedy of wit.

WHEN I CONSIDER LIFE

WHEN I consider life, 'tis all a cheat;
Yet, fooled with hope, men favour the deceit;
Trust on, and think to-morrow will repay:
To-morrow's falser than the former day;
Lies worse, and, while it says we shall be blest
With some new joys, cuts off what we possessed.
Strange cozenage! None would live past years again,
Yet all hope pleasure in what yet remain;
And, from the dregs of life, think to receive,
What the first sprightly running could not give.
I'm tired with waiting for this chymic[1] gold,
Which fools us young, and beggars us when old.

(From *Aureng-Zebe*, Act IV, sc. i.)

EPILOGUE TO THE CONQUEST OF GRANADA

(SECOND PART)

THEY who have best succeeded on the stage,
Have still conformed their genius to their age.
Thus Jonson did mechanic humour show
When men were dull, and conversation low.
Then comedy was faultless, but 'twas coarse;
Cobb's tankard was a jest, and Otter's horse.
And as their comedy, their love was mean;
Except, by chance, in some one laboured scene,

[1] chymic] alchemic, i.e. counterfeit

Which must atone for an ill-written play,
They rose, but at their height could seldom stay.
Fame then was cheap, and the firstcomer sped;[1]
And they have kept it since, by being dead,
But, were they now to write, when critics weigh
Each line, and every word, throughout a play,
None of 'em, no, not Jonson in his height,
Could pass, without allowing grains for weight.
Think it not envy, that these truths are told;
Our poet's not malicious, though he's bold.
'Tis not to brand 'em that their faults are shown,
But by their errors to excuse his own.
If love and honour now are higher rais'd,
'Tis not the poet, but the age is prais'd.
Wit's now arrived to a more high degree;
Our native language more refin'd and free;
Our ladies and our men now speak more wit
In conversation, than those poets writ.
Then, one of these is, consequently, true;
That what this poet writes comes short of you,
And imitates you ill (which most he fears)
Or else his writing is not worse than theirs.
Yet, though you judge (as sure the critics will)
That some before him writ with greater skill,
In this one praise he has their fame surpassed,
To please an age more gallant than the last.

LOVE

Love is that madness which all lovers have;
But yet 'tis sweet and pleasing so to rave:
'Tis an enchantment, where the reason's bound;
But paradise is in the enchanted ground;
A palace, void of envy, cares and strife,
Where gentle hours delude so much of life.
To take those charms away, and set me free,
Is but to send me into misery;
And prudence, of whose cure so much you boast,
Restores those pains which that sweet folly lost.

(*The Conquest of Granada*, pt. ii, Act iii, sc. iii.)

[1] sped] was successful

HUMAN HAPPINESS

In wishing nothing we enjoy still most;
For ever our wish is in possession lost:
Restless we wander to a new desire,
And burn ourselves by blowing of the fire:
We toss and turn about our feverish will,
When all our ease must come by lying still:
For all the happiness mankind can gain
Is not in pleasure, but in rest from pain.

(The Indian Emperor, IV. i.)

CLEOPATRA AND ANTONY

How shall I plead my cause, when you, my judge,
Already have condemned me? Shall I bring
The love you bore me for my advocate?
That now is turn'd against me, that destroys me;
For love, once past, is at the best forgotten;
But oftener sours to hate: 'twill please my lord
To ruin me, and therefore I'll be guilty.
But, could I once have thought it would have pleased you,
That you should pry, with narrow searching eyes
Into my faults, severe to my destruction,
And watching all advantages with care
That serve to make me wretched? Speak, my lord,
For I end here. Though I deserve this usage,
Was it like you to give it?

. . . O horror, horror!
Egypt has been; our latest hour is come:
The queen of nations, from her ancient seat
Is sunk for ever in the dark abyss:
Time hath unroll'd her glories to the last,
And now closed up the volume.

. . . O that I less could fear to lose this being,
Which, like a snowball in my coward hand,
The more 'tis grasped, the faster melts away.
Poor Reason! what a wretched aid art thou!
For still, in spite of thee,

These two long-lovers, soul and body, dread
Their final separation.

. . . Lie there, thou shadow of an emperor;
The place thou pressest on thy mother earth
Is all thy empire now: now it contains thee;
Some few days hence, and then 'twill be too large,
When thou'rt contracted in thy narrow urn,
Shrunk to a few cold ashes; then Octavia
(For Cleopatra will not live to see it),
Octavia then will have thee all her own,
And bear thee in her widowed hand to Caesar;
Caesar will weep, the crocodile will weep,
To see his rival of the universe
Lie still and peaceful there. I'll think no more on't.
(All for Love.)

SONG

FAREWELL ungrateful Traitor,
  Farewell my perjured swain,
Let never injur'd creature
  Believe a man again.
The pleasure of possessing
Surpasses all expressing,
But 'tis too short a blessing,
  And love too long a pain.

'Tis easy to deceive us
  In pity of your pain,
But when we love you leave us
  To rail at you in vain.
Before we have descried it,
There is no bliss beside it,
But she that once has tried it
  Will never love again.

The passion you pretended
  Was only to obtain,
But when the charm is ended
  The charmer you disdain.

155

Your love by ours we measure
Till we have lost our treasure,
But dying is a pleasure,
    When living is a pain.
          (From *The Spanish Friar*.)

AH, FADING JOY

AH fading joy, how quickly art thou past!
    Yet we thy ruin haste:
As if the cares of human life were few,
    We seek out new,
And follow fate that does too fast pursue.

See how on every bough the birds express
    In their sweet notes their happiness.
    They all enjoy and nothing spare;
But on their mother nature lay their care:
Why then should man, the lord of all below,
    Such troubles choose to know,
As none of all his subjects undergo?

Hark! hark! The waters fall, fall, fall,
    And with a murmuring sound
Dash, dash, upon the ground,
    To gentle slumbers call.
          (From *The Indian Emperor*.)

TO MY DEAR FRIEND, MR. CONGREVE

ON HIS COMEDY CALLED 'THE DOUBLE-DEALER'

WELL then, the promised hour is come at last;
The present age of wit obscures the past:
Strong were our sires, and as they fought they writ,
Conquering with force of arms and dint of wit:
Theirs was the giant race before the flood;
And thus, when Charles return'd, our empire stood.
Like Janus, he the stubborn soil manur'd,
With rules of husbandry the rankness cur'd:
Tamed us to manners, when the stage was rude,
And boistrous English wit with art indued.
Our age was cultivated thus at length;
But what we gain'd in skill we lost in strength;

Our builders were with want of genius cursed;
The second temple was not like the first;
Till you, the best Vitruvius, come at length,
Our beauties equal, but excel our strength.
Firm Doric pillars found your solid base,
The fair Corinthian crowns the higher space;
Thus all below is strength, and all above is grace.
In easy dialogue is Fletcher's praise:
He mov'd the mind, but had no power to raise.
Great Jonson did by strength of judgement please,
Yet, doubling Fletcher's force, he wants his ease.
In differing talents both adorn'd their age,
One for the study, t'other for the stage.
But both to Congreve justly shall submit,
One match'd in judgment, both o'er-match'd in wit.
In him all beauties of this age we see,
Etherege his courtship, Southern's purity,
The satire, wit, and strength of manly Wycherly.
All this in blooming youth you have achieved;
Nor are your foil'd contemporaries griev'd;
So much the sweetness of your manners move,
We cannot envy you, because we love.
Fabius might joy in Scipio, when he saw
A beardless consul made against the law,
And join his suffrage to the votes of Rome,
Though he with Hannibal was overcome.
Thus old Romano bow'd to Raphael's fame,
And scholar to the youth he taught, became.

O that your brows my laurel had sustain'd,
Well had I been depos'd, if you had reign'd!
The father had descended for the son,
For only you are lineal to the throne.
Thus, when the state one Edward did depose,
A greater Edward in his room arose:
But now, not I, but poetry is cursed,
For Tom the Second reigns like Tom the First.
But let 'em not mistake my patron's part
Nor call his charity their own desert.
Yet this I prophesy; thou shalt be seen,
(Tho' with some short parenthesis between)

High on the throne of wit; and, seated there,
Nor mine (that's little) but thy laurel wear.
Thy first attempt an early promise made;
That early promise this has more than paid.
So bold, yet so judiciously you dare,
That your least praise is to be regular.
Time, place, and action may with pains be wrought,
But genius must be born, and never can be taught.
This is your portion, this your native store:
Heav'n, that but once was prodigal before,
To Shakespeare gave as much; she could not give him more.
    Maintain your post: that's all the fame you need;
For 'tis impossible you should proceed.
Already I am worn with cares and age,
And just abandoning th' ungrateful stage:
Unprofitably kept at Heaven's expense,
I live a rent-charge on his providence:
But you, whom every muse and grace adorn,
Whom I foresee to better fortune born,
Be kind to my remains; and oh defend,
Against your judgment, your departed friend!
Let not the insulting foe my fame pursue;
But shade those laurels which descend to you:
And take for tribute what these lines express;
You merit more; nor could my love do less.

TO THE MEMORY OF MR. OLDHAM

FAREWELL, too little and too lately known,
Whom I began to think and call my own:
For sure our souls were near allied, and thine
Cast in the same poetic mould with mine.
One common note on either lyre did strike,
And knaves and fools we both abhorred alike.
To the same goal did both our studies drive:
The last set out the soonest did arrive.
Thus Nisus fell upon the slippery place,
Whilst his young friend performed and won the race.
O early ripe! to thy abundant store
What could advancing age have added more?

158

JOHN DRYDEN

It might (what Nature never gives the young)
Have taught the numbers of thy native tongue.
But satire needs not those, and wit will shine
Through the harsh cadence of a rugged line.
A noble error, and but seldom made,
When poets are by too much force betrayed.
Thy generous fruits, though gather'd ere their prime,
Still showed a quickness; and maturing time
But mellows what we write to the dull sweets of rhyme.
Once more, hail, and farewell! farewell, thou young,
But ah! too short, Marcellus of our tongue!
Thy brows with ivy and with laurels bound;
But Fate and gloomy night encompass thee around.

ALEXANDER'S FEAST;
OR, THE POWER OF MUSIC

AN ODE IN HONOUR OF ST. CECILIA'S DAY, 1697

'Twas at the royal feast, for Persia won
    By Philip's warlike son:
    Aloft in awful state
    The god-like hero sate
    On his imperial throne:
    His valiant peers were placed around,
Their brows with roses and with myrtles bound;
    (So should desert in arms be crown'd:)
    The lovely Thais, by his side,
    Sate like a blooming Eastern bride
    In flower of youth and beauty's pride.
    Happy, happy, happy pair!
        None but the brave,
        None but the brave,
None but the brave deserves the fair.

CHORUS

    Happy, happy, happy pair!
        None but the brave,
        None but the brave,
None but the brave deserves the fair.

Timotheus, placed on high
  Amid the tuneful choir,
  With flying fingers touch'd the lyre:
The trembling notes ascend the sky,
  And heavenly joys inspire.
The song began from Jove,
Who left his blissful seats above
(Such is the power of mighty love).
A dragon's fiery form belied the god:
Sublime on radiant spires he rode,
  When he to fair Olympia press'd:
  And while he sought her snowy breast:
Then round her slender waist he curl'd.
And stamp'd an image of himself, a sovereign of the
    world.
The listening crowd admire the lofty sound,
A present deity! they shout around:
A present deity! the vaulted roofs rebound.
            With ravish'd ears
            The monarch hears,
            Assumes the god,
            Affects to nod,
And seems to shake the spheres.

CHORUS

            With ravish'd ears
            The monarch hears,
            Assumes the god,
            Affects to nod,
And seems to shake the spheres.

The praise of Bacchus then the sweet musician sung,
  Of Bacchus ever fair and ever young:
    The jolly god in triumph comes;
    Sound the trumpets; beat the drums:
    Flush'd with a purple grace
    He shows his honest face:
Now give the hautboys breath. He comes! he comes!
    Bacchus, ever fair and young,

Drinking joys did first ordain;
Bacchus' blessings are a treasure,
Drinking is the soldier's pleasure:
    Rich the treasure,
    Sweet the pleasure,
Sweet is pleasure after pain.

CHORUS

Bacchus' blessings are a treasure,
Drinking is the soldier's pleasure:
    Rich the treasure,
    Sweet the pleasure,
Sweet is pleasure after pain.

Soothed with the sound the king grew vain;
    Fought all his battles o'er again;
And thrice he routed all his foes, and thrice he slew
    the slain.
The master saw the madness rise;
His glowing cheeks, his ardent eyes;
And while he heaven and earth defied,
Changed his hand, and check'd his pride.
    He chose a mournful muse,
    Soft pity to infuse:
He sung Darius, great and good,
    By too severe a fate
Fallen, fallen, fallen, fallen,
Fallen from his high estate,
    And welt'ring in his blood;
Deserted, at his utmost need,
By those his former bounty fed;
On the bare earth exposed he lies,
With not a friend to close his eyes.
With downcast looks the joyless victor sate,
    Revolving in his alter'd soul
      The various turns of chance below;
    And, now and then, a sigh he stole;
    And tears began to flow.

CHORUS

Revolving in his alter'd soul
  The various turns of chance below;
And, now and then, a sigh he stole;
  And tears began to flow.

The mighty master smiled, to see
That love was in the next degree;
'Twas but a kindred-sound to move,
For pity melts the mind to love.
  Softly sweet, in Lydian measures,
  Soon he soothed his soul to pleasures.
War, he sung, is toil and trouble;
Honour, but an empty bubble;
  Never ending, still beginning,
Fighting still, and still destroying:
  If the world be worth thy winning,
Think, oh think it worth enjoying:
  Lovely Thais sits beside thee,
Take the good the gods provide thee.
The many rend the skies with loud applause;
So Love was crown'd, but Music won the cause.
  The prince, unable to conceal his pain,
      Gazed on the fair
      Who caused his care,
  And sigh'd and look'd, sigh'd and look'd,
  Sigh'd and look'd, and sigh'd again:
At length, with love and wine at once oppress'd,
The vanquish'd victor sunk upon her breast.

CHORUS

  The prince, unable to conceal his pain,
      Gazed on the fair
      Who caused his care,
  And sigh'd and look'd, sigh'd and look'd,
  Sigh'd and look'd, and sigh'd again:
At length, with love and wine at once oppress'd,
The vanquish'd victor sunk upon her breast.

Now strike the golden lyre again:
A louder yet, and yet a louder strain.
　　Break his bands of sleep asunder,
　　And rouse him like a rattling peal of thunder.
　　　　　Hark, hark, the horrid sound
　　　　　　Has raised up his head:
　　　　　　As awaked from the dead,
　　　　　And amazed, he stares around.
　　Revenge! revenge! Timotheus cries,
　　　　See the furies arise!
　　　See the snakes that they rear,
　　　How they hiss in their hair!
　　And the sparkles that flash from their eyes!
　　　Behold a ghastly band,
　　　Each a torch in his hand!
Those are Grecian ghosts, that in battle were slain,
　　　　　And unburied remain,
　　　　　Inglorious on the plain:
　　　　　Give the vengeance due
　　　　　To the valiant crew.
Behold how they toss their torches on high,
　　How they point to the Persian abodes,
And glittering temples of their hostile gods.
The princes applaud with a furious joy;
And the king seized a flambeau with zeal to destroy;
　　　Thais led the way,
　　　To light him to his prey,
And, like another Helen, fired another Troy!

CHORUS

And the king seized a flambeau with zeal to destroy;
　　　Thais led the way,
　　　To light him to his prey,
And, like another Helen, fired another Troy!

　　　Thus long ago,
　　Ere heaving bellows learn'd to blow,
　　　While organs yet were mute,
　　　Timotheus, to his breathing flute,

And sounding lyre,
Could swell the soul to rage, or kindle soft desire.
At last divine Cecilia came,
Inventress of the vocal frame;
The sweet enthusiast, from her sacred store,
Enlarged the former narrow bounds,
And added length to solemn sounds,
With nature's mother-wit, and arts unknown before.
Let old Timotheus yield the prize,
Or both divide the crown;
He raised a mortal to the skies;
She drew an angel down.

GRAND CHORUS

At last divine Cecilia came,
Inventress of the vocal frame;
The sweet enthusiast, from her sacred store,
Enlarged the former narrow bounds,
And added length to solemn sounds,
With nature's mother-wit, and arts unknown before.
Let old Timotheus yield the prize,
Or both divide the crown;
He raised a mortal to the skies;
She drew an angel down.

ALEXANDER POPE

ALEXANDER POPE (1688–1744) was the son of a Roman Catholic linen-draper of London. His health was ruined and his figure distorted by a severe illness at the age of 12. He showed his precocious metrical skill in his *Pastorals* (1709) written, according to himself, when he was 16. His *Essay on Criticism*, (1711,) made him known to Addison's circle. His *Rape of the Lock* appeared in 1712. He issued in 1715 the first volume of his translation in heroic couplets of Homer's *Iliad*, which was completed in 1720. In 1723, four years after Addison's death, appeared Pope's portrait of Atticus, a satire on Addison, probably written some years earlier. In 1725 Pope published an edition of Shakespeare, the errors in which were pointed out in a pamphlet by Theobald. This led to the selection of Theobald by Pope as the hero of his *Dunciad*, a satire on Dullness, in three books, of which the first edition appeared anonymously in 1728. A complete *Dunciad* in four books appeared in 1743. Pope published a series of moral and philosophical poems, *An Essay on Man*, 1733–4; and *Moral Essays*. In 1733 he published the first of his miscellaneous satires, *Imitations of Horace*. The year 1735 saw the appearance of the *Epistle to Dr. Arbuthnot*, the prologue to the above Satires.

ONE has only to think of Blake, who stands in the other half of Pope's century, to see that Pope was in no sense revolutionary. No poet has ever been more dependent than he on the tradition established by his immediate predecessors. He carries on the work of those seventeenth-century poets of whom Denham and Waller were early examples and Dryden the latest and greatest. Describing an early glimpse of Dryden, Pope said, *Virgilium tantum vidi*, and his salute is useful as showing how, for him, the seventeenth century in England and the poets of Rome were two sides of the same medal. Almost all Pope's work is done in forms which the poets of Rome and of the seventeenth century in England (and France) had invented or practised. Pope begins as a boy by translations mainly from Latin. His earliest 'original' poems were pastorals. His *Essay on Criticism* looks back to Horace's *Ars Poetica* and the verse essays on literary themes which succeeded, to the *Art Poétique* of Boileau. His 'local poem' *Windsor Forest* imitates

Denham's *Cooper's Hill*. His *Temple of Fame* has many French and English predecessors besides Chaucer's *Hous of Fame* which is its immediate source. The *Rape of the Lock* and, later, the *Dunciad* belong to that mock-epic tradition which begins, as far as extant work is concerned, with Homer's *Battle of the Frogs and Mice*. *Eloisa to Abelard* follows Ovid's *Heroides*. The *Essay on Man* and the *Moral Essays* are virtually Horatian epistles, and the *Imitations of Horace* describe themselves accurately. Like Dryden, Pope hankers after writing an epic, and whereas Dryden translates the *Æneid*, Pope translates the *Iliad* and the *Odyssey*.

In all this Pope was doing what any of his contemporary poets could have chosen to do. He may be said to have allowed his age to dictate what poems he should write. And in the same way, there is nothing revolutionary in his metre. During the whole of the seventeenth century—to go no farther back—there had been conscious and continuous attempts to make the most of the heroic couplet, to discover or develop the 'rules' by which poets could be guided to write it 'correctly'. Pope seldom uses any other measure. His 'ten thousand verses', marvellously varied within their couplets, crown the experiments of a century.

Furthermore, there is nothing revolutionary in the 'content' of his poems. Pope deliberately drew his material from what was then called 'Nature', i.e. from that considerable part of every intelligent man's mind which is virtually identical with a considerable part of the mind of his fellows, past, present, and future. To invent an instance. If Pope, like Keats, had listened to a nightingale and had found himself believing that 'Now more than ever seems it rich to die', he would not have put the idea into a poem. He would have considered that, deeply as the idea might stir him, he was in this too much unlike his fellows to speak of it to them. He would also have seen that the idea had more force for him—Keats was consumptive—than for his fellows, and that tuberculosis, whatever it meant to him, was a barrier between him and them. When Pope heard nightingales, he heard them, of course, more sensitively than his fellows, but he only used that element in his perception which was, in kind at least, that of every man. And because such subjects did not often come in the way of ordinary men, he did not often write of them. The interests of ordinary men may be summarized as other men, personal relationships, manners, morals, politics, books, houses, food, &c. And so it is these themes with their loads of pointed, brilliant detail which occupy him most. It is for this reason that he looks back on the *Pastorals*, *Windsor Forest*, the *Rape of the Lock* as so much wandering 'in Fancy's maze', and on his essays and satires as 'truth', as concerned with fact, with 'WHATEVER IS'. Pope's later work, therefore, is rooted in man.

Within this human bound his poems explore a great variety of topics. To begin with, there are Pope's friends and men like the Man of Ross, who are praised; and there are his 'enemies' who are analysed as if with the sharpest instruments of the vivisectionist. The friends may seem to be posed in too golden a light, the enemies in too poisonous a limelight. Pope's scorn can be so intense that he seems to overstep the elected bounds of 'Nature' and write personally as a 'Romantic' poet. But his merciless, at times feminine, emphasis and his deadly quiet have the effect of sharpening the moral, the general truth. The immediate object is burnt up in a wider illumination. The praised or condemned figures do not remain individuals. They expand into summaries, into types. Often Pope arrives at types by another route, less personal than friends and enemies. *Of the Knowledge and Characters of Men* begins by considering the data offered by all individuals. Their characters are bundles of incoherent details. And yet continued scrutiny may discover some central spring which controls the whole ramshackle apparatus. And when more of these springs are found, resemblances among them will pattern out the type.

Pope touches the apex of the human pyramid when he leaves types for Man. Man is summarized with unexceptionable authority in the opening lines of the second Epistle of the *Essay on Man*.

Pope for the most part abides by what *oft* was thought, and his task is to express it *ne'er so well*.[1] He deliberates over the material existing in every man's mind till he finds that his own sense of its quality is prompting the perfect expression. It is in this best expression that Pope's originality most obviously shows itself. He is not out to surprise by his thoughts, his metre, his 'form'. And yet his poetry is full of surprises. These are often the surprises of finding a hot fire made out of a few sticks, and made out of the sticks which in the hands of other poets had remained uninflammable. The elements of his poetry are commonplace but suddenly rare. Pope, to use Joubert's words, was one of those 'spirits . . . who when they have an idea to put forth, brood long over it first, and wait patiently till it *shines*, as Buffon enjoined, when he defined genius to be the aptitude for patience'. Pope was tireless in his brooding over the inches of his poems. He found it 'as pleasant . . . to correct as to write'. But one feels that the series of his revisions have all the 'inspiration' that is associated with freer work. They often take the form of adding a new transparent element on top of an old, and it is this superimposition of strata that makes Pope's work difficult to see to the bottom of. Some of his most famous lines—for example, 'To err is human, to forgive divine'—are no doubt crystal clear. But usually Pope intends his meaning only to complete itself when the things attracted to it from outside are allowed their full say. He is sometimes spoken of as a poet without 'atmosphere', without 'suggestion'. But in truth he is a poet whose suggestion is unusually elaborate. The suggestion, however, is usually not so much pictorial as

[1] True Wit is Nature to advantage dress'd,
  What oft was thought, but ne'er so well express'd.
  (*Essay on Criticism*, ll. 297–8).

literary. Before one can appreciate Pope properly one has to know what contemporary readers knew. One needs a head full of earlier poetry and prose. Pope's very meaning, his tone, depend often on a comparison between what he writes and what his writing is echoing. In the *Dunciad*, for example, occur these lines:

> Silence, ye Wolves! while Ralph to Cynthia howls,
> And makes night hideous—Answer him, ye owls!

Without any special knowledge, the reader is instantly aware of the excellence of the comedy. But the comedy is deepened when he finds that Ralph wrote a poem called *Night*, and that the second line echoes Hamlet's sublime address to the ghost. The comic effect is still further deepened when one realizes that the couplet is also striking on the great bell of the *Psalms* and of the prayer in Book V of *Paradise Lost*. The sixteen words of that couplet represent a piling of Pelion on Ossa. The howls of Ralph jar a whole universe. One can never be sure that one has discovered everything that Pope put into his verses, and this is perhaps the reason that Lamb could read him 'over and over for ever'.[1]

But Pope was not always out for these layers of effect. Sometimes he elicits a simpler response, a response much more nearly confined to the emotions. In *Eloisa to Abelard*, for instance, and *The Elegy to the Memory of an Unfortunate Lady* the literary echoes (they never cease in Pope) are intended to be heard much less clearly, to have the vaguer emotional values they would have in nineteenth-century poetry. In these 'pathetic' pieces—the word was equivalent to our 'emotive'—Pope found an outlet for the extraordinary tenderness of feeling that is so amply attested by his friends. But even in these poems, moved as he himself is, he is still thinking of 'Nature', of how not only he, but all people,

---

[1] Cf. W. Macartney's *Walls have Mouths*, 1936, p. 213: 'One wild Leeds youth, Henderson [a convict] had a passion for Pope and would recite heroic couplets for hours and hours . . . while digging spuds.'

feel. He is still providing a human, rather than a personal, document. He seldom says directly that his own feeling is running high, except when he is standing publicly proud or indignant. He insinuates his own mood into a 'dramatic' piece, into the plight of Eloisa, or into an *Elegy* on a lady who never in fact existed. And it is because of this use of the 'objective co-relative' that his feeling never gets out of control. Nor does it exist apart from a sound 'sense'. When Eloisa cries,

> Ah hopeless, lasting flames! like those that burn
> To light the dead, and warm th' unfruitful urn,

the lines do not merely set us feeling their subtle blending of upheaval and resignation. They set us thinking. Feeling, indeed, deepens as thinking grows clearer. Eloisa's love *is* hopeless and lasting (Abelard is incapable of union with her, and she is incapable of forgetting him) and the images (not new in themselves but newly applied) which develop, and so reanimate, the commonplace image of 'flames' are not used merely because of their music, their 'atmosphere', their pictorial and literary suggestiveness. Nor are they used merely because they are, literally, flames which are hopeless and lasting. They are used also because they light the dead and warm the unfruitful. Pope's poetry exhibits always an equilibrium of many separate forces. One's response to it can never be a vague one.

GEOFFREY TILLOTSON.

ODE ON SOLITUDE

HAPPY the man, whose wish and care
  A few paternal acres bound,
Content to breathe his native air
      In his own ground.

Whose herds with milk, whose fields with bread,
  Whose flocks supply him with attire,
Whose trees in summer yield him shade,
      In winter fire.

Blest, who can unconcern'dly find
  Hours, days, and years slide soft away,
In health of body, peace of mind,
      Quiet by day,

Sound sleep by night; study and ease,
  Together mixt; sweet recreation:
And innocence, which most does please
      With meditation.

Thus let me live, unseen, unknown,
  Thus unlamented let me die,
Steal from the world, and not a stone
      Tell where I lie.

From AN ESSAY ON CRITICISM

'TIS hard to say, if greater want of skill
Appear in writing or in judging ill;
But, of the two, less dangerous is the offence
To tire our patience, than mislead our sense.
Some few in that, but numbers err in this,
Ten censure wrong for one who writes amiss;
A fool might once himself alone expose,
Now one in verse makes many more in prose.

. . . Yet, if we look more closely, we shall find
Most have the seeds of judgment in their mind:
Nature affords at least a glimmering light;

The lines, though touch'd but faintly, are drawn right.
But as the slightest sketch, if justly traced,
Is by ill colouring but the more disgraced,
So by false learning is good sense defaced;
Some are bewilder'd in the maze of schools,
And some made coxcombs Nature meant but fools.
In search of wit these lose their common sense,
And then turn critics in their own defence:
Each burns alike, who can, or cannot write,
Or with a rival's, or an eunuch's spite.
All fools have still an itching to deride,
And fain would be upon the laughing side.
If Maevius scribble in Apollo's spite,
There are who judge still worse than he can write.

. . . First follow Nature, and your judgment frame
By her just standard, which is still the same:
Unerring Nature, still divinely bright,
One clear, unchanged, and universal light,
Life, force, and beauty, must to all impart,
At once the source, and end, and test of Art.
Art from that fund each just supply provides;
Works without show, and without pomp presides:
In some fair body thus th' informing soul
With spirits feeds, with vigour fills the whole,
Each motion guides, and every nerve sustains;
Itself unseen, but in th' effects remains.
Some, to whom Heaven in wit has been profuse,
Want as much more to turn it to its use;
For wit and judgment often are at strife,
Though meant each other's aid, like man and wife.
'Tis more to guide, than spur the Muse's steed;
Restrain his fury, than provoke his speed:
The winged courser, like a generous horse,
Shows most true mettle when you check his course.

Those rules of old discover'd, not devised,
Are Nature still, but Nature methodized:
Nature, like liberty, is but restrain'd
By the same laws which first herself ordain'd.

. . . . Of all the causes which conspire to blind
Man's erring judgment, and misguide the mind,
What the weak head with strongest bias rules,
Is PRIDE, the never-failing vice of fools.
Whatever Nature has in worth denied,
She gives in large recruits of needless pride;
For as in bodies, thus in souls we find
What wants in blood and spirits, swell'd with wind:
Pride, where wit fails, steps in to our defence,
And fills up all the mighty void of sense.
If once right reason drives that cloud away,
Truth breaks upon us with resistless day.
Trust not yourself; but your defects to know,
Make use of every friend—and every foe.
A little learning is a dangerous thing;
Drink deep, or taste not the Pierian spring:
There shallow draughts intoxicate the brain,
And drinking largely sobers us again.
Fired at first sight with what the Muse imparts,
In fearless youth we tempt the height of arts,
While from the bounded level of our mind,
Short views we take, nor see the lengths behind;
But more advanced, behold with strange surprise
New distant scenes of endless science rise!
So pleased at first the towering Alps we try,
Mount o'er the vales, and seem to tread the sky,
The eternal snows appear already passed,
And the first clouds and mountains seem the last:
But, those attain'd, we tremble to survey
The growing labours of the lengthen'd way,
The increasing prospect tires our wandering eyes,
Hills peep o'er hills, and Alps on Alps arise!

. . . But most by numbers judge a poet's song;
And smooth or rough, with them, is right or wrong:
In the bright Muse, though thousand charms conspire,
Her voice is all these tuneful fools admire;
Who haunt Parnassus but to please their ear,
Not mend their minds; as some to church repair,
Not for the doctrine, but the music there.

These equal syllables alone require,
Though oft the ear the open vowels tire;
While expletives their feeble aid do join;
And ten low words oft creep in one dull line:
While they ring round the same unvaried chimes,
With sure returns of still expected rhymes;
Where'er you find 'the cooling western breeze',
In the next line, it 'whispers through the trees':
If crystal streams 'with pleasing murmurs creep':
The reader's threaten'd (not in vain) with 'sleep'.
Then, at the last and only couplet fraught
With some unmeaning thing they call a thought,
A needless Alexandrine ends the song,
That, like a wounded snake, drags its slow length along.
Leave such to tune their own dull rhymes, and know
What's roundly smooth, or languishingly slow;
And praise the easy vigour of a line,
Where Denham's strength and Waller's sweetness join.
True ease in writing comes from art, not chance,
As those move easiest who have learn'd to dance.
'Tis not enough no harshness gives offence,
The sound must seem an echo to the sense:
Soft is the strain when Zephyr gently blows,
And the smooth stream in smoother numbers flows;
But when loud surges lash the sounding shore,
The hoarse, rough verse should like the torrent roar.
When Ajax strives some rock's vast weight to throw,
The line too labours, and the words move slow:
Not so, when swift Camilla scours the plain,
Flies o'er the unbending corn, and skims along the main.
Hear how Timotheus' varied lays surprise,
And bid alternate passions fall and rise!
While, at each change, the son of Libyan Jove
Now burns with glory, and then melts with love;
Now his fierce eyes with sparkling fury glow,
Now sighs steal out, and tears begin to flow:
Persians and Greeks like turns of Nature found
And the world's victor stood subdued by sound!
The power of music all our hearts allow,
And what Timotheus was, is DRYDEN now.

ALEXANDER POPE

ELEGY

TO THE MEMORY OF AN UNFORTUNATE LADY

WHAT beckoning ghost along the moonlight shade
Invites my steps, and points to yonder glade?
'Tis she!—but why that bleeding bosom gored,
Why dimly gleams the visionary sword?
Oh, ever beauteous, ever friendly! tell,
Is it, in heaven, a crime to love too well?
To bear too tender or too firm a heart,
To act a lover's or a Roman's part?
Is there no bright reversion in the sky
For those who greatly think, or bravely die?
Why bade ye else, ye powers! her soul aspire
Above the vulgar flight of low desire?
Ambition first sprung from your blest abodes,
The glorious fault of angels and of gods:
Thence to their images on earth it flows,
And in the breasts of kings and heroes glows.
Most souls, 'tis true, but peep out once an age,
Dull, sullen prisoners in the body's cage:
Dim lights of life, that burn a length of years,
Useless, unseen, as lamps in sepulchres;
Like Eastern kings a lazy state they keep
And, close confined to their own palace, sleep.
From these perhaps (ere Nature bade her die)
Fate snatched her early to the pitying sky.
As into air the purer spirits flow,
And separate from their kindred dregs below;
So flew the soul to its congenial place,
Nor left one virtue to redeem her race.
But thou, false guardian of a charge too good,
Thou, mean deserter of thy brother's blood!
See on these ruby lips the trembling breath,
These cheeks now fading at the blast of death;
Cold is that breast which warm'd the world before,
And those love-darting eyes must roll no more.
Thus, if eternal justice rules the ball,
Thus shall your wives, and thus your children fall:

On all the line a sudden vengeance waits,
And frequent hearses shall besiege your gates;
There passengers shall stand, and pointing say,
(While the long funerals blacken all the way,)
'Lo! these were they, whose souls the Furies steel'd,
And cursed with hearts unknowing how to yield.'
Thus unlamented pass the proud away,
The gaze of fools, and pageant of a day!
So perish all, whose breast ne'er learn'd to glow
For others' good, or melt at others' woe.
What can atone (oh ever-injured shade!)
Thy fate unpitied, and thy rites unpaid?
No friend's complaint, no kind domestic tear
Pleased thy pale ghost, or graced thy mournful bier.
By foreign hands thy dying eyes were closed,
By foreign hands thy decent limbs composed,
By foreign hands thy humble grave adorn'd,
By strangers honour'd, and by strangers mourn'd!
What though no friends in sable weeds appear,
Grieve for an hour, perhaps, then mourn a year,
And bear about the mockery of woe
To midnight dances, and the public show?
What though no weeping loves thy ashes grace,
Nor polish'd marble emulate thy face?
What though no sacred earth allow thee room,
Nor hallow'd dirge be mutter'd o'er thy tomb?
Yet shall thy grave with rising flowers be dress'd,
And the green turf lie lightly on thy breast:
There shall the morn her earliest tears bestow,
There the first roses of the year shall blow;
While angels with their silver wings o'ershade
The ground now sacred by thy relics made.
So peaceful rests, without a stone, a name,
What once had beauty, titles, wealth, and fame.
How loved, how honour'd once, avails thee not,
To whom related, or by whom begot;
A heap of dust alone remains of thee,
'Tis all thou art, and all the proud shall be!
Poets themselves must fall, like those they sung,
Deaf the praised ear, and mute the tuneful tongue.

Even he, whose soul now melts in mournful lays,
Shall shortly want the generous tear he pays;
Then from his closing eyes thy form shall part,
And the last pang shall tear thee from his heart,
Life's idle business at one gasp be o'er,
The Muse forgot, and thou beloved no more!

THE RAPE OF THE LOCK

CANTO III

CLOSE by those meads, for ever crown'd with flowers,
Where Thames with pride surveys his rising towers,
There stands a structure of majestic frame,
Which from the neighb'ring Hampton takes its name.
Here Britain's statesmen oft the fall foredoom
Of foreign tyrants, and of nymphs at home;
Here thou, great Anna! whom three realms obey,
Dost sometimes counsel take—and sometimes tea.
Hither the heroes and the nymphs resort,
To taste a while the pleasures of a court;
In various talk th' instructive hours they pass'd,
Who gave the ball, or paid the visit last;
One speaks the glory of the British Queen,
And one describes a charming Indian screen;
A third interprets motion, looks, and eyes;
At every word a reputation dies.
Snuff, or the fan, supply each pause of chat,
With singing, laughing, ogling, *and all that*.
Meanwhile, declining from the noon of day,
The sun obliquely shoots his burning ray;
The hungry judges soon the sentence sign,
And wretches hang that jurymen may dine;
The merchant from th' exchange returns in peace,
And the long labours of the toilet cease.
Belinda now, whom thirst of fame invites,
Burns to encounter two adventurous knights,
At ombre singly to decide their doom;
And swells her breast with conquests yet to come.
Straight the three bands prepare in arms to join,
Each band the number of the sacred nine.

Soon as she spreads her hand, th' aërial guard
Descend, and sit on each important card:
First Ariel perch'd upon a Matadore,[1]
Then each according to the rank they bore;
For sylphs, yet mindful of their ancient race,
Are, as when women, wondrous fond of place.
Behold, four Kings in majesty revered,
With hoary whiskers and a forky beard;
And four fair Queens, whose hands sustain a flower,
Th' expressive emblem of their softer power;
Four knaves in garb succinct, a trusty band,
Caps on their heads, and halberts in their hand;
And party-colour'd troops, a shining train,
Drawn forth to combat on the velvet plain.
The skilful nymph reviews her force with care:
'Let Spades be trumps!' she said, and trumps they were.
Now move to war her sable Matadores,[1]
In show like leaders of the swarthy Moors.
Spadillio[2] first, unconquerable lord!
Led off two captive trumps, and swept the board.
As many more Manillio[3] forced to yield,
And march'd a victor from the verdant field.
Him Basto[4] follow'd; but his fate more hard
Gain'd but one trump, and one plebeian card.
With his broad sabre next, a chief in years,
The hoary Majesty of Spades appears,
Puts forth one manly leg, to sight reveal'd,
The rest, his many-colour'd robe conceal'd.
The rebel Knave, who dares his prince engage,
Proves the just victim of his royal rage.
Ev'n mighty Pam,[5] that kings and queens o'erthrew,
And mow'd down armies in the fights of Lu,[6]
Sad chance of war! now destitute of aid,
Falls undistinguish'd by the victor Spade!

[1] Matadores] In the game of Ombre, the three principal trumps were called Matadores.   [2] Spadillio] The ace of spades, the first trump at Ombre.   [3] Manillio] The deuce of trumps, when trumps are black, the seven when they are red. The second trump at Ombre.
[4] Basto] The ace of clubs, third trump at Ombre.   [5] Pam] In certain games the knave of clubs is called Pam.   [6] Lu] The game of Loo, in which Pam is the highest card.

Thus far both armies to Belinda yield;
Now to the baron fate inclines the field.
His warlike Amazon her host invades,
Th' imperial consort of the crown of Spades.
The Club's black tyrant first her victim dyed,
Spite of his haughty mien, and barb'rous pride:
What boots the regal circle on his head,
His giant limbs, in state unwieldy spread;
That long behind he trails his pompous robe,
And, of all monarchs, only grasps the globe?
The baron now his Diamonds pours apace;
Th' embroider'd King who shows but half his face,
And his refulgent Queen, with powers combined
Of broken troops an easy conquest find.
Clubs, Diamonds, Hearts, in wild disorder seen,
With throngs promiscuous strow the level green.
Thus when dispersed a routed army runs,
Of Asia's troops, and Afric's sable sons,
With like confusion different nations fly,
Of various habit, and of various dye,
The pierced battalions disunited fall,
In heaps on heaps; one fate o'erwhelms them all.

The Knave of Diamonds tries his wily arts,
And wins (oh shameful chance!) the Queen of Hearts.
At this, the blood the virgin's cheek forsook,
A livid paleness spreads o'er all her look;
She sees, and trembles at th' approaching ill,
Just in the jaws of ruin, and Codille.[1]
And now (as oft in some distemper'd state)
On one nice trick depends the gen'ral fate.
An Ace of Hearts steps forth: the King unseen
Lurk'd in her hand, and mourn'd his captive Queen:
He springs to vengeance with an eager pace,
And falls like thunder on the prostrate Ace.
The nymph exulting fills with shouts the sky;
The walls, the woods, and long canals reply.

[1] Codille] a term in Ombre and quadrille. When those who defend
the pool make more tricks than those who defend the game, they are
said to 'win the Codille'.

O thoughtless mortals! ever blind to fate,
Too soon dejected, and too soon elate.
Sudden, these honours shall be snatch'd away,
And cursed for ever this victorious day.
For lo! the board with cups and spoons is crown'd,
The berries crackle, and the mill turns round:
On shining altars of Japan they raise
The silver lamp; the fiery spirits blaze:
From silver spouts the grateful liquors glide,
While China's earth receives the smoking tide:
At once they gratify their scent and taste,
And frequent cups prolong the rich repast.
Straight hover round the fair her airy band;
Some, as she sipp'd, the fuming liquor fann'd,
Some o'er her lap their careful plumes display'd,
Trembling, and conscious of the rich brocade.
Coffee (which makes the politician wise,
And see through all things with his half-shut eyes)
Sent up in vapours to the baron's brain
New stratagems, the radiant lock to gain.
Ah cease, rash youth! desist ere 'tis too late,
Fear the just gods, and think of Scylla's fate!
Changed to a bird, and sent to flit in air,
She dearly pays for Nisus' injured hair!
But when to mischief mortals bend their will,
How soon they find fit instruments of ill!
Just then, Clarissa drew with tempting grace
A two-edged weapon from her shining case:
So ladies, in romance, assist their knight,
Present the spear, and arm him for the fight.
He takes the gift with reverence, and extends
The little engine on his fingers' ends;
This just behind Belinda's neck he spread,
As o'er the fragrant steams she bends her head.
Swift to the lock a thousand sprites repair,
A thousand wings, by turns, blow back the hair;
And thrice they twitch'd the diamond in her ear;
Thrice she look'd back, and thrice the foe drew near.
Just in that instant, anxious Ariel sought
The close recesses of the virgin's thought:

As on the nosegay in her breast reclin'd,
He watch'd th' ideas rising in her mind,
Sudden he view'd, in spite of all her art,
An earthly lover lurking at her heart.
Amazed, confused, he found his power expired,
Resign'd to fate, and with a sigh retired.
The peer now spreads the glitt'ring forfex[1] wide,
T' inclose the lock; now joins it, to divide.
Ev'n then, before the fatal engine closed,
A wretched sylph too fondly interposed;
Fate urged the shears, and cut the sylph in twain,
(But airy substance soon unites again)
The meeting points the sacred hair dissever
From the fair head, for ever, and for ever!
Then flash'd the living lightning from her eyes,
And screams of horror rend th' affrighted skies.
Not louder shrieks to pitying Heaven are cast,
When husbands or when lap-dogs breathe their last;
Or when rich China vessels, fall'n from high,
In glitt'ring dust and painted fragments lie!

ON MR. GAY

IN WESTMINSTER ABBEY, 1732

Of manners gentle, of affections mild;
In wit, a man; simplicity, a child:
With native humour tempering virtuous rage,
Form'd to delight at once and lash the age:
Above temptation in a low estate,
And uncorrupted, ev'n among the great:
A safe companion, and an easy friend,
Unblamed through life, lamented in thy end.
These are thy honours! not that here thy bust
Is mix'd with heroes, or with kings thy dust;
But that the worthy and the good shall say,
Striking their pensive bosoms—Here lies GAY.

---

[1] forfex] pair of scissors.

THE REIGN OF CHAOS

In vain, in vain—the all-composing hour
Resistless falls: the Muse obeys the pow'r.
She comes! she comes! the sable throne behold
Of Night primeval and of Chaos old!
Before her, fancy's gilded clouds decay,
And all its varying rainbows die away.
Wit shoots in vain its momentary fires,
The meteor drops, and in a flash expires.
As one by one, at dread Medea's strain,
The sick'ning stars fade off th' ethereal plain;
As Argus' eyes by Hermes' wand opprest,
Closed one by one to everlasting rest;
Thus at her felt approach, and secret might,
Art after art goes out, and all is night.
See skulking Truth to her old cavern fled,
Mountains of casuistry heaped o'er her head!
Philosophy, that leaned on Heaven before,
Shrinks to her second cause, and is no more.
Physic of metaphysic begs defence,
And metaphysic calls for aid on sense!
See mystery to mathematics fly!
In vain! they gaze, turn giddy, rave, and die.
Religion blushing veils her sacred fires,
And unawares morality expires.
For public flame, nor private, dares to shine,
Nor human spark is left, nor glimpse divine!
Lo! thy dread empire, Chaos, is restored;
Light dies before thy uncreating word;
Thy hand, great Anarch! lets the curtain fall,
And universal darkness buries all.

(*The Dunciad*, iv, ll. 627–56.)

ULYSSES AND HIS DOG

Thus, near the gates conferring as they drew,
Argus, the dog, his ancient master knew;
He, not unconscious of the voice, and tread,
Lifts to the sound his ear, and rears his head.

Bred by Ulysses, nourish'd at his board,
But ah! not fated long to please his Lord!
To him, his swiftness and his strength were vain;
The voice of Glory call'd him o'er the main.

Till then in every sylvan chase renown'd,
With Argus, Argus, rung the woods around;
With him the youth pursued, the goat or fawn,
Or traced the mazy leveret[1] o'er the lawn.
Now left to man's ingratitude he lay,
Unhous'd, neglected, in the public way;
And where on heaps the rich manure was spread,
Obscene with reptiles, took his sordid bed.

He knew his Lord; he knew, and strove to meet,
In vain he strove to crawl, and kiss his feet;
Yet (all he could) his tail, his ears, his eyes
Salute his master, and confess his joys.
Soft pity touch'd the mighty master's soul;
Adown his cheek a tear unbidden stole,
Stole unperceiv'd; he turn'd his head, and dried
The drop humane: then thus impassion'd cried:

'What noble beast in this abandon'd state
Lies here all helpless at Ulysses' gate?
His bulk and beauty speak no vulgar praise;
If, as he seems, he was in better days,
Some care his age deserved; or was he prized
For worthless beauty? therefore now despised?
Such dogs, and men there are, mere things of state,
And always cherish'd by their friends, the great.'

'Not Argus so,' *Eumæus* thus rejoin'd,
'But serv'd a master of a nobler kind,
Who never, never shall behold him more!
Long, long since perish'd on a distant shore!
Oh had you seen him, vigorous, bold and young,
Swift as a stag, and as a lion strong,
Him no fell savage on the plain withstood,
None 'scap'd him, bosom'd in the gloomy wood;

His eye how piercing, and his scent how true,
To wind the vapour in the tainted dew.

[1] leveret] a young hare

Such, when Ulysses left his natal coast;
Now years unnerve him, and his lord is lost!
The women keep the gen'rous creature bare,
A sleek and idle race is all their care:
The master gone, the servants what restrains?
Or dwells humanity where riot reigns?
Jove fix'd it certain, that whatever day
Makes man a slave, takes half his worth away.'
This said, the honest herdsman strode before:
The musing monarch pauses at the door:
The dog whom fate had granted to behold
His lord, when twenty tedious years had roll'd,
Takes a last look, and having seen him, dies;
So clos'd for ever faithful Argus' eyes!

(*Odyssey*, Bk. XVII.)

THE IDEALS OF SATIRE

. . . Our rural ancestors, with little blest,
Patient of labour when the end was rest,
Indulged the day that housed their annual grain,
With feasts, and offerings, and a thankful strain:
The joy their wives, their sons, and servants share,
Ease of their toil, and partners of their care:
The laugh, the jest, attendants on the bowl,
Smooth'd every brow, and open'd every soul:
With growing years the pleasing licence grew,
And taunts alternate innocently flew.
But times corrupt and Nature ill-inclined
Produced the point that left a sting behind;
Till friend with friend, and families at strife,
Triumphant malice raged through private life.
Who felt the wrong, or fear'd it, took the alarm,
Appeal'd to law, and justice lent her arm.
At length, by wholesome dread of statutes bound,
The poets learn'd to please, and not to wound:
Most warp'd to flattery's side; but some, more nice,
Preserved the freedom, and forbore the vice.
Hence Satire rose, that just the medium hit,
And heals with morals what it hurts with wit.

We conquer'd France, but felt our captive's charms;
Her arts victorious triumph'd o'er our arms:
Britain to soft refinements less a foe,
Wit grew polite, and numbers learn'd to flow.
Waller was smooth; but Dryden taught to join
The varying verse, the full-resounding line,
The long majestic march and energy divine.
Though still some traces of our rustic vein
And splayfoot verse remain'd, and will remain.
Late, very late, correctness grew our care,
When the tired nation breathed from civil war.
Exact Racine, and Corneille's noble fire,
Show'd us that France had something to admire.
Not but the tragic spirit was our own,
And full in Shakespeare, fair in Otway shone:
But Otway fail'd to polish or refine,
And fluent Shakespeare scarce effaced a line.
Even copious Dryden wanted, or forgot,
The last and greatest art, the art to blot.

(*Imitation of the First Epistle of the 2nd Book of Horace.*)

THE DEATH OF BUCKINGHAM

In the worst inn's worst room, with mat half-hung,
The floors of plaster, and the walls of dung,
On once a flock-bed, but repair'd with straw,
With tape-tied curtains never meant to draw,
The George and Garter dangling from that bed
Where tawdry yellow strove with dirty red,
Great Villiers lies,—alas! how changed from him,
That life of pleasure, and that soul of whim!
Gallant and gay, in Cliveden's proud alcove,
The bower of wanton Shrewsbury and love;
Or just as gay, at council, in a ring
Of mimick'd statesmen, and their merry King.
No wit to flatter left of all his store!
No fool to laugh at, which he valued more.
There, victor of his health, of fortune, friends,
And fame, this lord of useless thousands ends.

(*Moral Essays*, Ep. III, Of the Use of Riches.)

THE PROPER STUDY OF MANKIND

KNOW then thyself, presume not God to scan,
The proper study of mankind is man.
Placed on this isthmus of a middle state,
A being darkly wise, and rudely great:
With too much knowledge for the sceptic side,
With too much weakness for the stoic's pride,
He hangs between; in doubt to act, or rest;
In doubt to deem himself a god, or beast;
In doubt his mind or body to prefer;
Born but to die, and reasoning but to err;
Alike in ignorance, his reason such,
Whether he thinks too little, or too much:
Chaos of thought and passion, all confused;
Still by himself abused or disabused;
Created half to rise, and half to fall;
Great lord of all things, yet a prey to all;
Sole judge of truth, in endless error hurl'd:
The glory, jest, and riddle of the world!
Go, wondrous creature! mount where Science guides;
Go, measure earth, weigh air, and state the tides;
Instruct the planets in what orbs to run,
Correct old Time, and regulate the sun;
Go, soar with Plato to th' empyreal sphere,
To the first good, first perfect, and first fair;
Or tread the mazy round his followers trod,
And quitting sense call imitating God;
As Eastern priests in giddy circles run,
And turn their heads to imitate the sun.
Go, teach Eternal Wisdom how to rule—
Then drop into thyself, and be a fool!
(*Essay on Man*, Ep. II, Of the Nature and State of Man.)

HUMAN FOLLY

WHATE'ER the passion, knowledge, fame, or pelf,
Not one will change his neighbour with himself.
The learn'd is happy Nature to explore,
The fool is happy that he knows no more;

The rich is happy in the plenty given,
The poor contents him with the care of Heaven.
See the blind beggar dance, the cripple sing,
The sot a hero, lunatic a king;
The starving chemist in his golden views
Supremely blest, the poet in his Muse.
See some strange comfort every state attend,
And pride bestow'd on all, a common friend:
See some fit passion every age supply,
Hope travels through, nor quits us when we die.
Behold the child, by Nature's kindly law,
Pleased with a rattle, tickled with a straw:
Some livelier plaything gives his youth delight,
A little louder, but as empty quite:
Scarfs, garters, gold, amuse his riper stage,
And beads and prayer-books are the toys of age:
Pleased with this bauble still, as that before;
Till tired he sleeps, and life's poor play is o'er.

(Essay on Man, Ep. II.)

From EPISTLE TO DR. ARBUTHNOT

WHY did I write? what sin to me unknown
Dipp'd me in ink, my parents', or my own?
As yet a child, nor yet a fool to fame,
I lisp'd in numbers, for the numbers came.
I left no calling for this idle trade,
No duty broke, no father disobey'd:
The Muse but served to ease some friend, not wife,
To help me through this long disease, my life;
To second, ARBUTHNOT! thy art and care,
And teach the being you preserved to bear.
But why then publish? Granville the polite,
And knowing Walsh, would tell me I could write;
Well-natured Garth inflamed with early praise,
And Congreve loved, and Swift endured my lays;
The courtly Talbot, Somers, Sheffield read,
Even mitred Rochester would nod the head,
And St. John's self (great Dryden's friend before)
With open arms received one poet more.

Happy my studies, when by these approved!
Happier their author, when by these beloved!
From these the world will judge of men and books,
Not from the Burnets, Oldmixons, and Cookes.
Soft were my numbers; who could take offence
While pure description held the place of sense?
Like gentle Fanny's was my flowery theme,
A painted mistress, or a purling stream.
Yet then did Gildon draw his venal quill;
I wish'd the man a dinner, and sate still.
Yet then did Dennis rave in furious fret;
I never answer'd—I was not in debt.
If want provoked, or madness made them print,
I waged no war with Bedlam or the Mint.
Did some more sober critic come abroad—
If wrong, I smiled; if right, I kiss'd the rod.
Pains, reading, study, are their just pretence,
And all they want is spirit, taste, and sense.
Commas and points they set exactly right,
And 'twere a sin to rob them of their mite;
Yet ne'er one sprig of laurel graced these ribalds,
From slashing Bentley down to piddling Tibbalds:
Each wight, who reads not, and but scans and spells,
Each word-catcher, that lives on syllables,
Even such small critics some regard may claim,
Preserved in Milton's or in Shakespeare's name.
Pretty! in amber to observe the forms
Of hairs, or straws, or dirt, or grubs, or worms!
The things we know are neither rich nor rare,
But wonder how the devil they got there.
Were others angry—I excused them too;
Well might they rage, I gave them but their due.
A man's true merit 'tis not hard to find;
But each man's secret standard in his mind,
That casting-weight pride adds to emptiness,
This, who can gratify, for who can guess?
The bard whom pilfer'd Pastorals renown,
Who turns a Persian tale for half-a-crown,
Just writes to make his barrenness appear,
And strains from hard-bound brains eight lines a-year;

He, who still wanting, though he lives on theft,
Steals much, spends little, yet has nothing left:
And he, who now to sense, now nonsense leaning,
Means not, but blunders round about a meaning:
And he, whose fustian's so sublimely bad,
It is not poetry, but prose run mad:
All these, my modest satire bade translate,
And own'd that nine such poets made a Tate.
How did they fume, and stamp, and roar, and chafe!
And swear, not Addison himself was safe.

Peace to all such! but were there one whose fires
True genius kindles, and fair fame inspires;
Blest with each talent, and each art to please,
And born to write, converse, and live with ease;
Should such a man, too fond to rule alone,
Bear, like the Turk, no brother near the throne,
View him with scornful, yet with jealous eyes,
And hate for arts that caused himself to rise;
Damn with faint praise, assent with civil leer,
And, without sneering, teach the rest to sneer;
Willing to wound, and yet afraid to strike,
Just hint a fault, and hesitate dislike;
Alike reserved to blame, or to commend,
A timorous foe, and a suspicious friend;
Dreading e'en fools, by flatterers besieged,
And so obliging, that he ne'er obliged;
Like Cato, give his little senate laws,
And sit attentive to his own applause;
While wits and Templars every sentence raise,
And wonder with a foolish face of praise—
Who but must laugh, if such a man there be?
Who would not weep, if Atticus were he?

EPITAPH ON SIR ISAAC NEWTON

NATURE and Nature's laws lay hid in night:
God said, Let Newton be! and all was light.

WILLIAM COWPER

WILLIAM COWPER, (pron. Cooper), (1731–1800), was articled to a solicitor and was called to the bar in 1754. He suffered from fits of depression, which developed into mania, and he tried to commit suicide. Of this mania he was cured, but he thereafter lived in retirement. In 1765 he became a boarder in the house of Morley Unwin at Huntingdon, where the simple life perfectly suited him, and after Unwin's death he removed with Mary, Unwin's widow, to Olney. At the suggestion of Mrs. Unwin he wrote eight satires which were published in 1782, *John Gilpin* (1782), and, in 1784, *The Task*. Mrs. Unwin died in 1794 and her loss left Cowper shattered in mind and body. The fine but gloomy poem *The Castaway* was written shortly before his death.

OF all the poets in this selection Cowper is perhaps the smallest in poetical stature. He would probably have counted himself lucky to figure in such grand company; and indeed, he can hardly be reckoned a poet in the full sense in which Spenser and Pope and Wordsworth were poets. Poetry to Cowper was not the business of his life; it was his diversion. His friends gave him subjects to write about, and he wrote. *The Task*, he tells us, was written because 'a lady, fond of blank verse, demanded a poem of that kind from the Author, and gave him the SOFA for a subject. He obeyed . . . .' That statement is not without significance, but it should not be exaggerated. Many great poems have sprung from the chance suggestions of friends; the origin of *The Ancient Mariner*, for instance, appears to have been a dream of one of Coleridge's friends, and for the albatross and some other important points he was indebted to later suggestions by Wordsworth. It is not so much the immediate origin of a poem that matters as the question of how and why it is written. In his whole attitude to poetry Cowper differs fundamentally from a poet like Coleridge— from the Coleridge, at any rate, who wrote *The Ancient Mariner* and *Kubla Khan*. If Coleridge, on his own confession, gave up the writing of poetry because he found the strain of imaginative composition too great for his physical powers, Cowper took to poetry as a means of escape from the pressure of thoughts and feelings that threatened his very sanity. The one fled from poetry to metaphysics, the other from theological speculations and religious agonies to poetry. But if Cowper found a refuge in poetry, it could only be by keeping resolutely to a world of familiar and friendly appearances, by averting his gaze from those terrible shapes that haunted his dreams and more than once overset his brain—in short, by remaining as far as possible on the plane of intelligent observation and commentary, and by denying his imagination that liberty of action the consequences of which he knew only too well. Through poetry Cowper may have preserved his sanity, but sanity alone will not preserve poetry. What he has given us is often acute, sensitively observed, gentle, civilized; but, to make use of a phrase of Coleridge's (which he does not, however, apply to Cowper), it is rarely more than 'the poetry of the milder muse'.

Cowper's work, in fact, often makes an appeal that is not strictly poetical at all. One is interested in his mild but convinced praise of liberty, in his never uncritical patriotism, in his sympathy with the poor and the humble, in his kindness to animals (though, as a sensible eighteenth-century poet, he keeps his head about them, and tells us when a beetle or a spider may be innocently destroyed), in his satirical observation of his fellow men, and in his frequent, if not quite unfailing, good sense. Above all, one is interested in Cowper himself. The charm of *John Gilpin* lies partly in the whimsical author behind the tale; the lines *On the Receipt of My Mother's Picture* owe much of their appeal to the revelation of a sensitive and even morbid nature. Cowper the poet has, in fact, much of the charm that one finds in the more personal of the eighteenth-century essayists, and in the great personal essayist of the early nineteenth century, Charles Lamb. He writes frankly and intimately about himself, his own peculiar thoughts and feelings, his likes and dislikes, his recollections of his own childhood. To the literary historian, Cowper is an interesting link between the old confident world of the eighteenth century that was passing away, and the new and untried world that was soon to be ushered in by the French Revolution. There is certainly a good deal that is new in Cowper, though the literature of the early eighteenth century will afford many parallels to what is often thought of as most modern in his work. It is instructive, for instance, to compare the lines *On the Receipt of My Mother's Picture* with the *Tatler* (No. 181), in which Steele described a little boy's recollections of the death of his father. In the essay, as in the poem, the child's uncomprehending dismay in the presence of death—'rather amazed at what all the house meant, than possessed with a real understanding why nobody was willing to play with me'—is realized with touching simplicity. Cowper's mind, indeed, is a meeting-ground for many conflicting tendencies and movements—Rousseauism, evangelicalism, old-fashioned Whig principles—but Cowper himself is more than the sum total of his beliefs. If he cannot reconcile all the varied sides of his nature—who can?—he yet emerges a real and coherent personality, struggling earnestly and sometimes passionately to get his own private universe into order. It is the man and the struggle that engage our attention to-day, quite as much as the poetry which was the by-product of that struggle. The very range of his interests often leads him in such poems as *Table Talk* or *The Task* to write what is neither prose nor poetry, but a series of versified ideas. Indeed, the stream of his poetry flowed 'much mingled and defiled', carrying on its surface all sorts of odd chips of argument and commentary.

It is when he forgets to preach or to argue, and allows himself to contemplate the beauty of the English countryside, that he is most surely a poet. Reading such passages as that in *The Winter Walk at Noon*,

The night was winter in his roughest mood;
The morning sharp and clear. . . .

one realizes anew that man is not interested only in man. The natural scene, the seasons, cloud, wind, the waving branch, the snowflake falling, the robin 'flitting light from spray to spray'—those are sufficient; the human mind is capable of being moved, and moved deeply, by those alone. That was not, of course, Cowper's discovery; but in his perfect confidence in the thing seen and heard he looks forward to Wordsworth more often than he looks back to James Thomson. In such passages, too, his blank verse develops a new power; it frees itself from the artificiality that often clings to it when he is arguing or expounding his views on contemporary affairs, and it vibrates with the emotion of a man delighting in the thing he contemplates. For once there is no inhibition; the whole soul of the poet is brought into activity.

'There is a pleasure in poetic pains,' he tells us in *The Task*, and in his longer poems one is sometimes too conscious of them. Even in his shorter and more lyrical compositions the right word is occasionally 'coy and difficult to win'. Often, as in the Hymns, it is too easily won; the conventional word or image presents itself boldly to the poet, and is accepted. But Cowper has one or two striking successes. Among the Hymns, *God moves in a mysterious way*, with its exhortation to the saints to take courage—

Ye fearful saints, fresh courage take,
    The clouds ye so much dread
Are big with mercy, and shall break
    In blessings on your head. . .

is an achievement that one surely does not need to be a Christian to admire. The manly and affecting lines, *On the Loss of the 'Royal George'*, have the monotonous beat of a passing bell; there is a muffled sorrow in the very sound of the words. Finally, there is *John Gilpin*. One is apt to underestimate the very real art of this poem because it is in Cowper's lightest vein; but the tone of breathless jollity is perfectly sustained throughout, and the excitement rises in a steady crescendo to the close. Cowper might surely have said of this poem what Wordsworth said of his *Idiot Boy*: 'I never wrote anything with so much glee.' If only his conscience, or his temperament, or his principles had allowed him to write more *John Gilpin*'s, he would have contributed even more remarkably than he has done to the sum total of human happiness. In the hundred and fifty odd years that have passed since *John Gilpin* was written, how many faces must have brightened at the adventures of the citizen of famous London town! Cowper could not have failed to approve; for there is perhaps no other poem in the English language which has provided such heartfelt, and—what was to him all-important—such innocent, amusement.

JAMES SUTHERLAND.

194

AN EPISTLE TO ROBERT LLOYD, ESQ.

'Tis not that I design to rob
Thee of thy birthright, gentle Bob,
For thou art born sole heir, and single,
Of dear Mat Prior's easy jingle;
Nor that I mean, while thus I knit
My thread-bare sentiments together,
To show my genius or my wit,
When God and you know I have neither;
Or such, as might be better shown
By letting poetry alone.
'Tis not with either of these views,
That I presume t' address the Muse:
But to divert a fierce banditti
(Sworn foes to ev'ry thing that's witty),
That, with a black infernal train,
Make cruel inroads in my brain,
And daily threaten to drive thence
My little garrison of sense:
The fierce banditti, which I mean,
Are gloomy thoughts led on by Spleen.
Then there's another reason yet,
Which is, that I may fairly quit
The debt, which justly became due
The moment when I heard from you:
And you might grumble, crony mine,
If paid in any other coin;
Since twenty sheets of lead, God knows,
(I would say twenty sheets of prose,)
Can ne'er be deem'd worth half so much
As one of gold, and yours was such.
Thus, the preliminaries settled,
I fairly find myself pitch-kettled;[1]
And cannot see, though few see better,
How I shall hammer out a letter.
First, for a thought—since all agree—
A thought—I have it—let me see—·

[1] pitch-kettled] non-plussed

'Tis gone again—plague on't! I thought
I had it—but I have it not.
Dame Gurton thus, and Hodge her son,
That useful thing, her needle, gone,
Rake well the cinders—sweep the floor,
And sift the dust behind the door;
While eager Hodge beholds the prize
In old Grimalkin's glaring eyes;
And Gammer finds it on her knees
In every shining straw she sees.
This simile were apt enough;
But I've another, critic-proof!
The virtuoso thus, at noon,
Broiling beneath a July sun,
The gilded butterfly pursues
O'er hedge and ditch, through gaps and mews;
And after many a vain essay
To captivate the tempting prey,
Gives him at length the lucky pat,
And has him safe beneath his hat:
Then lifts it gently from the ground.
But ah! 'tis lost as soon as found;
Culprit his liberty regains;
Flits out of sight and mocks his pains.
The sense was dark; 'twas therefore fit
With simile t' illustrate it;
But as too much obscures the sight,
As often as too little light,
We have our similes cut short,
For matters of more grave import.

That Matthew's numbers run with ease
Each man of common-sense agrees;
All men of common-sense allow,
That Robert's lines are easy too;
Where then the preference shall we place,
Or how do justice in this case?
Matthew, (says Fame) with endless pains
Smooth'd and refin'd the meanest strains;
Nor suffer'd one ill-chosen rhyme
T' escape him, at the idlest time;

And thus o'er all a lustre cast,
That, while the language lives, shall last.
An't please your Ladyship (quoth I,
For 'tis my business to reply;)
Sure so much labour, so much toil,
Bespeak at least a stubborn soil.
Theirs be the laurel-wreath decreed,
Who both write well and write full-speed!
Who throw their Helicon about
As freely as a conduit spout!
Friend Robert, thus like *chien scavant*,
Lets fall a poem *en passant*,
Nor needs his genuine ore refine;
'Tis ready polish'd from the mine.

ALEXANDER SELKIRK

I AM monarch of all I survey,
    My right there is none to dispute;
From the centre all round to the sea,
    I am lord of the fowl and the brute.
Oh, solitude! where are the charms
    That sages have seen in thy face?
Better dwell in the midst of alarms,
    Than reign in this horrible place.

I am out of humanity's reach,
    I must finish my journey alone,
Never hear the sweet music of speech;
    I start at the sound of my own.
The beasts that roam over the plain,
    My form with indifference see;
They are so unacquainted with man,
    Their tameness is shocking to me.

Society, friendship, and love,
    Divinely bestow'd upon man,
Oh, had I the wings of a dove,
    How soon would I taste you again!

My sorrows I then might assuage
   In the ways of religion and truth,
Might learn from the wisdom of age,
   And be cheer'd by the sallies of youth.

Religion! what treasure untold
   Resides in that heavenly word!
More precious than silver and gold,
   Or all that this earth can afford.
But the sound of the church-going bell
   These valleys and rocks never heard,
Ne'er sigh'd at the sound of a knell,
   Or smil'd when a sabbath appear'd.

Ye winds, that have made me your sport,
   Convey to this desolate shore
Some cordial endearing report
   Of a land I shall visit no more.
My friends, do they now and then send
   A wish or a thought after me?
O tell me I yet have a friend,
   Though a friend I am never to see.

How fleet is a glance of the mind!
   Compar'd with the speed of its flight,
The tempest itself lags behind,
   And the swift winged arrows of light.
When I think of my own native land,
   In a moment I seem to be there;
But alas! recollection at hand
   Soon hurries me back to despair.

But the sea-fowl is gone to her nest,
   The beast is laid down in his lair,
Ev'n here is a season of rest,
   And I to my cabin repair.
There is mercy in every place;
   And mercy, encouraging thought!
Gives even affliction a grace,
   And reconciles man to his lot.

ON THE LOSS OF THE *ROYAL GEORGE*

Toll for the brave—
The brave! that are no more:
  All sunk beneath the wave,
Fast by their native shore.
  Eight hundred of the brave,
Whose courage well was tried,
  Had made the vessel heel
And laid her on her side;
  A land-breeze shook the shrouds,
And she was overset;
  Down went the *Royal George*,
With all her crew complete.

Toll for the brave—
Brave Kempenfelt is gone,
  His last sea-fight is fought,
His work of glory done.
  It was not in the battle,
No tempest gave the shock,
  She sprang no fatal leak,
She ran upon no rock;
  His sword was in the sheath,
His fingers held the pen,
  When Kempenfelt went down
With twice four hundred men.

Weigh the vessel up,
Once dreaded by our foes,
  And mingle with your cup
The tears that England owes;
  Her timbers yet are sound,
And she may float again,
  Full charg'd with England's thunder.
And plough the distant main;
  But Kempenfelt is gone,
His victories are o'er;
  And he and his Eight hundred
Must plough the wave no more.

OH! FOR A CLOSER WALK WITH GOD

Oh! for a closer walk with God,
  A calm and heav'nly frame;
A light to shine upon the road
  That leads me to the Lamb!

Where is the blessedness I knew
  When first I saw the Lord?
Where is the soul-refreshing view
  Of Jesus, and his word?

What peaceful hours I once enjoy'd!
  How sweet their mem'ry still!
But they have left an aching void,
  The world can never fill.

Return, O holy Dove, return,
  Sweet messenger of rest;
I hate the sins that made thee mourn,
  And drove thee from my breast.

The dearest idol I have known,
  Whate'er that idol be;
Help me to tear it from thy throne,
  And worship only thee.

So shall my walk be close with God,
  Calm and serene my frame;
So purer light shall mark the road
  That leads me to the Lamb.

GOD MOVES IN A MYSTERIOUS WAY

God moves in a mysterious way,
  His wonders to perform;
He plants his footsteps in the sea,
  And rides upon the storm.

Deep in unfathomable mines
  Of never-failing skill,
He treasures up his bright designs,
  And works his sovereign will.

Ye fearful saints, fresh courage take,
  The clouds ye so much dread
Are big with mercy, and shall break
  In blessings on your head.

Judge not the LORD by feeble sense,
  But trust him for his grace;
Behind a frowning providence,
  He hides a smiling face.

His purposes will ripen fast,
  Unfolding ev'ry hour;
The bud may have a bitter taste,
  But sweet will be the flow'r.

Blind unbelief is sure to err,
  And scan his work in vain;
GOD is his own interpreter,
  And he will make it plain.

EPITAPH ON A HARE

HERE lies, whom hound did ne'er pursue,
  Nor swifter greyhound follow,
Whose foot ne'er tainted morning dew,
  Nor ear heard huntsman's hallo,

Old Tiney, surliest of his kind,
  Who, nursed with tender care,
And to domestic bounds confined,
  Was still a wild Jack-hare.

Though duly from my hand he took
  His pittance every night,
He did it with a jealous look,
  And, when he could, would bite.

His diet was of wheaten bread,
  And milk, and oats, and straw,
Thistles, or lettuces instead,
  With sand to scour his maw.

On twigs of hawthorn he regaled,
  On pippins' russet peel;
And, when his juicy salads failed,
  Sliced carrot pleased him well.

A Turkey carpet was his lawn,
  Whereon he lov'd to bound,
To skip and gambol like a fawn,
  And swing his rump around.

His frisking was at evening hours,
  For then he lost his fear;
But most before approaching show'rs,
  Or when a storm drew near.

Eight years and five round-rolling moons
  He thus saw steal away,
Dozing out all his idle noons,
  And ev'ry night at play.

I kept him for his humour's sake,
  For he would oft beguile
My heart of thoughts that made it ache,
  And force me to a smile.

But now, beneath this walnut-shade
  He finds his long, last home,
And waits in snug concealment laid,
  'Till gentler Puss shall come.

He, still more aged, feels the shocks
  From which no care can save,
And, partner once of Tiney's box,
  Must soon partake his grave.

THE POPLAR-FIELD

THE poplars are fell'd, farewell to the shade
And the whispering sound of the cool colonnade,
The winds play no longer, and sing in the leaves,
Nor Ouse on his bosom their image receives.

Twelve years have elaps'd since I first took a view
Of my favourite field and the bank where they grew,
And now in the grass behold they are laid,
And the tree is my seat that once lent me a shade.

The blackbird has fled to another retreat
Where the hazels afford him a screen from the heat,
And the scene where his melody charm'd me before,
Resounds with his sweet-flowing ditty no more.

My fugitive years are all hasting away,
And I must ere long lie as lowly as they,
With a turf on my breast, and a stone at my head,
Ere another such grove shall arise in its stead.

'Tis a sight to engage me, if any thing can,
To muse on the perishing pleasures of man;
Though his life be a dream, his enjoyments, I see,
Have a being less durable even than he.

THE DIVERTING HISTORY OF JOHN GILPIN

SHOWING HOW HE WENT FARTHER THAN HE INTENDED,
AND CAME SAFE HOME AGAIN

JOHN GILPIN was a citizen
   Of credit and renown,
A train-band captain eke was he
   Of famous London town.

John Gilpin's spouse said to her dear—
   Though wedded we have been
These twice ten tedious years, yet we
   No holiday have seen.

To-morrow is our wedding-day,
    And we will then repair
Unto the Bell at Edmonton
    All in a chaise and pair.

My sister, and my sister's child,
    Myself, and children three,
Will fill the chaise; so you must ride
    On horseback after we.

He soon replied—I do admire
    Of womankind but one,
And you are she, my dearest dear,
    Therefore it shall be done.

I am a linen-draper bold,
    As all the world doth know,
And my good friend the calender
    Will lend his horse to go.

Quoth Mrs. Gilpin—That's well said;
    And, for that wine is dear,
We will be furnish'd with our own,
    Which is both bright and clear.

John Gilpin kiss'd his loving wife;
    O'erjoy'd was he to find
That, though on pleasure she was bent,
    She had a frugal mind.

The morning came, the chaise was brought,
    But yet was not allow'd
To drive up to the door, lest all
    Should say that she was proud.

So three doors off the chaise was stay'd,
    Where they did all get in;
Six precious souls, and all agog
    To dash through thick and thin!

Smack went the whip, round went the wheels,
    Were never folk so glad;
The stones did rattle underneath,
    As if Cheapside were mad.

John Gilpin at his horse's side
   Seiz'd fast the flowing mane,
And up he got, in haste to ride,
   But soon came down again;

For saddle-tree scarce reach'd had he,
   His journey to begin,
When, turning round his head, he saw
   Three customers come in.

So down he came; for loss of time,
   Although it griev'd him sore,
Yet loss of pence, full well he knew,
   Would trouble him much more.

'Twas long before the customers
   Were suited to their mind,
When Betty screaming came down stairs—
   'The wine is left behind!'

Good lack! quoth he—yet bring it me,
   My leathern belt likewise,
In which I bear my trusty sword
   When I do exercise.

Now mistress Gilpin (careful soul!)
   Had two stone bottles found,
To hold the liquor that she lov'd,
   And keep it safe and sound.

Each bottle had a curling ear,
   Through which the belt he drew,
And hung a bottle on each side,
   To make his balance true.

Then, over all, that he might be
   Equipp'd from top to toe,
His long red cloak, well brush'd and neat,
   He manfully did throw.

Now see him mounted once again
   Upon his nimble steed,
Full slowly pacing o'er the stones,
   With caution and good heed!

But, finding soon a smoother road
   Beneath his well-shod feet,
The snorting beast began to trot,
   Which gall'd him in his seat.

So, Fair and softly, John he cried,
   But John he cried in vain;
That trot became a gallop soon
   In spite of curb and rein.

So stooping down, as needs he must
   Who cannot sit upright,
He grasp'd the mane with both his hands,
   And eke with all his might.

His horse, who never in that sort
   Had handled been before,
What thing upon his back had got
   Did wonder more and more.

Away went Gilpin, neck or nought;
   Away went hat and wig!—
He little dreamt, when he set out,
   Of running such a rig!

The wind did blow, the cloak did fly,
   Like streamer long and gay,
Till, loop and button failing both,
   At last it flew away.

Then might all people well discern
   The bottles he had slung;
A bottle swinging at each side,
   As hath been said or sung.

The dogs did bark, the children scream'd,
   Up flew the windows all;
And ev'ry soul cried out—Well done!
   As loud as he could bawl.

Away went Gilpin—who but he?
   His fame soon spread around—
He carries weight! he rides a race
   'Tis for a thousand pound!

And still, as fast as he drew near,
   'Twas wonderful to view
How in a trice the turnpike-men
   Their gates wide open threw.

And now, as he went bowing down
   His reeking head full low,
The bottles twain behind his back
   Were shatter'd at a blow.

Down ran the wine into the road,
   Most piteous to be seen,
Which made his horse's flanks to smoke
   As they had basted been.

But still he seem'd to carry weight,
   With leathern girdle brac'd;
For all might see the bottle-necks
   Still dangling at his waist.

Thus all through merry Islington
   These gambols he did play,
And till he came unto the Wash
   Of Edmonton so gay.

And there he threw the wash about
   On both sides of the way,
Just like unto a trundling mop,
   Or a wild goose at play.

At Edmonton his loving wife
   From the balcony spied
Her tender husband, wond'ring much
   To see how he did ride.

Stop, stop, John Gilpin!—Here's the house—
   They all at once did cry;
The dinner waits, and we are tir'd:
   Said Gilpin—So am I!

But yet his horse was not a whit
   Inclin'd to tarry there;
For why?—his owner had a house
   Full ten miles off, at Ware.

So like an arrow swift he flew,
   Shot by an archer strong;
So did he fly—which brings me to
   The middle of my song.

Away went Gilpin, out of breath,
   And sore against his will,
Till at his friend the calender's,
   His horse at last stood still.

The calender, amaz'd to see
   His neighbour in such trim,
Laid down his pipe, flew to the gate,
   And thus accosted him:—

What news? what news? your tidings tell;
   Tell me you must and shall—
Say why bare-headed you are come,
   Or why you come at all?

Now Gilpin had a pleasant wit,
   And lov'd a timely joke;
And thus unto the calender
   In merry guise he spoke:—

I came because your horse would come;
   And, if I well forebode,
My hat and wig will soon be here—
   They are upon the road.

The calender, right glad to find
   His friend in merry pin,[1]
Return'd him not a single word,
   But to the house went in;

Whence straight he came with hat and wig;
   A wig that flow'd behind,
A hat not much the worse for wear,
   Each comely in its kind.

He held them up, and, in his turn,
   Thus show'd his ready wit—
My head is twice as big as yours,
   They therefore needs must fit.

[1] in merry pin] in a merry humour

But let me scrape the dirt away
  That hangs upon your face;
And stop and eat, for well you may
  Be in a hungry case.

Said John—It is my wedding-day,
  And all the world would stare,
If wife should dine at Edmonton
  And I should dine at Ware!

So, turning to his horse, he said—
  I am in haste to dine;
'Twas for your pleasure you came here,
  You shall go back for mine.

Ah, luckless speech, and bootless boast!
  For which he paid full dear;
For, while he spake, a braying ass
  Did sing most loud and clear;

Whereat his horse did snort, as he
  Had heard a lion roar,
And gallop'd off with all his might,
  As he had done before.

Away went Gilpin, and away
  Went Gilpin's hat and wig!
He lost them sooner than at first—
  For why?—they were too big!

Now, mistress Gilpin, when she saw
  Her husband posting down
Into the country far away,
  She pull'd out half a crown;

And thus unto the youth she said
  That drove them to the Bell—
This shall be yours when you bring back
  My husband safe and well.

The youth did ride, and soon did meet
  John coming back amain;
Whom in a trice he tried to stop,
  By catching at his rein;

But, not performing what he meant,
　　And gladly would have done,
The frighted steed he frighted more,
　　And made him faster run.

Away went Gilpin, and away
　　Went post-boy at his heels!—
The post-boy's horse right glad to miss
　　The lumb'ring of the wheels.

Six gentlemen upon the road,
　　Thus seeing Gilpin fly,
With post-boy scamp'ring in the rear,
　　They rais'd the hue and cry:

Stop thief! stop thief!—a highwayman!
　　Not one of them was mute;
And all and each that pass'd that way
　　Did join in the pursuit.

And now the turnpike gates again
　　Flew open in short space;
The toll-men thinking, as before,
　　That Gilpin rode a race.

And so he did—and won it too!—
　　For he got first to town;
Nor stopp'd till where he had got up
　　He did again get down.

Now let us sing—Long live the king,
　　And Gilpin long live he;
And, when he next doth ride abroad,
　　May I be there to see!

ON THE RECEIPT OF MY MOTHER'S PICTURE

Oh that those lips had language! Life has pass'd
With me but roughly since I heard thee last.
Those lips are thine—thy own sweet smiles I see,
The same that oft in childhood solaced me;
Voice only fails, else, how distinct they say,
'Grieve not, my child, chase all thy fears away!'
The meek intelligence of those dear eyes
(Blest be the art that can immortalize,

The art that baffles Time's tyrannic claim
To quench it) here shines on me still the same
   Faithful remembrancer of one so dear,
Oh welcome guest, though unexpected, here!
Who bidd'st me honour with an artless song,
Affectionate, a mother lost so long,
I will obey, not willingly alone,
But gladly, as the precept were her own;
And, while that face renews my filial grief,
Fancy shall weave a charm for my relief—
Shall steep me in Elysian reverie,
A momentary dream, that thou art she.

   My mother! when I learn'd that thou wast dead,
Say, wast thou conscious of the tears I shed?
Hover'd thy spirit o'er thy sorrowing son,
Wretch even then, life's journey just begun?
Perhaps thou gav'st me, though unfelt, a kiss;
Perhaps a tear, if souls can weep in bliss—
Ah that maternal smile! it answers—Yes.
I heard the bell toll'd on thy burial day,
I saw the hearse that bore thee slow away,
And, turning from my nurs'ry window, drew
A long, long sigh, and wept a last adieu!
But was it such?—It was.—Where thou art gone
Adieus and farewells are a sound unknown.
May I but meet thee on that peaceful shore,
The parting sound shall pass my lips no more!
Thy maidens, griev'd themselves at my concern,
Oft gave me promise of thy quick return.
What ardently I wish'd, I long believ'd,
And, disappointed still, was still deceiv'd;
By expectation every day beguil'd,
Dupe of *to-morrow* even from a child.
Thus many a sad to-morrow came and went,
Till, all my stock of infant sorrow spent,
I learn'd at last submission to my lot;
But, though I less deplor'd thee, ne'er forgot.

   Where once we dwelt our name is heard no more,
Children not thine have trod my nurs'ry floor;

And where the gard'ner Robin, day by day,
Drew me to school along the public way,
Delighted with my bauble coach, and wrapt
In scarlet mantle warm, and velvet capt,
'Tis now become a history little known,
That once we call'd the past'ral house our own.
Short-liv'd possession! but the record fair
That mem'ry keeps of all thy kindness there,
Still outlives many a storm that has effac'd
A thousand other themes less deeply trac'd.
Thy nightly visits to my chamber made,
That thou might'st know me safe and warmly laid;
Thy morning bounties ere I left my home,
The biscuit, or confectionary plum;
The fragrant waters on my cheeks bestow'd
By thy own hand, till fresh they shone and glow'd;
All this, and more endearing still than all,
Thy constant flow of love, that knew no fall,
Ne'er roughen'd by those cataracts and brakes
That humour interpos'd too often makes;
All this still legible in mem'ry's page,
And still to be so, to my latest age,
Adds joy to duty, makes me glad to pay
Such honours to thee as my numbers may;
Perhaps a frail memorial, but sincere,
Not scorn'd in heav'n, though little notic'd here.
    Could Time, his flight revers'd, restore the hours,
When, playing with thy vesture's tissued flow'rs,
The violet, the pink, and jessamine,
I prick'd them into paper with a pin,
(And thou wast happier than myself the while,
Would'st softly speak, and stroke my head and smile)
Could those few pleasant hours again appear,
Might one wish bring them, would I wish them here?
I would not trust my heart—the dear delight
Seems so to be desir'd, perhaps I might.
But no—what here we call our life is such,
So little to be lov'd, and thou so much,
That I should ill requite thee to constrain
Thy unbound spirit into bonds again.

GOD MADE THE COUNTRY

God made the country, and man made the town.
What wonder then that health and virtue, gifts
That can alone make sweet the bitter draught
That life holds out to all, should most abound
And least be threaten'd in the fields and groves?
Possess ye, therefore, ye, who, borne about
In chariots and sedans, know no fatigue
But that of idleness, and taste no scenes
But such as art contrives, possess ye still
Your element; there only can ye shine,
There only minds like yours can do no harm.
Our groves were planted to console at noon
The pensive wand'rer in their shades. At eve
The moon-beam, sliding softly in between
The sleeping leaves, is all the light they wish,
Birds warbling all the music. We can spare
The splendour of your lamps; they but eclipse
Our softer satellite. Your songs confound
Our more harmonious notes: the thrush departs
Scar'd, and th' offended nightingale is mute.
There is a public mischief in your mirth;
It plagues your country. Folly such as yours,
Grac'd with a sword, and worthier of a fan,
Has made, what enemies could ne'er have done,
Our arch of empire, stedfast but for you,
A mutilated structure, soon to fall.

(*The Task*, Bk. I.)

ENGLAND

England, with all thy faults, I love thee still—
My country! and, while yet a nook is left
Where English minds and manners may be found,
Shall be constrain'd to love thee. Though thy clime
Be fickle, and thy year most part deform'd
With dripping rains, or wither'd by a frost,
I would not yet exchange thy sullen skies,

And fields without a flow'r, for warmer France
With all her vines; nor for Ausonia's groves
Of golden fruitage, and her myrtle bow'rs.
To shake thy senate, and from heights sublime
Of patriot eloquence to flash down fire
Upon thy foes, was never meant my task:
But I can feel thy fortunes, and partake
Thy joys and sorrows, with as true a heart
As any thund'rer there.

(The Task, Bk. II.)

POETIC PAINS

THERE is a pleasure in poetic pains
Which only poets know. The shifts and turns,
Th' expedients and inventions, multiform,
To which the mind resorts, in chase of terms
Though apt, yet coy, and difficult to win—
T' arrest the fleeting images that fill
The mirror of the mind, and hold them fast,
And force them sit till he has pencil'd off
A faithful likeness of the forms he views;
Then to dispose his copies with such art,
That each may find its most propitious light,
And shine by situation, hardly less
Than by the labour and the skill it cost;
Are occupations of the poet's mind
So pleasing, and that steal away the thought
With such address from themes of sad import,
That, lost in his own musings, happy man!
He feels th' anxieties of life, denied
Their wonted entertainment, all retire.
Such joys has he that sings. But ah! not such,
Or seldom such, the hearers of his song.
Fastidious, or else listless, or perhaps
Aware of nothing arduous in a task
They never undertook, they little note
His dangers or escapes, and haply find
There least amusement where he found the most.

(The Task, Bk. II.)

THE STRICKEN DEER

I was a stricken deer, that left the herd
Long since; with many an arrow deep infixt
My panting side was charg'd, when I withdrew
To seek a tranquil death in distant shades.
There was I found by one who had himself
Been hurt by th' archers. In his side he bore,
And in his hands and feet, the cruel scars.
With gentle force soliciting the darts,
He drew them forth, and heal'd, and bade me live.
Since then, with few associates, in remote
And silent woods I wander, far from those
My former partners of the peopled scene;
With few associates, and not wishing more.

(*The Task*, Bk. III.)

THE POST-BOY

Hark! 'tis the twanging horn o'er yonder bridge,
That with its wearisome but needful length
Bestrides the wintry flood, in which the moon
Sees her unwrinkled face reflected bright;—
He comes, the herald of a noisy world,
With spatter'd boots, strapp'd waist, and frozen locks;
News from all nations lumb'ring at his back.
True to his charge, the close-pack'd load behind,
Yet careless what he brings, his one concern
Is to conduct it to the destin'd inn:
And, having dropp'd th' expected bag, pass on.
He whistles as he goes, light-hearted wretch,
Cold and yet cheerful: messenger of grief
Perhaps to thousands, and of joy to some;
To him indiff'rent whether grief or joy.
Houses in ashes, and the fall of stocks,
Births, deaths, and marriages, epistles wet
With tears, that trickled down the writer's cheeks
Fast as the periods from his fluent quill,
Or charg'd with am'rous sighs of absent swains,

Or nymphs responsive, equally affect
His horse and him, unconscious of them all.
But oh th' important budget! usher'd in
With such heart-shaking music, who can say
What are its tidings? have our troops awak'd?
Or do they still, as if with opium drugg'd,
Snore to the murmurs of th' Atlantic wave?
Is India free? and does she wear her plum'd
And jewell'd turban with a smile of peace,
Or do we grind her still? The grand debate,
The popular harangue, the tart reply,
The logic, and the wisdom, and the wit,
And the loud laugh—I long to know them all;
I burn to set th' imprison'd wranglers free,
And give them voice and utt'rance once again.
  Now stir the fire, and close the shutters fast,
Let fall the curtains, wheel the sofa round,
And, while the bubbling and loud-hissing urn
Throws up a steamy column, and the cups,
That cheer but not inebriate, wait on each,
So let us welcome peaceful ev'ning in.

(The Task, Bk. IV.)

LINES WRITTEN DURING A PERIOD OF INSANITY

HATRED and vengeance, my eternal portion,
Scarce can endure delay of execution,
Wait, with impatient readiness, to seize my
                    Soul in a moment.

Damn'd below Judas: more abhorr'd than he was,
Who for a few pence sold his holy Master.
Twice betrayed Jesus me, the last delinquent,
                    Deems the profanest.

Man disavows, and Deity disowns me:
Hell might afford my miseries a shelter;
Therefore hell keeps her ever hungry mouths all
                    Bolted against me.

Hard lot! encompass'd with a thousand dangers;
Weary, faint, trembling with a thousand terrors;
I'm called, if vanquish'd, to receive a sentence
                Worse than Abiram's.

Him the vindictive rod of angry justice
Sent quick and howling to the centre headlong;
I, fed with judgment, in a fleshly tomb, am
                Buried above ground.

THE CASTAWAY

OBSCUREST night involv'd the sky,
  Th' Atlantic billows roar'd,
When such a destin'd wretch as I,
  Wash'd headlong from on board,
Of friends, of hope, of all bereft,
His floating home for ever left.

No braver chief could Albion boast
  Than he with whom he went,
Nor ever ship left Albion's coast,
  With warmer wishes sent.
He lov'd them both, but both in vain,
Nor him beheld, nor her again.

Not long beneath the whelming brine,
  Expert to swim, he lay;
Nor soon he felt his strength decline,
  Or courage die away;
But wag'd with death a lasting strife,
Supported by despair of life.

He shouted: nor his friends had fail'd
  To check the vessel's course,
But so the furious blast prevail'd,
  That, pitiless perforce,
They left their outcast mate behind,
And scudded still before the wind.

Some succour yet they could afford;
   And, such as storms allow,
The cask, the coop, the floated cord,
   Delay'd not to bestow.
But he (they knew) nor ship, nor shore,
Whate'er they gave, should visit more.

Nor, cruel as it seem'd, could he
   Their haste himself condemn,
Aware that flight, in such a sea,
   Alone could rescue them;
Yet bitter felt it still to die
Deserted, and his friends so nigh.

He long survives, who lives an hour
   In ocean, self-upheld;
And so long he, with unspent pow'r,
   His destiny repell'd;
And ever, as the minutes flew,
Entreated help, or cried—Adieu!

At length, his transient respite past,
   His comrades, who before
Had heard his voice in ev'ry blast,
   Could catch the sound no more.
For then, by toil subdued, he drank
The stifling wave, and then he sank.

No poet wept him: but the page
   Of narrative sincere,
That tells his name, his worth, his age,
   Is wet with Anson's tear.
And tears by bards or heroes shed
Alike immortalize the dead.

I therefore purpose not, or dream,
   Descanting on his fate,
To give the melancholy theme
   A more enduring date:
But misery still delights to trace
Its 'semblance in another's case.

No voice divine the storm allay'd,
    No light propitious shone;
When, snatch'd from all effectual aid,
    We perish'd, each alone:
But I beneath a rougher sea,
And whelm'd in deeper gulphs than he.

TO MARY

THE twentieth year is well-nigh past,
Since first our sky was overcast;
Ah would that this might be the last!
                My Mary!

Thy spirits have a fainter flow,
I see thee daily weaker grow—
'Twas my distress that brought thee low,
                My Mary!

Thy needles, once a shining store,
For my sake restless heretofore,
Now rust disus'd, and shine no more,
                My Mary!

For though thou gladly wouldst fulfil
The same kind office for me still,
Thy sight now seconds not thy will,
                My Mary!

But well thou play'd'st the housewife's part,
And all thy threads with magic art
Have wound themselves about this heart,
                My Mary!

Thy indistinct expressions seem
Like language utter'd in a dream;
Yet me they charm, whate'er the theme,
                My Mary!

Thy silver locks, once auburn bright,
Are still more lovely in my sight
Than golden beams of orient light,
My Mary!

For could I view nor them nor thee,
What sight worth seeing could I see?
The sun would rise in vain for me,
My Mary!

Partakers of thy sad decline,
Thy hands their little force resign;
Yet, gently prest, press gently mine,
My Mary!

And then I feel that still I hold
A richer store ten thousandfold
Than misers fancy in their gold,
My Mary!

Such feebleness of limbs thou prov'st,
That now at every step thou mov'st
Upheld by two; yet still thou lov'st,
My Mary!

And still to love, though prest with ill,
In wintry age to feel no chill,
With me is to be lovely still,
My Mary!

But ah! by constant heed I know
How oft the sadness that I show
Transforms thy smiles to looks of woe,
My Mary!

And should my future lot be cast
With much resemblance of the past,
Thy worn-out heart will break at last,
My Mary!

WILLIAM WORDSWORTH

WILLIAM WORDSWORTH (1770–1850) was educated at the grammar school of Hawkshead and St. John's College, Cambridge. In 1790 he went on a walking tour in France, the Alps, and Italy. He returned to France late in 1791 and spent a year there; the revolutionary movement was then at its height and exercised a strong influence on his mind. While in France he fell in love with the daughter of a surgeon at Blois, Annette Vallon, who bore him a daughter. When the French Revolution was followed by the English declaration of war and the Terror, Wordsworth's republican enthusiasm gave place to a period of pessimism. In 1795 he made the acquaintance of S. T. Coleridge. A close and long-enduring friendship developed between the poets, and Wordsworth, with his sister Dorothy and Mr. and Mrs. Coleridge, lived for a year in close intercourse at Alfoxden and Stowey in Somerset. Together the poets published in 1798 *Lyrical Ballads*, which marked a revival in English poetry. Together also, at the end of the same year, the poets went to Germany, Wordsworth and his sister wintering at Goslar. Here Wordsworth began *The Prelude* and wrote *Ruth*, *Lucy Gray*, the lines on *Lucy*, and other poems. He married in 1802 Mary Hutchinson of Penrith. Events abroad now changed his political attitude to one of patriotic enthusiasm. In 1805 he completed *The Prelude* which, however, was not published until after his death. In 1807 he moved to Rydal Mount, Grasmere, which he occupied till his death. In 1843 he succeeded Southey as Poet Laureate and died in 1850.

'TAKIN' his family out in a string and never geein' the dearest bit of notice to 'em; standin' by hisself and stoppin' behind agapin', with his jaws workin' the whoal time; but niver no crackin' wi 'em, nor no pleasure in 'em—a desolate-minded man, ye kna—it was potry as did it'—thus it was that Wordsworth struck the critical eye of his local innkeeper. Chaucer, likewise, cut no great figure in the opinion of Chaucer's Host; still a far less unhappy figure than this.

And yet one of the essential things about Wordsworth is, precisely, his happiness. Few men, certainly few poets, have found so much of it as the writer of *The Happy Warrior*. And, to complete his happiness, he was himself aware of it. He was not, like Virgil's rustics, ignorant of his own bliss. 'No one,' he said, 'has completely understood me—not even

Coleridge. He is not happy enough.[1] I am myself one of the happiest of men, and no man who lives a life of constant bustle and whose happiness depends on the opinions of others can possibly comprehend the best of my poems.'

What, then, was Wordsworth's secret? He was born with no silver spoon in his mouth. In youth he suffered both poverty and unhappy passion; nor was his the happy-go-lucky temper of a Leigh Hunt—he felt too violently. 'Had I been a writer of love-poetry, it would have been natural to me to write it with a degree of warmth which could hardly have been approved of by my principles, and which might have been undesirable for the reader.' Indeed, in *The Borderers* there are moments as savagely embittered as Beddoes, as gloomy as modern Europe:

> We look
> But at the surfaces of things; we hear
> Of towns in flames, fields ravaged, young and old
> Driven out in troops to want and nakedness:
> Then grasp our swords and rush upon a cure
> That flatters us because it asks not thought:
> The deeper malady is better hid,
> *The world is poisoned at the heart.*

Nor, again, did the key to Wordsworth's happiness lie simply in his poetic gift. History is full of 'mighty poets in their misery dead'. For as often as not this gift of Apollo can prove a curse like Cassandra's. Nor was it his poetic success. For by thirty, it is said, Wordsworth had earned only £10, then earned no more till sixty-five; while if reviews could kill. . . .

No, Wordsworth doggedly trod out his own path to happiness; because he knew himself, and how to find himself and, above all, how to lose himself.

[1] Cf., for instance, Coleridge's rather owlish complaint that Wordsworth ascribed an exaggerated delight to dancing with daffodils, as compared with 'the joy of retrospection, when the images and virtuous actions of a whole well-spent life pass before that conscience which' etc. a joy of which, in any case, poor Coleridge cannot have known much; and which uncomfortably suggests a pleasant Sunday afternoon at Mr. Pecksniff's.

'Il nous faut nous abestir pour nous assagir,' 'In order to become sages, we must first become beasts' observes the wise Montaigne. 'I have been too hard on my brother the ass,' said the dying St. Francis of his body. The author of *Peter Bell* made no such mistake. He realized betimes how much the cities of our modern civilization are Cities of Destruction: he fled, with all the fervour of Bunyan's Pilgrim, from the snares of material 'Progress.'

No doubt all civilization must be an encroachment on Nature. Those who think it an argument against anything to call it 'unnatural' should for consistency fling off their clothes and skip up the nearest tree. Yet encroach on Nature one step *too* far, and her revenges are terrible. She cannot prevent the giant-city smoking where once waved her woods; but her slow retribution sets its mark on paling cheeks and failing nerves, on foreheads haggard with the rush of modern life, on childless hearths. This is no new revelation. Theocritus, Virgil, Horace, Montaigne, Ronsard, Cowley, Rousseau, Walt Whitman, W. H. Davies, D. H. Lawrence—all of them in their different times and ways have heard 'above the roar of streets' the voice of her whom we may at moments imagine we have tamed, but who can still destroy the minds and souls, as well as the bodies, of all who outrage her.

Yet Wordsworth, in his return to her, never grew morbid like Rousseau, or animal like D. H. Lawrence. 'Love had he found in huts where poor men lie.'[1] He did not try, like Whitman, 'to turn and live with the *animals*'. So to-day his is still a living voice, crying in the wilderness its prophetic protest, not only against the unhealthiness of all over-civilization, but also against the drab brutality of the machine-world and of the mass-state. (He was not always a pleasant individual: but he was always individual.) He

---

[1] Mr. J. M. Keynes has told me how at Versailles in 1919 General Smuts, meeting him one day, equally oppressed by the squalid intrigues of the Conference, quoted this line with its contrasting sense of peace.

wrote no poem more characteristic than *Resolution and Independence*. And in our herd-age he still stands out in passionate opposition, as one who vindicates unceasingly the freedom of soul not only of Shakespeare and Milton, but even of leech-gatherers and old shepherds like Michael; the individual worth, to the eye of vision, of even the meanest flower, even the commonest clod.

> Long have I loved what I behold,
> The night that calms, the day that cheers;
> The common growth of mother earth
> Suffices me—her tears, her mirth,
> Her humblest mirth and tears.

No doubt in later years he ossified. It is always one of the hardest things in life to hold the balance between letting the world be 'too much with us', and too little: and Wordsworth tended to grow too much the Hermit of Grasmere, the Grand Lama of the Lakes. But at least he never renounced his conviction that it is only states of mind and feeling that really matter; not things, nor machinery, nor even books (that was poor Southey's mistake)—for books, too, are machines, however good ones.

This is the true Wordsworth who has ministered to so many minds diseased; not the defender of Capital Punishment or of the Irish Church. This is the Wordsworth who was happy; so far as man can be. Happiness consists largely, as in a grim boutade Johnson once suggested, in being drunk. But not in Johnson's literal sense; for that brings headache and repentance. 'Enivrez-vous; enivrez-vous sans cesse! De vin, de vertu, ou de poésie, à votre guise.' Wordsworth, happier than Baudelaire, was a man intoxicated, not with wine, but with brook-water; with the burn tumbling from Glaramara, with the wind across Helvellyn, with the spin of his own healthy Cumberland blood. And these leave no stings behind.

Hence his appeal to souls like J. S. Mill, who had grown from an infant-prodigy, nourished on book-dust and ink, into a desiccated, depressed young man. Hence his power over many minds, as the founder almost of a new church, prophet as well as poet; wiser than Rousseau, though less wise, I feel, than Montaigne. Because of this simple strength his work endures, without any of the rainbow magic of Coleridge, or the kiss of La Belle Dame sans Merci on the pale lips of Keats, or the sun-shimmering mists of Shelley's vision, or the calling clarions of Scott, or the passionate gloom of Byron, or Landor's quiet, proud grace. He goes his own way, this grey, homespun man, who *would* wear his woollen stockings even to Court, under his silk ones: he goes his own way, but he does not lose it.

As a 'pure poet' he is easy to criticize. We can well understand how, at exasperated moments, he seemed even to admirers like Tennyson and Arnold 'thick-ankled' and 'a boor'; to FitzGerald, 'Daddy Wordsworth'; to Swinburne, 'a Philistine'; to Rossetti, 'good, you know, but unbearable'; to Meredith in *Richard Feverel*, 'a superior donkey reclaimed from the heathen'. His famous theory of style is merely a natural revulsion frozen into a foolish rule; and his style in practice is often the very opposite of his own theory, without being any the better for that. Even in his best years he could vandalize the simple beauty of Helen of Kirkconnel into the unspeakable—

> Proud Gordon, maddened by the thoughts
> That through his brain are travelling,
> Rushed forth and at the heart of Bruce
> He launched a deadly javelin! . . .
>
> And Bruce, as soon as he had slain
> The Gordon, sailed away to Spain
> And fought with rage incessant
> Against the Moorish crescent.

He was seldom good at telling a story. He was seldom good at characters (unless, like Michael, they were kin to his own). His children, in particular, are often odious. Even his central ideas are sometimes thin and parochial—above all, his worship of Nature as a sort of gentle Quakeress, which forgets how a few thousand miles to southward she becomes a gaudy murderess.

And yet he remains a standing example of that mystery and miracle—inspiration, the power of the unconscious levels of the mind. As J. K. Stephen said, there are two wholly different Wordsworths. Suddenly in this rough block of granite the mica flashes out, like diamond, beneath the moon; on this blunt, whale-headed fell the sunset strikes, like a great transfiguration, athwart the grey, crawling rags of mist, until

> the sky seems not a sky
> Of earth—and with what motion move the clouds!

Like a great lonely ram he stalks across his moorlands; and to some souls he has been like the ram of Odysseus, carrying them out of their prisoning darkness to the light of deliverance. The bell about his neck tolls on, deep-toned and moving; though our hearts, indeed, can seldom dance to it.

But Landor has said it all better, in words not the less true for being half humorous (as all English hexameters, willy-nilly, tend to be):

> Equable was he and plain, but wandering a little in wisdom,
> Sometimes flying from blood and sometimes pouring it freely.
> Yet he was English at heart. If his words were too many; if Fancy's
> Furniture lookt rather scant in a whitewashed homely apartment;
> If in his mural designs there is sameness and tameness; if often
> Feebleness is there for breadth; if his pencil wants rounding and pointing;
> Few in this age or the last stand out on the like elevation.
> There is a sheepfold he rais'd which my memory loves to revisit,
> Sheepfold whose walls shall endure when there is not a stone of the palace.

F. L. Lucas.

LUCY GRAY

OFT I had heard of Lucy Gray:
And, when I crossed the wild,
I chanced to see at break of day
The solitary child.

No mate, no comrade Lucy knew;
She dwelt on a wide moor,
—The sweetest thing that ever grew
Beside a human door!

You yet may spy the fawn at play,
The hare upon the green;
But the sweet face of Lucy Gray
Will never more be seen.

'To-night will be a stormy night—
You to the town must go;
And take a lantern, Child, to light
Your mother through the snow.'

'That, Father! will I gladly do:
'Tis scarcely afternoon—
The minster-clock has just struck two,
And yonder is the moon!'

At this the Father raised his hook,
And snapped a faggot-band;
He plied his work;—and Lucy took
The lantern in her hand.

Not blither is the mountain roe:
With many a wanton stroke
Her feet disperse the powdery snow,
That rises up like smoke.

The storm came on before its time:
She wandered up and down;
And many a hill did Lucy climb:
But never reached the town.

The wretched parents all that night
Went shouting far and wide;
But there was neither sound nor sight
To serve them for a guide.

At day-break on a hill they stood
That overlooked the moor;
And thence they saw the bridge of wood,
A furlong from their door.

They wept—and, turning homeward, cried,
'In heaven we all shall meet;'
—When in the snow the mother spied
The print of Lucy's feet.

Then downwards from the steep hill's edge
They tracked the footmarks small;
And through the broken hawthorn hedge,
And by the long stone-wall;

And then an open field they crossed:
The marks were still the same;
They tracked them on, nor ever lost;
And to the bridge they came.

They followed from the snowy bank
Those footmarks, one by one,
Into the middle of the plank;
And further there were none!

—Yet some maintain that to this day
She is a living child;
That you may see sweet Lucy Gray
Upon the lonesome wild.

O'er rough and smooth she trips along,
And never looks behind;
And sings a solitary song
That whistles in the wind.

LUCY

I

STRANGE fits of passion have I known:
And I will dare to tell,
But in the Lover's ear alone,
What once to me befell.

When she I loved looked every day
Fresh as a rose in June,
I to her cottage bent my way,
Beneath an evening-moon.

Upon the moon I fixed my eye,
All over the wide lea;
With quickening pace my horse drew nigh
Those paths so dear to me.

And now we reached the orchard-plot;
And, as we climbed the hill,
The sinking moon to Lucy's cot
Came near, and nearer still.

In one of those sweet dreams I slept,
Kind Nature's gentlest boon!
And all the while my eyes I kept
On the descending moon.

My horse moved on; hoof after hoof
He raised, and never stopped:
When down behind the cottage-roof,
At once, the bright moon dropped.

What fond and wayward thoughts will slide
Into a Lover's head!
'O mercy!' to myself I cried,
'If Lucy should be dead!'

II

I TRAVELLED among unknown men,
    In lands beyond the sea;
Nor, England! did I know till then
    What love I bore to thee.

'Tis past, that melancholy dream!
Nor will I quit thy shore
A second time; for still I seem
To love thee more and more.

Among thy mountains did I feel
The joy of my desire;
And she I cherished turned her wheel
Beside an English fire.

Thy mornings showed, thy nights concealed,
The bowers where Lucy played;
And thine too is the last green field
That Lucy's eyes surveyed.

III

SHE dwelt among the untrodden ways
Beside the springs of Dove,
A Maid whom there were none to praise
And very few to love:

A violet by a mossy stone
Half hidden from the eye!
—Fair as a star, when only one
Is shining in the sky.

She lived unknown, and few could know
When Lucy ceased to be;
But she is in her grave, and, oh,
The difference to me!

IV

THREE years she grew in sun and shower,
Then Nature said, 'A lovelier flower
On earth was never sown;
This Child I to myself will take;
She shall be mine, and I will make
A Lady of my own.

'Myself will to my darling be
Both law and impulse: and with me
The Girl, in rock and plain,
In earth and heaven, in glade and bower,
Shall feel an overseeing power
To kindle or restrain.

'She shall be sportive as the fawn
That wild with glee across the lawn
Or up the mountain springs;
And hers shall be the breathing balm,
And hers the silence and the calm
Of mute insensate things.

'The floating clouds their state shall lend
To her; for her the willow bend;
Nor shall she fail to see
Even in the motions of the Storm
Grace that shall mould the Maiden's form
By silent sympathy.

'The stars of midnight shall be dear
To her; and she shall lean her ear
In many a secret place
Where rivulets dance their wayward round,
And beauty born of murmuring sound
Shall pass into her face.

'And vital feelings of delight
Shall rear her form to stately height,
Her virgin bosom swell;
Such thoughts to Lucy I will give
While she and I together live
Here in this happy dell.'

Thus Nature spake—The work was done—
How soon my Lucy's race was run!
She died, and left to me
This heath, this calm, and quiet scene;
The memory of what has been,
And never more will be.

V

A SLUMBER did my spirit seal;
    I had no human fears:
She seemed a thing that could not feel
    The touch of earthly years.

No motion has she now, no force;
    She neither hears nor sees;
Rolled round in earth's diurnal course,
    With rocks, and stones, and trees.

THE FRENCH REVOLUTION

AS IT APPEARED TO ENTHUSIASTS AT ITS COMMENCEMENT.

OH! pleasant exercise of hope and joy!
For mighty were the auxiliars which then stood
Upon our side, we who were strong in love!
Bliss was it in that dawn to be alive,
But to be young was very heaven!—Oh! times,
In which the meagre, stale, forbidding ways
Of custom, law, and statute, took at once
The attraction of a country in romance!
When Reason seemed the most to assert her rights,
When most intent on making of herself
A prime Enchantress—to assist the work
Which then was going forward in her name!
Not favoured spots alone, but the whole earth,
The beauty wore of promise, that which sets
(As at some moment might not be unfelt
Among the bowers of paradise itself)
The budding rose above the rose full blown.
What temper at the prospect did not wake
To happiness unthought of? The inert
Were roused, and lively natures rapt away!
They who had fed their childhood upon dreams,
The playfellows of fancy, who had made
All powers of swiftness, subtilty, and strength

Their ministers—who in lordly wise had stirred
Among the grandest objects of the sense,
And dealt with whatsoever they found there
As if they had within some lurking right
To wield it;—they, too, who, of gentle mood,
Had watched all gentle motions, and to these
Had fitted their own thoughts, schemers more mild,
And in the region of their peaceful selves;—
Now was it that both found, the meek and lofty
Did both find, helpers to their heart's desire,
And stuff at hand, plastic as they could wish;
Were called upon to exercise their skill,
Not in Utopia, subterranean fields,
Or some secreted island, Heaven knows where!
But in the very world, which is the world
Of all of us,—the place where in the end
We find our happiness, or not at all!

TO THE CUCKOO

O BLITHE Newcomer! I have heard,
I hear thee and rejoice.
O Cuckoo! shall I call thee Bird,
Or but a wandering Voice?

While I am lying on the grass
Thy twofold shout I hear;
From hill to hill it seems to pass
At once far off and near.

Though babbling only to the Vale,
Of sunshine and of flowers,
Thou bringest unto me a tale
Of visionary hours.

Thrice welcome, darling of the Spring!
Even yet thou art to me
No bird, but an invisible thing,
A voice, a mystery;

The same whom in my schoolboy days
I listened to; that Cry
Which made me look a thousand ways
In bush, and tree, and sky.

To seek thee did I often rove
Through woods and on the green;
And thou wert still a hope, a love;
Still longed for, never seen.

And I can listen to thee yet;
Can lie upon the plain
And listen, till I do beget
That golden time again.

O blessèd Bird! the earth we pace
Again appears to be
An unsubstantial, faery place;
That is fit home for Thee!

DAFFODILS

I WANDERED lonely as a cloud
That floats on high o'er vales and hills,
When all at once I saw a crowd,
A host, of golden daffodils;
Beside the lake, beneath the trees,
Fluttering and dancing in the breeze.

Continuous as the stars that shine
And twinkle on the milky way,
They stretched in never-ending line
Along the margin of a bay:
Ten thousand saw I at a glance,
Tossing their heads in sprightly dance.

The waves beside them danced; but they
Out-did the sparkling waves in glee:
A poet could not but be gay,
In such a jocund company:
I gazed—and gazed—but little thought
What wealth the show to me had brought:

For oft, when on my couch I lie
In vacant or in pensive mood,
They flash upon that inward eye
Which is the bliss of solitude;
And then my heart with pleasure fills,
And dances with the daffodils.

LINES

COMPOSED A FEW MILES ABOVE TINTERN ABBEY, ON REVISITING
THE BANKS OF THE WYE DURING A TOUR. JULY 13, 1798.

FIVE years have past; five summers, with the length
Of five long winters! and again I hear
These waters, rolling from their mountain-springs
With a soft inland murmur.—Once again
Do I behold these steep and lofty cliffs,
That on a wild secluded scene impress
Thoughts of more deep seclusion; and connect
The landscape with the quiet of the sky.
The day is come when I again repose
Here, under this dark sycamore, and view
These plots of cottage-ground, these orchard-tufts,
Which at this season, with their unripe fruits,
Are clad in one green hue, and lose themselves
'Mid groves and copses. Once again I see
These hedge-rows, hardly hedge-rows, little lines
Of sportive wood run wild: these pastoral farms,
Green to the very door; and wreaths of smoke
Sent up, in silence, from among the trees!
With some uncertain notice, as might seem
Of vagrant dwellers in the houseless woods,
Or of some Hermit's cave, where by his fire
The Hermit sits alone.

          These beauteous forms,
Through a long absence, have not been to me
As is a landscape to a blind man's eye:
But oft, in lonely rooms, and 'mid the din
Of towns and cities, I have owed to them,
In hours of weariness, sensations sweet,

235

Felt in the blood, and felt along the heart;
And passing even into my purer mind,
With tranquil restoration:—feelings too
Of unremembered pleasure: such, perhaps,
As have no slight or trivial influence
On that best portion of a good man's life,
His little, nameless, unremembered acts
Of kindness and of love. Nor less, I trust,
To them I may have owed another gift,
Of aspect more sublime; that blessed mood,
In which the burthen of the mystery,
In which the heavy and the weary weight
Of all this unintelligible world,
Is lightened:—that serene and blessed mood,
In which the affections gently lead us on,—
Until, the breath of this corporeal frame
And even the motion of our human blood
Almost suspended, we are laid asleep
In body, and become a living soul:
While with an eye made quiet by the power
Of harmony, and the deep power of joy,
We see into the life of things.

                                        If this
Be but a vain belief, yet, oh! how oft—
In darkness and amid the many shapes
Of joyless daylight; when the fretful stir
Unprofitable, and the fever of the world
Have hung upon the beatings of my heart—
How oft, in spirit, have I turned to thee,
O sylvan Wye! thou wanderer thro' the woods,
How often has my spirit turned to thee!

    And now, with gleams of half-extinguished thought,
With many recognitions dim and faint,
And somewhat of a sad perplexity,
The picture of the mind revives again:
While here I stand, not only with the sense
Of present pleasure, but with pleasing thoughts
That in this moment there is life and food
For future years. And so I dare to hope,

Though changed, no doubt, from what I was when first
I came among these hills; when like a roe
I bounded o'er the mountains, by the sides
Of the deep rivers, and the lonely streams,
Wherever nature led: more like a man
Flying from something that he dreads than one
Who sought the thing he loved. For nature then
(The coarser pleasures of my boyish days,
And their glad animal movements all gone by)
To me was all in all.—I cannot paint
What then I was. The sounding cataract
Haunted me like a passion: the tall rock,
The mountain, and the deep and gloomy wood,
Their colours and their forms, were then to me
An appetite; a feeling and a love,
That had no need of a remoter charm,
By thought supplied, nor any interest
Unborrowed from the eye.—That time is past,
And all its aching joys are now no more,
And all its dizzy raptures. Not for this
Faint I, nor mourn nor murmur; other gifts
Have followed; for such loss, I would believe,
Abundant recompense. For I have learned
To look on nature, not as in the hour
Of thoughtless youth; but hearing oftentimes
The still, sad music of humanity,
Nor harsh nor grating, though of ample power
To chasten and subdue. And I have felt
A presence that disturbs me with the joy
Of elevated thoughts; a sense sublime
Of something far more deeply interfused,
Whose dwelling is the light of setting suns,
And the round ocean and the living air,
And the blue sky, and in the mind of man:
A motion and a spirit, that impels
All thinking things, all objects of all thought,
And rolls through all things. Therefore am I still
A lover of the meadows and the woods,
And mountains; and of all that we behold
From this green earth; of all the mighty world

Of eye, and ear,—both what they half create,
And what perceive; well pleased to recognise
In nature and the language of the sense
The anchor of my purest thoughts, the nurse,
The guide, the guardian of my heart, and soul
Of all my moral being.
                              Nor perchance,
If I were not thus taught, should I the more
Suffer my genial spirits to decay:
For thou art with me here upon the banks
Of this fair river; thou my dearest Friend,
My dear, dear Friend; and in thy voice I catch
The language of my former heart, and read
My former pleasures in the shooting lights
Of thy wild eyes. Oh! yet a little while
May I behold in thee what I was once,
My dear, dear Sister! and this prayer I make,
Knowing that Nature never did betray
The heart that loved her; 'tis her privilege,
Through all the years of this our life, to lead
From joy to joy: for she can so inform
The mind that is within us, so impress
With quietness and beauty, and so feed
With lofty thoughts, that neither evil tongues,
Rash judgements, nor the sneers of selfish men,
Nor greetings where no kindness is, nor all
The dreary intercourse of daily life,
Shall e'er prevail against us, or disturb
Our cheerful faith, that all which we behold
Is full of blessings. Therefore let the moon
Shine on thee in thy solitary walk;
And let the misty mountain-winds be free
To blow against thee: and, in after years,
When these wild ecstasies shall be matured
Into a sober pleasure, when thy mind
Shall be a mansion for all lovely forms,
Thy memory be as a dwelling-place
For all sweet sounds and harmonies; oh! the
If olitude, or fear, or pain, or grief,
Should be thy portion, with what healing thoughts

Of tender joy wilt thou remember me,
And these my exhortations! Nor, perchance—
If I should be where I no more can hear
Thy voice, nor catch from thy wild eyes these gleams
Of past existence—wilt thou then forget
That on the banks of this delightful stream
We stood together; and that I, so long
A worshipper of Nature, hither came
Unwearied in that service: rather say
With warmer love—oh! with far deeper zeal
Of holier love. Nor wilt thou then forget
That after many wanderings, many years
Of absence, these steep woods and lofty cliffs,
And this green pastoral landscape, were to me
More dear, both for themselves and for thy sake!

IT IS A BEAUTEOUS EVENING

It is a beauteous evening, calm and free,
The holy time is quiet as a Nun
Breathless with adoration; the broad sun
Is sinking down in its tranquillity;
The gentleness of heaven broods o'er the Sea:
Listen! the mighty Being is awake,
And doth with his eternal motion make
A sound like thunder—everlastingly.
Dear Child! dear Girl! that walkest with me here,
If thou appear untouched by solemn thought,
Thy nature is not therefore less divine:
Thou liest in Abraham's bosom all the year;
And worshipp'st at the Temple's inner shrine,
God being with thee when we know it not.

THE WORLD IS TOO MUCH WITH US

The world is too much with us; late and soon,
Getting and spending, we lay waste our powers:
Little we see in Nature that is ours;
We have given our hearts away, a sordid boon!
This Sea that bares her bosom to the moon;
The winds that will be howling at all hours,
And are up-gathered now like sleeping flowers;
For this, for everything, we are out of tune;

It moves us not.—Great God! I'd rather be
A Pagan suckled in a creed outworn;
So might I, standing on this pleasant lea,
Have glimpses that would make me less forlorn;
Have sight of Proteus rising from the sea;
Or hear old Triton blow his wreathèd horn.

SONNET

COMPOSED UPON WESTMINSTER BRIDGE, SEPTEMBER 3, 1802.

EARTH has not anything to show more fair:
Dull would he be of soul who could pass by
A sight so touching in its majesty:
This City now doth, like a garment, wear
The beauty of the morning; silent, bare,
Ships, towers, domes, theatres, and temples lie
Open unto the fields, and to the sky;
All bright and glittering in the smokeless air.
Never did sun more beautifully steep,
In his first splendour, valley, rock, or hill;
Ne'er saw I, never felt, a calm so deep!
The river glideth at his own sweet will:
Dear God! the very houses seem asleep;
And all that mighty heart is lying still!

LONDON, 1802.

MILTON! thou shouldst be living at this hour:
England hath need of thee: she is a fen
Of stagnant waters: altar, sword, and pen,
Fireside, the heroic wealth of hall and bower,
Have forfeited their ancient English dower
Of inward happiness. We are selfish men;
Oh! raise us up, return to us again;
And give us manners, virtue, freedom, power.
Thy soul was like a Star, and dwelt apart;
Thou hadst a voice whose sound was like the sea:
Pure as the naked heavens, majestic, free,
So didst thou travel on life's common way,
In cheerful godliness; and yet thy heart
The lowliest duties on herself did lay.

IT IS NOT TO BE THOUGHT OF THAT THE FLOOD

IT is not to be thought of that the Flood
Of British freedom, which, to the open sea
Of the world's praise, from dark antiquity
Hath flowed, 'with pomp of waters, unwithstood,'
Roused though it be full often to a mood
Which spurns the check of salutary bands,
That this most famous Stream in bogs and sands
Should perish; and to evil and to good
Be lost for ever. In our halls is hung
Armoury of the invincible Knights of old:
We must be free or die, who speak the tongue
That Shakespeare spake; the faith and morals hold
Which Milton held.—In every thing we are sprung
Of Earth's first blood, have titles manifold.

THE SOLITARY REAPER

BEHOLD her, single in the field,
Yon solitary Highland Lass!
Reaping and singing by herself;
Stop here, or gently pass!
Alone she cuts and binds the grain,
And sings a melancholy strain;
O listen! for the Vale profound
Is overflowing with the sound.
No Nightingale did ever chaunt
More welcome notes to weary bands
Of travellers in some shady haunt,
Among Arabian sands:
A voice so thrilling ne'er was heard
In spring-time from the Cuckoo-bird,
Breaking the silence of the seas
Among the farthest Hebrides.

Will no one tell me what she sings?—
Perhaps the plaintive numbers flow
For old, unhappy, far-off things,
And battles long ago:

Or is it some more humble lay,
Familiar matter of to-day?
Some natural sorrow, loss, or pain,
That has been, and may be again?

Whate'er the theme, the Maiden sang
As if her song could have no ending;
I saw her singing at her work,
And o'er the sickle bending;—
I listened, motionless and still;
And, as I mounted up the hill,
The music in my heart I bore,
Long after it was heard no more.

ODE

INTIMATIONS OF IMMORTALITY FROM RECOLLECTIONS OF

EARLY CHILDHOOD.

> The Child is father of the Man;
> And I could wish my days to be
> Bound each to each by natural piety.

THERE was a time when meadow, grove, and stream,
The earth, and every common sight,
　　To me did seem
　　Apparelled in celestial light,
The glory and the freshness of a dream.
It is not now as it hath been of yore;—
　　Turn wheresoe'er I may,
　　By night or day,
The things which I have seen I now can see no more.

　　The Rainbow comes and goes,
　　And lovely is the Rose,
　　The Moon doth with delight
Look round her when the heavens are bare,
　　Waters on a starry night
　　Are beautiful and fair;
　The sunshine is a glorious birth;
　But yet I know, where'er I go,
That there hath past away a glory from the earth.

Now, while the birds thus sing a joyous song,
  And while the young lambs bound
    As to the tabor's sound,
To me alone there came a thought of grief:
A timely utterance gave that thought relief,
    And I again am strong:
The cataracts blow their trumpets from the steep;
No more shall grief of mine the season wrong;
I hear the Echoes through the mountains throng,
The Winds come to me from the fields of sleep,
    And all the earth is gay;
      Land and sea
  Give themselves up to jollity,
    And with the heart of May
  Doth every Beast keep holiday;—
    Thou Child of Joy,
Shout round me, let me hear thy shouts, thou happy Shep-
                           [herd-boy!

Ye blessèd Creatures, I have heard the call
  Ye to each other make; I see
The heavens laugh with you in your jubilee;
  My heart is at your festival,
    My head hath its coronal,
The fulness of your bliss, I feel—I feel it all.
    Oh evil day! if I were sullen
    While Earth herself is adorning,
      This sweet May-morning,
    And the Children are culling
      On every side,
    In a thousand valleys far and wide,
    Fresh flowers; while the sun shines warm,
And the Babe leaps up on his Mother's arm:—
    I hear, I hear, with joy I hear!
    —But there's a Tree, of many, one,
A single Field which I have looked upon,
Both of them speak of something that is gone:
    The Pansy at my feet
    Doth the same tale repeat:
Whither is fled the visionary gleam?
Where is it now, the glory and the dream?

Our birth is but a sleep and a forgetting:
The Soul that rises with us, our life's Star,
    Hath had elsewhere its setting,
      And cometh from afar:
    Not in entire forgetfulness,
    And not in utter nakedness,
But trailing clouds of glory do we come
    From God, who is our home:
Heaven lies about us in our infancy!
Shades of the prison-house begin to close
    Upon the growing Boy,
But he beholds the light, and whence it flows,
    He sees it in his joy;
The Youth, who daily farther from the east
    Must travel, still is Nature's Priest,
    And by the vision splendid
    Is on his way attended;
At length the Man perceives it die away,
And fade into the light of common day.

Earth fills her lap with pleasures of her own;
Yearnings she hath in her own natural kind,
And, even with something of a Mother's mind,
    And no unworthy aim,
    The homely Nurse doth all she can
To make her Foster-child, her Inmate Man,
    Forget the glories he hath known,
And that imperial palace whence he came.

Behold the Child among his new-born blisses,
A six years' Darling of a pigmy size!
See, where 'mid work of his own hand he lies,
Fretted by sallies of his mother's kisses,
With light upon him from his father's eyes!
See, at his feet, some little plan or chart,
Some fragment from his dream of human life,
Shaped by himself with newly-learnèd art;
    A wedding or a festival,
    A mourning or a funeral;
    And this hath now his heart,

And unto this he frames his song:
  Then will he fit his tongue
To dialogues of business, love, or strife;
  But it will not be long
  Ere this be thrown aside,
  And with new joy and pride
The little Actor cons another part;
Filling from time to time his 'humorous stage'
With all the Persons, down to palsied Age,
That Life brings with her in her equipage;
  As if his whole vocation
  Were endless imitation.

Thou, whose exterior semblance doth belie
  Thy Soul's immensity;
Thou best Philosopher, who yet dost keep
Thy heritage, thou Eye among the blind,
That, deaf and silent, read'st the eternal deep,
Haunted for ever by the eternal mind,—
  Mighty Prophet! Seer blest!
  On whom those truths do rest,
Which we are toiling all our lives to find,
In darkness lost, the darkness of the grave;
Thou, over whom thy Immortality
Broods like the Day, a Master o'er a Slave,
A Presence which is not to be put by;
  [To whom the grave
Is but a lonely bed without the sense or sight
  Of day or the warm light,
A place of thought where we in waiting lie;]
Thou little Child, yet glorious in the might
Of heaven-born freedom on thy being's height,
Why with such earnest pains dost thou provoke
The years to bring the inevitable yoke,
Thus blindly with thy blessedness at strife?
Full soon thy Soul shall have her earthly freight,
And custom lie upon thee with a weight,
Heavy as frost, and deep almost as life!

O joy! that in our embers
Is something that doth live,
That nature yet remembers
What was so fugitive!
The thought of our past years in me doth breed
Perpetual benediction: not indeed
For that which is most worthy to be blest;
Delight and liberty, the simple creed
Of Childhood, whether busy or at rest,
With new-fledged hope still fluttering in his breast:—
      Not for these I raise
      The song of thanks and praise;
    But for those obstinate questionings
    Of sense and outward things,
      Fallings from us, vanishings;
      Blank misgivings of a Creature
Moving about in worlds not realised,
High instincts before which our mortal Nature
Did tremble like a guilty Thing surprised:
      But for those first affections,
      Those shadowy recollections,
    Which, be they what they may,
Are yet the fountain-light of all our day,
Are yet a master-light of all our seeing;
      Uphold us, cherish, and have power to make
Our noisy years seem moments in the being
Of the eternal Silence: truths that wake,
      To perish never:
Which neither listlessness, nor mad endeavour,
      Nor Man nor Boy,
Nor all that is at enmity with joy,
Can utterly abolish or destroy!
      Hence in a season of calm weather,
      Though inland far we be,
Our Souls have sight of that immortal sea
      Which brought us hither,
      Can in a moment travel thither,
And see the Children sport upon the shore,
And hear the mighty waters rolling evermore.

Then sing, ye Birds, sing, sing a joyous song!
    And let the young Lambs bound
    As to the tabor's sound!
We in thought will join your throng,
    Ye that pipe and ye that play,
    Ye that through your hearts to-day
    Feel the gladness of the May!
What though the radiance which was once so bright
Be now for ever taken from my sight,
    Though nothing can bring back the hour
Of splendour in the grass, of glory in the flower;
    We will grieve not, rather find
    Strength in what remains behind;
    In the primal sympathy
    Which having been must ever be;
    In the soothing thoughts that spring
    Out of human suffering;
    In the faith that looks through death,
In years that bring the philosophic mind.

And O, ye Fountains, Meadows, Hills, and Groves,
Forebode not any severing of our loves!
Yet in my heart of hearts I feel your might;
I only have relinquished one delight
To live beneath your more habitual sway.
I love the Brooks, which down their channels fret,
Even more than when I tripped lightly as they;
The innocent brightness of a new-born Day
    Is lovely yet;
The Clouds that gather round the setting sun
Do take a sober colouring from an eye
That hath kept watch o'er man's mortality;
Another race hath been, and other palms are won.
Thanks to the human heart by which we live,
Thanks to its tenderness, its joys, and fears,
To me the meanest flower that blows can give
Thoughts that do often lie too deep for tears.

ONE SUMMER EVENING

One summer evening (led by her)[1] I found
A little boat tied to a willow tree
Within a rocky cave, its usual home.
Straight I unloosed her chain, and stepping in
Pushed from the shore. It was an act of stealth
And troubled pleasure, nor without the voice
Of mountain-echoes did my boat move on;
Leaving behind her still, on either side,
Small circles glittering idly in the moon,
Until they melted all into one track
Of sparkling light. But now, like one who rows,
Proud of his skill, to reach a chosen point
With an unswerving line, I fixed my view
Upon the summit of a craggy ridge,
The horizon's utmost boundary; for above
Was nothing but the stars and the grey sky.
She was an elfin pinnace; lustily
I dipped my oars into the silent lake,
And, as I rose upon the stroke, my boat
Went heaving through the water like a swan;
When, from behind that craggy steep, till then,
The horizon's bound, a huge peak, black and huge,
As if with voluntary power instinct,
Upreared its head. I struck and struck again,
And, growing still in stature, the grim shape
Towered up between me and the stars, and still,
For so it seemed, with purpose of its own
And measured motion like a living thing,
Strode after me. With trembling oars I turned,
And through the silent water stole my way
Back to the covert of the willow tree;
There in her mooring-place I left my bark,—
And through the meadows homeward went, in grave
And serious mood; but after I had seen
That spectacle, for many days, my brain
Worked with a dim and undetermined sense
Of unknown modes of being; o'er my thoughts

[1] her] Nature

There hung a darkness, call it solitude
Or blank desertion. No familiar shapes
Remained, no pleasant images of trees,
Of sea or sky, no colours of green fields;
But huge and mighty forms, that do not live
Like living men, moved slowly through the mind
By day, and were a trouble to my dreams.

(Prelude, i, ll. 357–400.)

WINANDER LAKE

THERE was a Boy: ye knew him well, ye cliffs
And islands of Winander!—many a time
At evening, when the earliest stars began
To move along the edges of the hills,
Rising or setting, would he stand alone
Beneath the trees or by the glimmering lake,
And there, with fingers interwoven, both hands
Pressed closely palm to palm, and to his mouth
Uplifted, he, as through an instrument,
Blew mimic hootings to the silent owls,
That they might answer him; and they would shout
Across the watery vale, and shout again,
Responsive to his call, with quivering peals,
And long halloos and screams, and echoes loud,
Redoubled and redoubled, concourse wild
Of jocund din; and, when a lengthened pause
Of silence came and baffled his best skill,
Then sometimes, in that silence while he hung
Listening, a gentle shock of mild surprise
Has carried far into his heart the voice
Of mountain torrents; or the visible scene
Would enter unawares into his mind,
With all its solemn imagery, its rocks,
Its woods, and that uncertain heaven, received
Into the bosom of the steady lake.

(Prelude, v, ll. 364–88.)

IMAGINATION

IMAGINATION—here the Power so called
Through sad incompetence of human speech,
That awful Power rose from the mind's abyss
Like an unfathered vapour that enwraps,
At once, some lonely traveller. I was lost;
Halted without an effort to break through;
But to my conscious soul I now can say—
'I recognise thy glory'; in such strength
Of usurpation, when the light of sense
Goes out, but with a flash that has revealed
The invisible world, doth greatness make abode,
There harbours; whether we be young or old,
Our destiny, our being's heart and home,
Is with infinitude, and only there;
With hope it is, hope that can never die,
Effort, and expectation, and desire,
And something evermore about to be.

Under such banners militant, the soul
Seeks for no trophies, struggles for no spoils
That may attest her prowess, blest in thoughts
That are their own perfection and reward,
Strong in herself and in beatitude
That hides her, like the mighty flood of Nile
Poured from his fount of Abyssinian clouds
To fertilise the whole Egyptian plain.

The melancholy slackening that ensued
Upon those tidings by the peasant given
Was soon dislodged. Downwards we hurried fast,
And, with the half-shaped road which we had missed,
Entered a narrow chasm. The brook and road
Were fellow-travellers in this gloomy strait,
And with them did we journey several hours
At a slow pace. The immeasurable height
Of woods decaying, never to be decayed,
The stationary blasts of waterfalls,
And in the narrow rent at every turn
Winds thwarting winds, bewildered and forlorn,

The torrents shooting from the clear blue sky,
The rocks that muttered close upon our ears,
Black drizzling crags that spake by the way-side
As if a voice were in them, the sick sight
And giddy prospect of the raving stream,
The unfettered clouds and region of the Heavens,
Tumult and peace, the darkness and the light—
Were all like workings of one mind, the features
Of the same face, blossoms upon one tree;
Characters of the great Apocalypse,
The types and symbols of Eternity,
Of first, and last, and midst, and without end.

(Prelude, vi, ll. 592–640.)

OH! MYSTERY OF MAN

OH! mystery of man, from what a depth
Proceed thy honours. I am lost, but see
In simple childhood something of the base
On which thy greatness stands; but this I feel,
That from thyself it comes, that thou must give,
Else never canst receive. The days gone by
Return upon me almost from the dawn
Of life: the hiding-places of man's power
Open; I would approach them, but they close.
I see by glimpses now; when age comes on,
May scarcely see at all; and I would give,
While yet we may, as far as words can give,
Substance and life to what I feel, enshrining,
Such is my hope, the spirit of the Past
For future restoration.   (<i>Prelude</i>, xii, ll. 272–286.)

EXTEMPORE EFFUSION UPON THE DEATH OF JAMES HOGG

WHEN first, descending from the moorlands,
I saw the Stream of Yarrow glide
Along a bare and open valley,
The Ettrick Shepherd was my guide.

When last along its banks I wandered,
Through groves that had begun to shed
Their golden leaves upon the pathways,
My steps the Border-minstrel led.

The mighty Minstrel breathes no longer,
'Mid mouldering ruins low he lies;
And death, upon the braes of Yarrow,
Has closed the Shepherd-poet's eyes:

Nor has the rolling year twice measured,
From sign to sign, its steadfast course,
Since every mortal power of Coleridge
Was frozen at its marvellous source;

The rapt One, of the godlike forehead,
The heaven-eyed creature sleeps in earth:
And Lamb, the frolic and the gentle,
Has vanished from his lonely hearth.

Like clouds that rake the mountain-summits,
Or waves that own no curbing hand,
How fast has brother followed brother,
From sunshine to the sunless land!

Yet I, whose lids from infant slumber
Were earlier raised, remain to hear
A timid voice, that asks in whispers,
'Who next will drop and disappear?'

Our haughty life is crowned with darkness,
Like London with its own black wreath,
On which with thee, O Crabbe! forth-looking,
I gazed from Hampstead's breezy heath.

As if but yesterday departed,
Thou too art gone before; but why,
O'er ripe fruit, seasonably gathered,
Should frail survivors heave a sigh?

Mourn rather for that holy Spirit,
Sweet as the spring, as ocean deep;
For Her[1] who, ere her summer faded,
Has sunk into a breathless sleep.

No more of old romantic sorrows,
For slaughtered Youth or love-lorn Maid!
With sharper grief is Yarrow smitten,
And Ettrick mourns with her their Poet dead.

[1] her] Mrs. Hemans

SAMUEL TAYLOR COLERIDGE

SAMUEL TAYLOR COLERIDGE (1772–1834), son of the vicar of Ottery St. Mary, Devon, was educated at Christ's Hospital (Lamb, in his *Elia* essay, describes him there) and at Jesus College, Cambridge. In 1795 he made the acquaintance of Wordsworth, and the two poets lived for about a year at Nether Stowey and Alfoxden in Somerset. Their *Lyrical Ballads*, containing Coleridge's *Ancient Mariner*, appeared in 1798. Coleridge wrote the first part of *Christabel* and *Kubla Khan* in 1797, and some of his best poems during 1798–1802. *Dejection* was written in 1802. In 1804 he travelled to Malta and Italy, returning in 1806 broken in health and a prey to the use of opium. He spent much of the latter part of his life in the houses of friends; after 1816, of a kindly surgeon, James Gillman, at Highgate. In 1817 appeared his *Biographia Literaria* or literary autobiography, and in 1825 his *Aids to Reflection*, in the first of which he did much to introduce German philosophy to English thinkers. He died in 1834.

> You will see Coleridge—he who sits obscure
> In the exceeding lustre and the pure
> Intense irradiation of a mind,
> Which, with its own internal lightnings blind,
> Flags wearily through darkness and despair.

'COLERIDGE was a muddle-brained metaphysician, who by some strange freak of fortune turned out a few real poems amongst the dreary flood of inanity which was his wont. It is these real poems only which must be selected, or we burden the world with another useless book. . . . There is no difficulty in making the selection—the difference between his poetry and his drivel is so striking.'

The first estimate is that of Shelley, writing characteristically penetrating, aerially imaginative, poetry to Maria Gisborne. The second is that of William Morris, writing characteristically swashbuckling and robustly dogmatic prose to the Kelmscott Press about a selection from Coleridge. But the two approach each other more closely in substance than they do in manner. Both stress Coleridge's preoccupation with the things of the mind, and both stress his lack of stamina, his inability to sustain his flight at its highest pitch. Even those who doubt whether Coleridge is one of the greatest of English critics will readily admit that he is one of the most brilliantly illuminating; but even in this field the brilliance is spasmodic. Truth springs out clear-cut, silhouetted for a moment on the sky-line by the lightning-flash of the sudden phrase; but the lightning is transitory and the tree merges again into the shades of night.

Something the same is true of his poetry, though with this difference, that he produces his best criticism at those moments when his mind is kindled by his imagination, but his best poetry when his mind is as nearly as may be laid asleep. He wrote three poems which are by common consent among the most notable in our language, in their own kind, indeed, unapproachable. Besides these he turned out a great body of work, a good deal of it trivial, and the bulk of it competent enough versifying, but characterless, no better and no worse than could have been turned out by plenty of other poets. Morris was no doubt extravagant in depreciation, but he was right in this that Coleridge of all poets is the easiest from whom to select. He stands or falls, as a poet, by three poems, and a most remarkable and imperishable trio they are, remarkable not only for their excellence, but also for their diversity in excellence. All three present the supernatural, the world of faerie and of dreams, but each presents it in its own distinctive way.

Of all modern poems *The Rime of the Ancient Mariner* comes nearest to achieving an impossible, the impossibility for the modern writer of writing a genuine 'ballad'. Coleridge at least grazes the clout because, for all that he applies to the task a sophisticated and inevitably imitative technique, he can throw back to the true ballad spirit and maintain it, the spirit which is content to record vividly and leave it to the hearer to comment, which will record the extraordinary with as matter-of-fact a nonchalance as the hum-drum. It is a mistake to suppose that the ballad-writers did not regard the supernatural as supernatural; they did; but they also regarded it as, given the necessary conditions, normal. If at the dead hour of the night you heard the bridles ring, the bridles were elfin and the hair of your head stood up; but if you were unlucky enough, or foolhardy enough, to be at the right place at the right hour, you were likely, in the normal course of events, to hear the elfin bridles. *The Ancient Mariner* is a masterpiece of vivid description, but nothing in it is more remarkable than the way in which the transition from the detailed, matter-of-fact, and accurate description of the voyage towards and from the South Pole to the equally matter-of-fact description of the avowedly supernatural manifestation of the phantom ship is managed with so little change of tone that one hardly, in a rapid reading, realizes that the transition has been made. If one has unwisely shot an albatross, then sooner or later strange things will happen. But the strange things will be described with the same clear circumstantial detail as the rising of the sun upon the other hand. There is no question of an incursion, a border raid, of the supernatural on the natural; both are parts of a whole.

Christabel is wholly different in spirit; the two realms are sharply defined, and the denizens of the one trespass on the confines of the other. It is different also in method, and those who, with Keats, dislike poetry that has a palpable design upon them dislike it, for the design is palpable in conception and gross in execution. Coleridge is as determined as the fat boy to make his readers' flesh creep, and he proposes to do it not by the method of plain statement but by the method of 'suggestion'. This method can be terrifyingly effective when used with restraint, but Coleridge's determination is so relentless that he loses all finesse. Hence the vagueness, hence the frequent appeals to the Heavenly powers, hence the mastiff-bitch, that irritating hound. And in one instance Coleridge perfectly betrays his method for inspection. He wrote first

> Behold! her bosom and half her side
> Are lean and old and foul of hue.

Surprising, no doubt, and repellent, but direct. This is the technique of *The Ancient Mariner* and this therefore will never do. So Coleridge rewrites it, with a suggestive aposiopesis (incidentally sacrificing an essential rhyme and forgetting in the second part that he has rewritten it)

> Behold! her bosom and half her side—
> A sight to dream of, not to tell!

And we either shiver deliciously or turn away from the too patent garden-path according to temperament. *Christabel* is a masterpiece, but to many readers an exasperating masterpiece.

Kubla Khan is a masterpiece of another, and, I think, far higher order, though 'masterpiece' is probably too conscious a word to describe rightly so unconscious a poem. There is no valid reason to doubt Coleridge's own account of its composition. It is true that the most of us, if we write anything in dreams, write unpublishable doggerel. But take a man with as peculiarly associative a mind as Coleridge's (*The Road to Xanadu* showed its singularly 'prehensile, amalgamating' quality), a man with an adequate training in poetic technique, and a man in whom the subconscious was so much less far below the threshold of consciousness than with most of us; put this man under opium, and there is no reason why the outcome should not be *Kubla Khan*, that most perfect of all records of dreamexperience, with the coherent incoherence of a dream. One may or may not like it; it is 'fanciful'; it is 'intangible'; it 'has no relation to life as ordinary men and women live it'; but no one who is not deaf to the music of poetry, and blind to the images of poetic fancy, can deny that in its own kind it is beyond criticism, securely *hors concours*; storing in one vial all the sorceries of 'Romanticism', distilled by a process of which only Keats and Coleridge fully knew the secret.

> A savage place! as holy and enchanted
> As e'er beneath a waning moon was haunted
> By woman wailing for her demon lover!

Kipling, who, amongst many other things, was himself a master of words and a sensitive literary critic takes the two famous lines of Keats on the magic casements and these three of Coleridge, and he says, 'Remember that in all the millions permitted there are no more than five—five little lines—of which one can say: "These are the pure Magic. These are the clear Vision. The rest is only poetry." '

M. R. RIDLEY.

THE RIME OF THE ANCIENT MARINER

IN SEVEN PARTS

ARGUMENT

How a Ship having passed the Line was driven by storms to the cold Country towards the South Pole; and how from thence she made her course to the tropical Latitude of the Great Pacific Ocean; how the Ancient Mariner cruelly and in contempt of the laws of hospitality killed a Sea-bird and how he was followed by many and strange Judgements: and in what manner he came back to his own Country.

PART I

An ancient Mariner meeteth three Gallants bidden to a wedding-feast, and detaineth one.

IT is an ancient Mariner,
And he stoppeth one of three.
'By thy long grey beard and glittering eye,
Now wherefore stopp'st thou me?

The Bridegroom's doors are opened wide,
And I am next of kin;
The guests are met, the feast is set:
May'st hear the merry din.'

He holds him with his skinny hand,
'There was a ship,' quoth he.
'Hold off! unhand me, grey-beard loon!'
Eftsoons his hand dropt he.

The Wedding-Guest is spellbound by the eye of the old seafaring man, and constrained to hear his tale.

He holds him with his glittering eye—
The Wedding-Guest stood still,
And listens like a three years' child:
The Mariner hath his will.

The Wedding-Guest sat on a stone:
He cannot choose but hear;
And thus spake on that ancient man,
The bright-eyed Mariner.

'The ship was cheered, the harbour cleared;
Merrily did we drop
Below the kirk, below the hill,
Below the lighthouse top.

The Sun came up upon the left,
Out of the sea came he!
And he shone bright, and on the right
Went down into the sea.

Higher and higher every day,
Till over the mast at noon—'
The Wedding-Guest here beat his breast,
For he heard the loud bassoon.

The bride hath paced into the hall,
Red as a rose is she;
Nodding their heads before her goes
The merry minstrelsy.

The Wedding-Guest he beat his breast,
Yet he cannot choose but hear;
And thus spake on that ancient man,
The bright-eyed Mariner.

'And now the STORM-BLAST came, and he
Was tyrannous and strong:
He struck with his o'ertaking wings,
And chased us south along.

With sloping masts and dipping prow,
As who pursued with yell and blow
Still treads the shadow of his foe,
And forward bends his head,
The ship drove fast, loud roared the blast,
And southward aye we fled.

And now there came both mist and snow,
And it grew wondrous cold:
And ice, mast-high, came floating by,
As green as emerald.

The Mariner tells how the ship sailed southward with a good wind and fair weather, till it reached the line.

The Wedding-Guest heareth the bridal music; but the Mariner continueth his tale.

The ship driven by a storm toward the south pole.

258

The land of
ice, and of
fearful sounds
where no
living thing
was to be seen.

And through the drifts the snowy clifts
Did send a dismal sheen:
Nor shapes of men nor beasts we ken—
The ice was all between.

The ice was here, the ice was there,
The ice was all around:
It cracked and growled, and roared and howled,
Like noises in a swound!

Till a great
sea-bird,
called the
Albatross,
came through
the snow-fog,
and was
received with
great joy and
hospitality.

At length did cross an Albatross,
Thorough the fog it came;
As if it had been a Christian soul,
We hailed it in God's name.

It ate the food it ne'er had eat,
And round and round it flew.
The ice did split with a thunder-fit;
The helmsman steered us through!

And lo! the
Albatross
proveth a bird
of good omen,
and followeth
the ship as it
returned
northward
through fog
and floating
ice.

And a good south wind sprung up behind;
The Albatross did follow,
And every day, for food or play,
Came to the mariner's hollo!

In mist or cloud, on mast or shroud,
It perched for vespers nine;
Whiles all the night, through fog-smoke white,
Glimmered the white Moon-shine.'

'God save thee, ancient Mariner!
From the fiends, that plague thee thus!—
Why look'st thou so?'—'With my cross-bow
I shot the ALBATROSS.'

PART II

The ancient
Mariner
inhospitably
killeth the
pious bird of
good omen.

The Sun now rose upon the right:
Out of the sea came he,
Still hid in mist, and on the left
Went down into the sea.

And the good south wind still blew behind,
But no sweet bird did follow,
Nor any day for food or play
Came to the mariners' hollo!

259

His shipmates cry out against the ancient Mariner, for killing the bird of good luck.

And I had done a hellish thing,
And it would work 'em woe:
For all averred I had killed the bird
That made the breeze to blow.
Ah wretch! said they, the bird to slay,
That made the breeze to blow!

But when the fog cleared off, they justify the same, and thus make themselves accomplices in the crime.

Nor dim nor red, like God's own head,
The glorious Sun uprist:
Then all averred I had killed the bird
That brought the fog and mist.
'Twas right, said they, such birds to slay,
That bring the fog and mist.

The fair breeze continues; the ship enters the Pacific Ocean, and sails northward, even till it reaches the Line.

The fair breeze blew, the white foam flew,
The furrow followed free;
We were the first that ever burst
Into that silent sea.

The ship hath been suddenly becalmed.

Down dropt the breeze, the sails dropt down,
'Twas sad as sad could be;
And we did speak only to break
The silence of the sea!

All in a hot and copper sky,
The bloody Sun, at noon,
Right up above the mast did stand,
No bigger than the Moon.

Day after day, day after day,
We stuck, nor breath nor motion;
As idle as a painted ship
Upon a painted ocean.

And the Albatross begins to be avenged.

Water, water, everywhere,
And all the boards did shrink;
Water, water, everywhere,
Nor any drop to drink.

The very deep did rot: O Christ!
That ever this should be!
Yea, slimy things did crawl with legs
Upon the slimy sea.

About, about, in reel and rout
The death-fires danced at night;
The water, like a witch's oils,
Burnt green, and blue and white.

A Spirit had
followed them;
one of the in-
visible inhabi-
tants of this
planet, neither
departed souls

And some in dreams assuréd were
Of the Spirit that plagued us so;
Nine fathom deep he had followed us
From the land of mist and snow.

nor angels; concerning whom the learned Jew, Josephus, and the Platonic
Constantinopolitan, Michael Psellus, may be consulted. They are very numerous,
and there is no climate or element without one or more.

And every tongue, through utter drought,
Was withered at the root;
We could not speak, no more than if
We had been choked with soot.

The shipmates,
in their sore
distress, would
fain throw the
whole guilt on
the ancient
Mariner: in

Ah! well-a-day! what evil looks
Had I from old and young!
Instead of the cross, the Albatross
About my neck was hung.

sign whereof they hang the dead sea-bird round his neck.

PART III

There passed a weary time. Each throat
Was parched, and glazed each eye.
A weary time! a weary time!
How glazed each weary eye,
When looking westward, I beheld
A something in the sky.

The ancient
Mariner be-
holdeth a sign
in the element
afar off.

At first it seemed a little speck,
And then it seemed a mist;
It moved and moved, and took at last
A certain shape, I wist.

A speck, a mist, a shape, I wist!
And still it neared and neared:
As if it dodged a water-sprite,
It plunged and tacked and veered.

At its nearer
approach, it
seemeth him
to be a ship;
and at a dear
ransom he
freeth his
speech from
the bonds of
thirst.

With throats unslaked, with black lips baked,
We could not laugh nor wail;
Through utter drought all dumb we stood!
I bit my arm, I sucked the blood,
And cried, A sail! a sail!

With throats unslaked, with black lips baked,
Agape they heard me call:

A flash of joy;

Gramercy! they for joy did grin,
And all at once their breath drew in,
As they were drinking all.

And horror
follows. For
can it be a
ship that
comes onward
without wind
or tide?

See! see! (I cried) she tacks no more!
Hither to work us weal;
Without a breeze, without a tide,
She steadies with upright keel!

The western wave was all a-flame.
The day was well-nigh done!
Almost upon the western wave
Rested the broad bright Sun;
When that strange shape drove suddenly
Betwixt us and the Sun.

It seemeth
him but the
skeleton of
a ship.

And straight the Sun was flecked with bars,
(Heaven's Mother send us grace!)
As if through a dungeon-grate he peered
With broad and burning face.

And its ribs
are seen as
bars on the
face of the
setting Sun.

Alas! (thought I, and my heart beat loud)
How fast she nears and nears!
Are those her sails that glance in the Sun,
Like restless gossameres?

The Spectre-
Woman and
her Death-
mate, and no
other on
board the
skeleton ship.

Are those her ribs through which the Sun
Did peer, as through a grate?
And is that Woman all her crew?
Is that a DEATH? and are there two?
Is DEATH that woman's mate?

Like vessel, like crew!
Death and Life-in-Death have diced for the ship's crew, and she (the latter) winneth the ancient Mariner.

Her lips were red, her looks were free,
Her locks were yellow as gold:
Her skin was as white as leprosy,
The Night-mare LIFE-IN-DEATH was she,
Who thicks man's blood with cold.

The naked hulk alongside came,
And the twain were casting dice;
'The game is done! I've won! I've won!'
Quoth she, and whistles thrice.

No twilight within the courts of the Sun.

The Sun's rim dips; the stars rush out:
At one stride comes the dark;
With far-heard whisper, o'er the sea,
Off shot the spectre-bark.

At the rising of the Moon,

We listened and looked sideways up!
Fear at my heart, as at a cup,
My life-blood seemed to sip!
The stars were dim, and thick the night,
The steersman's face by his lamp gleamed white;
From the sails the dew did drip—
Till clomb above the eastern bar
The hornéd Moon, with one bright star
Within the nether tip.

one after another,

One after one, by the star-dogged Moon,
Too quick for groan or sigh,
Each turned his face with a ghastly pang,
And cursed me with his eye.

his shipmates drop down dead.

Four times fifty living men,
(And I heard nor sigh nor groan)
With heavy thump, a lifeless lump,
They dropped down one by one.

But Life-in-Death begins her work on the ancient Mariner.

The souls did from their bodies fly,—
They fled to bliss or woe!
And every soul, it passed me by,
Like the whizz of my cross-bow!

263

PART IV

The Wedding-Guest feareth that a Spirit is talking to him;

'I fear thee, ancient Mariner!
I fear thy skinny hand!
And thou art long, and lank, and brown,
As is the ribbed sea-sand.

I fear thee and thy glittering eye,
And thy skinny hand, so brown.'—
but the ancient Mariner assureth him of his bodily life, and proceedeth to relate his horrible penance.
'Fear not, fear not, thou Wedding-Guest!
This body dropt not down.

Alone, alone, all, all alone,
Alone on a wide wide sea!
And never a saint took pity on
My soul in agony.

He despiseth the creatures of the calm,
The many men, so beautiful!
And they all dead did lie:
And a thousand thousand slimy things
Lived on; and so did I.

and envieth that *they* should live, and so many lie dead.
I looked upon the rotting sea,
And drew my eyes away;
I looked upon the rotting deck,
And there the dead men lay.

I looked to heaven, and tried to pray;
But or ever a prayer had gusht,
A wicked whisper came, and made
My heart as dry as dust.

I closed my lids, and kept them close,
And the balls like pulses beat;
For the sky and the sea, and the sea and the sky,
Lay like a load on my weary eye,
And the dead were at my feet.

But the curse liveth for him in the eye of the dead men.
The cold sweat melted from their limbs,
Nor rot nor reek did they:
The look with which they looked on me
Had never passed away.

An orphan's curse would drag to hell
A spirit from on high;
But oh! more horrible than that
Is the curse in a dead man's eye!
Seven days, seven nights, I saw that curse,
And yet I could not die.

In his lone-
liness and
fixedness he
yearneth to-
wards the
journeying
Moon, and the
stars that still
sojourn, yet
still move
onward; and
every where
the blue sky
belongs to
them, and is
their appointed
rest, and their native country and their own natural homes, which they enter un-
announced, as lords that are certainly expected and yet there is a silent joy at their
arrival.

The moving Moon went up the sky,
And nowhere did abide:
Softly she was going up,
And a star or two beside—

Her beams bemocked the sultry main,
Like April hoar-frost spread;
But where the ship's huge shadow lay,
The charméd water burnt alway
A still and awful red.

By the light
of the Moon he
beholdeth
God's crea-
tures of the
great calm.

Beyond the shadow of the ship,
I watched the water-snakes:
They moved in tracks of shining white,
And when they reared, the elfish light
Fell off in hoary flakes.

Within the shadow of the ship
I watched their rich attire:
Blue, glossy green, and velvet black,
They coiled and swam; and every track
Was a flash of golden fire.

Their beauty
and their
happiness.

O happy living things! no tongue
Their beauty might declare:
A spring of love gushed from my heart,
And I blessed them unaware:

He blesseth
them in his
heart.

Sure my kind saint took pity on me,
And I blessed them unaware.

The spell
begins to
break.

The self-same moment I could pray;
And from my neck so free
The Albatross fell off, and sank
Like lead into the sea.

Part V

Oh sleep! it is a gentle thing,
Beloved from pole to pole!
To Mary Queen the praise be given!
She sent the gentle sleep from Heaven,
That slid into my soul.

By grace of
the holy
Mother, the
ancient
Mariner is
refreshed with
rain.

The silly buckets on the deck,
That had so long remained,
I dreamt that they were filled with dew;
And when I awoke, it rained.

My lips were wet, my throat was cold,
My garments all were dank;
Sure I had drunken in my dreams,
And still my body drank.

I moved, and could not feel my limbs:
I was so light—almost
I thought that I had died in sleep,
And was a blessèd ghost.

He heareth
sounds and
seeth strange
sights and
commotions in
the sky and
the element.

And soon I heard a roaring wind:
It did not come anear;
But with its sound it shook the sails,
That were so thin and sere.

The upper air burst into life!
And a hundred fire-flags sheen,
To and fro they were hurried about!
And to and fro, and in and out,
The wan stars danced between.

And the coming wind did roar more loud,
And the sails did sigh like sedge;
And the rain poured down from one black
    cloud;
The Moon was at its edge.

The thick black cloud was cleft, and still
The Moon was at its side:
Like waters shot from some high crag,
The lightning fell with never a jag,
A river steep and wide.

266

The bodies of the ship's crew are inspired and the ship moves on;

The loud wind never reached the ship,
Yet now the ship moved on!
Beneath the lightning and the Moon
The dead men gave a groan.

They groaned, they stirred, they all uprose,
Nor spake, nor moved their eyes;
It had been strange, even in a dream,
To have seen those dead men rise.

The helmsman steered, the ship moved on;
Yet never a breeze up-blew;
The mariners all 'gan work the ropes,
Where they were wont to do;
They raised their limbs like lifeless tools—
We were a ghastly crew.

The body of my brother's son
Stood by me, knee to knee:
The body and I pulled at one rope,
But he said nought to me.'

but not by the souls of the men, nor by dæmons of earth or middle air, but by a blessed troop of angelic spirits, sent down by the invocation of the guardian saint.

'I fear thee, ancient Mariner!'
'Be calm, thou Wedding-Guest!
'Twas not those souls that fled in pain,
Which to their corses came again,
But a troop of spirits blest:

For when it dawned—they dropped their arms,
And clustered round the mast;
Sweet sounds rose slowly through their mouths,
And from their bodies passed.

Around, around, flew each sweet sound,
Then darted to the Sun;
Slowly the sounds came back again,
Now mixed, now one by one.

Sometimes a-dropping from the sky
I heard the sky-lark sing;
Sometimes all little birds that are,
How they seemed to fill the sea and air
With their sweet jargoning!

SAMUEL TAYLOR COLERIDGE

And now 'twas like all instruments,
Now like a lonely flute;
And now it is an angel's song,
That makes the heavens be mute.

It ceased; yet still the sails made on
A pleasant noise till noon,
A noise like of a hidden brook
In the leafy month of June,
That to the sleeping woods all night
Singeth a quiet tune.

Till noon we quietly sailed on,
Yet never a breeze did breathe:
Slowly and smoothly went the ship,
Moved onward from beneath.

The lonesome Spirit from the south-pole carries on the ship as far as the Line, in obedience to the angelic troop, but still requireth vengeance.

Under the keel nine fathom deep,
From the land of mist and snow,
The Spirit slid: and it was he
That made the ship to go.
The sails at noon left off their tune,
And the ship stood still also.

The Sun, right up above the mast,
Had fixed her to the ocean:
But in a minute she 'gan stir,
With a short uneasy motion—
Backwards and forwards half her length
With a short uneasy motion.

Then like a pawing horse let go,
She made a sudden bound:
It flung the blood into my head,
And I fell down in a swound.

The Polar Spirit's fellow-dæmons, the invisible inhabitants of the element, take part in his wrong;

How long in that same fit I lay,
I have not to declare;
But ere my living life returned,
I heard and in my soul discerned
Two voices in the air.

and two of them relate one to the other, that penance long and heavy for the ancient Mariner hath been accorded to the Polar Spirit, who returneth southward.

268

"Is it he?" quoth one, "Is this the man?
By Him who died on cross,
With his cruel bow he laid full low
The harmless Albatross.

The Spirit who bideth by himself
In the land of mist and snow,
He loved the bird that loved the man
Who shot him with his bow."

The other was a softer voice,
As soft as honey-dew:
Quoth he, "The man hath penance done,
And penance more will do."

PART VI

FIRST VOICE

"But tell me, tell me! speak again,
Thy soft response renewing—
What makes that ship drive on so fast?
What is the ocean doing?"

SECOND VOICE

"Still as a slave before his lord,
The ocean hath no blast;
His great bright eye most silently
Up to the Moon is cast—

If he may know which way to go;
For she guides him smooth or grim.
See, brother, see! how graciously
She looketh down on him."

FIRST VOICE

"But why drives on that ship so fast,
Without or wave or wind?"

SECOND VOICE

"The air is cut away before,
And closes from behind.

The Mariner hath been cast into a trance; for the angelic power causeth the vessel to drive northward faster than human life could endure.

269

Fly, brother, fly! more high, more high!
Or we shall be belated:
For slow and slow that ship will go,
When the Mariner's trance is abated."

The supernatural motion is retarded; the Mariner awakes, and his penance begins anew.

I woke, and we were sailing on
As in a gentle weather:
'Twas night, calm night, the moon was high;
The dead men stood together.

All stood together on the deck,
For a charnel-dungeon fitter:
All fixed on me their stony eyes,
That in the Moon did glitter.

The pang, the curse, with which they died,
Had never passed away:
I could not draw my eyes from theirs,
Nor turn them up to pray.

The curse is finally expiated.

And now this spell was snapt: once more
I viewed the ocean green,
And looked far forth, yet little saw
Of what had else been seen—

Like one, that on a lonesome road
Doth walk in fear and dread,
And having once turned round walks on,
And turns no more his head;
Because he knows a frightful fiend
Doth close behind him tread.

But soon there breathed a wind on me,
Nor sound nor motion made:
Its path was not upon the sea,
In ripple or in shade.

It raised my hair, it fanned my cheek
Like a meadow-gale of spring—
It mingled strangely with my fears,
Yet it felt like a welcoming.

Swiftly, swiftly flew the ship,
Yet she sailed softly too:
Sweetly, sweetly blew the breeze—
On me alone it blew.

Oh! dream of joy! is this indeed
The light-house top I see?
Is this the hill? is this the kirk?
Is this mine own countree?

We drifted o'er the harbour-bar,
And I with sobs did pray—
O let me be awake, my God!
Or let me sleep alway.

The harbour-bar was clear as glass,
So smoothly it was strewn!
And on the bay the moonlight lay,
And the shadow of the Moon.

The rock shone bright, the kirk no less,
That stands above the rock:
The moonlight steeped in silentness
The steady weathercock.

And the bay was white with silent light,
Till rising from the same,

Full many shapes, that shadows were,
In crimson colours came.

A little distance from the prow

Those crimson shadows were:
I turned my eyes upon the deck—
Oh, Christ! what saw I there!

Each corse lay flat, lifeless and flat,
And, by the holy rood!
A man all light, a seraph-man,
On every corse there stood.

This seraph-band, each waved his hand:
It was a heavenly sight!
They stood as signals to the land,
Each one a lovely light;

This seraph-band, each waved his hand,
No voice did they impart—
No voice; but oh! the silence sank
Like music on my heart.

But soon I heard the dash of oars,
I heard the Pilot's cheer;
My head was turned perforce away,
And I saw a boat appear.

The Pilot and the Pilot's boy,
I heard them coming fast:
Dear Lord in Heaven! it was a joy
The dead men could not blast.

I saw a third—I heard his voice:
It is the Hermit good!
He singeth loud his godly hymns
That he makes in the wood.
He'll shrieve my soul, he'll wash away
The Albatross's blood.

Part VII

The Hermit of the Wood,

This Hermit good lives in that wood
Which slopes down to the sea.
How loudly his sweet voice he rears!
He loves to talk with marineres
That come from a far countree.

He kneels at morn, and noon, and eve—
He hath a cushion plump:
It is the moss that wholly hides
The rotted old oak-stump.

The skiff-boat neared: I heard them talk,
"Why, this is strange, I trow!
Where are those lights so many and fair,
That signal made but now?"

"Strange, by my faith!" the Hermit said—
"And they answered not our cheer!
The planks looked warped! and see those sails,
How thin they are and sere!
I never saw aught like to them,
Unless perchance it were

Brown skeletons of leaves that lag
My forest-brook along;
When the ivy-tod is heavy with snow,
And the owlet whoops to the wolf below,
That eats the she-wolf's young."

"Dear Lord! it hath a fiendish look—
(The Pilot made reply)
I am a-feared"—"Push on, push on!"
Said the Hermit cheerily.

The boat came closer to the ship,
But I nor spake nor stirred;
The boat came close beneath the ship,
And straight a sound was heard.

Under the water it rumbled on,
Still louder and more dread:
It reached the ship, it split the bay;
The ship went down like lead.

Stunned by that loud and dreadful sound,
Which sky and ocean smote
Like one that hath been seven days drowned
My body lay afloat;
But swift as dreams, myself I found
Within the Pilot's boat.

Upon the whirl, where sank the ship,
The boat spun round and round;
And all was still, save that the hill
Was telling of the sound.

I moved my lips—the Pilot shrieked
And fell down in a fit;
The holy Hermit raised his eyes,
And prayed where he did sit.

I took the oars: the Pilot's boy,
Who now doth crazy go,
Laughed loud and long, and all the while
His eyes went to and fro.
"Ha! ha!" quoth he, "full plain I see,
The Devil knows how to row."

And now, all in my own countree,
I stood on the firm land!
The Hermit stepped forth from the boat,
And scarcely he could stand.

The ancient Mariner earnestly entreateth the Hermit to shrieve him; and the penance of life falls on him.

"O shrieve me, shrieve me, holy man!"
The Hermit crossed his brow.
"Say quick," quoth he, "I bid thee say—
What manner of man art thou?"

Forthwith this frame of mine was wrenched
With a woful agony,
Which forced me to begin my tale;
And then it left me free.

And ever and anon throughout his future life an agony constraineth him to travel from land to land;

Since then, at an uncertain hour,
That agony returns:
And till my ghastly tale is told,
This heart within me burns.

I pass, like night, from land to land;
I have strange power of speech;
That moment that his face I see,
I know the man that must hear me:
To him my tale I teach.

What loud uproar bursts from the door!
The wedding-guests are there:
But in the garden-bower the bride
And bride-maids singing are:
And hark the little vesper bell,
Which biddeth me to prayer!

O Wedding-Guest! this soul hath been
Alone on a wide wide sea:
So lonely 'twas, that God himself
Scarce seeméd there to be.

274

O sweeter than the marriage-feast,
'Tis sweeter far to me,
To walk together to the kirk
With a goodly company!—

To walk together to the kirk,
And all together pray,
While each to his great Father bends,
Old men, and babes, and loving friends
And youths and maidens gay!

And to teach,
by his own
example, love
and reverence
to all things
that God made
and loveth.

Farewell, farewell! but this I tell
To thee, thou Wedding-Guest!
He prayeth well, who loveth well
Both man and bird and beast.

He prayeth best, who loveth best
All things both great and small;
For the dear God who loveth us,
He made and loveth all.'

The Mariner, whose eye is bright,
Whose beard with age is hoar,
Is gone: and now the Wedding-Guest
Turned from the bridegroom's door.

He went like one that hath been stunned,
And is of sense forlorn:
A sadder and a wiser man,
He rose the morrow morn.

KUBLA KHAN

In Xanadu did Kubla Khan
A stately pleasure-dome decree:
Where Alph, the sacred river, ran
Through caverns measureless to man
   Down to a sunless sea.
So twice five miles of fertile ground
With walls and towers were girdled round:
And there were gardens bright with sinuous rills,
Where blossomed many an incense-bearing tree;
And here were forests ancient as the hills,
Enfolding sunny spots of greenery.

275

But oh! that deep romantic chasm which slanted
Down the green hill athwart a cedarn cover!
A savage place! as holy and enchanted
As e'er beneath a waning moon was haunted
By woman wailing for her demon-lover!
And from this chasm, with ceaseless turmoil seething,
As if this earth in fast thick pants were breathing,
A mighty fountain momently was forced:
Amid whose swift half-intermitted burst
Huge fragments vaulted like rebounding hail,
Or chaffy grain beneath the thresher's flail:
And 'mid these dancing rocks at once and ever
It flung up momently the sacred river.
Five miles meandering with a mazy motion
Through wood and dale the sacred river ran,
Then reached the caverns measureless to man,
And sank in tumult to a lifeless ocean:
And 'mid this tumult Kubla heard from far
Ancestral voices prophesying war!
   The shadow of the dome of pleasure
   Floated midway on the waves;
   Where was heard the mingled measure
   From the fountain and the caves.
It was a miracle of rare device,
A sunny pleasure-dome with caves of ice!

   A damsel with a dulcimer
   In a vision once I saw:
   It was an Abyssinian maid,
   And on her dulcimer she played,
   Singing of Mount Abora.
   Could I revive within me
   Her symphony and song,
   To such a deep delight 'twould win me,
That with music loud and long,
I would build that dome in air,
That sunny dome! those caves of ice!
And all who heard should see them there,
And all should cry, Beware! Beware!
His flashing eyes, his floating hair!

Weave a circle round him thrice,
And close your eyes with holy dread,
For he on honey-dew hath fed,
And drunk the milk of Paradise.

CHRISTABEL
(Part I.)

'Tis the middle of night by the castle clock,
And the owls have awakened the crowing cock;
Tu—whit!——Tu—whoo!
And hark, again! the crowing cock,
How drowsily it crew.

Sir Leoline, the Baron rich
Hath a toothless mastiff bitch;
From her kennel beneath the rock
She maketh answer to the clock,
Four for the quarters, and twelve for the hour;
Ever and aye, by shine and shower,
Sixteen short howls, not over loud;
Some say, she sees my lady's shroud.

Is the night chilly and dark?
The night is chilly, but not dark.
The thin gray cloud is spread on high,
It covers but not hides the sky.
The moon is behind, and at the full;
And yet she looks both small and dull.
The night is chill, the cloud is gray:
'Tis a month before the month of May,
And the Spring comes slowly up this way.

The lovely lady, Christabel,
Whom her father loves so well,
What makes her in the wood so late,
A furlong from the castle gate?
She had dreams all yesternight
Of her own betrothéd knight;
And she in the midnight wood will pray
For the weal of her lover that's far away.

She stole along, she nothing spoke,
The sighs she heaved were soft and low,
And naught was green upon the oak
But moss and rarest misletoe:
She kneels beneath the huge oak tree,
And in silence prayeth she.

The lady sprang up suddenly,
The lovely lady, Christabel!
It moaned as near, as near can be,
But what it is she cannot tell.—
On the other side it seems to be,
Of the huge, broad-breasted, old oak tree.

The night is chill; the forest bare;
Is it the wind that moaneth bleak?
There is not wind enough in the air
To move away the ringlet curl
From the lovely lady's cheek—
There is not wind enough to twirl
The one red leaf, the last of its clan,
That dances as often as dance it can,
Hanging so light, and hanging so high,
On the topmost twig that looks up at the sky.

Hush, beating heart of Christabel!
Jesu, Maria, shield her well!
She folded her arms beneath her cloak,
And stole to the other side of the oak.
    What sees she there?

There she sees a damsel bright,
Drest in a silken robe of white,
That shadowy in the moonlight shone:
The neck that made that white robe wan,
Her stately neck and arms were bare;
Her blue-veined feet unsandal'd were,
And wildly glittered here and there
The gems entangled in her hair.

I guess, 'twas frightful there to see
A lady so richly clad as she—
Beautiful exceedingly!

'Mary mother, save me now!'
(Said Christabel,) 'And who art thou?'

The lady strange made answer meet,
And her voice was faint and sweet:—
'Have pity on my sore distress,
I scarce can speak for weariness:
Stretch forth thy hand, and have no fear!'
Said Christabel, 'How camest thou here?'
And the lady, whose voice was faint and sweet,
Did thus pursue her answer meet:—

'My sire is of a noble line,
And my name is Geraldine:
Five warriors seized me yestermorn,
Me, even me, a maid forlorn:
They choked my cries with force and fright,
And tied me on a palfrey white.
The palfrey was as fleet as wind,
And they rode furiously behind.

They spurred amain, their steeds were white:
And once we crossed the shade of night.
As sure as Heaven shall rescue me,
I have no thought what men they be;
Nor do I know how long it is
(For I have lain entranced I wis)
Since one, the tallest of the five,
Took me from the palfrey's back,
A weary woman, scarce alive.
Some muttered words his comrades spoke:
He placed me underneath this oak;
He swore they would return with haste;
Whither they went I cannot tell—
I thought I heard, some minutes past,
Sounds as of a castle bell.
Stretch forth thy hand' (thus ended she),
'And help a wretched maid to flee.'

Then Christabel stretched forth her hand,
And comforted fair Geraldine:
'O well, bright dame! may you command
The service of Sir Leoline;
And gladly our stout chivalry
Will he send forth and friends withal
To guide and guard you safe and free
Home to your noble father's hall.'

She rose: and forth with steps they passed
That strove to be, and were not, fast.
Her gracious stars the lady blest,
And thus spake on sweet Christabel:
'All our household are at rest,
The hall as silent as the cell;
Sir Leoline is weak in health,
And may not well awakened be,
And we will move as if in stealth,
And I beseech your courtesy,
This night, to share your couch with me.'

They crossed the moat, and Christabel
Took the key that fitted well;
A little door she opened straight,
All in the middle of the gate;
The gate that was ironed within and without,
Where an army in battle array had marched out.
The lady sank, belike through pain,
And Christabel with might and main
Lifted her up, a weary weight,
Over the threshold of the gate:
Then the lady rose again,
And moved, as she were not in pain.

So free from danger, free from fear,
They crossed the court: right glad they were.
And Christabel devoutly cried
To the lady by her side,
'Praise we the Virgin all divine
Who hath rescued thee from thy distress!'

'Alas, alas!' said Geraldine,
'I cannot speak for weariness.'
So free from danger, free from fear,
They crossed the court: right glad they were.

Outside her kennel, the mastiff old
Lay fast asleep, in moonshine cold.
The mastiff old did not awake,
Yet she an angry moan did make!
And what can ail the mastiff bitch?
Never till now she uttered yell
Beneath the eye of Christabel.
Perhaps it is the owlet's scritch:
For what can ail the mastiff bitch?

They passed the hall, that echoes still,
Pass as lightly as you will!
The brands were flat, the brands were dying,
Amid their own white ashes lying;
But when the lady passed, there came
A tongue of light, a fit of flame;
And Christabel saw the lady's eye,
And nothing else saw she thereby,
Save the boss of the shield of Sir Leoline tall,
Which hung in a murky old niche in the wall.
'O softly tread,' said Christabel,
'My father seldom sleepeth well.'

Sweet Christabel her feet doth bare,
And jealous of the listening air
They steal their way from stair to stair,
Now in glimmer, and now in gloom,
And now they pass the Baron's room,
As still as death, with stifled breath!
And now have reached her chamber door;
And now doth Geraldine press down
The rushes of the chamber floor.

The moon shines dim in the open air,
And not a moonbeam enters here.
But they without its light can see
The chamber carved so curiously,

Carved with figures strange and sweet,
All made out of the carver's brain,
For a lady's chamber meet:
The lamp with twofold silver chain
Is fastened to an angel's feet.

The silver lamp burns dead and dim;
But Christabel the lamp will trim.
She trimmed the lamp, and made it bright,
And left it swinging to and fro,
While Geraldine, in wretched plight,
Sank down upon the floor below.

'O weary lady, Geraldine,
I pray you, drink this cordial wine!
It is a wine of virtuous powers;
My mother made it of wild flowers.'

'And will your mother pity me,
Who am a maiden most forlorn?'
Christabel answered—'Woe is me!
She died the hour that I was born.
I have heard the grey-haired friar tell
How on her death-bed she did say,
That she should hear the castle-bell
Strike twelve upon my wedding-day.
O mother dear! that thou wert here!'
'I would,' said Geraldine, 'she were!'

But soon with altered voice, said she—
'Off, wandering mother! Peak and pine!
I have power to bid thee flee.'
Alas! what ails poor Geraldine?
Why stares she with unsettled eye?
Can she the bodiless dead espy?
And why with hollow voice cries she,
'Off, woman, off! this hour is mine—
Though thou her guardian spirit be,
Off, woman, off! 'tis given to me.'

Then Christabel knelt by the lady's side,
And raised to heaven her eyes so blue—
Alas! said she, this ghastly ride—

282

Dear lady! it hath wildered you!
The lady wiped her moist cold brow,
And faintly said, ' 'tis over now!'

Again the wild-flower wine she drank:
Her fair large eyes 'gan glitter bright,
And from the floor whereon she sank,
The lofty lady stood upright:
She was most beautiful to see,
Like a lady of a far countrée.

And thus the lofty lady spake—
'All they who live in the upper sky,
Do love you, holy Christabel!
And you love them, and for their sake
And for the good which me befel,
Even I in my degree will try,
Fair maiden, to requite you well.
But now unrobe yourself; for I
Must pray, ere yet in bed I lie.'

Quoth Christabel, 'So let it be!'
And as the lady bade, did she.
Her gentle limbs did she undress,
And lay down in her loveliness.

But through her brain of weal and woe
So many thoughts moved to and fro,
That vain it were her lids to close;
So half-way from the bed she rose,
And on her elbow did recline
To look at the lady Geraldine.

Beneath the lamp the lady bowed,
And slowly rolled her eyes around;
Then drawing in her breath aloud,
Like one that shuddered, she unbound
The cincture from beneath her breast:
Her silken robe, and inner vest,
Dropt to her feet, and full in view,
Behold! her bosom and half her side——
A sight to dream of, not to tell!
O shield her! shield sweet Christabel!

Yet Geraldine nor speaks nor stirs;
Ah! what a stricken look was hers!
Deep from within she seems half-way
To lift some weight with sick assay,
And eyes the maid and seeks delay;
Then suddenly, as one defied,
Collects herself in scorn and pride,
And lay down by the Maiden's side!—
And in her arms the maid she took,
      Ah wel-a-day!
And with low voice and doleful look
These words did say:
'In the touch of this bosom there worketh a spell,
Which is lord of thy utterance, Christabel!
Thou knowest to-night, and wilt know to-morrow,
This mark of my shame, this seal of my sorrow;
     But vainly thou warrest,
      For this is alone in
     Thy power to declare,
      That in the dim forest
     Thou heard'st a low moaning,
And found'st a bright lady, surpassingly fair;
And didst bring her home with thee in love and in charity
To shield her and shelter her from the damp air.'

DEJECTION: AN ODE

[WRITTEN APRIL 4, 1802]

> Late, late yestreen I saw the new Moon,
> With the old Moon in her arms;
> And I fear, I fear, my Master dear!
> We shall have a deadly storm.
> *Ballad of Sir Patrick Spence.*

WELL! If the Bard was weather-wise, who made
  The grand old ballad of Sir Patrick Spence,
  This night, so tranquil now, will not go hence
Unroused by winds, that ply a busier trade

Than those which mould yon cloud in lazy flakes,
Or the dull sobbing draft, that moans and rakes
Upon the strings of this Aeolian lute,
    Which better far were mute.
  For lo! the New-moon winter-bright!
  And overspread with phantom light,
  (With swimming phantom light o'erspread
  But rimmed and circled by a silver thread)
I see the old Moon in her lap, foretelling
  The coming-on of rain and squally blast.
And oh! that even now the gust were swelling,
  And the slant night-shower driving loud and fast!
Those sounds which oft have raised me, whilst they awed,
    And sent my soul abroad,
Might now perhaps their wonted impulse give,
Might startle this dull pain, and make it move and live!

A grief without a pang, void, dark, and drear,
  A stifled, drowsy, unimpassioned grief,
  Which finds no natural outlet, no relief,
    In word, or sigh, or tear—
O Lady! in this wan and heartless mood,
To other thoughts by yonder throstle woo'd,
  All this long eve, so balmy and serene,
Have I been gazing on the western sky,
  And its peculiar tint of yellow green:
And still I gaze—and with how blank an eye!
And those thin clouds above, in flakes and bars,
That give away their motion to the stars;
Those stars, that glide behind them or between,
Now sparkling, now bedimmed, but always seen:
Yon crescent Moon, as fixed as if it grew
In its own cloudless, starless lake of blue;
I see them all so excellently fair,
I see, not feel, how beautiful they are!

    My genial spirits fail;
    And what can these avail
To lift the smothering weight from off my breast?
    It were a vain endeavour,
    Though I should gaze for ever

On that green light that lingers in the west:
I may not hope from outward forms to win
The passion and the life, whose fountains are within.

O Lady! we receive but what we give,
And in our life alone does Nature live:
Ours is her wedding garment, ours her shroud!
   And would we aught behold, of higher worth,
Than that inanimate cold world allowed
To the poor loveless ever-anxious crowd,
   Ah! from the soul itself must issue forth
A light, a glory, a fair luminous cloud
      Enveloping the Earth—
And from the soul itself must there be sent
   A sweet and potent voice, of its own birth,
Of all sweet sounds the life and element!

O pure of heart! thou need'st not ask of me
What this strong music in the soul may be!
What, and wherein it doth exist,
This light, this glory, this fair luminous mist,
This beautiful and beauty-making power.
   Joy, virtuous Lady! Joy that ne'er was given,
Save to the pure, and in their purest hour,
Life, and Life's effluence, cloud at once and shower,

Joy, Lady! is the spirit and the power,
Which wedding Nature to us gives in dower
   A new Earth and new Heaven,
Undreamt of by the sensual and the proud—
Joy is the sweet voice, Joy the luminous cloud—
      We in ourselves rejoice!
And thence flows all that charms or ear or sight,
   All melodies the echoes of that voice,
All colours a suffusion from that light.

There was a time when, though my path was rough,
   This joy within me dallied with distress,
And all misfortunes were but as the stuff
   Whence Fancy made me dreams of happiness:
For hope grew round me, like the twining vine,
And fruits, and foliage, not my own, seemed mine.

But now afflictions bow me down to earth:
Nor care I that they rob me of my mirth;
  But oh! each visitation
Suspends what nature gave me at my birth,
  My shaping spirit of Imagination.
For not to think of what I needs must feel,
  But to be still and patient, all I can;
And haply by abstruse research to steal
  From my own nature all the natural man—
  This was my sole resource, my only plan:
Till that which suits a part infects the whole,
And now is almost grown the habit of my soul.

Hence, viper thoughts, that coil around my mind,
    Reality's dark dream!
I turn from you, and listen to the wind,
  Which long has raved unnoticed. What a scream
Of agony by torture lengthened out
That lute sent forth! Thou Wind, that rav'st without,
  Bare crag, or mountain-tarn, or blasted tree,
Or pine-grove whither woodman never clomb,
Or lonely house, long held the witches' home,
  Methinks were fitter instruments for thee,
Mad Lutanist! who in this month of showers,
Of dark-brown gardens, and of peeping flowers,
Mak'st Devils' yule, with worse than wintry song,
The blossoms, buds, and timorous leaves among.
  Thou Actor, perfect in all tragic sounds!
Thou mighty Poet, e'en to frenzy bold!
    What tell'st thou now about?
    'Tis of the rushing of an host in rout,
With groans of trampled men, with smarting wounds—
At once they groan with pain, and shudder with the cold!
But hush! there is a pause of deepest silence!
  And all that noise, as of a rushing crowd,
With groans, and tremulous shudderings—all is over—
It tells another tale, with sounds less deep and loud!
    A tale of less affright,
    And tempered with delight,

As Otway's self had framed the tender lay,—
  'Tis of a little child
  Upon a lonesome wild,
Not far from home, but she hath lost her way:
And now moans low in bitter grief and fear,
And now screams loud, and hopes to make her mother hear.

'Tis midnight, but small thoughts have I of sleep:
Full seldom may my friend such vigils keep!
Visit her, gentle Sleep! with wings of healing,
 And may this storm be but a mountain-birth,
May all the stars hang bright above her dwelling,
 Silent as though they watched the sleeping Earth!
  With light heart may she rise,
  Gay fancy, cheerful eyes,
 Joy lift her spirit, joy attune her voice;
To her may all things live, from pole to pole,
Their life the eddying of her living soul!
  O simple spirit, guided from above,
Dear Lady! friend devoutest of my choice,
Thus mayest thou ever, evermore rejoice.

FROST AT MIDNIGHT

 THE Frost performs its secret ministry,
Unhelped by any wind. The owlet's cry
Came loud—and hark, again! loud as before.
The inmates of my cottage, all at rest,
Have left me to that solitude, which suits
Abstruser musings: save that at my side
My cradled infant slumbers peacefully.
'Tis calm indeed! so calm, that it disturbs
And vexes meditation with its strange
And extreme silentness. Sea, hill, and wood,
This populous village! Sea, and hill, and wood,
With all the numberless goings-on of life,
Inaudible as dreams! the thin blue flame
Lies on my low-burnt fire, and quivers not;
Only that film, which fluttered on the grate,
Still flutters there, the sole unquiet thing.

Methinks, its motion in this hush of nature
Gives it dim sympathies with me who live,
Making it a companionable form,
Whose puny flaps and freaks the idling Spirit
By its own moods interprets, every where
Echo or mirror seeking of itself,
And makes a toy of Thought.

               But O! how oft,
How oft, at school, with most believing mind,
Presageful, have I gazed upon the bars,
To watch that fluttering *stranger*! and as oft
With unclosed lids, already had I dreamt
Of my sweet birth-place, and the old church-tower,
Whose bells, the poor man's only music, rang
From morn to evening, all the hot Fair-day,
So sweetly, that they stirred and haunted me
With a wild pleasure, falling on mine ear
Most like articulate sounds of things to come!
So gazed I, till the soothing things I dreamt,
Lulled me to sleep, and sleep prolonged my dreams!
And so I brooded all the following morn,
Awed by the stern preceptor's face, mine eye
Fixed with mock study on my swimming book:
Save if the door half opened, and I snatched
A hasty glance, and still my heart leaped up,
For still I hoped to see the *stranger's* face,
Townsman, or aunt, or sister more beloved,
My play-mate when we both were clothed alike!

    Dear Babe, that sleepest cradled by my side,
Whose gentle breathings, heard in this deep calm,
Fill up the interspersèd vacancies
And momentary pauses of the thought!
My babe so beautiful! it thrills my heart
With tender gladness, thus to look at thee,
And think that thou shalt learn far other lore,
And in far other scenes! For I was reared
In the great city, pent 'mid cloisters dim,
And saw nought lovely but the sky and stars.
But *thou*, my babe! shalt wander like a breeze

By lakes and sandy shores, beneath the crags
Of ancient mountain, and beneath the clouds,
Which image in their bulk both lakes and shores
And mountain crags: so shalt thou see and hear
The lovely shapes and sounds intelligible
Of that eternal language, which thy God
Utters, who from eternity doth teach
Himself in all, and all things in himself.
Great universal Teacher! he shall mould
Thy spirit, and by giving make it ask.

Therefore all seasons shall be sweet to thee,
Whether the summer clothe the general earth
With greenness, or the redbreast sit and sing
Betwixt the tufts of snow on the bare branch
Of mossy apple-tree, while the nigh thatch
Smokes in the sun-thaw; whether the eave-drops fall
Heard only in the trances of the blast,
Or if the secret ministry of frost
Shall hang them up in silent icicles,
Quietly shining to the quiet Moon.

YOUTH AND AGE

Verse, a breeze mid blossoms straying,
Where Hope clung feeding, like a bee—
Both were mine! Life went a-maying
    With Nature, Hope, and Poesy,
        When I was young!

When I was young?—Ah, woful When!
Ah! for the change 'twixt Now and Then!
This breathing house not built with hands,
This body that does me grievous wrong,
O'er aery cliffs and glittering sands,
How lightly then it flashed along:—
Like those trim skiffs, unknown of yore,
On winding lakes and rivers wide,
That ask no aid of sail or oar,
That fear no spite of wind or tide!

Nought cared this body for wind or weather
When Youth and I lived in't together.
Flowers are lovely; Love is flower-like;
Friendship is a sheltering tree;
O! the joys, that came down shower-like,
Of Friendship, Love, and Liberty,
     Ere I was old!

Ere I was old? Ah woful Ere,
Which tells me, Youth's no longer here!
O Youth! for years so many and sweet,
'Tis known that Thou and I were one,
I'll think it but a fond conceit—
It cannot be that Thou art gone!
Thy vesper-bell hath not yet toll'd:—
And thou wert aye a masker bold!
What strange disguise hast now put on,
To make believe that thou art gone?
I see these locks in silvery slips,
This drooping gait, this altered size:
But Spring-tide blossoms on thy lips,
And tears take sunshine from thine eyes!
Life is but thought: so think I will
That Youth and I are house-mates still

Dew-drops are the gems of morning,
But the tears of mournful eve!
Where no hope is, life's a warning
That only serves to make us grieve,
     When we are old:

That only serves to make us grieve
With oft and tedious taking-leave,
Like some poor nigh-related guest,
That may not rudely be dismist;
Yet hath outstay'd his welcome while,
And tells the jest without the smile.

WHAT IS LIFE?

RESEMBLES life what once was deem'd of light,
Too ample in itself for human sight?
An absolute self—an element ungrounded—
All that we see, all colours of all shade
By encroach of darkness made?—
Is very life by consciousness unbounded?
And all the thoughts, pains, joys of mortal breath,
A war-embrace of wrestling life and death?

EPITAPH

STOP, Christian passer-by!—Stop, child of God,
And read with gentle breast. Beneath this sod
A poet lies, or that which once seem'd he.
O, lift one thought in prayer for S.T.C.;
That he who many a year with toil of breath
Found death in life, may here find life in death!
Mercy for praise—to be forgiven for fame[1]
He ask'd, and hoped, through Christ. Do thou the same!

WORK WITHOUT HOPE

ALL Nature seems at work. Slugs leave their lair—
The bees are stirring—birds are on the wing—
And Winter slumbering in the open air,
Wears on his smiling face a dream of Spring!
And I the while, the sole unbusy thing,
Nor honey make, nor pair, nor build, nor sing.

Yet well I ken the banks where amaranths blow,
Have traced the founts whence streams of nectar flow.
Bloom, O ye amaranths! bloom for whom ye may,
For me ye bloom not! Glide rich streams away!
With lips unbrightened, wreathless brow I stroll:
And would you learn the spells that drowse my soul?
Work without Hope draws nectar in a sieve,
And Hope without an object cannot live.

[1] 'N.B. "for" in the sense of "instead of" ' [Coleridge's own note].

GEORGE GORDON BYRON

GEORGE GORDON BYRON, 6th Baron (1788–1824), son of Captain John Byron, a profligate, was educated at Harrow and Trinity College, Cambridge. From 1809 to 1811 he travelled abroad, visiting Portugal, Spain, Greece, and the Levant. On his return he published the first two cantos of *Childe Harold*. During the next four years appeared a series of narrative poems. In 1815 Byron married Anne Isabella Milbanke, an heiress, from whom he was separated in 1816. He left England, never to return, embittered by the strictures of what he regarded as a hypocritical society. In company part of the time with the Shelleys, he travelled to Switzerland and Venice, which, with Ravenna, Pisa, and Genoa, became his head-quarters. Canto iii of *Childe Harold* appeared in 1816, canto iv in 1818. Byron wrote the first five cantos of *Don Juan* in 1818–20; *Beppo* appeared in 1818. In 1822 appeared *The Vision of Judgment*, an outcome of his feud with Southey. In 1823 Byron set out to join the Greek insurgents, and died of fever at Missolonghi in April 1824.

G EORGE GORDON BYRON, one of the three English writers with a European reputation, the other two being Shakespeare and Oscar Wilde, was born in respectable lodgings in London on January 22nd, 1788, and died in Greece thirty-six years later, a major poet, a brilliant letter-writer, and a rich man, after a lifetime of unhappiness, travel, and love-affairs.

On neither side was the stock particularly stable. The Byrons were sensual, irresponsible, and charming. His uncle spent days fighting toy naval battles with his man-servant, and used to stage races of cockroaches up and down his own body. His father eloped with a married woman, and on her death, married the poet's mother for her money, which he soon spent.

The Gordons were passionate, unhappy, and cruel; many of them had ended on the scaffold. Catherine Gordon fell wildly in love with Captain Byron, a love that he did not return, and when their son was born, they had already separated, meeting only to have violent rows. Owing, probably, to the carelessness of the midwife, George Gordon Byron was born with a deformed foot.

At the age of ten he succeeded to the title and left Aberdeen Grammar School for the more select Harrow. Cambridge followed Harrow; and, soon after, came a Grand Tour of Portugal, Albania, and Greece, during which he wrote the first two cantos of *Childe Harold*, the publication of which in 1812 made him the literary lion of fashionable London.

At the beginning of 1815 he married an heiress, Miss Milbanke; but, as had been the case with Byron's own parents, the lady was more in love with him than he with her, and within little more than a year they had parted, and there was a scandal. Socially ruined, he left England for good to settle in Italy, where he wrote his greatest poem, *Don Juan*. In 1823 he was drawn into politics, into the struggle of the Greeks to win independence from Turkey. He left Italy to join the Greek Army at Missolonghi; three months later he caught a chill and died on April 19th, 1824. There is little doubt that the popular feeling aroused by his death was an important factor in determining the decision of the British Government to support the Greek cause.

The source of the poetic gift is a mystery: it is possible that, had Byron's foot been cured by modern surgery, or had his parents got on with each other, he would never have written a line. On the other hand, there are plenty of cripples and children of unhappy parents who write bad poetry or none. The study of a poet's biography or psychology or social status cannot explain why he writes well, but it can help us to understand why his poetry is of a particular kind, why he succeeds at one thing and fails at another: no study of Byron the man, for example, will ever explain the excellence of *A Vision of Judgment*, but it will partially explain why *A Vision of Judgment* is unlike the *Ode on the Intimations of Immortality in Early Childhood*.

Byron spent his early years in comparative poverty with a mother who alternately hit him and covered him with kisses, and a Calvinist nurse who spoke to him of Hell-fire and predestined damnation. Periodically there were visits from his father and parental rows. Unhappiness sharpens a child's wits, and he soon realized that his parents were violent and odd people, that his ancestors were violent and odd too, and that his deformity made him different from other children. Further, as usually happens when the parents are separated, he idealized the absent one, the father. Out of this background came the Byronic Hero: father made him handsome and dashing, mother made him passionate, nanny made him doomed, ancestors and the little lame foot made him aristocratic yet the bitter enemy of society.

He is a dream-figure and, like all dream-figures, even Dante's Beatrice, theatrical and a bit of a bore, which is why *Childe Harold* and *Manfred*, in spite of great incidental beauties, have not worn well. *Don Juan*, on the other hand, is a success because in that poem the hero is not really the hero at all, but a passive figure to whom certain experiences happen, a device enabling Byron to get down to the business for which his talents were really suited, a satirical panorama of the ruling classes of his time.

Byron was an egoist and, like all egoists, capable of falling in love with a succession of dream-figures, but incapable of genuine love or fidelity which accepts a personality completely. This did not prevent his writing good love poetry like *Hebrew Melodies*. In fact, nearly all love poetry is dream-figure poetry. Love may stimulate an artist indirectly and intensify his general vision of life; it does not often make him write love poems: their source is more commonly egoism or frustrated lust.

But Byron was not only an egoist; he was also acutely conscious of guilt and sin. Sometimes these two traits ran in harness, and their conjunction brought out the worst in him, both in his personal life and in his art; the self-conscious Satanism of his affairs, and the worst parts of *The Corsair*. At other times they were in opposition, and the conflict brought out the best; *Don Juan* and the Greek expedition.

Byron had one great virtue which everyone recognized in him from his earliest years; he had immense physical and moral courage. Even his worst errors were those of a brave man; he was never cautious or afraid of making a fool of himself either in his art or his life, nor was he a disingenuous careerist, qualities which distinguish him from a greater poet whom in many ways he resembles, Alexander Pope, who could have written the attack on Southey, but never the great lines against the Duke of Wellington.

No egoist can become a mature writer until he has learnt to recognize and to accept, a little ruefully perhaps, his egoism. When Byron had ceased to identify his moral sense with himself and had discovered how to extract the Byronic Satanism from his lonely hero and to turn it into the Byronic Irony which illuminated the whole setting, when he realized that he was a little ridiculous, but also not as odd as he had imagined, he became a great poet. For Byron was not really odd like Wordsworth; his experiences were those of the ordinary man. He had no unusual emotional or intellectual vision, and his distinctive contribution to English poetry was to be, not the defiant thunder of the rebel angel, but the speaking voice of the tolerant man-about-town.

His literary influences were Pope, Gay, Tom Moore, Hookham Frere, and perhaps Chateaubriand: from these he fashioned a style of poetry which for speed, wit, and moral seriousness combined with lack of pulpit pomposity is unique, and a lesson to all young would-be writers who are conscious of similar temptations and defects.

W. H. AUDEN.

WHEN WE TWO PARTED

WHEN we two parted
   In silence and tears,
Half broken-hearted
   To sever for years,
Pale grew thy cheek and cold,
   Colder thy kiss;
Truly that hour foretold
   Sorrow to this.

The dew of the morning
   Sunk chill on my brow—
It felt like the warning
   Of what I feel now.
Thy vows are all broken,
   And light is thy fame:
I hear thy name spoken,
   And share in its shame.

They name thee before me,
   A knell to mine ear;
A shudder comes o'er me—
   Why wert thou so dear?
They know not I knew thee,
   Who knew thee too well:—
Long, long shall I rue thee,
   Too deeply to tell.

In secret we met—
   In silence I grieve,
That thy heart could forget,
   Thy spirit deceive.
If I should meet thee
   After long years,
How should I greet thee?—
   With silence and tears.

SHE WALKS IN BEAUTY

She walks in beauty, like the night
   Of cloudless climes and starry skies;
And all that's best of dark and bright
   Meet in her aspect and her eyes:
Thus mellow'd to that tender light
   Which heaven to gaudy day denies.

One shade the more, one ray the less,
   Had half impair'd the nameless grace
Which waves in every raven tress,
   Or softly lightens o'er her face;
Where thoughts serenely sweet express
   How pure, how dear their dwelling-place.

And on that cheek, and o'er that brow,
   So soft, so calm, yet eloquent,
The smiles that win, the tints that glow,
   But tell of days in goodness spent,
A mind at peace with all below,
   A heart whose love is innocent!

(Hebrew Melodies)

OH! SNATCH'D AWAY IN BEAUTY'S BLOOM

Oh! snatch'd away in beauty's bloom,
On thee shall press no ponderous tomb;
   But on thy turf shall roses rear
   Their leaves, the earliest of the year;
And the wild cypress wave in tender gloom:

And oft by yon blue gushing stream
   Shall Sorrow lean her drooping head,
And feed deep thought with many a dream,
   And lingering pause and lightly tread;
   Fond wretch! as if her step disturb'd the dead!

Away! we know that tears are vain,
   That death nor heeds nor hears distress:
Will this unteach us to complain?
   Or make one mourner weep the less?
And thou—who tell'st me to forget,
Thy looks are wan, thine eyes are wet.

(Hebrew Melodies)

STANZAS FOR MUSIC

THERE be none of Beauty's daughters
  With a magic like thee;
And like music on the waters
  Is thy sweet voice to me:
When, as if its sound were causing
The charmed ocean's pausing,
The waves lie still and gleaming,
And the lull'd winds seem dreaming:

And the midnight moon is weaving
  Her bright chain o'er the deep;
Whose breast is gently heaving,
  As an infant's asleep:
So the spirit bows before thee,
To listen and adore thee;
With a full but soft emotion,
Like the swell of Summer's ocean.

SONNET ON CHILLON

ETERNAL Spirit of the chainless Mind!
  Brightest in dungeons, Liberty! thou art,
  For there thy habitation is the heart—
The heart which love of thee alone can bind;
And when thy sons to fetters are consign'd—
  To fetters, and the damp vault's dayless gloom,
  Their country conquers with their martyrdom,
And Freedom's fame finds wings on every wind.
Chillon! thy prison is a holy place,
  And thy sad floor an altar—for 'twas trod,
Until his very steps have left a trace
  Worn, as if thy cold pavement were a sod,
By Bonnivard! May none those marks efface!
  For they appeal from tyranny to God.

THE WANDERING OUTLAW

In my youth's summer I did sing of One,
The wandering outlaw of his own dark mind;
Again I seize the theme, then but begun,
And bear it with me, as the rushing wind
Bears the cloud onwards: in that Tale I find
The furrows of long thought, and dried-up tears,
Which, ebbing, leave a sterile track behind,
O'er which all heavily the journeying years
Plod the last sands of life,—where not a flower appears.

Since my young days of passion—joy, or pain,
Perchance my heart and harp have lost a string,
And both may jar: it may be, that in vain
I would essay as I have sung to sing.
Yet, though a dreary strain, to this I cling;
So that it wean me from the weary dream
Of selfish grief or gladness—so it fling
Forgetfulness around me—it shall seem
To me, though to none else, a not ungrateful theme.

He, who grown aged in this world of woe,
In deeds, not years, piercing the depths of life,
So that no wonder waits him; nor below
Can love or sorrow, fame, ambition, strife,
Cut to his heart again with the keen knife
Of silent, sharp endurance: he can tell
Why thought seeks refuge in lone caves, yet rife
With airy images, and shapes which dwell
Still unimpair'd, though old, in the soul's haunted cell.

'T is to create, and in creating live
A being more intense that we endow
With form our fancy, gaining as we give
The life we image, even as I do now.
What am I? Nothing: but not so art thou,
Soul of my thought! with whom I traverse earth,
Invisible but gazing, as I glow
Mix'd with thy spirit, blended with thy birth,
And feeling still with thee in my crush'd feelings' dearth.

Yet must I think less wildly:—I *have* thought
Too long and darkly, till my brain became,
In its own eddy boiling and o'erwrought,
A whirling gulf of phantasy and flame:
And thus, untaught in youth my heart to tame,
My springs of life were poison'd. 'Tis too late!
Yet am I changed; though still enough the same
In strength to bear what time cannot abate,
And feed on bitter fruits without accusing Fate.
(*Childe Harold's Pilgrimage*, canto iii, stanzas 3–7.)

WATERLOO

THERE was a sound of revelry by night,
And Belgium's capital had gather'd then
Her Beauty and her Chivalry, and bright
The lamps shone o'er fair women and brave men;
A thousand hearts beat happily; and when
Music arose with its voluptuous swell,
Soft eyes look'd love to eyes which spake again,
And all went merry as a marriage bell;
But hush! hark! a deep sound strikes like a rising knell!

Did ye not hear it?—No; 't was but the wind,
Or the car rattling o'er the stony street;
On with the dance! let joy be unconfined;
No sleep till morn, when Youth and Pleasure meet
To chase the glowing Hours with flying feet—
But hark!—that heavy sound breaks in once more,
As if the clouds its echo would repeat;
And nearer, clearer, deadlier than before!
Arm! Arm! it is—it is—the cannon's opening roar!

Within a window'd niche of that high hall
Sate Brunswick's fated chieftain; he did hear
That sound the first amidst the festival,
And caught its tone with Death's prophetic ear;
And when they smiled because he deem'd it near,
His heart more truly knew that peal too well
Which stretch'd his father on a bloody bier,
And roused the vengeance blood alone could quell;
He rush'd into the field, and, foremost fighting, fell.

Ah! then and there was hurrying to and fro,
And gathering tears, and tremblings of distress,
And cheeks all pale, which but an hour ago
Blush'd at the praise of their own loveliness;
And there were sudden partings, such as press
The life from out young hearts, and choking sighs
Which ne'er might be repeated; who could guess
If ever more should meet those mutual eyes,
Since upon night so sweet such awful morn could rise!

And there was mounting in hot haste: the steed,
The mustering squadron, and the clattering car,
Went pouring forward with impetuous speed,
And swiftly forming in the ranks of war;
And the deep thunder peal on peal afar;
And near, the beat of the alarming drum
Roused up the soldier ere the morning star;
While throng'd the citizens with terror dumb,
Or whispering, with white lips—'The foe! they come!
      they come!'

And wild and high the 'Camerons' gathering' rose!
The war-note of Lochiel, which Albyn's hills
Have heard, and heard, too, have her Saxon foes:—
How in the noon of night that pibroch thrills,
Savage and shrill! But with the breath which fills
Their mountain-pipe, so fill the mountaineers
With the fierce native daring which instils
The stirring memory of a thousand years,
And Evan's, Donald's fame rings in each clansman's ears!

And Ardennes waves above them her green leaves,
Dewy with nature's tear-drops as they pass,
Grieving, if aught inanimate e'er grieves,
Over the unreturning brave,—alas!
Ere evening to be trodden like the grass
Which now beneath them, but above shall grow
In its next verdure, when this fiery mass
Of living valour, rolling on the foe
And burning with high hope, shall moulder cold and low.

Last noon beheld them full of lusty life,
Last eve in Beauty's circle proudly gay,
The midnight brought the signal-sound of strife,
The morn the marshalling in arms,—the day
Battle's magnificently stern array!
The thunder-clouds close o'er it, which when rent
The earth is cover'd thick with other clay,
Which her own clay shall cover, heaped and pent,
Rider and horse,—friend, foe,—in one red burial blent!

(*Childe Harold's Pilgrimage*, canto iii, stanzas 21–8.)

FAME

FROM mighty wrongs to petty perfidy
Have I not seen what human things could do?
From the loud roar of foaming calumny
To the small whisper of the as paltry few,
And subtler venom of the reptile crew,
The Janus glance of whose significant eye,
Learning to lie with silence, would *seem* true,
And without utterance, save the shrug or sigh,
Deal round to happy fools its speechless obloquy.

But I have lived, and have not lived in vain:
My mind may lose its force, my blood its fire,
And my frame perish even in conquering pain;
But there is that within me which shall tire
Torture and Time, and breathe when I expire;
Something unearthly, which they deem not of,
Like the remember'd tone of a mute lyre,
Shall on their soften'd spirits sink, and move
In hearts all rocky now the late remorse of love.

(*Childe Harold's Pilgrimage*, canto iv, stanzas 136–7.)

ROLL ON, THOU DEEP AND DARK BLUE OCEAN

THERE is a pleasure in the pathless woods,
There is a rapture on the lonely shore,
There is society, where none intrudes,
By the deep Sea, and music in its roar:

I love not Man the less, but Nature more,
From these our interviews, in which I steal
From all I may be, or have been before,
To mingle with the Universe, and feel
What I can ne'er express, yet cannot all conceal.

Roll on, thou deep and dark blue Ocean—roll!
Ten thousand fleets sweep over thee in vain;
Man marks the earth with ruin—his control
Stops with the shore; upon the watery plain
The wrecks are all thy deed, nor doth remain
A shadow of man's ravage, save his own,
When, for a moment, like a drop of rain,
He sinks into thy depths with bubbling groan,
Without a grave, unknell'd, uncoffin'd, and unknown.

His steps are not upon thy paths,—thy fields
Are not a spoil for him,—thou dost arise
And shake him from thee; the vile strength he wields
For earth's destruction thou dost all despise,
Spurning him from thy bosom to the skies,
And send'st him, shivering in thy playful spray
And howling, to his Gods, where haply lies
His petty hope in some near port or bay,
And dashest him again to earth:—there let him lay.

The armaments which thunderstrike the walls
Of rock-built cities, bidding nations quake,
And monarchs tremble in their capitals,
The oak leviathans, whose huge ribs make
Their clay creator the vain title take
Of lord of thee, and arbiter of war—
These are thy toys, and, as the snowy flake,
They melt into thy yeast of waves, which mar
Alike the Armada's pride or spoils of Trafalgar.

Thy shores are empires, changed in all save thee—
Assyria, Greece, Rome, Carthage, what are they?
Thy waters wash'd them power while they were free,
And many a tyrant since; their shores obey
The stranger, slave, or savage; their decay

Has dried up realms to deserts:—not so thou;—
Unchangeable, save to thy wild waves' play,
Time writes no wrinkle on thine azure brow:
Such as creation's dawn beheld, thou rollest now.

Thou glorious mirror, where the Almighty's form
Glasses itself in tempests; in all time,—
Calm or convulsed, in breeze, or gale, or storm,
Icing the pole, or in the torrid clime
Dark-heaving—boundless, endless, and sublime,
The image of eternity, the throne
Of the Invisible; even from out thy slime
The monsters of the deep are made; each zone
Obeys thee; thou goest forth, dread, fathomless, alone.

(*Childe Harold's Pilgrimage*, canto iv, stanzas 78–83)

FRAGMENT

I WOULD to heaven that I were so much clay,
    As I am blood, bone, marrow, passion, feeling—
Because at least the past were pass'd away—
    And for the future—(but I write this reeling,
Having got drunk exceedingly to-day,
    So that I seem to stand upon the ceiling)
I say—the future is a serious matter—
    And so—for God's sake—hock and soda-water!

DEDICATION TO THE POET LAUREATE

BOB SOUTHEY! You're a poet—Poet-laureate,
    And representative of all the race;
Although 'tis true that you turn'd out a Tory at
    Last,—yours has lately been a common case;
And now, my Epic Renegade! what are ye at?
    With all the Lakers, in and out of place?
A nest of tuneful persons, to my eye
Like 'four and twenty Blackbirds in a pye;

'Which pye being open'd they began to sing'
   (This old song and new simile holds good),
'A dainty dish to set before the King,'
   Or Regent, who admires such kind of food;—
And Coleridge, too, has lately taken wing,
   But like a hawk encumber'd with his hood,—
Explaining metaphysics to the nation—
I wish he would explain his Explanation.

You, Bob! are rather insolent, you know,
   At being disappointed in your wish
To supersede all warblers here below,
   And be the only Blackbird in the dish;
And then you overstrain yourself, or so,
   And tumble downward like the flying fish
Gasping on deck, because you soar too high, Bob,
And fall, for lack of moisture quite a-dry, Bob!

And Wordsworth, in a rather long 'Excursion'
   (I think the quarto holds five hundred pages),
Has given a sample from the vasty version
   Of his new system to perplex the sages;
'Tis poetry—at least by his assertion,
   And may appear so when the dog-star rages—
And he who understands it would be able
To add a story to the Tower of Babel.

You—Gentlemen! by dint of long seclusion
   From better company, have kept your own
At Keswick, and, through still continued fusion
   Of one another's minds, at last have grown
To deem as a most logical conclusion,
   That Poesy has wreaths for you alone:
There is a narrowness in such a notion,
Which makes me wish you'd change your lakes for ocean.

. . . If, fallen in evil days on evil tongues,
   Milton appealed to the Avenger, Time,
If Time, the Avenger, execrates his wrongs,
   And makes the word 'Miltonic' mean 'sublime,'

He deign'd not to belie his soul in songs,
  Nor turn his very talent to a crime;
He did not loathe the Sire to laud the Son,
But closed the tyrant-hater he begun.

Think'st thou, could he—the blind Old Man—arise,
  Like Samuel from the grave, to freeze once more
The blood of monarchs with his prophecies,
  Or be alive again—again all hoar
With time and trials, and those helpless eyes,
  And heartless daughters—worn—and pale—and poor;
Would *he* adore a sultan? *he* obey
The intellectual eunuch Castlereagh?

Cold-blooded, smooth-faced, placid miscreant!
  Dabbling its sleek young hands in Erin's gore,
And thus for wider carnage taught to pant,
  Transferr'd to gorge upon a sister shore,
The vulgarest tool that Tyranny could want,
  With just enough of talent, and no more,
To lengthen fetters by another fix'd,
And offer poison long already mix'd.

An orator of such set trash of phrase
  Ineffably—legitimately vile,
That even its grossest flatterers dare not praise,
  Nor foes—all nations—condescend to smile;
Not even a sprightly blunder's spark can blaze
  From that Ixion grindstone's ceaseless toil,
That turns and turns to give the world a notion
Of endless torments and perpetual motion.

A bungler even in its disgusting trade,
  And botching, patching, leaving still behind
Something of which its masters are afraid,
  States to be curb'd, and thoughts to be confined,
Conspiracy or Congress to be made—
  Cobbling at manacles for all mankind——
A tinkering slave-maker, who mends old chains,
With God and man's abhorrence for its gains.

. . . Where shall I turn me not to *view* its bonds,
 For I will never *feel* them;—Italy!
Thy late reviving Roman soul desponds
 Beneath the lie this State-thing breathed o'er thee—
Thy clanking chain, and Erin's yet green wounds,
 Have voices—tongues to cry aloud for me.
Europe has slaves, allies, kings, armies still,
And Southey lives to sing them very ill.

Meantime, Sir Laureate, I proceed to dedicate,
 In honest simple verse, this song to you.
And, if in flattering strains I do not predicate,
 'Tis that I still retain my 'buff and blue;'
My politics as yet are all to educate:
 Apostasy's so fashionable, too,
To keep *one* creed's a task grown quite Herculean:
Is it not so, my Tory, Ultra-Julian?

VENICE, *September 16, 1818.*
(Dedication to *Don Juan.*)

POETICAL COMMANDMENTS

IF ever I should condescend to prose,
 I'll write poetical commandments, which
Shall supersede beyond all doubt all those
 That went before; in these I shall enrich
My text with many things that no one knows,
 And carry precept to the highest pitch:
I'll call the work 'Longinus o'er a Bottle,
Or, Every Poet his *own* Aristotle.'

Thou shalt believe in Milton, Dryden, Pope;
 Thou shalt not set up Wordsworth, Coleridge, Southey;
Because the first is crazed beyond all hope,
 The second drunk, the third so quaint and mouthy:
With Crabbe it may be difficult to cope,
 And Campbell's Hippocrene is somewhat drouthy:
Thou shalt not steal from Samuel Rogers, nor
Commit—flirtation with the muse of Moore.

(*Don Juan*, canto i, stanzas 204–5.)

AT THIRTY YEARS

'*Non ego hoc ferrem calida juventâ*
    Consule Planco,' Horace said, and so
Say I; by which quotation there is meant a
    Hint that some six or seven good years ago
(Long ere I dreamt of dating from the Brenta)
    I was most ready to return a blow,
And would not brook at all this sort of thing
In my hot youth—when George the Third was King.

But now at thirty years my hair is gray—
    (I wonder what it will be like at forty?
I thought of a peruke the other day—)
    My heart is not much greener; and, in short, I
Have squander'd my whole summer while 'twas May,
    And feel no more the spirit to retort; I
Have spent my life, both interest and principal,
And deem not, what I deem'd, my soul invincible.

No more—no more—Oh! never more on me
    The freshness of the heart can fall like dew,
Which out of all the lovely things we see
    Extracts emotions beautiful and new;
Hived in our bosoms like the bag o' the bee.
    Think'st thou the honey with those objects grew?
Alas! 'twas not in them, but in thy power
To double even the sweetness of a flower.
                    (*Don Juan*, canto i, stanzas 212–14.)

ROMANTIC TO BURLESQUE

NOTHING so difficult as a beginning
    In poesy, unless perhaps the end;
For oftentimes when Pegasus seems winning
    The race, he sprains a wing, and down we tend,
Like Lucifer when hurl'd from heaven for sinning;
    Our sin the same, and hard as his to mend,
Being pride, which leads the mind to soar too far,
Till our own weakness shows us what we are.

309

But time, which brings all beings to their level,
  And sharp Adversity, will teach at last
Man,—and, as we would hope,—perhaps the devil,
  That neither of their intellects are vast:
While youth's hot wishes in our red veins revel,
  We know not this—the blood flows on too fast:
But as the torrent widens towards the ocean,
We ponder deeply on each past emotion.

As boy, I thought myself a clever fellow,
  And wish'd that others held the same opinion;
They took it up when my days grew more mellow,
  And other minds acknowledged my dominion:
Now my sere fancy 'falls into the yellow
  Leaf,' and Imagination droops her pinion,
And the sad truth which hovers o'er my desk
Turns what was once romantic to burlesque.

                    (*Don Juan*, canto iv, stanzas 1–3.)

THE ISLES OF GREECE

The isles of Greece, the isles of Greece!
  Where burning Sappho loved and sung,
Where grew the arts of war and peace,
  Where Delos rose, and Phœbus sprung!
Eternal summer gilds them yet,
But all, except their sun, is set.

The Scian and the Teian muse,
  The hero's harp, the lover's lute,
Have found the fame your shores refuse:
  Their place of birth alone is mute
To sounds which echo further west
Than your sires' 'Islands of the Blest.'

The mountains look on Marathon—
  And Marathon looks on the sea;
And musing there an hour alone,
  I dream'd that Greece might still be free;
For standing on the Persians' grave,
I could not deem myself a slave.

A king sate on the rocky brow
  Which looks o'er sea-born Salamis;
And ships, by thousands, lay below,
  And men in nations;—all were his!
He counted them at break of day—
And when the sun set where were they?

And where are they? and where art thou,
  My country? On thy voiceless shore
The heroic lay is tuneless now—
  The heroic bosom beats no more!
And must thy lyre, so long divine,
Degenerate into hands like mine?

'Tis something, in the dearth of fame,
  Though link'd among a fetter'd race,
To feel at least a patriot's shame,
  Even as I sing, suffuse my face;
For what is left the poet here?
For Greeks a blush—for Greece a tear.

Must *we* but weep o'er days more blest?
  Must *we* but blush?—Our fathers bled.
Earth! render back from out thy breast
  A remnant of our Spartan dead!
Of the three hundred grant but three,
To make a new Thermopylae!

What, silent still? and silent all?
  Ah! no;—the voices of the dead
Sound like a distant torrent's fall,
  And answer, 'Let one living head,
But one arise,—we come, we come!'
'Tis but the living who are dumb.

In vain—in vain: strike other chords;
  Fill high the cup with Samian wine!
Leave battles to the Turkish hordes,
  And shed the blood of Scio's vine!
Hark! rising to the ignoble call—
How answers each bold Bacchanal!

You have the Pyrrhic dance as yet;
    Where is the Pyrrhic phalanx gone?
Of two such lessons, why forget
    The nobler and the manlier one?
You have the letters Cadmus gave—
Think ye he meant them for a slave?

Fill high the bowl with Samian wine!
    We will not think of themes like these!
It made Anacreon's song divine:
    He served—but served Polycrates—
A tyrant; but our masters then
Were still, at least, our countrymen.

The tyrant of the Chersonese
    Was freedom's best and bravest friend;
That tyrant was Miltiades!
    Oh! that the present hour would lend
Another despot of the kind!
Such chains as his were sure to bind.

Fill high the bowl with Samian wine!
    On Suli's rock, and Parga's shore,
Exists the remnant of a line
    Such as the Doric mothers bore;
And there, perhaps, some seed is sown,
The Heracleidan blood might own.

Trust not for freedom to the Franks—
    They have a king who buys and sells;
In native swords, and native ranks,
    The only hope of courage dwells:
But Turkish force, and Latin fraud,
Would break your shield, however broad.

Fill high the bowl with Samian wine!
    Our virgins dance beneath the shade—
I see their glorious black eyes shine;
    But gazing on each glowing maid,
My own the burning tear-drop laves,
To think such breasts must suckle slaves.

Place me on Sunium's marbled steep,
　　Where nothing, save the waves and I,
May hear our mutual murmurs sweep;
　　There, swan-like, let me sing and die:
A land of slaves shall ne'er be mine—
Dash down yon cup of Samian wine!
　　　　　　　　　　(*Don Juan*, canto iii.)

THE DEATH OF HAIDÉE

SHE woke at length, but not as sleepers wake,
　　Rather the dead, for life seem'd something new,
A strange sensation which she must partake
　　Perforce, since whatsoever met her view
Struck not on memory, though a heavy ache
　　Lay at her heart, whose earliest beat still true
Brought back the sense of pain without the cause,
For, for a while, the furies made a pause.

She look'd on many a face with vacant eye,
　　On many a token without knowing what;
She saw them watch her without asking why,
　　And reck'd not who around her pillow sat;
Not speechless, though she spoke not; not a sigh
　　Relieved her thoughts; dull silence and quick chat
Were tried in vain by those who served; she gave
No sign, save breath, of having left the grave.

Her handmaids tended, but she heeded not;
　　Her father watch'd, she turn'd her eyes away;
She recognised no being, and no spot,
　　However dear or cherish'd in their day;
They changed from room to room, but all forgot,
　　Gentle, but without memory she lay;
At length those eyes, which they would fain be weaning
Back to old thoughts, wax'd full of fearful meaning.

And then a slave bethought her of a harp;
　　The harper came, and tuned his instrument;
At the first notes, irregular and sharp,
　　On him her flashing eyes a moment bent,

313

Then to the wall she turn'd as if to warp
  Her thoughts from sorrow through her heart re-sent,
And he began a long low island song
Of ancient days, ere tyranny grew strong.

Anon her thin wan fingers beat the wall
  In time to his old tune; he changed the theme,
And sung of love; the fierce name struck through all
  Her recollection; on her flash'd the dream
Of what she was, and is, if ye could call
  To be so being; in a gushing stream
The tears rush'd forth from her o'erclouded brain,
Like mountain mists at length dissolved in rain.

Short solace, vain relief!—thought came too quick,
  And whirl'd her brain to madness; she arose
As one who ne'er had dwelt among the sick,
  And flew at all she met, as on her foes;
But no one ever heard her speak or shriek,
  Although her paroxysm drew towards its close;—
Hers was a phrensy which disdain'd to rave,
Even when they smote her, in the hope to save.

Yet she betray'd at times a gleam of sense;
  Nothing could make her meet her father's face,
Though on all other things with looks intense
  She gazed, but none she ever could retrace;
Food she refused, and raiment; no pretence
  Avail'd for either; neither change of place,
Nor time, nor skill, nor remedy, could give her
Senses to sleep—the power seem'd gone for ever.

Twelve days and nights she wither'd thus; at last,
  Without a groan, or sigh, or glance, to show
A parting pang, the spirit from her passed:
  And they who watch'd her nearest could not know
The very instant, till the change that cast
  Her sweet face into shadow, dull and slow,
Glazed o'er her eyes—the beautiful, the black—
Oh! to possess such lustre—and then lack!

She died, but not alone; she held within
   A second principle of life, which might
Have dawned a fair and sinless child of sin;
   But closed its little being without light,
And went down to the grave unborn, wherein
   Blossom and bough lie wither'd with one blight;
In vain the dews of Heaven descend above
The bleeding flower and blasted fruit of love.

Thus lived—thus died she; never more on her
   Shall sorrow light, or shame. She was not made
Through years or moons the inner weight to bear,
   Which colder hearts endure till they are laid
By age in earth: her days and pleasures were
   Brief, but delightful—such as had not staid
Long with her destiny; but she sleeps well
By the sea-shore, whereon she loved to dwell.

That isle is now all desolate and bare,
   Its dwellings down, its tenants pass'd away;
None but her own and father's grave is there,
   And nothing outward tells of human clay;
Ye could not know where lies a thing so fair,
   No stone is there to show, no tongue to say,
What was; no dirge, except the hollow sea's,
Mourns o'er the beauty of the Cyclades.
            (*Don Juan*, canto iv, stanzas 62–72.)

ON WELLINGTON

OH, Wellington! (or 'Villainton') for Fame
   Sounds the heroic syllables both ways;
France could not even conquer your great name,
   But punn'd it down to this facetious phrase—
Beating or beaten she will laugh the same,)
   You have obtain'd great pensions and much praise:
Glory like yours should any dare gainsay,
Humanity would rise, and thunder 'Nay!'

*   *   *   *   *

Though Britain owes (and pays you too) so much,
  Yet Europe doubtless owes you greatly more:
You have repair'd Legitimacy's crutch,
  A prop not quite so certain as before:
The Spanish, and the French, as well as Dutch,
  Have seen, and felt, how strongly you *restore*;
And Waterloo has made the world your debtor
(I wish your bards would sing it rather better).

* * * * *

I am no flatterer—you've supp'd full of flattery:
  They say you like it too—'tis no great wonder.
He whose whole life has been assault and battery,
  At last may get a little tired of thunder;
And swallowing eulogy much more than satire, he
  May like being praised for every lucky blunder,
Call'd 'Saviour of the Nations'—not yet saved,
And 'Europe's Liberator'—still enslaved.

I've done. Now go and dine from off the plate
  Presented by the Prince of the Brazils,
And send the sentinel before your gate
  A slice or two from your luxurious meals:
He fought, but has not fed so well of late.
  Some hunger, too, they say the people feels:—
There is no doubt that you deserve your ration,
But pray give back a little to the nation.

* * * * *

Never had mortal man such opportunity,
  Except Napoleon, or abused it more:
You might have freed fallen Europe from the unity
  Of tyrants, and been blest from shore to shore:
And *now*—what *is* your fame? Shall the Muse tune it ye?
  Now—that the rabble's first vain shouts are o'er?
Go! hear it in your famish'd country's cries!
Behold the world! and curse your victories!

              (*Don Juan*, canto ix, stanzas 1, 3, 5, 7 & 9.)

JUAN IN ENGLAND

Don Juan had got out on Shooter's Hill;
　Sunset the time, the place the same declivity
Which looks along that vale of good and ill
　Where London streets ferment in full activity;
While everything around was calm and still,
　Except the creak of wheels, which on their pivot he
Heard,—and that bee-like, bubbling, busy hum
Of cities, that boil over with their scum:—

I say, Don Juan, wrapt in contemplation,
　Walk'd on behind his carriage, o'er the summit,
And lost in wonder of so great a nation,
　Gave way to 't, since he could not overcome it.
'And here,' he cried, 'is Freedom's chosen station;
　Here peals the people's voice, nor can entomb it
Racks, prisons, inquisitions; resurrection
Awaits it, each new meeting or election.

'Here are chaste wives, pure lives; here people pay
　But what they please; and if that things be dear,
'Tis only that they love to throw away
　Their cash, to show how much they have a year.
Here laws are all inviolate; none lay
　Traps for the traveller; every highway's clear;
Here'—he was interrupted by a knife,
With—'Damn your eyes! your money or your life!'—

These freeborn sounds proceeded from four pads
　In ambush laid, who had perceived him loiter
Behind his carriage; and, like handy lads,
　Had seized the lucky hour to reconnoitre,
In which the heedless gentleman who gads
　Upon the road, unless he prove a fighter,
May find himself within that isle of riches
Exposed to lose his life as well as breeches.

317

Juan, who did not understand a word
   Of English, save their shibboleth, 'God damn!'
And even that he had so rarely heard,
   He sometimes thought 't was only their 'Salām,'
Or 'God be with you!'—and 't is not absurd
   To think so: for half English as I am
(To my misfortune), never can I say
I heard them wish 'God with you,' save that way;—

Juan yet quickly understood their gesture,
   And being somewhat choleric and sudden,
Drew forth a pocket-pistol from his vesture,
   And fired it into one assailant's pudding—
Who fell, as rolls an ox o'er in his pasture,
   And roar'd out, as he writhed his native mud in,
Unto his nearest follower or henchman,
'Oh Jack! I'm floored by that 'ere bloody Frenchman!'

On which Jack and his train set off at speed,
   And Juan's suite, late scatter'd at a distance,
Came up, all marvelling at such a deed,
   And offering, as usual, late assistance.
Juan, who saw the moon's late minion bleed
   As if his veins would pour out his existence,
Stood calling out for bandages and lint,
And wish'd he had been less hasty with his flint.

'Perhaps,' thought he, 'it is the country's wont
   To welcome foreigners in this way: now
I recollect some innkeepers who don't
   Differ, except in robbing with a bow,
In lieu of a bare blade and brazen front.
   But what is to be done? I can't allow
The fellow to lie groaning on the road:
So take him up; I'll help you with the load.'

But ere they could perform this pious duty,
   The dying man cried, 'Hold! I've got my gruel!
Oh! for a glass of *max*! We've miss'd our booty;
   Let me die where I am!' And as the fuel
Of life shrunk in his heart, and thick and sooty

318

The drops fell from his death-wound, and he drew ill
His breath,—he from his swelling throat untied
A kerchief, crying 'Give Sal that!'—and died.

(*Don Juan*, canto xi, stanzas 8–16.)

GEORGE THE THIRD

LET's skip a few short years of hollow peace,
    Which peopled earth no better, hell as wont,
And heaven none—they form the tyrant's lease,
    With nothing but new names subscribed upon 't;
'T will one day finish: meantime they increase,
    'With seven heads and ten horns,' and all in front,
Like Saint John's foretold beast; but ours are born
Less formidable in the head than horn.

In the first year of freedom's second dawn
    Died George the Third; although no tyrant, one
Who shielded tyrants, till each sense withdrawn
    Left him nor mental nor external sun:
A better farmer ne'er brush'd dew from lawn,
    A worse king never left a realm undone!
He died—but left his subjects still behind,
One half as mad—and t'other no less blind.

He died! his death made no great stir on earth:
    His burial made some pomp; there was profusion
Of velvet, gilding, brass, and no great dearth
    Of aught but tears—save those shed by collusion.
For these things may be bought at their true worth;
    Of elegy there was the due infusion—
Bought also; and the torches, cloaks, and banners,
Heralds, and relics of old Gothic manners,

Form'd a sepulchral melodrame. Of all
    The fools who flock'd to swell or see the show,
Who cared about the corpse? The funeral
    Made the attraction, and the black the woe.
There throbb'd not there a thought which pierced the pall;
    And when the gorgeous coffin was laid low,
It seem'd the mockery of hell to fold
The rottenness of eighty years in gold.

319

. . . 'Look to the earth, I said, and say again:
When this old, blind, mad, helpless, weak, poor worm
Began in youth's first bloom and flush to reign,
The world and he both wore a different form,
And much of earth and all the watery plain
Of ocean call'd him king: through many a storm
His isles had floated on the abyss of time;
For the rough virtues chose them for their clime.

'He came to his sceptre young; he leaves it old:
Look to the state in which he found his realm,
And left it; and his annals too behold,
How to a minion first he gave the helm;
How grew upon his heart a thirst for gold,
The beggar's vice, which can but overwhelm
The meanest hearts; and for the rest, but glance
Thine eye along America and France.

''Tis true, he was a tool from first to last
(I have the workmen safe); but as a tool
So let him be consumed. From out the past
Of ages, since mankind have known the rule
Of monarchs—from the bloody rolls amass'd
Of sin and slaughter—from the Cæsar's school,
Take the worst pupil; and produce a reign
More drench'd with gore, more cumber'd with the slain.

'He ever warr'd with freedom and the free:
Nations as men, home subjects, foreign foes,
So that they utter'd the word "Liberty!"
Found George the Third their first opponent. Whose
History was ever stain'd as his will be
With national and individual woes?
I grant his household abstinence; I grant
His neutral virtues, which most monarchs want;

'I know he was a constant consort; own
He was a decent sire, and middling lord.
All this is much, and most upon a throne;
As temperance, if at Apicius' board,
Is more than at an anchorite's supper shown.

I grant him all the kindest can accord;
And this was well for him, but not for those
Millions who found him what oppression chose.

'The New World shook him off; the Old yet groans
   Beneath what he and his prepared, if not
Completed: he leaves heirs on many thrones
   To all his vices, without what begot
Compassion for him—his tame virtues; drones
   Who sleep, or despots who have now forgot
A lesson which shall be re-taught them, wake
Upon the thrones of earth; but let them quake!'
                  (*The Vision of Judgment.*)

SO, WE'LL GO NO MORE A ROVING

So, we'll go no more a roving
   So late into the night,
Though the heart be still as loving,
   And the moon be still as bright.

For the sword outwears its sheath,
   And the soul wears out the breast,
And the heart must pause to breathe,
   And love itself have rest.

Though the night was made for loving,
   And the day returns too soon,
Yet we'll go no more a roving
   By the light of the moon.

ON THIS DAY I COMPLETE MY THIRTY-SIXTH YEAR

'Tis time this heart should be unmoved,
   Since others it hath ceased to move:
Yet, though I cannot be beloved,
   Still let me love!

My days are in the yellow leaf;
   The flowers and fruits of love are gone;
The worm, the canker, and the grief
   Are mine alone!

The fire that on my bosom preys
  Is lone as some volcanic isle;
No torch is kindled at its blaze—
    A funeral pile.

The hope, the fear, the jealous care,
  The exalted portion of the pain
And power of love, I cannot share,
    But wear the chain.

But 'tis not *thus*—and 'tis not *here*—
  Such thoughts should shake my soul, nor *now*,
Where glory decks the hero's bier,
    Or binds his brow.

The sword, the banner, and the field,
  Glory and Greece, around me see!
The Spartan, borne upon his shield,
    Was not more free.

Awake! (not Greece—she *is* awake!)
  Awake, my spirit! Think through *whom*
Thy life-blood tracks its parent lake,
    And then strike home!

Tread those reviving passions down,
  Unworthy manhood!—unto thee
Indifferent should the smile or frown
    Of beauty be.

If thou regrett'st thy youth, *why live*?
  The land of honourable death
Is here:—up to the field, and give
    Away thy breath!

Seek out—less often sought than found
  A soldier's grave, for thee the best;
Then look around, and choose thy ground,
    And take thy rest.

PERCY BYSSHE SHELLEY

PERCY BYSSHE SHELLEY (1792–1822), was educated at Eton and University College, Oxford. From Oxford he was sent down in 1811 after circulating a pamphlet on *The Necessity of Atheism*. In the same year he married Harriet Westbrook, who was aged sixteen, and from whom he separated after three years of a wandering life. He left England in 1814 with Mary Wollstonecraft, to whom he was married after the unhappy Harriet had, in 1816, drowned herself in the Serpentine. Shelley's *Alastor* was published in 1816. In the same year began his friendship with Byron. In 1818 Shelley left England for Italy. He visited Byron at Venice, and in the same year wrote the *Stanzas written in dejection*. Early in 1819, stirred to indignation by the political events at home, he wrote *The Mask of Anarchy*, an indictment of Castlereagh's administration. He also published *Peter Bell the Third*, a satire on Wordsworth. The same year, 1819, saw the publication of *The Cenci* and the composition of his great lyrical drama, *Prometheus Unbound* (1820). At the end of 1819 the Shelleys moved to Pisa, and it was now that he wrote some of his best-known lyrics, including the *Ode to the West Wind*, *To a Skylark*, and *The Cloud*. On 8 July 1822 he was drowned, in his thirtieth year, while sailing near Spezzia.

THE early years of Shelley, which were so fruitful in personal calamities, did not establish him among the unmistakable poets of the age. In his boyish state of intellectual excitement, darting here and there as new ideas and speculations attracted him, he poured forth abundance of prose and verse with little suspicion that the art of writing needed severe study and selectiveness. His first important composition, *Queen Mab*, the production of his twentieth year, exhibited not merely the critic of human bondage but also the too facile follower of the new versification, much better understood by his model Robert Southey. To the end of his life, Shelley was inclined to slide into poetical declamation and to merit the implied censure of Keats, under the advice of curbing magnanimity and loading every rift with ore.

'Mr. Shelley's defects as a poet are obscurity, inartificial and yet not natural economy, violation of custom, and too great a sameness and gratuitousness of image and metaphor.' The criticism was that of a friend, who also complained of the excessively metaphysical content of Shelley's biggest attempts. It is now being revealed that many of this poet's strangest and seemingly most superficial figures are his presentations of scientific fact as it was accepted in his day. The electrical apparatus with which he diverted his leisure at Eton was in its way the source of later imagery, intended to have an exact significance; but without a key few will perceive in *The Witch of Atlas* more than a wandering from caprice to caprice. Even Mary Shelley described that poem as 'a brilliant congregation of ideas such as his senses gathered, and his fancy coloured, during his rambles in the sunny land he so much loved'. He himself warns us not to 'unveil my Witch', but without some detection of her place in nature, among his 'genii of the elements', she may be sent into the wilderness of man's vanished dreamings, like any other child of Idlesse.

In every poet of extensive and incisive performance, there is found a characteristic recurrence of symbol and allusion. A life-work of serious aim is naturally developed from a first choice of things that matter to the individual, alike as subjects and as means of statement. A fabric is provided, upon the firmness of which all changes of mood and occasion and artistic adventure may ultimately rest. With Shelley this deep, distinguishing, persisting frame of principal terms is obvious. Once past his preliminary manœuvres—even in those—he displays a world of his own, intensely his own:

> Within that circle none durst walk but he.

There is no likelihood of his verse being ascribed to Francis Bacon, or even to his 'nearest mate' Samuel Taylor Coleridge:

> Glorious shapes have life in thee,
> Earth, and all earth's company;
>   Living globes which ever throng
> Thy deep chasms and wildernesses;
>   And green worlds that glide along;

> And swift stars with flashing tresses;
> And icy moons most cold and bright,
> And mighty suns beyond the night,
> Atoms of intensest light.

And still, without bating a jot of gratitude for a spirit so majestical, so radiant, we may wish that Shelley had had time or inclination to discipline his recurrence to certain terms. If, every time he was tempted to introduce into his verse, by way of illustration, an Eagle, a Serpent, a Wreck, a Sunrise, there had come a Worm into the area of his manuscript, then perhaps the horrid warning would have made him more naturally economical of his giant forms, and those would not have become too familiar and miscellaneous in their reference. Few of our poets have been fit to talk in terms of Eagles: Shelley was one. But he was careless of his final power (poor Shelley, so little read or commended in his life) when he could indifferently apply the Eagle to William Godwin (or as some say Leigh Hunt), to a cosmic vision, and roughly speaking to something in every poem of any length that he wrote. In the same free way Shelley rang upon his epithets until their best, their most vivid appearances were dimmed by the cloud of repetitions. The quotation above begins with one of them, 'glorious', and he could seldom resist that Shelleyan word wherever the least chance appeared; similarly with 'gentle', 'azure', 'aethereal', 'dizzy', 'liquid', and a hundred more.

So far, then, the charge-sheet against this poet includes unnecessary, or at least inhuman obscurity, and artistic monotony. Perhaps the present is not a very well-chosen moment for an attack on a poet because he is difficult to decipher. Still, if poets will appeal to an audience of more than one, they must expect a little heckling on their less explicit proposals. Shelley expected it, and ascribed it to dullness, but the man has yet to be born who can at first hearing expound the opening couplet of *Epipsychidion*:

> Sweet Spirit! Sister of that orphan one,
> Whose empire is the name thou weepest on.

Not many can do more than admire the poet, when Panthea presents

> A sphere, which is as many thousand spheres,
> Solid as crystal, yet through all its mass
> Flow, as through empty space, music and light;
> Ten thousand orbs involving and involved,
> Purple and azure, white, and green, and golden,
> Sphere within sphere; and every space between
> Peopled with unimaginable shapes,
> Such as ghosts dream dwell in the lampless deep,
> Yet each inter-transpicuous. . . .

'Such as ghosts dream'; suddenly Shelley is beating the compact poets in effective laconics. Perhaps he is surpassing Coleridge in the dream question; Coleridge had written of 'that strange thing, an infant's dream'. But, to revert to the other point—Shelley's facility with his own essential colours; was it a fatal facility?

I should answer, not so fatal as indolent reviewers would wish. It would be so comfortable to clear away so many of the old authors. Some have even suggested a total conflagration, a holocaust of all that was formerly written, in order that the world's great age might begin anew (but Shelley wrote that). Others would be happy with a compromise. In the ordinary way, Shelley is not discarded because he repeats himself so often (like several of my contemporaries) in his large, rapid passion for central beliefs. His detail is often subject to easy prediction, but often not. In *Prometheus Unbound* (Act iv) Panthea continues the astonishing conversation of which a few lines have been quoted, and certainly she uses some expected Shelleyana, 'swords of azure fire, or golden spears', orb, abyss, cavern, 'unimagined gems'. But she breaks away to mention 'armorial beasts round which death laughed', shapes 'split, jammed in the hard black deep', 'the jaggèd alligator', and certain 'monarch beasts' which tenanted the primeval world

> till the blue globe
> Wrapped deluge round it like a cloak, and they
> Yelled, gasped, and were abolished.

Shelley believed in the potentialities of long poems as agents in modern civilization, as addresses to the general heart of man. Even *The Mask of Anarchy*, which he intended for popular reading and democratic stimulus, is a lengthy item. In that startling appeal, it is true, he resorted to a plainer mode of speech than most of his longer poems show: he refused to consider dragoons as vultures, but more usefully observed,

> Every woman in the land
> Will point at them as they stand—
> They will hardly dare to greet
> Their acquaintance in the street.

And in general, though it is too often forgotten, Shelley could write with the keenest simplicity and still be Shelley. His contribution to the English inheritance of *immediate* poems is as great as anybody's. As he neared the close of his life, not altogether unaware of the event (for indeed there was something supernatural about Shelley), he relied considerably on a style of poem which did not need unriddling. Goethe has given us an immense parable of Faust, and yet he has quite as sure a place in our devotion for his brief 'dying falls' of music, which spell enchantment and purity; so it is with Goethe's disciple Shelley. Shelley's ambitious myths of freedom, suffering, darkness, lucidity are for the few; his melodies of feeling and acceptance are for the many, and perhaps, could he revisit this plane of existence, he would commend the preference of the majority. What he wrote in dejection has delighted more of us than all that he invented in projection. We may not follow him through his altitudes, but the knowledge, the evidence that he outsoars the shadow of our night adds compulsion, friendship, love to his simplest songs of human concern.

Critics of Shelley have hurled their turnips at him, on occasion, with boomerang effect. There is an inherited idea that he was without humour, which might not be of much consequence, if it were only related to his biography;

but it spoils the access to his poetry. Shelley did not take up every subject for verse in the solemn, neutral way which we scholiasts are liable to ascribe to him. Much has been written on his address *To a Skylark*, and much without proper recognition of his actual occasion. Shelley, in that poem, was *talking*, at least at the point of departure. He was capable, there, of joking (for there is a free state of mind, which may not resemble the comic spirit of the *New Yorker*, or perhaps it may—but it is truly random); he did not start as an automatic machine delivering the weight and fortune of skylarks.

> Hail to thee, blithe Spirit!

A skylark: but he refuses to believe the natural historian's limited definition. 'Bird thou never wert.' He also rejects the Shakespearean location of Heaven, or else is willing to play upon the neighbourhood ('Hark, hark, the lark at Heaven's gate sings') with his

> That *from Heaven, or near it,*
> Pourest thy full heart. . . .

The numerous comparisons in the poem, which have been treated like realistic equations, are in fact so much talk, the gestures of a mind in play, the sportive balloon-flying of one who does not really wish to catch his lark.

There are several surviving protests against Shelley. He ought at all costs to have finished *The Boat on the Serchio*, a poem which, so far as it goes, seems to combine all his mystery and concept of our universe, and all his social grace and observation. When he set out on his last voyage, *mutatis mutandis* this is how he went; the biographers need not deplore the want of a log-book or a dictaphone; here is the voice, stir, and fascination of Shelley putting out to sea. Another complaint is that he set sail at such an inauspicious moment. He was, at the time, entering upon a new chapter of intellectual astuteness. In his last long poem, *The Triumph of Life*, though the confusion and agglomeration of his younger manner have not quite disappeared, there is a sinewy and ironic force which makes him jump almost a century. But apart from that, he was beginning to live, and to cease to be 'at war with life'. Disturbance still embittered him, but exceptionally: a faultless ease was stealing upon his poetry,

> The clearest echoes of the hills,
> The softest notes of falling rills,
> The melodies of birds and bees,
> The murmurings of summer seas,
> And pattering rain, and breathing dew,
> And airs of evening; and it knew
> That seldom-heard mysterious sound
> Which, driven on its diurnal round,
> As it floats through boundless day,
> Our world enkindles on its way.

E. BLUNDEN.

From ALASTOR

EARTH, ocean, air, belovèd brotherhood!
If our great Mother has imbued my soul
With aught of natural piety to feel
Your love, and recompense the boon with mine;
If dewy morn, and odorous noon, and even,
With sunset and its gorgeous ministers,
And solemn midnight's tingling silentness;
If autumn's hollow sighs in the sere wood,
And winter robing with pure snow and crowns
Of starry ice the grey grass and bare boughs;
If spring's voluptuous pantings when she breathes
Her first sweet kisses, have been dear to me;
If no bright bird, insect, or gentle beast
I consciously have injured, but still loved
And cherished these my kindred; then forgive
This boast, belovèd brethren, and withdraw
No portion of your wonted favour now!

Mother of this unfathomable world!
Favour my solemn song, for I have loved
Thee ever, and thee only; I have watched
Thy shadow, and the darkness of thy steps,

And my heart ever gazes on the depth
Of thy deep mysteries. I have made my bed
In charnels and on coffins, where black death
Keeps record of the trophies won from thee,
Hoping to still these obstinate questionings
Of thee and thine, by forcing some lone ghost,
Thy messenger, to render up the tale
Of what we are. In lone and silent hours,
When night makes a weird sound of its own stillness,
Like an inspired and desperate alchymist
Staking his very life on some dark hope,
Have I mixed awful talk and asking looks
With my most innocent love, until strange tears
Uniting with those breathless kisses, made
Such magic as compels the charmèd night
To render up thy charge: . . . and, though ne'er yet
Thou hast unveiled thy inmost sanctuary,
Enough from incommunicable dream,
And twilight phantasms, and deep noon-day thought,
Has shone within me, that serenely now
And moveless, as a long-forgotten lyre
Suspended in the solitary dome
Of some mysterious and deserted fane,
I wait thy breath, Great Parent, that my strain
May modulate with murmurs of the air,
And motions of the forests and the sea,
And voice of living beings, and woven hymns
Of night and day, and the deep heart of man.

STANZAS.—APRIL, 1814

AWAY! the moor is dark beneath the moon,
  Rapid clouds have drunk the last pale beam of even:
Away! the gathering winds will call the darkness soon,
  And profoundest midnight shroud the serene lights of
    heaven.

Pause not! The time is past! Every voice cries, Away!
  Tempt not with one last tear thy friend's ungentle mood:
Thy lover's eye, so glazed and cold, dares not entreat thy stay:
  Duty and dereliction guide thee back to solitude.

Away, away! to thy sad and silent home;
    Pour bitter tears on its desolated hearth;
Watch the dim shades as like ghosts they go and come,
    And complicate strange webs of melancholy mirth.

The leaves of wasted autumn woods shall float around thine
      head:
    The blooms of dewy spring shall gleam beneath thy feet:
But thy soul or this world must fade in the frost that binds
      the dead,
    Ere midnight's frown and morning's smile, ere thou and
      peace may meet.

The cloud shadows of midnight possess their own repose,
    For the weary winds are silent, or the moon is in the deep:
Some respite to its turbulence unresting ocean knows;
    Whatever moves, or toils, or grieves, hath its appointed
      sleep.

Thou in the grave shalt rest—yet till the phantoms flee
    Which that house and heath and garden made dear to
      thee erewhile,
Thy remembrance, and repentance, and deep musings are
      not free
    From the music of two voices and the light of one sweet
      smile.

TO WORDSWORTH

Poet of Nature, thou hast wept to know
That things depart which never may return:
Childhood and youth, friendship and love's first glow,
Have fled like sweet dreams, leaving thee to mourn.
These common woes I feel. One loss is mine
Which thou too feel'st, yet I alone deplore.
Thou wert as a lone star, whose light did shine
On some frail bark in winter's midnight roar:
Thou hast like to a rock-built refuge stood
Above the blind and battling multitude:

In honoured poverty thy voice did weave
Songs consecrate to truth and liberty,—
Deserting these, thou leavest me to grieve,
Thus having been, that thou shouldst cease to be.

WHEN THE LAMP IS SHATTERED

When the lamp is shattered
The light in the dust lies dead—
　When the cloud is scattered
The rainbow's glory is shed.
　When the lute is broken,
Sweet tones are remembered not;
　When the lips have spoken,
Loved accents are soon forgot.

　As music and splendour
Survive not the lamp and the lute,
　The heart's echoes render
No song when the spirit is mute:—
　No song but sad dirges,
Like the wind through a ruined cell,
　Or the mournful surges
That ring the dead seaman's knell.

　When hearts have once mingled
Love first leaves the well-built nest;
　The weak one is singled
To endure what it once possessed.
　O Love! who bewailest
The frailty of all things here,
　Why choose you the frailest
For your cradle, your home, and your bier?

　Its passions will rock thee
As the storms rock the ravens on high;
　Bright reason will mock thee,
Like the sun from a wintry sky.
　From thy nest every rafter
Will rot, and thine eagle home
　Leave thee naked to laughter,
When leaves fall and cold winds come.

LOVE

One word is too often profaned
    For me to profane it,
One feeling too falsely disdained
    For thee to disdain it;
One hope is too like despair
    For prudence to smother,
And pity from thee more dear
    Than that from another.

I can give not what men call love,
    But wilt thou accept not
The worship the heart lifts above
    And the Heavens reject not,—
The desire of the moth for the star,
    Of the night for the morrow,
The devotion to something afar
    From the sphere of our sorrow?

TO ———

Music, when soft voices die,
Vibrates in the memory—
Odours, when sweet violets sicken,
Live within the sense they quicken.

Rose leaves, when the rose is dead,
Are heaped for the belovèd's bed;
And so thy thoughts, when thou art gone,
Love itself shall slumber on.

From ADONAIS

I weep for Adonais—he is dead!
O, weep for Adonais! though our tears
Thaw not the frost which binds so dear a head!
And thou, sad Hour, selected from all years
To mourn our loss, rouse thy obscure compeers,
And teach them thine own sorrow, say: 'With me
Died Adonais; till the Future dares
Forget the Past, his fate and fame shall be
An echo and a light unto eternity!'

*   *   *   *   *

Thus ceased she: and the mountain shepherds came,
Their garlands sere, their magic mantles rent;
The Pilgrim of Eternity, whose fame
Over his living head like Heaven is bent,
An early but enduring monument,
Came, veiling all the lightnings of his song
In sorrow; from her wilds Ierne sent
The sweetest lyrist of her saddest wrong,
And Love taught Grief to fall like music from his tongue.

Midst others of less note, came one frail Form,
A phantom among men; companionless
As the last cloud of an expiring storm
Whose thunder is its knell; he, as I guess,
Had gazed on Nature's naked loveliness,
Actaeon-like, and now he fled astray
With feeble steps o'er the world's wilderness,
And his own thoughts, along that rugged way,
Pursued, like raging hounds, their father and their prey.

A pardlike Spirit beautiful and swift—
A Love in desolation masked;—a Power
Girt round with weakness;—it can scarce uplift
The weight of the superincumbent hour;
It is a dying lamp, a falling shower,
A breaking billow;—even whilst we speak
Is it not broken? On the withering flower
The killing sun smiles brightly: on a cheek
The life can burn in blood, even while the heart may break.

* * * * *

Peace, peace! he is not dead, he doth not sleep—
He hath awakened from the dream of life—
'Tis we, who, lost in stormy visions, keep
With phantoms an unprofitable strife,
And in mad trance, strike with our spirit's knife
Invulnerable nothings.—*We* decay
Like corpses in a charnel; fear and grief
Convulse us and consume us day by day,
And cold hopes swarm like worms within our living clay.

He has outsoared the shadow of our night;
Envy and calumny and hate and pain,
And that unrest which men miscall delight,
Can touch him not and torture not again;
From the contagion of the world's slow stain
He is secure, and now can never mourn
A heart grown cold, a head grown gray in vain;
Nor, when the spirit's self has ceased to burn,
With sparkless ashes load an unlamented urn.

He lives, he wakes—'tis Death is dead, not he;
Mourn not for Adonais.—Thou young Dawn,
Turn all thy dew to splendour, for from thee
The spirit thou lamentest is not gone;
Ye caverns and ye forests, cease to moan!
Cease, ye faint flowers and fountains, and thou Air,
Which like a mourning veil thy scarf hadst thrown
O'er the abandoned Earth, now leave it bare
Even to the joyous stars which smile on its despair!

He is made one with Nature: there is heard
His voice in all her music, from the moan
Of thunder to the song of night's sweet bird;
He is a presence to be felt and known
In darkness and in light, from herb and stone,
Spreading itself where'er that Power may move
Which has withdrawn his being to its own;
Which wields the world with never-wearied love,
Sustains it from beneath, and kindles it above.

He is a portion of the loveliness
Which once he made more lovely: he doth bear
His part, while the one Spirit's plastic stress
Sweeps through the dull dense world, compelling there
All new successions to the forms they wear;
Torturing th' unwilling dross that checks its flight
To its own likeness, as each mass may bear;
And bursting in its beauty and its might
From trees and beasts and men into the Heaven's light.

*   *   *   *   *

The One remains, the many change and pass;
Heaven's light forever shines, Earth's shadows fly;
Life, like a dome of many-coloured glass,
Stains the white radiance of Eternity,
Until Death tramples it to fragments.—Die,
If thou wouldst be with that which thou dost seek!
Follow where all is fled!—Rome's azure sky,
Flowers, ruins, statues, music, words, are weak
The glory they transfuse with fitting truth to speak.

*   *   *   *   *

The breath whose might I have invoked in song
Descends on me; my spirit's bark is driven,
Far from the shore, far from the trembling throng
Whose sails were never to the tempest given;
The massy earth and spherèd skies are riven!
I am borne darkly, fearfully, afar;
Whilst, burning through the inmost veil of Heaven,
The soul of Adonais, like a star,
Beacons from the abode where the Eternal are.

OZYMANDIAS

I MET a traveller from an antique land
Who said: Two vast and trunkless legs of stone
Stand in the desert. Near them, on the sand,
Half sunk, a shattered visage lies, whose frown,
And wrinkled lip, and sneer of cold command,
Tell that its sculptor well those passions read
Which yet survive, stamped on these lifeless things,
The hand that mocked them, and the heart that fed:
And on the pedestal these words appear:
'My name is Ozymandias, king of kings:
Look on my works, ye Mighty, and despair!'
Nothing beside remains. Round the decay
Of that colossal wreck, boundless and bare,
The lone and level sands stretch far away.

THE WORLD'S GREAT AGE BEGINS ANEW

THE world's great age begins anew,
    The golden years return,
    The earth doth like a snake renew

Her winter weeds outworn:
Heaven smiles, and faiths and empires gleam,
Like wrecks of a dissolving dream.

A brighter Hellas rears its mountains
    From waves serener far;
A new Peneus rolls his fountains
    Against the morning star.
Where fairer Tempes bloom, there sleep
Young Cyclads on a sunnier deep.

A loftier Argo cleaves the main,
    Fraught with a later prize;
Another Orpheus sings again,
    And loves, and weeps, and dies.
A new Ulysses leaves once more
Calypso for his native shore.

Oh, write no more the tale of Troy,
    If earth Death's scroll must be!
Nor mix with Laian rage the joy
    Which dawns upon the free:
Although a subtler Sphinx renew
Riddles of death Thebes never knew.

Another Athens shall arise,
    And to remoter time
Bequeath, like sunset to the skies,
    The splendour of its prime;
And leave, if nought so bright may live,
All earth can take or Heaven can give.

Saturn and Love their long repose
    Shall burst, more bright and good
Than all who fell, than One who rose,
    Than many unsubdued:
Not gold, not blood, their altar dowers,
But votive tears and symbol flowers.

Oh, cease! must hate and death return?
    Cease! must men kill and die?
Cease! drain not to its dregs the urn

Of bitter prophecy.
The world is weary of the past,
Oh, might it die or rest at last!

(Chorus from *Hellas*.)

SONG TO THE MEN OF ENGLAND

MEN of England, wherefore plough
For the lords who lay ye low?
Wherefore weave with toil and care
The rich robes your tyrants wear?

Wherefore feed, and clothe, and save,
From the cradle to the grave,
Those ungrateful drones who would
Drain your sweat—nay, drink your blood?

Wherefore, Bees of England, forge
Many a weapon, chain, and scourge,
That these stingless drones may spoil
The forced produce of your toil?

Have ye leisure, comfort, calm,
Shelter, food, love's gentle balm?
Or what is it ye buy so dear
With your pain and with your fear?

The seed ye sow, another reaps;
The wealth ye find, another keeps;
The robes ye weave, another wears;
The arms ye forge, another bears.

Sow seed,—but let no tyrant reap;
Find wealth,—let no impostor heap;
Weave robes,—let not the idle wear;
Forge arms,—in your defence to bear.

Shrink to your cellars, holes, and cells;
In halls ye deck another dwells.
Why shake the chains ye wrought? Ye see
The steel ye tempered glance on ye.

With plough and spade, and hoe and loom,
Trace your grave, and build your tomb,
And weave your winding-sheet, till fair
England be your sepulchre!

SONNET: ENGLAND IN 1819

An old, mad, blind, despised, and dying king,—
Princes, the dregs of their dull race, who flow
Through public scorn,—mud from a muddy spring,—
Rulers who neither see, nor feel, nor know,
But leech-like to their fainting country cling,
Till they drop, blind in blood, without a blow,—
A people starved and stabbed in the untilled field,—
An army, which liberticide and prey
Makes as a two-edged sword to all who wield,—
Golden and sanguine laws which tempt and slay;
Religion Christless, Godless—a book sealed;
A Senate,—Time's worst statute unrepealed,—
Are graves, from which a glorious Phantom may
Burst, to illumine our tempestuous day.

ODE TO THE WEST WIND

I

O wild West Wind, thou breath of Autumn's being,
Thou, from whose unseen presence the leaves dead
Are driven, like ghosts from an enchanter fleeing,

Yellow, and black, and pale, and hectic red,
Pestilence-stricken multitudes: O thou,
Who chariotest to their dark wintry bed

The wingèd seeds, where they lie cold and low,
Each like a corpse within its grave, until
Thine azure sister of the Spring shall blow

Her clarion o'er the dreaming earth, and fill
(Driving sweet buds like flocks to feed in air)
With living hues and odours plain and hill:

Wild Spirit, which art moving everywhere;
Destroyer and preserver; hear, oh, hear!

II

Thou on whose stream, mid the steep sky's commotion,
Loose clouds like earth's decaying leaves are shed,
Shook from the tangled boughs of Heaven and Ocean,

Angels of rain and lightning: there are spread
On the blue surface of thine aëry surge,
Like the bright hair uplifted from the head

Of some fierce Maenad, even from the dim verge
Of the horizon to the zenith's height,
The locks of the approaching storm. Thou dirge

Of the dying year, to which this closing night
Will be the dome of a vast sepulchre,
Vaulted with all thy congregated might

Of vapours, from whose solid atmosphere
Black rain, and fire, and hail will burst: oh, hear!

III

Thou who didst waken from his summer dreams
The blue Mediterranean, where he lay,
Lulled by the coil of his crystálline streams,

Beside a pumice isle in Baiae's bay,
And saw in sleep old palaces and towers
Quivering within the wave's intenser day,

All overgrown with azure moss and flowers
So sweet, the sense faints picturing them! Thou
For whose path the Atlantic's level powers

Cleave themselves into chasms, while far below
The sea-blooms and the oozy woods which wear
The sapless foliage of the ocean, know

Thy voice, and suddenly grow gray with fear,
And tremble and despoil themselves: oh, hear!

IV

If I were a dead leaf thou mightest bear;
If I were a swift cloud to fly with thee;
A wave to pant beneath thy power, and share

The impulse of thy strength, only less free
Than thou, O uncontrollable! If even
I were as in my boyhood, and could be

340

'The comrade of thy wanderings over Heaven,
As then, when to outstrip thy skiey speed
Scarce seemed a vision; I would ne'er have striven

As thus with thee in prayer in my sore need.
Oh, lift me as a wave, a leaf, a cloud!
I fall upon the thorns of life! I bleed!

A heavy weight of hours has chained and bowed
One too like thee: tameless, and swift, and proud.

v

Make me thy lyre, even as the forest is:
What if my leaves are falling like its own!
The tumult of thy mighty harmonies

Will take from both a deep, autumnal tone,
Sweet though in sadness. Be thou, Spirit fierce,
My spirit! Be thou me, impetuous one!

Drive my dead thoughts over the universe
Like withered leaves to quicken a new birth!
And, by the incantation of this verse,

Scatter, as from an unextinguished hearth
Ashes and sparks, my words among mankind!
Be through my lips to unawakened earth

The trumpet of a prophecy! O, Wind,
If Winter comes, can Spring be far behind?

LINES TO AN INDIAN AIR

I ARISE from dreams of thee
In the first sweet sleep of night,
When the winds are breathing low,
And the stars are shining bright:
I arise from dreams of thee,
And a spirit in my feet
Hath led me—who knows how?
To thy chamber window, Sweet!

341

The wandering airs they faint
On the dark, the silent stream—
The Champak odours fail
Like sweet thoughts in a dream;
The nightingale's complaint,
It dies upon her heart;—
As I must on thine,
Oh, belovèd as thou art!

Oh lift me from the grass!
I die! I faint! I fail!
Let thy love in kisses rain
On my lips and eyelids pale.
My cheek is cold and white, alas!
My heart beats loud and fast;—
Oh! press it to thine own again,
Where it will break at last.

STANZAS WRITTEN IN DEJECTION

THE sun is warm, the sky is clear,
　　The waves are dancing fast and bright,
Blue isles and snowy mountains wear
　　The purple noon's transparent might,
　　The breath of the moist earth is light,
Around its unexpanded buds;
　　Like many a voice of one delight,
The winds, the birds, the ocean floods,
The City's voice itself is soft like Solitude's.

I see the Deep's untrampled floor
　　With green and purple seaweeds strown;
I see the waves upon the shore,
　　Like light dissolved in star-showers, thrown:
　　I sit upon the sands alone,—
The lightning of the noontide ocean
　　Is flashing round me, and a tone
Arises from its measured motion,
How sweet! did any heart now share in my emotion.

Alas! I have nor hope nor health,
  Nor peace within nor calm around,
Nor that content surpassing wealth
  The sage in meditation found,
  And walked with inward glory crowned—
Nor fame, nor power, nor love, nor leisure.
  Others I see whom these surround—
Smiling they live, and call life pleasure;—
To me that cup has been dealt in another measure.

Yet now despair itself is mild,
  Even as the winds and waters are;
I could lie down like a tired child,
  And weep away the life of care
  Which I have borne and yet must bear,
Till death like sleep might steal on me,
  And I might feel in the warm air
My cheek grow cold, and hear the sea
Breathe o'er my dying brain its last monotony.

Some might lament that I were cold,
  As I, when this sweet day is gone,
Which my lost heart, too soon grown old,
  Insults with this untimely moan;
  They might lament—for I am one
Whom men love not,—and yet regret,
  Unlike this day, which, when the sun
Shall on its stainless glory set,
Will linger, though enjoyed, like joy in memory yet.

THE QUESTION

I DREAMED that, as I wandered by the way,
  Bare Winter suddenly was changed to Spring,
And gentle odours led my steps astray,
  Mixed with a sound of waters murmuring
Along a shelving bank of turf, which lay
  Under a copse, and hardly dared to fling
Its green arms round the bosom of the stream,
But kissed it and then fled, as thou mightest in dream.

343

There grew pied wind-flowers and violets,
  Daisies, those pearled Arcturi of the earth,
The constellated flower that never sets;
  Faint oxslips; tender bluebells, at whose birth
The sod scarce heaved; and that tall flower that wets—
  Like a child, half in tenderness and mirth—
Its mother's face with Heaven's collected tears,
When the low wind, its playmate's voice, it hears.

And in the warm hedge grew lush eglantine,
  Green cowbind and the moonlight-coloured may,
And cherry-blossoms, and white cups, whose wine
  Was the bright dew yet drained not by the day;
And wild roses, and ivy serpentine,
  With its dark buds and leaves, wandering astray;
And flowers azure, black, and streaked with gold,
Fairer than any wakened eyes behold.

And nearer to the river's trembling edge
  There grew broad flag-flowers, purple pranked with white,
And starry river buds among the sedge,
  And floating water-lilies, broad and bright,
Which lit the oak that overhung the hedge
  With moonlight beams of their own watery light;
And bulrushes, and reeds of such deep green
As soothed the dazzled eye with sober sheen.

Methought that of these visionary flowers
  I made a nosegay, bound in such a way
That the same hues, which in their natural bowers
  Were mingled or opposed, the like array
Kept these imprisoned children of the Hours
  Within my hand,—and then, elate and gay,
I hastened to the spot whence I had come,
That I might there present it!—Oh! to whom?

PROMETHEUS

MONARCH of Gods and Dæmons, and all Spirits
But One, who throng those bright and rolling worlds
Which Thou and I alone of living things
Behold with sleepless eyes! regard this Earth

Made multitudinous with thy slaves, whom thou
Requitest for knee-worship, prayer, and praise,
And toil, and hecatombs of broken hearts,
With fear and self-contempt and barren hope.
Whilst me, who am thy foe, eyeless in hate,
Hast thou made reign and triumph to thy scorn,
O'er mine own misery and thy vain revenge.
Three thousand years of sleep-unsheltered hours,
And moments aye divided by keen pangs
Till they seemed years, torture and solitude,
Scorn and despair,—these are mine empire:—
More glorious far than that which thou surveyest
From thine unenvied throne, O Mighty God!
Almighty, had I deigned to share the shame
Of thine ill tyranny, and hung not here
Nailed to this wall of eagle-baffling mountain,
Black, wintry, dead, unmeasured; without herb,
Insect, or beast, or shape or sound of life.
Ah me! alas, pain, pain ever, for ever!

No change, no pause, no hope! Yet I endure.
I ask the Earth, have not the mountains felt?
I ask yon Heaven, the all-beholding Sun,
Has it not seen? The Sea, in storm or calm,
Heaven's ever-changing Shadow, spread below,
Have its deaf waves not heard my agony?
Ah me! alas, pain, pain ever, for ever!

The crawling glaciers pierce me with the spears
Of their moon-freezing crystals, the bright chains
Eat with their burning cold into my bones.
Heaven's wingèd hound, polluting from thy lips
His beak in poison not his own, tears up
My heart; and shapeless sights come wandering by,
The ghastly people of the realm of dream,
Mocking me: and the Earthquake-fiends are charged
To wrench the rivets from my quivering wounds
When the rocks split and close again behind:
While from their loud abysses howling throng
The genii of the storm, urging the rage
Of whirlwind, and afflict me with keen hail.

And yet to me welcome is day and night,
Whether one breaks the hoar frost of the morn,
Or starry, dim, and slow, the other climbs
The leaden-coloured east; for then they lead
The wingless, crawling hours, one among whom
—As some dark Priest hales the reluctant victim—
Shall drag thee, cruel King, to kiss the blood
From these pale feet, which then might trample thee
If they disdained not such a prostrate slave.
Disdain! Ah no! I pity thee. What ruin
Will hunt thee undefended through wide Heaven!
How will thy soul, cloven to its depth with terror,
Gape like a hell within! I speak in grief,
Not exultation, for I hate no more,
As then ere misery made me wise. The curse
Once breathed on thee I would recall. Ye Mountains,
Whose many-voicèd Echoes, through the mist
Of cataracts, flung the thunder of that spell!
Ye icy Springs, stagnant with wrinkling frost,
Which vibrated to hear me, and then crept
Shuddering through India! Thou serenest Air,
Through which the Sun walks burning without beams!
And ye swift Whirlwinds, who on poisèd wings
Hung mute and moveless o'er yon hushed abyss,
As thunder, louder than your own, made rock
The orbèd world! If then my words had power,
Though I am changed so that aught evil wish
Is dead within; although no memory be
Of what is hate, let them not lose it now!
What was that curse? for ye all heard me speak.

(Prometheus, Act i, ll. 1–73.)

ON A POET'S LIPS I SLEPT

On a poet's lips I slept
Dreaming like a love-adept
In the sound his breathing kept;
Nor seeks nor finds he mortal blisses,
But feeds on the aëreal kisses

346

Of shapes that haunt thought's wildernesses.
He will watch from dawn to gloom
The lake-reflected sun illume
The yellow bees in the ivy-bloom,
Nor heed nor see, what things they be;
But from these create he can
Forms more real than living man,
Nurslings of immortality!
One of these awakened me,
And I sped to succour thee.

(Prometheus, Act i, ll. 737–51.)

LIFE OF LIFE

LIFE of Life! thy lips enkindle
  With their love the breath between them;
And thy smiles before they dwindle
  Make the cold air fire; then screen them
In those looks, where whoso gazes
Faints, entangled in their mazes.

Child of Light! thy limbs are burning
  Through the vest which seems to hide them;
As the radiant lines of morning
  Through the clouds ere they divide them;
And this atmosphere divinest
Shrouds thee wheresoe'er thou shinest.

Fair are others; none beholds thee,
  But thy voice sounds low and tender
Like the fairest, for it folds thee
  From the sight, that liquid splendour,
And all feel, yet see thee never,
As I feel now, lost for ever!

Lamp of Earth! where'er thou movest
  Its dim shapes are clad with brightness,
And the souls of whom thou lovest

347

Walk upon the winds with lightness,
Till they fail, as I am failing,
Dizzy, lost, yet unbewailing!
(*Prometheus*, Act. ii, Scene 5.)

PROMETHEUS
(Spirit of the Hour loquitur)

I WANDERING went

Among the haunts and dwellings of mankind,
And first was disappointed not to see
Such mighty change as I had felt within
Expressed in outward things; but soon I looked,
And behold, thrones were kingless, and men walked
One with the other even as spirits do,
None fawned, none trampled; hate, disdain, or fear,
Self-love or self-contempt, on human brows
No more inscribed, as o'er the gate of hell,
'All hope abandon ye who enter here;'
None frowned, none trembled, none with eager fear
Gazed on another's eye of cold command,
Until the subject of a tyrant's will
Became, worse fate, the abject of his own,
Which spurred him, like an outspent horse, to death.
None wrought his lips in truth-entangling lines
Which smiled the lie his tongue disdained to speak;
None, with firm sneer, trod out in his own heart
The sparks of love and hope till there remained
Those bitter ashes, a soul self-consumed,
And the wretch crept a vampire among men,
Infecting all with his own hideous ill;
None talked that common, false, cold, hollow talk
Which makes the heart deny the *yes* it breathes,
Yet question that unmeant hypocrisy
With such a self-mistrust as has no name.
And women, too, frank, beautiful, and kind
As the free heaven which rains fresh light and dew
On the wide earth, past; gentle radiant forms,
From custom's evil taint exempt and pure;
Speaking the wisdom once they could not think,
Looking emotions once they feared to feel,

348

And changed to all which once they dared not be,
Yet being now, made earth like heaven; nor pride,
Nor jealousy, nor envy, nor ill shame,
The bitterest of those drops of treasured gall,
Spoilt the sweet taste of the nepenthe, love.

Thrones, altars, judgement-seats, and prisons; wherein,
And beside which, by wretched men were borne
Sceptres, tiaras, swords, and chains, and tomes
Of reasoned wrong, glozed on by ignorance,
Were like those monstrous and barbaric shapes,
The ghosts of a no-more-remembered fame,
Which, from their unworn obelisks, look forth
In triumph o'er the palaces and tombs
Of those who were their conquerors: mouldering round,
These imaged to the pride of kings and priests
A dark yet mighty faith, a power as wide
As is the world it wasted, and are now
But an astonishment; even so the tools
And emblems of its last captivity,
Amid the dwellings of the peopled earth,
Stand, not o'erthrown, but unregarded now.
And those foul shapes, abhorred by god and man,—
Which, under many a name and many a form
Strange, savage, ghastly, dark and execrable,
Were Jupiter, the tyrant of the world;
And which the nations, panic-stricken, served
With blood, and hearts broken by long hope, and love
Dragged to his altars soiled and garlandless,
And slain amid men's unreclaiming tears,
Flattering the thing they feared, which fear was hate,—
Frown, mouldering fast, o'er their abandoned shrines:
The painted veil, by those who were, called life,
Which mimicked, as with colours idly spread,
All men believed or hoped, is torn aside;
The loathsome mask has fallen, the man remains
Sceptreless, free, uncircumscribed, but man
Equal, unclassed, tribeless, and nationless,
Exempt from awe, worship, degree, the king
Over himself; just, gentle, wise: but man

Passionless?——no, yet free from guilt or pain,
Which were, for his will made or suffered them,
Nor yet exempt, though ruling them like slaves,
From chance, and death, and mutability,
The clogs of that which else might oversoar
The loftiest star of unascended heaven,
Pinnacled dim in the intense inane.

(*Prometheus*, end of Act iii.)

BEATRICE'S LAST WORDS

Beatrice.   Farewell, my tender brother. Think
Of our sad fate with gentleness, as now:
And let mild, pitying thoughts lighten for thee
Thy sorrow's load. Err not in harsh despair,
But tears and patience. One thing more, my child:
For thine own sake be constant to the love
Thou bearest us; and to the faith that I,
Though wrapped in a strange cloud of crime and shame,
Lived ever holy and unstained. And though
Ill tongues shall wound me, and our common name
Be as a mark stamped on thine innocent brow
For men to point at as they pass, do thou
Forbear, and never think a thought unkind
Of those, who perhaps love thee in their graves.
So mayest thou die as I do; fear and pain
Being subdued. Farewell! Farewell! Farewell!
    Bernardo. I cannot say, farewell!
    Camillo.   Oh, Lady Beatrice!
    Beatrice.   Give yourself no unnecessary pain,
My dear Lord Cardinal. Here, Mother, tie
My girdle for me, and bind up this hair
In any simple knot; ay, that does well.
And yours I see is coming down. How often
Have we done this for one another! Now
We shall not do it any more. My Lord,
We are quite ready. Well, 'tis very well.

(End of *The Cenci*.)

JOHN KEATS

JOHN KEATS (1795–1821), the son of a livery-stable keeper in London, acquired a knowledge of Latin and history, and some French, but no Greek. He became intimate with Hazlitt and Leigh Hunt, who printed a sonnet for him in the *Examiner* in May 1816, and in whose house he met Shelley. He published in 1817 *Poems by John Keats*, which were financially a failure. In the course of 1818 Keats wrote *Endymion* which was savagely criticized in *Blackwood's Magazine* and the *Quarterly*; and commenced *Hyperion*. He began *The Eve of St. Agnes* early in 1819, and wrote *La Belle Dame sans Merci* and the unfinished *Eve of St. Mark*. About the same time he wrote his great odes *On a Grecian Urn*, *To a Nightingale*, and *To Autumn*; and those *On Melancholy*, *On Indolence*, and *To Psyche*. By 1820 Keats was seriously ill with consumption. He sailed for Italy in September 1820, reached Rome in November, and died there.

THE most notable characteristic of Keats is his youth; he died at the age of twenty-five. Less than three years before his death he wrote in the Preface to *Endymion*: 'The imagination of a boy is healthy, and the mature imagination of a man is healthy; but there is a space of life in between, in which the soul is in a ferment, the character undecided, the way of life uncertain, the ambition thick-sighted: thence proceeds mawkishness, and all the thousand bitters which those men I speak of must necessarily taste in going over the following pages.' In fact, he represents himself as an adolescent writing for adolescents. In the same year (1818) he invented in a letter his famous image of the Chamber of Maiden-thought, which represents (*a*) the awakening of the mind from the thoughtlessness of childhood and with it a quickening of the sensuous man, but (*b*) a recognition of evil and doubt, a feeling of frustration—'We see not the balance of good and evil; we are in a mist. . . .' Keats never moved out of the Chamber of Maiden-thought; till his death he was still in a mist.

The two poetic idols of schoolboys are Keats and Shelley. I remember a very young master at my preparatory school, just down from Oxford, telling the boys that

Keats was the only poet in the world who really mattered. We were a little too young to endorse that opinion, and the master, no doubt, was only just young enough to hold it. We liked the pictures in Keats—

'sweet peas on tip-toe for a flight',

the confectionery—

> 'jellies soother than the creamy curd,
> And lucent syrops tinct with cinnamon';

we liked the sound of the lines and the diction (as Keats said, 'I look upon fine phrases like a lover.') But Keats's erotic nostalgia and violent self-pity are things which the average boy will not find sympathetic till he is about sixteen. At the same age one tends to be swept off one's feet by the equally adolescent crusading fervour of Shelley.

It would be a great mistake to belittle any poet's work (as Byron did with Keats—'this miserable self-polluter of the human Mind') because it is founded on self-pity, nostalgia, or feelings of frustration in general. Poetry is *making*, and we must consider what things of positive value a poet can make, starting from his own negations. Keats in life could not have the world he wanted; he tried to build up a world in poetry. The value of such a world depends upon how egocentric its author is or rather, perhaps, upon how far he is a man like other men. Keats we might at first sight think very egocentric, but we should then have to remember that Keats was not a very peculiar person and that therefore his egocentricity, whatever its degree, would not necessarily isolate him from his fellows. Keats as a person was far less isolated than Shelley. The sensuous nostalgia of the *Ode to a Nightingale* is much more of an everyday experience than the mystical-metaphysical, would-be political yearnings of *Prometheus Unbound*. As for Keats's self-pity, it is not merely defeatist; it does not find the world merely unprofitable nor does it exclude pity for others—

> For them the Ceylon diver held his breath,
> And went all naked to the hungry shark.

However ignoble or selfish our emotions may appear to be, they usually contain some wider reference or are capable of expansion, of redirection. The same impulse which makes the adolescent mope in a corner can later become his driving-force in facing the problems of life. Thus Euripides appears in the *Rhesus* (which I assume was his work) mainly as a lover of fine phrases and pictures, slightly as a sentimentalist. But love of words or pictures is not properly divorced from love of beauty in general, and sentiments of pity are properly an earnest of a humane but critical world-view. We find these fuller developments in Euripides' later work. Keats's poetry, if he had not become ill and died, would, I feel, have grown tougher, more critical, more objective; it would then have been also more fully representative of Keats himself—of the man whom we meet in his letters, a good mixer with ordinary people. Keats, I think, like Mr. Yeats, might well have set out to make his poetry less 'poetic'. He did indeed take steps in this direction: compare *Hyperion* with *Endymion* and notice his emendations in *The Eve of St. Agnes*; in one stanza in the first draft he twice used the word 'gules', then cut it out in both places. Gerard Manley Hopkins remarks in a letter that Keats's school used 'mediaeval keepings. . . . They were also great realists and observers of nature.' Keats's logical progress, if he had not died, was towards more realism and less gules. His hellenism also would have grown less hellenistic.

But, considering Keats's poetry as it is, what do we find in it of value? No one can deny that Keats had a very good eye and a remarkable feeling for the music of words (on both scores he makes a very pleasant change from Shelley); as a sensuous poet he falls into line with Marlowe and Tennyson. But there is no such thing as a merely sensuous poet. Keats's reactions to Nature had not been worked out into a philosophy like Wordsworth's ('Beauty is truth' can hardly be called a philosophy), but it seems clear that Keats was what may be called a mystic through the medium of the senses (the divorce of the sensuous man from the mystic is a popular fallacy based on the experiences of the Christian saints but not always borne out by those experiences; consider St. Francis and his praises of the visible creation). I would agree up to a point, therefore, with the Abbé Brémond that there is something in Keats's poetry akin to prayer, a kind of religious incantation, though I would not agree that all true poetry must be of this kind.

Keats then is a sensuous mystic. Few major poets, however, have lived by mysticism—or by the senses—alone. Aeschylus is a mystic but he has a mystical *view* approved by his brain. Keats had not been bred up to such a view (he was not a poet working within a tradition accepted by his community) nor had he yet developed one. Witness his own description of the poetical character—'it is not itself—it has no self—it is every thing and nothing—it has no character—it enjoys light and shade—it lives in gusto. . . . A Poet is the most unpoetical of any thing in existence, because he has no Identity; he is continually infor[ming], and filling, some other Body.' This is obviously true of Keats himself, but it does not seem true of Sophocles or Dante. That a poet has no identity is a useful half-truth, for it counteracts the common opinion that a poet is some one hawking his own personality. Many poets, however, have had an identity as spokesmen for a congenial community or for a tradition that was still functioning. Keats, without these assets, lives in gusto. But we cannot deny that he lives.

Louis MacNeice.

SONNET

WHEN I have fears that I may cease to be
  Before my pen has glean'd my teeming brain,
Before high-pilèd books, in charact'ry,
  Hold like rich garners the full-ripen'd grain;
When I behold, upon the night's starr'd face,
  Huge cloudy symbols of a high romance,
And think that I may never live to trace
  Their shadows, with the magic hand of chance;
And when I feel, fair creature of an hour!
  That I shall never look upon thee more,
Never have relish in the faery power
  Of unreflecting love;—then on the shore
Of the wide world I stand alone, and think
Till love and fame to nothingness do sink.

LA BELLE DAME SANS MERCI

'O WHAT can ail thee, knight-at-arms,
    Alone and palely loitering?
The sedge is wither'd from the lake,
    And no birds sing.

'O what can ail thee, knight-at-arms,
  So haggard and so woe-begone?
The squirrel's granary is full,
    And the harvest's done.

'I see a lily on thy brow
  With anguish moist and fever dew;
And on thy cheek a fading rose
    Fast withereth too.'

'I met a lady in the meads,
  Full beautiful—a faery's child.
Her hair was long, her foot was light,
    And her eyes were wild.

'I made a garland for her head,
  And bracelets too, and fragrant zone;
She look'd at me as she did love,
    And made sweet moan.

'I set her on my pacing steed
　　And nothing else saw all day long,
For sideways would she lean, and sing
　　　　A faery's song.

'She found me roots of relish sweet,
　　And honey wild and manna dew,
And sure in language strange she said,
　　　　"I love thee true!"

'She took me to her elfin grot,
　　And there she wept and sigh'd full sore;
And there I shut her wild, wild eyes
　　　　With kisses four.

'And there she lullèd me asleep,
　　And there I dream'd—Ah! woe betide!
The latest dream I ever dream'd
　　　　On the cold hill's side.

'I saw pale kings and princes too,
　　Pale warriors, death-pale were they all;
Who cried—"La belle Dame sans Merci
　　　　Hath thee in thrall!"

'I saw their starved lips in the gloam
　　With horrid warning gapèd wide,
And I awoke and found me here
　　　　On the cold hill's side.

'And this is why I sojourn here
　　Alone and palely loitering,
Though the sedge is wither'd from the lake,
　　　　And no birds sing.'

ON FIRST LOOKING INTO CHAPMAN'S HOMER

Much have I travell'd in the realms of gold,
　　And many goodly states and kingdoms seen;
　　Round many western islands have I been
Which bards in fealty to Apollo hold.

Oft of one wide expanse had I been told
  That deep-brow'd Homer ruled as his demesne;
  Yet did I never breathe its pure serene
Till I heard Chapman speak out loud and bold:
Then felt I like some watcher of the skies
  When a new planet swims into his ken;
Or like stout Cortez when with eagle eyes
  He star'd at the Pacific—and all his men
Look'd at each other with a wild surmise—
  Silent, upon a peak in Darien.

MEG MERRILIES

OLD Meg she was a Gipsey,
  And liv'd upon the Moors:
Her bed it was the brown heath turf,
  And her house was out of doors.

Her apples were swart blackberries,
  Her currants, pods o' broom;
Her wine was dew of the wild white rose,
  Her book a churchyard tomb.

Her Brothers were the craggy hills,
  Her Sisters larchen trees;
Alone with her great family
  She liv'd as she did please.

No breakfast had she many a morn,
  No dinner many a noon,
And, 'stead of supper, she would stare
  Full hard against the Moon.

But every morn, of woodbine fresh
  She made her garlanding,
And, every night, the dark glen Yew
  She wove, and she would sing.

And with her fingers, old and brown,
  She plaited Mats o' Rushes,
And gave them to the Cottagers
  She met among the Bushes.

Old Meg was brave as Margaret Queen
　　And tall as Amazon;
An old red blanket cloak she wore;
　　A chip hat had she on.
God rest her aged bones somewhere!
　　She died full long agone!

ODE ON A GRECIAN URN

THOU still unravish'd bride of quietness,
　　Thou foster-child of silence and slow time,
Sylvan historian, who canst thus express
　　A flowery tale more sweetly than our rhyme:
What leaf-fring'd legend haunts about thy shape
　　Of deities or mortals, or of both,
　　　　In Tempe or the dales of Arcady?
　　What men or gods are these? What maidens loth?
What mad pursuit? What struggle to escape?
　　　　What pipes and timbrels? What wild ecstasy?

Heard melodies are sweet, but those unheard
　　Are sweeter; therefore, ye soft pipes, play on;
Not to the sensual ear, but, more endear'd,
　　Pipe to the spirit ditties of no tone:
Fair youth, beneath the trees, thou canst not leave
　　Thy song, nor ever can those trees be bare;
　　　　Bold Lover, never, never canst thou kiss,
Though winning near the goal—yet, do not grieve;
　　　　She cannot fade, though thou hast not thy bliss,
　　For ever wilt thou love, and she be fair!

Ah, happy, happy boughs! that cannot shed
　　Your leaves, nor ever bid the Spring adieu;
And, happy melodist, unwearied,
　　For ever piping songs for ever new;
More happy love! more happy, happy love!
　　For ever warm and still to be enjoy'd,

358

For ever panting, and for ever young;
All breathing human passion far above,
That leaves a heart high-sorrowful and cloy'd,
A burning forehead, and a parching tongue.

Who are these coming to the sacrifice?
To what green altar, O mysterious priest,
Lead'st thou that heifer lowing at the skies,
And all her silken flanks with garlands drest?
What little town by river or sea shore,
Or mountain-built with peaceful citadel,
Is emptied of its folk, this pious morn?
And, little town, thy streets for evermore
Will silent be; and not a soul to tell
Why thou art desolate, can e'er return.

O Attic shape! Fair attitude! with brede [1]
Of marble men and maidens overwrought,
With forest branches and the trodden weed;
Thou, silent form, dost tease us out of thought
As doth eternity: Cold Pastoral!
When old age shall this generation waste,
Thou shalt remain, in midst of other woe
Than ours, a friend to man, to whom thou say'st,
'Beauty is truth, truth beauty,'—that is all
Ye know on earth, and all ye need to know.

ODE TO A NIGHTINGALE

My heart aches, and a drowsy numbness pains
My sense, as though of hemlock I had drunk,
Or emptied some dull opiate to the drains
One minute past, and Lethe-wards had sunk:
'Tis not through envy of thy happy lot,
But being too happy in thine happiness,—
That thou, light-winged Dryad of the trees,
In some melodious plot
Of beechen green, and shadows numberless,
Singest of summer in full-throated ease.

[1] brede] interlaced design

359

O, for a draught of vintage! that hath been
  Cool'd a long age in the deep-delved earth,
Tasting of Flora and the country green,
  Dance, and Provençal song, and sunburnt mirth!
O for a beaker full of the warm South,
  Full of the true, the blushful Hippocrene,
    With beaded bubbles winking at the brim,
      And purple-stained mouth;
  That I might drink, and leave the world unseen,
    And with thee fade away into the forest dim:

Fade far away, dissolve, and quite forget
  What thou among the leaves hast never known,
The weariness, the fever, and the fret
  Here, where men sit and hear each other groan;
Where palsy shakes a few, sad, last gray hairs,
  Where youth grows pale, and spectre-thin, and dies;
    Where but to think is to be full of sorrow
      And leaden-eyed despairs,
  Where Beauty cannot keep her lustrous eyes,
    Or new Love pine at them beyond to-morrow.

Away! away! for I will fly to thee,
  Not charioted by Bacchus and his pards,
But on the viewless wings of Poesy,
  Though the dull brain perplexes and retards:
Already with thee! tender is the night,
  And haply the Queen-Moon is on her throne,
    Cluster'd around by all her starry Fays;
      But here there is no light,
  Save what from heaven is with the breezes blown
    Through verdurous glooms and winding mossy ways.

I cannot see what flowers are at my feet,
  Nor what soft incense hangs upon the boughs,
But, in embalmed darkness, guess each sweet
  Wherewith the seasonable month endows
The grass, the thicket, and the fruit-tree wild;
  White hawthorn, and the pastoral eglantine;

Fast fading violets cover'd up in leaves;
  And mid-May's eldest child,
The coming musk-rose, full of dewy wine,
  The murmurous haunt of flies on summer eves.

Darkling I listen; and, for many a time
  I have been half in love with easeful Death,
Call'd him soft names in many a mused rhyme,
  To take into the air my quiet breath;
Now more than ever seems it rich to die,
  To cease upon the midnight with no pain,
    While thou art pouring forth thy soul abroad
      In such an ecstasy!
  Still wouldst thou sing, and I have ears in vain—
    To thy high requiem become a sod.

Thou wast not born for death, immortal Bird!
  No hungry generations tread thee down;
The voice I hear this passing night was heard
  In ancient days by emperor and clown:
Perhaps the self-same song that found a path
  Through the sad heart of Ruth, when, sick for home,
    She stood in tears amid the alien corn;
      The same that oft-times hath
  Charm'd magic casements, opening on the foam
  Of perilous seas, in faery lands forlorn.

Forlorn! the very word is like a bell
  To toll me back from thee to my sole self!
Adieu! the fancy cannot cheat so well
  As she is fam'd to do, deceiving elf.
Adieu! adieu! thy plaintive anthem fades
  Past the near meadows, over the still stream,
    Up the hill-side; and now 'tis buried deep
      In the next valley-glades:
  Was it a vision, or a waking dream?
    Fled is that music:—Do I wake or sleep?

ODE ON MELANCHOLY

No, no, go not to Lethe, neither twist
  Wolf's-bane, tight-rooted, for its poisonous wine;
Nor suffer thy pale forehead to be kiss'd
  By nightshade, ruby grape of Proserpine;
Make not your rosary of yew-berries,
    Nor let the beetle, nor the death-moth be
      Your mournful Psyche, nor the downy owl
A partner in your sorrow's mysteries;
    For shade to shade will come too drowsily,
      And drown the wakeful anguish of the soul.

But when the melancholy fit shall fall
  Sudden from heaven like a weeping cloud,
That fosters the droop-headed flowers all,
  And hides the green hill in an April shroud;
Then glut thy sorrow on a morning rose,
    Or on the rainbow of the salt sand-wave,
      Or on the wealth of globed peonies;
Or if thy mistress some rich anger shows,
    Emprison her soft hand, and let her rave,
      And feed deep, deep upon her peerless eyes.

She dwells with Beauty—Beauty that must die;
  And Joy, whose hand is ever at his lips
Bidding adieu; and aching Pleasure nigh,
  Turning to Poison while the bee-mouth sips:
Ay, in the very temple of Delight,
    Veil'd Melancholy has her sovran shrine,
      Though seen of none save him whose strenuous tongue
Can burst Joy's grape against his palate fine;
    His soul shall taste the sadness of her might,
      And be among her cloudy trophies hung.

TO AUTUMN

Season of mists and mellow fruitfulness,
  Close bosom-friend of the maturing sun;
Conspiring with him how to load and bless
  With fruit the vines that round the thatch-eves run;
To bend with apples the moss'd cottage-trees,
  And fill all fruit with ripeness to the core;
    To swell the gourd, and plump the hazel shells
  With a sweet kernel; to set budding more,
And still more, later flowers for the bees,
Until they think warm days will never cease,
    For Summer has o'er-brimm'd their clammy cells.

Who hath not seen thee oft amid thy store?
  Sometimes whoever seeks abroad may find
Thee sitting careless on a granary floor,
  Thy hair soft-lifted by the winnowing wind;
Or on a half-reap'd furrow sound asleep,
  Drows'd with the fume of poppies, while thy hook
    Spares the next swath and all its twined flowers:
And sometimes like a gleaner thou dost keep
  Steady thy laden head across a brook;
  Or by a cyder-press, with patient look,
    Thou watchest the last oozings hours by hours.

Where are the songs of Spring? Ay, where are they?
  Think not of them, thou hast thy music too,—
While barred clouds bloom the soft-dying day,
  And touch the stubble-plains with rosy hue;
Then in a wailful choir the small gnats mourn
  Among the river sallows, borne aloft
    Or sinking as the light wind lives or dies;
And full-grown lambs loud bleat from hilly bourn;
  Hedge-crickets sing; and now with treble soft
  The red-breast whistles from a garden-croft;
    And gathering swallows twitter in the skies.

A THING OF BEAUTY

A THING of beauty is a joy for ever:
Its loveliness increases; it will never
Pass into nothingness; but still will keep
A bower quiet for us, and a sleep
Full of sweet dreams, and health, and quiet breathing.
Therefore, on every morrow, are we wreathing
A flowery band to bind us to the earth,
Spite of despondence, of the inhuman dearth
Of noble natures, of the gloomy days,
Of all the unhealthy and o'er-darkened ways
Made for our searching: yes, in spite of all,
Some shape of beauty moves away the pall
From our dark spirits. Such the sun, the moon,
Trees old and young, sprouting a shady boon
For simple sheep; and such are daffodils
With the green world they live in; and clear rills
That for themselves a cooling covert make
'Gainst the hot season; the mid forest brake,
Rich with a sprinkling of fair musk-rose blooms:
And such too is the grandeur of the dooms
We have imagined for the mighty dead;
All lovely tales that we have heard or read:
An endless fountain of immortal drink,
Pouring unto us from the heaven's brink,

  Nor do we merely feel these essences
For one short hour; no, even as the trees
That whisper round a temple become soon
Dear as the temple's self, so does the moon,
The passion poesy, glories infinite,
Haunt us till they become a cheering light
Unto our souls, and bound to us so fast,
That, whether there be shine, or gloom o'ercast,
They alway must be with us, or we die.
  Therefore, 'tis with full happiness that I
Will trace the story of Endymion.

The very music of the name has gone
Into my being, and each pleasant scene
Is growing fresh before me as the green
Of our own vallies: so I will begin
Now while I cannot hear the city's din;
Now while the early budders are just new,
And run in mazes of the youngest hue
About old forests; while the willow trails
Its delicate amber; and the dairy pails
Bring home increase of milk. And, as the year
Grows lush in juicy stalks, I'll smoothly steer
My little boat, for many quiet hours,
With streams that deepen freshly into bowers.
Many and many a verse I hope to write,
Before the daisies, vermeil rimm'd and white,
Hide in deep herbage; and ere yet the bees
Hum about globes of clover and sweet peas,
I must be near the middle of my story.
O may no wintry season, bare and hoary,
See it half finished: but let Autumn bold,
With universal tinge of sober gold,
Be all about me when I make an end.
And now at once, adventuresome, I send
My herald thought into a wilderness:
There let its trumpet blow, and quickly dress
My uncertain path with green, that I may speed
Easily onward, thorough flowers and weed.

(Endymion, ll. 1–62.)

THE EVE OF ST. AGNES

St. Agnes' Eve—Ah, bitter chill it was!
The owl, for all his feathers, was a-cold;
The hare limp'd trembling through the frozen grass,
And silent was the flock in woolly fold:
Numb were the Beadsman's fingers, while he told
His rosary, and while his frosted breath,
Like pious incense from a censer old,
Seem'd taking flight for heaven, without a death,
Past the sweet Virgin's picture, while his prayer he saith.

His prayer he saith, this patient, holy man;
Then takes his lamp, and riseth from his knees,
And back returneth, meagre, barefoot, wan,
Along the chapel aisle by slow degrees:
The sculptur'd dead, on each side, seem to freeze,
Emprison'd in black, purgatorial rails:
Knights, ladies, praying in dumb orat'ries,
He passeth by; and his weak spirit fails
To think how they may ache in icy hoods and mails.

Northward he turneth through a little door,
And scarce three steps, ere Music's golden tongue
Flatter'd to tears this aged man and poor;
But no—already had his death-bell rung;
The joys of all his life were said and sung:
His was harsh penance on St. Agnes' Eve:
Another way he went, and soon among
Rough ashes sat he for his soul's reprieve,
And all night kept awake, for sinners' sake to grieve.

That ancient Beadsman heard the prelude soft;
And so it chanc'd, for many a door was wide,
From hurry to and fro. Soon, up aloft,
The silver, snarling trumpets 'gan to chide:
The level chambers, ready with their pride,
Were glowing to receive a thousand guests:
The carved angels, ever eager-eyed,
Star'd, where upon their heads the cornice rests,
With hair blown back, and wings put cross-wise on their
      breasts.

At length burst in the argent revelry,
With plume, tiara, and all rich array,
Numerous as shadows haunting fairily
The brain, new stuff'd, in youth, with triumphs gay
Of old romance. These let us wish away,
And turn, sole-thoughted, to one Lady there,
Whose heart had brooded, all that wintry day,
On love, and wing'd St. Agnes' saintly care,
As she had heard old dames full many times declare.

366

They told her how, upon St. Agnes' Eve,
Young virgins might have visions of delight,
And soft adorings from their loves receive
Upon the honey'd middle of the night,
If ceremonies due they did aright;
As, supperless to bed they must retire,
And couch supine their beauties, lily white;
Nor look behind, nor sideways, but require
Of Heaven with upward eyes for all that they desire.

Full of this whim was thoughtful Madeline:
The music, yearning like a God in pain,
She scarcely heard: her maiden eyes divine,
Fix'd on the floor, saw many a sweeping train
Pass by—she heeded not at all: in vain
Came many a tiptoe, amorous cavalier,
And back retir'd, not cool'd by high disdain;
But she saw not: her heart was otherwhere:
She sigh'd for Agnes' dreams, the sweetest of the year.

. . . So, purposing each moment to retire,
She linger'd still. Meantime, across the moors,
Had come young Porphyro, with heart on fire
For Madeline. Beside the portal doors,
Buttress'd from moonlight, stands he, and implores
All saints to give him sight of Madeline,
But for one moment in the tedious hours,
That he might gaze and worship all unseen;
Perchance speak, kneel, touch, kiss—in sooth such things
        have been.

He ventures in: let no buzz'd whisper tell:
All eyes be muffled, or a hundred swords
Will storm his heart, Love's fev'rous citadel:
For him, those chambers held barbarian hordes,
Hyena foemen, and hot-blooded lords,
Whose very dogs would execrations howl
Against his lineage: not one breast affords
Him any mercy, in that mansion foul,
Save one old beldame, weak in body and in soul.

Ah, happy chance! the aged creature came,
Shuffling along with ivory-headed wand,
To where he stood, hid from the torch's flame,
Behind a broad hall-pillar, far beyond
The sound of merriment and chorus bland:
He startled her; but soon she knew his face,
And grasp'd his fingers in her palsied hand,
Saying, 'Mercy, Porphyro! hie thee from this place;
They are all here to-night, the whole blood-thirsty race!

'Get hence! get hence! there's dwarfish Hildebrand;
He had a fever late, and in the fit
He cursed thee and thine, both house and land:
Then there's that old Lord Maurice, not a whit
More tame for his gray hairs—Alas me! flit!
Flit like a ghost away.'—'Ah, Gossip dear,
We're safe enough; here in this arm-chair sit,
And tell me how'—'Good Saints! not here, not here;
Follow me, child, or else these stones will be thy bier.'

He follow'd through a lowly arched way,
Brushing the cobwebs with his lofty plume,
And as she mutter'd 'Well-a—well-a-day!'
He found him in a little moonlight room,
Pale, lattic'd, chill, and silent as a tomb.
'Now tell me where is Madeline,' said he,
'O tell me, Angela, by the holy loom
Which none but secret sisterhood may see,
When they St. Agnes' wool are weaving piously.'

'St. Agnes! Ah! it is St. Agnes' Eve—
Yet men will murder upon holy days:
Thou must hold water in a witch's sieve,
And be liege-lord of all the Elves and Fays,
To venture so: it fills me with amaze
To see thee, Porphyro!—St. Agnes' Eve!
God's help! my lady fair the conjuror plays
This very night: good angels her deceive!
But let me laugh awhile, I've mickle time to grieve.'

368

Feebly she laugheth in the languid moon,
While Porphyro upon her face doth look,
Like puzzled urchin on an aged crone
Who keepeth clos'd a wond'rous riddle-book,
As spectacled she sits in chimney nook.
But soon his eyes grew brilliant, when she told
His lady's purpose; and he scarce could brook
Tears, at the thought of those enchantments cold,
And Madeline asleep in lap of legends old.

Sudden a thought came like a full-blown rose,
Flushing his brow, and in his pained heart
Made purple riot: then doth he propose
A stratagem, that makes the beldame start:
'A cruel man and impious thou art:
Sweet lady, let her pray, and sleep, and dream
Alone with her good angels, far apart
From wicked men like thee. Go, go!—I deem
Thou canst not surely be the same that thou didst seem.

. . . Ah! why wilt thou affright a feeble soul?
A poor, weak, palsy-stricken, churchyard thing,
Whose passing-bell may ere the midnight toll;
Whose prayers for thee, each morn and evening,
Were never miss'd.'—Thus plaining, doth she bring
A gentler speech from burning Porphyro;
So woful, and of such deep sorrowing,
That Angela gives promise she will do
Whatever he shall wish, betide her weal or woe.

Which was, to lead him, in close secrecy,
Even to Madeline's chamber, and there hide
Him in a closet, of such privacy
That he might see her beauty unespied,
And win perhaps that night a peerless bride,
While legion'd faeries pac'd the coverlet,
And pale enchantment held her sleepy-eyed.
Never on such a night have lovers met,
Since Merlin paid his Demon all the monstrous debt.

'It shall be as thou wishest,' said the Dame:
'All cates and dainties shall be stored there
Quickly on this feast-night: by the tambour frame
Her own lute thou wilt see: no time to spare,
For I am slow and feeble, and scarce dare
On such a catering trust my dizzy head.
Wait here, my child, with patience; kneel in prayer
The while: Ah! thou must needs the lady wed,
Or may I never leave my grave among the dead.'

So saying, she hobbled off with busy fear.
The lover's endless minutes slowly pass'd;
The dame return'd, and whisper'd in his ear
To follow her; with aged eyes aghast
From fright of dim espial. Safe at last,
Through many a dusky gallery, they gain
The maiden's chamber, silken, hush'd, and chaste;
Where Porphyro took covert, pleas'd amain.
His poor guide hurried back with agues in her brain.

Her falt'ring hand upon the balustrade,
Old Angela was feeling for the stair,
When Madeline, St. Agnes' charmed maid,
Rose, like a mission'd spirit, unaware:
With silver taper's light, and pious care,
She turn'd, and down the aged gossip led
To a safe level matting. Now prepare,
Young Porphyro, for gazing on that bed;
She comes, she comes again, like ring-dove fray'd and fled.

Out went the taper as she hurried in;
Its little smoke, in pallid moonshine, died:
She clos'd the door, she panted, all akin
To spirits of the air, and visions wide:
No uttered syllable, or, woe betide!
But to her heart, her heart was voluble,
Paining with eloquence her balmy side;
As though a tongueless nightingale should swell
Her throat in vain, and die, heart-stifled, in her dell.

A casement high and triple-arch'd there was,
All garlanded with carven imag'ries
Of fruits, and flowers, and bunches of knot-grass,
And diamonded with panes of quaint device,
Innumerable of stains and splendid dyes,
As are the tiger-moth's deep-damask'd wings;
And in the midst, 'mong thousand heraldries,
And twilight saints, and dim emblazonings,
A shielded scutcheon blush'd with blood of queens and
  kings.

Full on this casement shone the wintry moon,
And threw warm gules on Madeline's fair breast,
As down she knelt for heaven's grace and boon;
Rose-bloom fell on her hands, together prest,
And on her silver cross soft amethyst,
And on her hair a glory, like a saint:
She seem'd a splendid angel, newly drest,
Save wings, for heaven:—Porphyro grew faint:
She knelt, so pure a thing, so free from mortal taint.

Anon his heart revives: her vespers done,
Of all its wreathed pearls her hair she frees;
Unclasps her warmed jewels one by one;
Loosens her fragrant boddice; by degrees
Her rich attire creeps rustling to her knees:
Half-hidden, like a mermaid in sea-weed,
Pensive awhile she dreams awake, and sees,
In fancy, fair St. Agnes in her bed,
But dares not look behind, or all the charm is fled.

Soon trembling in her soft and chilly nest,
In sort of wakeful swoon, perplex'd she lay,
Until the poppied warmth of sleep oppress'd
Her soothed limbs, and soul fatigued away;
Flown, like a thought, until the morrow-day;
Blissfully haven'd both from joy and pain;
Clasp'd like a missal where swart Paynims pray;
Blinded alike from sunshine and from rain,
As though a rose should shut, and be a bud again.

Stol'n to this paradise, and so entranced,
Porphyro gazed upon her empty dress,
And listen'd to her breathing, if it chanced
To waken into a slumberous tenderness;
Which when he heard, that minute did he bless,
And breath'd himself: then from the closet crept,
Noiseless as fear in a wide wilderness,
And over the hush'd carpet, silent, stept,
And 'tween the curtains peep'd, where, lo!—how fast she
    slept.

. . . Awakening up, he took her hollow lute,—
Tumultuous,—and, in chords that tenderest be,
He play'd an ancient ditty, long since mute,
In Provence call'd, 'La belle dame sans mercy:'
Close to her ear touching the melody;—
Wherewith disturb'd, she utter'd a soft moan:
He ceased—she panted quick—and suddenly
Her blue affrayed eyes wide open shone:
Upon his knees he sank, pale as smooth-sculptured stone.

Her eyes were open, but she still beheld,
Now wide awake, the vision of her sleep:
There was a painful change, that nigh expell'd
The blisses of her dream so pure and deep
At which fair Madeline began to weep,
And moan forth witless words with many a sigh;
While still her gaze on Porphyro would keep;
Who knelt, with joined hands and piteous eye,
Fearing to move or speak, she look'd so dreamingly.

'Ah, Porphyro!' said she, 'but even now
Thy voice was at sweet tremble in mine ear,
Made tuneable with every sweetest vow;
And those sad eyes were spiritual and clear:
How chang'd thou art! how pallid, chill, and drear!
Give me that voice again, my Porphyro,
Those looks immortal, those complainings dear!
Oh leave me not in this eternal woe,
For if thou diest, my Love, I know not where to go.'

. . . 'Tis dark: quick pattereth the flaw-blown sleet:
'This is no dream, my bride, my Madeline!'
'Tis dark: the iced gusts still rave and beat:
'No dream, alas! alas! and woe is mine!
Porphyro will leave me here to fade and pine.—
Cruel! what traitor could thee hither bring?
I curse not, for my heart is lost in thine,
Though thou forsakest a deceived thing;—
A dove forlorn and lost with sick unpruned wing.'

. . . 'Hark! 'tis an elfin-storm from faery land,
Of haggard seeming, but a boon indeed:
Arise—arise! the morning is at hand;—
The bloated wassaillers will never heed:—
Let us away, my love, with happy speed;
There are no ears to hear, or eyes to see,—
Drown'd all in Rhenish and the sleepy mead:
Awake! arise! my love, and fearless be,
For o'er the southern moors I have a home for thee.'

She hurried at his words, beset with fears,
For there were sleeping dragons all around,
At glaring watch, perhaps, with ready spears—
Down the wide stairs a darkling way they found.—
In all the house was heard no human sound.
A chain-droop'd lamp was flickering by each door;
The arras, rich with horseman, hawk, and hound,
Flutter'd in the besieging wind's uproar;
And the long carpets rose along the gusty floor.

They glide, like phantoms, into the wide hall;
Like phantoms, to the iron porch, they glide;
Where lay the Porter, in uneasy sprawl,
With a huge empty flaggon by his side:
The wakeful bloodhound rose, and shook his hide,
But his sagacious eye an inmate owns:
By one, and one, the bolts full easy slide:—
The chains lie silent on the footworn stones;—
The key turns, and the door upon its hinges groans.

And they are gone: aye, ages long ago
These lovers fled away into the storm.
That night the Baron dreamt of many a woe,
And all his warrior-guests, with shade and form
Of witch, and demon, and large coffin-worm,
Were long be-nightmar'd. Angela the old
Died palsy-twitch'd, with meagre face deform;
The Beadsman, after thousand aves told,
For aye unsought for slept among his ashes cold.

HYPERION

DEEP in the shady sadness of a vale
Far sunken from the healthy breath of morn,
Far from the fiery noon, and eve's one star,
Sat gray-hair'd Saturn, quiet as a stone.
Still as the silence round about his lair;
Forest on forest hung about his head
Like cloud on cloud. No stir of air was there,
Not so much life as on a summer's day
Robs not one light seed from the feather'd grass,
But where the dead leaf fell, there did it rest.
A stream went voiceless by, still deadened more
By reason of his fallen divinity
Spreading a shade: the Naiad 'mid her reeds
Press'd her cold finger closer to her lips.

Along the margin-sand large foot-marks went,
No further than to where his feet had stray'd,
And slept there since. Upon the sodden ground
His old right hand lay nerveless, listless, dead,
Unsceptred; and his realmless eyes were closed;
While his bow'd head seem'd list'ning to the Earth,
His ancient mother, for some comfort yet.

It seem'd no force could wake him from his place;
But there came one, who with a kindred hand
Touch'd his wide shoulders, after bending low
With reverence, though to one who knew it not.
She was a Goddess of the infant world;

By her in stature the tall Amazon
Had stood a pigmy's height: she would have ta'en
Achilles by the hair and bent his neck;
Or with a finger stay'd Ixion's wheel.
Her face was large as that of Memphian sphinx,
Pedestal'd haply in a palace court,
When sages look'd to Egypt for their lore.
But oh! how unlike marble was that face:
How beautiful, if sorrow had not made
Sorrow more beautiful than Beauty's self.
There was a listening fear in her regard,
As if calamity had but begun;
As if the vanward clouds of evil days
Had spent their malice, and the sullen rear
Was with its stored thunder labouring up.
One hand she press'd upon that aching spot
Where beats the human heart, as if just there,
Though an immortal, she felt cruel pain:
The other upon Saturn's bended neck
She laid, and to the level of his ear
Leaning with parted lips, some words she spake
In solemn tenour and deep organ tone:
Some mourning words, which in our feeble tongue
Would come in these like accents; O how frail
To that large utterance of the early Gods!
'Saturn, look up!—though wherefore, poor old King?
I have no comfort for thee, no, not one:
I cannot say, "O wherefore sleepest thou?"
For heaven is parted from thee, and the earth
Knows thee not, thus afflicted, for a God;
And ocean too, with all its solemn noise,
Has from thy sceptre pass'd; and all the air
Is emptied of thine hoary majesty.
Thy thunder, conscious of the new command,
Rumbles reluctant o'er our fallen house;
And thy sharp lightning in unpractis'd hands
Scorches and burns our once serene domain.
O aching time! O moments big as years!
All as ye pass swell out the monstrous truth,
And press it so upon our weary griefs

That unbelief has not a space to breathe.
Saturn, sleep on:—O thoughtless, why did I
Thus violate thy slumbrous solitude?
Why should I ope thy melancholy eyes?
Saturn, sleep on! while at thy feet I weep.'

    As when, upon a tranced summer-night,
Those green-rob'd senators of mighty woods,
Tall oaks, branch-charmed by the earnest stars,
Dream, and so dream all night without a stir,
Save from one gradual solitary gust
Which comes upon the silence, and dies off,
As if the ebbing air had but one wave;
So came these words and went; the while in tears
She touch'd her fair large forehead to the ground,
Just where her falling hair might be outspread
A soft and silken mat for Saturn's feet.
One moon, with alteration slow, had shed
Her silver seasons four upon the night,
And still these two were postured motionless,
Like natural sculpture in cathedral cavern;
The frozen God still couchant on the earth,
And the sad Goddess weeping at his feet:
Until at length old Saturn lifted up
His faded eyes, and saw his kingdom gone,
And all the gloom and sorrow of the place,
And that fair kneeling Goddess; and then spake,
As with a palsied tongue, and while his beard
Shook horrid with such aspen-malady:
'O tender spouse of gold Hyperion,
Thea, I feel thee ere I see thy face;
Look up, and let me see our doom in it;
Look up, and tell me if this feeble shape
Is Saturn's; tell me, if thou hear'st the voice
Of Saturn; tell me, if this wrinkling brow,
Naked and bare of its great diadem,
Peers like the front of Saturn. Who had power
To make me desolate? whence came the strength?
How was it nurtur'd to such bursting forth,
While Fate seem'd strangled in my nervous grasp?

But it is so; and I am smother'd up,
And buried from all godlike exercise
Of influence benign on planets pale,
Of admonitions to the winds and seas,
Of peaceful sway above man's harvesting,
And all those acts which Deity supreme
Doth ease its heart of love in.—I am gone
Away from my own bosom: I have left
My strong identity, my real self,
Somewhere between the throne, and where I sit
Here on this spot of earth. Search, Thea, search!
Open thine eyes eterne, and sphere them round
Upon all space: space starr'd, and lorn of light;
Space region'd with life-air; and barren void;
Spaces of fire, and all the yawn of hell.—
Search, Thea, search! and tell me, if thou seest
A certain shape or shadow, making way
With wings or chariot fierce to repossess
A heaven he lost erewhile: it must—it must
Be of ripe progress—Saturn must be King.
Yes, there must be a golden victory;   [blown
There must be Gods thrown down, and trumpets
Of triumph calm, and hymns of festival
Upon the gold clouds metropolitan,
Voices of soft proclaim, and silver stir
Of strings in hollow shells; and there shall be
Beautiful things made new, for the surprise
Of the sky-children; I will give command:
Thea! Thea! Thea! where is Saturn?'

    This passion lifted him upon his feet,
And made his hands to struggle in the air,
His Druid locks to shake and ooze with sweat,
His eyes to fever out, his voice to cease.
He stood, and heard not Thea's sobbing deep;
A little time, and then again he snatch'd
Utterance thus.—'But cannot I create?
Cannot I form? Cannot I fashion forth
Another world, another universe,
To overbear and crumble this to naught?

Where is another chaos? Where?'—That word
Found way unto Olympus, and made quake
The rebel three.—Thea was startled up,
And in her bearing was a sort of hope,
As thus she quick-voic'd spake, yet full of awe.
'This cheers our fallen house: come to our friends,
O Saturn! come away, and give them heart;
I know the covert, for thence came I hither.'
Thus brief; then with beseeching eyes she went
With backward footing through the shade a space:
He follow'd, and she turn'd to lead the way
Through aged boughs, that yielded like the mist
Which eagles cleave upmounting from their nest.

Meanwhile in other realms big tears were shed,
More sorrow like to this, and such like woe,
Too huge for mortal tongue or pen of scribe:
The Titans fierce, self-hid, or prison-bound,
Groan'd for the old allegiance once more,
And listen'd in sharp pain for Saturn's voice.
But one of the whole mammoth-brood still kept
His sov'reignty, and rule, and majesty;—
Blazing Hyperion on his orbed fire
Still sat, still snuff'd the incense, teeming up
From man to the sun's God; yet unsecure:
For as among us mortals omens drear
Fright and perplex, so also shuddered he—
Not at dog's howl, or gloom-bird's hated screech,
Or the familiar visiting of one
Upon the first toll of his passing-bell,
Or prophesyings of the midnight lamp;
But horrors, portion'd to a giant nerve,
Oft made Hyperion ache. His palace bright
Bastion'd with pyramids of glowing gold,
And touch'd with shade of bronzed obelisks,
Glar'd a blood-red through all its thousand courts,
Arches, and domes, and fiery galleries;
And all its curtains of Aurorian clouds
Flush'd angerly: while sometimes eagle's wings,
Unseen before by Gods or wondering men,

Darken'd the place; and neighing steeds were heard,
Not heard before by Gods or wondering men.
Also, when he would taste the spicy wreaths
Of incense, breath'd aloft from sacred hills,
Instead of sweets, his ample palate took
Savour of poisonous brass and metal sick:
And so, when harbour'd in the sleepy west,
After the full completion of fair day,—
For rest divine upon exalted couch
And slumber in the arms of melody,
He pac'd away the pleasant hours of ease
With stride colossal, on from hall to hall;
While far within each aisle and deep recess,
His winged minions in close clusters stood,
Amaz'd and full of fear; like anxious men
Who on wide plains gather in panting troops,
When earthquakes jar their battlements and towers.
Even now, while Saturn, rous'd from icy trance,
Went step for step with Thea through the woods,
Hyperion, leaving twilight in the rear,
Came slope upon the threshold of the west;
Then, as was wont, his palace-door flew ope
In smoothest silence, save what solemn tubes,
Blown by the serious Zephyrs, gave of sweet
And wandering sounds, slow-breathed melodies;
And like a rose in vermeil tint and shape,
In fragrance soft, and coolness to the eye,
That inlet to severe magnificence
Stood full blown, for the God to enter in.

He enter'd, but he enter'd full of wrath;
His flaming robes stream'd out beyond his heels,
And gave a roar, as if of earthly fire,
That scar'd away the meek ethereal Hours
And made their dove-wings tremble. On he flared,
From stately nave to nave, from vault to vault,
Through bowers of fragrant and enwreathed light,
And diamond-paved lustrous long arcades,
Until he reach'd the great main cupola;
There standing fierce beneath, he stamped his foot,

And from the basements deep to the high towers
Jarr'd his own golden region; and before
The quavering thunder thereupon had ceas'd,
His voice leapt out, despite of godlike curb,
To this result: 'O dreams of day and night!
O monstrous forms! O effigies of pain!
O spectres busy in a cold, cold gloom!
O lank-ear'd Phantoms of black-weeded pools!
Why do I know ye? why have I seen ye? why
Is my eternal essence thus distraught
To see and to behold these horrors new?
Saturn is fallen, am I too to fall?
Am I to leave this haven of my rest,
This cradle of my glory, this soft clime,
This calm luxuriance of blissful light,
These crystalline pavilions, and pure fanes,
Of all my lucent empire? It is left
Deserted, void, nor any haunt of mine.
The blaze, the splendor, and the symmetry,
I cannot see—but darkness, death and darkness.
Even here, into my centre of repose,
The shady visions come to domineer,
Insult, and blind, and stifle up my pomp.—
Fall!—No, by Tellus and her briny robes!
Over the fiery frontier of my realms
I will advance a terrible right arm
Shall scare that infant thunderer, rebel Jove,
And bid old Saturn take his throne again.'—
He spake, and ceas'd, the while a heavier threat
Held struggle with his throat but came not forth;
For as in theatres of crowded men
Hubbub increases more they call out 'Hush!'
So at Hyperion's words the Phantoms pale
Bestirr'd themselves, thrice horrible and cold;
And from the mirror'd level where he stood
A mist arose, as from a scummy marsh.
At this, through all his bulk an agony
Crept gradual, from the feet unto the crown,
Like a lithe serpent vast and muscular
Making slow way, with head and neck convuls'd

From over-strained might. Releas'd, he fled
To the eastern gates, and full six dewy hours
Before the dawn in season due should blush,
He breath'd fierce breath against the sleepy portals,
Clear'd them of heavy vapours, burst them wide
Suddenly on the ocean's chilly streams.
The planet orb of fire, whereon he rode
Each day from east to west the heavens through,
Spun round in sable curtaining of clouds;
Not therefore veiled quite, blindfold, and hid,
But ever and anon the glancing spheres,
Circles, and arcs, and broad-belting colure,
Glow'd through, and wrought upon the muffling dark
Sweet-shaped lightnings from the nadir deep
Up to the zenith,—hieroglyphics old
Which sages and keen-eyed astrologers
Then living on the earth, with labouring thought
Won from the gaze of many centuries:
Now lost, save what we find on remnants huge
Of stone, or marble swart; their import gone,
Their wisdom long since fled.—Two wings this orb
Possess'd for glory, two fair argent wings,
Ever exalted at the God's approach:
And now, from forth the gloom their plumes immense
Rose, one by one, till all outspreaded were;
While still the dazzling globe maintain'd eclipse,
Awaiting for Hyperion's command.
Fain would he have commanded, fain took throne
And bid the day begin, if but for change.
He might not:—No, though a primeval God:
The sacred seasons might not be disturb'd.
Therefore the operations of the dawn
Stay'd in their birth, even as here 'tis told.
Those silver wings expanded sisterly,
Eager to sail their orb; the porches wide
Open'd upon the dusk demesnes of night;
And the bright Titan, phrenzied with new woes,
Unus'd to bend, by hard compulsion bent
His spirit to the sorrow of the time;
And all along a dismal rack of clouds,

Upon the boundaries of day and night,
He stretch'd himself in grief and radiance faint.
There as he lay, the Heaven with its stars
Look'd down on him with pity, and the voice
Of Cœlus, from the universal space,
Thus whisper'd low and solemn in his ear.
'O brightest of my children dear, earth-born
And sky-engender'd, Son of Mysteries
All unrevealed even to the powers
Which met at thy creating; at whose joys
And palpitations sweet, and pleasures soft,
I, Cœlus, wonder, how they came and whence;
And at the fruits thereof what shapes they be,
Distinct, and visible; symbols divine,
Manifestations of that beauteous life
Diffus'd unseen throughout eternal space:
Of these new-form'd art thou, oh brightest child!
Of these, thy brethren and the Goddesses!
There is sad feud among ye, and rebellion
Of son against his sire. I saw him fall,
I saw my first-born tumbled from his throne!
To me his arms were spread, to me his voice
Found way from forth the thunders round his head!
Pale wox I, and in vapours hid my face.
Art thou, too, near such doom? vague fear there is:
For I have seen my sons most unlike Gods.
Divine ye were created, and divine
In sad demeanour, solemn, undisturb'd,
Unruffled, like high Gods, ye liv'd and ruled:
Now I behold in you fear, hope, and wrath;
Actions of rage and passion; even as
I see them, on the mortal world beneath,
In men who die.—This is the grief, O Son!
Sad sign of ruin, sudden dismay, and fall!
Yet do thou strive; as thou art capable,
As thou canst move about, an evident God;
And canst oppose to each malignant hour
Ethereal presence:—I am but a voice;
My life is but the life of winds and tides,
No more than winds and tides can I avail:—

But thou canst.—Be thou therefore in the van
Of circumstance; yea, seize the arrow's barb
Before the tense string murmur.—To the earth!
For there thou wilt find Saturn, and his woes.
Meantime I will keep watch on thy bright sun,
And of thy seasons be a careful nurse.'—
Ere half this region-whisper had come down,
Hyperion arose, and on the stars
Lifted his curved lids, and kept them wide
Until it ceas'd; and still he kept them wide:
And still they were the same bright, patient stars.
Then with a slow incline of his broad breast,
Like to a diver in the pearly seas,
Forward he stoop'd over the airy shore,
And plung'd all noiseless into the deep night.

SONNET

Bright star, would I were stedfast as thou art—
    Not in lone splendour hung aloft the night
And watching, with eternal lids apart,
    Like nature's patient, sleepless Eremite,
The moving waters at their priestlike task
    Of pure ablution round earth's human shores,
Or gazing on the new soft-fallen mask
    Of snow upon the mountains and the moors—
No—yet still stedfast, still unchangeable,
    Pillow'd upon my fair love's ripening breast,
To feel for ever its soft fall and swell,
    Awake for ever in a sweet unrest,
Still, still to hear her tender-taken breath,
And so live ever—or else swoon to death.

ALFRED TENNYSON

ALFRED TENNYSON, first Baron Tennyson (1809–92), was educated at Trinity College, Cambridge. *Poems, by Two Brothers* (1827) contains some of his earlier and unimportant verse. In 1830 he published *Poems, chiefly Lyrical* which were unfavourably reviewed. His friend A. H. Hallam died in 1833, and in that year Tennyson began his *In Memoriam*, expressive of his grief for his lost friend. In 1833 he published a further volume of *Poems*, containing *The Two Voices*, *Œnone*, *The Lotos-Eaters*, *A Dream of Fair Women* (*Tithonus*, published in 1860, belongs also to this period); and in 1842 an edition of his poems in two volumes, which included some of his finest work: the *Morte d'Arthur* (the germ of the *Idylls*), *Locksley Hall*, *Ulysses*, *St. Simeon Stylites*, &c. In 1847 he published *The Princess* and in 1850 *In Memoriam*, and was appointed poet laureate in succession to Wordsworth in the latter year. He continued to publish volumes of verse until his death in 1892.

TENNYSON was born in 1809, and died in 1892. His first volume of verse, written with two of his brothers, was published in 1827, one year before he went to Cambridge: his last in 1892. He had, therefore, a writing-life of sixty-five years, and for nearly half a century he was the unchallenged head of English poetry.

No other poet has, during his lifetime, reigned so long, and none was, in consequence, after his death more certain to encounter a sharp and continuing decline. His only serious rival during the years of his laureateship was Browning. Posterity has rightly acclaimed the author of *The Ring and the Book* as the greater poet, but their verdict would have been laughed to scorn by Victorian England. Tennyson was, as a poet should be, the expositor of his age, and his age gratefully found its reflection heightened and enriched in his glowing page.

It was only when the shadows of the end of the century began to creep round his feet that the first challenges assailed him. Swinburne pelted his reputation with poisoned rose-leaves. After the appearance of *Poems and Ballads* Tennyson's honey had been effectually out-honeyed. For his limited romance had been substituted raptures so unbridled that to the admirers of the younger poet the Laureate had almost the air of a Sunday-school teacher. But Swinburne, chastised with the great courage of anonymity by honest John Morley, shocked and alarmed the majority. His time was not yet. He had to wait for support till the nineties, when the apostles of decay called the heroes of France to aid them in their assault on the English oak.

Steadily thereafter in the beginning of the twentieth century the revolt against Tennyson's dictatorship asserted itself. Tennyson had represented the industrial age in its years of self-complacency and self-satisfaction, mitigated by the doubts occasioned by satiety. The new writers were beginning to be aware of the cruel wounds that that age had inflicted on the spirit of man. They were no mere long-haired aesthetes, trilling rondeaux and offering absinthe to a thirsty world. They were men aware of something fast and fateful sweeping on to some disastrous consummation. The great poets of the period, Housman, de la Mare, and Yeats all played to a low and troubled note. Only Chesterton challenged the approach of doom, but, no less than the others, he saw the darkness on the horizon.

In such a world Tennyson's grace and classic charm began to be dismissed as facile sweetness. All the security which he reflected was in imminent danger, and, impatient as always, youth turned from him not because he wrote ill, but because he wrote of things they had not experienced and could not understand. Their distaste for one of the most material periods in man's history was turned unfairly against its great interpreter.

The pendulum has begun to swing a little. It is nearly half a century since Tennyson died, and in that time the world has died once, risen from the dead, and is again in the death-throes. The times in which we live are so impossibly remote from his that it is possible to consider him as calmly as though he were an Elizabethan. So far from us are the calm, measured, and leisured days which were sedulously and ignorantly, out of their wealth and ease, calling down the angry retribution of the gods.

In this recaptured impartiality we can re-possess one of the greatest writers of lyrics in the language, and we can understand how first he shook, and then held, the heart of England through the Victorian era. In considering him, we must distinguish the writer of lyrics and the technician from the thinker. We must also note the chronology of his works. It has been said that Tennyson died with the publication of *Maud* in 1855 and that he was succeeded by Alfred, who devoted himself to cooking cakes over the kitchen-fire for the rest of his life. This, like most such sayings, is silly, but, as we shall see, is not without some vestige of truth.

We shall do well to begin our assessment of Tennyson as a writer of lyrics by examining the two volumes published in 1830 and 1833—that is, when the poet was twenty-one and twenty-four respectively. We shall find here not only the seeds of all that he was to accomplish later, but, what is surprising, we shall find that before he was twenty-five he had written three or four of the most memorable poems of his life. This will enforce the conclusion, which will be urged, that Tennyson was one of the thrushes who have their first fine careless rapture. They can, and do, repeat it, but they cannot enlarge it, because to the gift of song is not added the ultimate vision. Let us also remember that those who have the bird-song at its purest and clearest can be counted on one's hands. They include Marvell and Herrick. This is no mean company for Tennyson.

In the 1830 volume we find *Mariana*, *The Poet*, and *Oriana*. In the 1833 volume there are *The Lady of Shalott*, *The Miller's Daughter*, *Oenone*, *The May Queen*, and *The Lotos-Eaters*. If we take *Mariana* first it is true that we find the influence of Keats so obvious as to make the poem almost derivative. It is right and natural in a poet of twenty-one to follow the masters, but Tennyson did more than follow. Let us look at one verse only:

> All day within the dreamy house
> 　The doors upon their hinges creak'd;
> The blue fly sang in the pane. The mouse
> Behind the mouldering wainscot shriek'd,
> 　Or from the crevice peeped about.
> 　Old faces glimmer'd thro' the doors.
> 　Old footsteps trod the upper floors.
> 　Old voices called her from without.
> She only said, 'My life is dreary,
> 　He cometh not,' she said;
> She said, 'I am aweary, aweary,
> 　I would that I were dead.'

First dismiss Keats from your mind, and then listen for another dim, elfin echo,

> 'Is there anybody there?' said the Traveller.

Yes, it is de la Mare syllabling forty years before he was born. That is one of Tennyson's tricks—to stalk the unborn spring. But consider further the mingling of the actual and the dream. There are things as palpable as 'hinges', 'blue fly', 'mouse', and 'wainscot'. No modernist poet could have asked for more prosaic nouns, and yet the young Tennyson by virtue of inner music gives them a deep and clinging substance of reality turned round upon itself. This inner music is new in English lyric verse; it has, over and above its strict accuracy, a lovely slipping of the cadence. The last line but one should read,

> She said I am aweary, weary.

Tennyson, by adding a syllable, ties his cobweb to a star.

This same mixture of texture and technique is displayed in *Oriana* with the broken repetition of the name. As Keats said of the wind, these syllables, so often spoken, so drawing, so retreating in slow ebb,

> Come upon the silence and die off,
> As though the ebbing air had but one wave.

And what was hinted and tried in 1830 comes to superb

consummation in 1833 with *The Lady of Shalott*. Let us note, before we consider its lyrical quality, one particular point of interest in this great poem. It deals with the Arthurian legend, and thus foreshadows the lifelong interest of its author in the Round Table, which culminated in *The Idylls of the King*. It is not necessary to quote. The reader may turn from these dull words to the lovely, lit page in which the young Merlin is at his magic. Everything is there that the most experienced poet could have learnt—rhyme that flowers from the line like a bud from a rose-bush, a scansion that is as sweet as bells and never cloys, and a sense all the time of beauty pouring in like light through a stained-glass window. But there is more in it than skill's lovely pageantry; truth can, and does, see herself in the fairy mirror before it cracks.

> 'I am half sick of shadows.' said
> The Lady of Shalott.

So all sit before their mirror; so all see life in its silver-foiled deception rolling by; so all grow weary of shadow, and so for all, when eyes are turned from the shadow to that which cast it, the mirror is split so that none will ever look in its fraudulent face again.

The Poet is a second string to the lyricist's bow. It has enough phrase-making to atone for the rather dim intellectual content and enough thought to stiffen what might otherwise be a rather limp beauty;

> Dower'd with the hate of hate, the scorn of scorn,
> The love of love,

are two lines, important in themselves, which indicate the highest point in this climate that Tennyson was destined to reach. It foreshadows those passages in *In Memoriam* when the poet is tempering emotion with plausible thought. It is an exposition, not too difficult and with an alien colour, of what many may have thought, and had wished to say half as well. And in spite of its essential commonplace it has the vitality born of a hot dream. Tennyson did not think very deep or very hard; but he plunged his thoughts in the flame. They glowed at the edges like hot iron.

Next we have in *The Miller's Daughter* and *The May Queen* companion-pictures to Sir John Millais' *Bubbles*. The great craftsman is not stooping to the popular taste; he is experiencing and sharing it. It is as little like the true Tennyson as Kipling's jingling *Recessional* was fair to the immortal author of *Valour and Innocence* and *There is no road through the Wood*. But in this mood Tennyson spoke to Kipling across half a century, as he did in another to de la Mare. He reverted to it often in his life, as in *The Charge of the Light Brigade* and the still more dreadful *Form, Riflemen, Form!* But in Tennyson, as in Kipling, this strain of coarseness only showed that under the genius was the common man, who stood eagerly by the side of the table picking up the crumbs. Need we insist that he should starve?

Last we have in *Oenone* and *The Lotos-Eaters* the first of the poems on classical themes which culminated in the triumphs of *Ulysses* and *Lucretius*. *Oenone*, as the work of a man under twenty-five, is staggering and unbeatable at any age. Let us observe, first, that after blank verse had died for nearly two centuries, Tennyson at a stroke gave it new and lovely being. It returned not as a hoary Rip Van Winkle, trailing dead moss and old twigs from some grave in the Forest of Arden, but it stepped out as gay as Rosalind and as free-spoken as Rosalind. If it has a fault it is in Tennyson's excessive preoccupation with broad vowel-sounds, which became almost a disease in *The Idylls of the King*. That is the only blemish in a cadence as deep and slow-swinging as waves in a gentle sea.

These were something to build on, and he built on each till he reached his lyric high-water mark in the songs in *The Princess* and that supreme passage in *Maud* (xviii) in which he anticipated half the developments in later verse and reached a point on which no tide of beauty since has lapped. *The Princess* is of particular historical interest. It belongs to the period when, after the death of Hallam, Tennyson had it half in mind to smash the lute. It is true that nine years after the tragedy he published a collection. It should be noted, however, that practically all volume i was reprints and that volume ii contains only two poems of major value, *Ulysses* and *Break, break, break*.

In *The Princess*, however, song by song, he was finding his way back not only to health and love but to the undisputed kingdom of lyric verse. Here are three of the greatest lyrics in the language: *Now sleeps the crimson petal, now the white, The Splendour falls on Castle Walls*, and *Tears, idle tears*. Let it not be forgotten that the first and the last have tuned blank verse to the fiddle. Here the mode, borrowed from France for the Elizabethan stage, throws off all fetters and soars, dips, and rises like the water-cry of the fiddle at the world's end. Skill, colour, beauty, cadence, and the thing beyond all these that attaches to them in the high moment of genius are all there.

> O hark, O hear! how thin and clear
> And thinner, clearer, farther going!
> O sweet and far from cliff and scar
> The horns of Elfland faintly blowing!

These are the authentic notes. It is not given to any poet to do more than overhear, and thus, imperishably, ensnare them.

It is an ungrateful task to come down with the shepherd-maid from the mountain-heights and stumble along the plains of Tennyson's thought even if, as compensation, the doves are moaning onomatopœically in the immemorial elms. The truth about Tennyson in this regard was admitted in 1830 when he wrote that dismal tract, *Confessions of a Second-rate Sensitive Mind*. He never in thought was more than a reflection, and he attempted to disguise the fact that he was a mirror by burnishing its surface continually. But that, alas! only made it more a mirror than ever.

There are, for example, long passages of contemplation

in *In Memoriam* which, it is recorded, gave much satisfaction to Mr. Gladstone. It was right that they should, because they set out neatly the doubts of the ordinary man without adding one inner ray of illumination. Tennyson, indeed, as a thinker could only summarize, and summaries delivered with a whisk of the prophetic cloak are dull and, to be frank, sometimes comic reading.

Nor can we pretend that his supreme lyric gift, unsupported by a deeply constructive mind, fitted him to attempt an epic. *The Idylls of the King* are a tribute to Tennyson's extreme pertinacity rather than to his genius. He outwrote everything in that long and painstaking chronicle in the single *Lady of Shalott*. There his genius, like a kingfisher, glittered and shone by his native stream. He could not lift a dead world with him on the wings of eagles.

What then do we conclude? Simply that Tennyson as a lyric poet, pure and simple, is among the first in the language. He cannot, it will be urged, live with Shakespeare, Milton, Wordsworth, Shelley, and Browning? No, he cannot; but in the supreme house of verse there are many mansions, some great with turrets on seas forlorn, others light and open to the winds and the scent of flowers. Tennyson occasionally knocked at the great iron doors. They refused him. He did not need to knock at the others. They were open and waiting when he came.

HUMBERT WOLFE.

THE POET'S SONG

THE rain had fallen, the Poet arose,
    He pass'd by the town and out of the street;
A light wind blew from the gates of the sun,
    And waves of shadow went over the wheat,
And he sat him down in a lonely place,
    And chanted a melody loud and sweet,
That made the wild-swan pause in her cloud,.
    And the lark drop down at his feet.

The swallow stopt as he hunted the bee,
    The snake slipt under a spray,
The wild hawk stood with the down on his beak,
    And stared, with his foot on the prey,
And the nightingale thought, 'I have sung many songs,
    But never a one so gay,
For he sings of what the world will be
    When the years have died away.'

THE LADY OF SHALOTT

PART I

On either side the river lie
Long fields of barley and of rye,
That clothe the wold and meet the sky;
And thro' the field the road runs by
        To many-tower'd Camelot;
And up and down the people go,
Gazing where the lilies blow
Round an island there below,
        The island of Shalott.

Willows whiten, aspens quiver,
Little breezes dusk and shiver
Thro' the wave that runs for ever
By the island in the river
        Flowing down to Camelot.
Four grey walls, and four grey towers,
Overlook a space of flowers,
And the silent isle imbowers
        The Lady of Shalott.

By the margin, willow-veil'd,
Slide the heavy barges trail'd
By slow horses; and unhail'd
The shallop flitteth silken-sail'd
        Skimming down to Camelot:
But who hath seen her wave her hand?
Or at the casement seen her stand?
Or is she known in all the land,
        The Lady of Shalott?

Only reapers, reaping early
In among the bearded barley,
Hear a song that echoes cheerly
From the river winding clearly,
　　　　Down to tower'd Camelot:
And by the moon the reaper weary,
Piling sheaves in uplands airy,
Listening, whispers ''Tis the fairy
　　　　Lady of Shalott.'

Part II

There she weaves by night and day
A magic web with colours gay.
She has heard a whisper say,
A curse is on her if she stay
　　　　To look down to Camelot.
She knows not what the curse may be,
And so she weaveth steadily,
And little other care hath she,
　　　　The Lady of Shalott.

And moving thro' a mirror clear
That hangs before her all the year,
Shadows of the world appear.
There she sees the highway near
　　　　Winding down to Camelot:
There the river eddy whirls,
And there the surly village-churls,
And the red cloaks of market girls,
　　　　Pass onward from Shalott.

Sometimes a troop of damsels glad,
An abbot on an ambling pad,
Sometimes a curly shepherd-lad,
Or long-hair'd page in crimson clad,
　　　　Goes by to tower'd Camelot;
And sometimes thro' the mirror blue
The knights come riding two and two:
She hath no loyal knight and true,
　　　　The Lady of Shalott.

393

But in her web she still delights
To weave the mirror's magic sights,
For often thro' the silent nights
A funeral, with plumes and lights
      And music, went to Camelot:
Or when the moon was overhead,
Came two young lovers lately wed;
'I am half sick of shadows,' said
      The Lady of Shalott.

Part III

A bow-shot from her bower-eaves,
He rode between the barley-sheaves,
The sun came dazzling thro' the leaves
And flamed upon the brazen greaves
      Of bold Sir Lancelot.
A red-cross knight for ever kneel'd
To a lady in his shield,
That sparkled on the yellow field,
      Beside remote Shalott.

The gemmy bridle glitter'd free,
Like to some branch of stars we see
Hung in the golden Galaxy.
The bridle bells rang merrily
      As he rode down to Camelot:
And from his blazon'd baldric slung
A mighty silver bugle hung,
And as he rode his armour rung,
      Beside remote Shalott.

All in the blue unclouded weather
Thick-jewell'd shone the saddle-leather,
The helmet and the helmet-feather
Burn'd like one burning flame together,
      As he rode down to Camelot.
As often thro' the purple night,
Below the starry clusters bright,
Some bearded meteor, trailing light,
      Moves over still Shalott.

His broad clear brow in sunlight glow'd;
On burnish'd hooves his war-horse trode;
From underneath his helmet flow'd
His coal-black curls as on he rode,
      As he rode down to Camelot.
From the bank and from the river
He flash'd into the crystal mirror,
'Tirra lirra,' by the river
      Sang Sir Lancelot.

She left the web, she left the loom,
She made three paces thro' the room,
She saw the water-lily bloom,
She saw the helmet and the plume,
      She look'd down to Camelot.
Out flew the web and floated wide;
The mirror crack'd from side to side;
'The curse is come upon me,' cried
      The Lady of Shalott.

Part IV

In the stormy east-wind straining,
The pale yellow woods were waning,
The broad stream in his banks complaining,
Heavily the low sky raining
      Over tower'd Camelot;
Down she came and found a boat
Beneath a willow left afloat,
And round about the prow she wrote
      The Lady of Shalott.

And down the river's dim expanse—
Like some bold seer in a trance,
Seeing all his own mischance—
With a glassy countenance
      Did she look to Camelot.
And at the closing of the day
She loosed the chain, and down she lay;
The broad stream bore her far away,
      The Lady of Shalott.

Lying, robed in snowy white
That loosely flew to left and right—
The leaves upon her falling light—
Thro' the noises of the night
        She floated down to Camelot:
And as the boat-head wound along
The willowy hills and fields among,
They heard her singing her last song,
        The Lady of Shalott.

Heard a carol, mournful, holy,
Chanted loudly, chanted lowly,
Till her blood was frozen slowly,
And her eyes were darken'd wholly,
        Turn'd to tower'd Camelot.
For ere she reach'd upon the tide
The first house by the water-side,
Singing in her song she died,
        The Lady of Shalott.

Under tower and balcony,
By garden-wall and gallery,
A gleaming shape she floated by,
Dead-pale between the houses high,
        Silent into Camelot.
Out upon the wharfs they came,
Knight and burgher, lord and dame,
And round the prow they read her name,
        The Lady of Shalott.

Who is this? and what is here?
And in the lighted palace near
Died the sound of royal cheer;
And they cross'd themselves for fear,
        All the knights at Camelot:
But Lancelot mused a little space;
He said, 'She has a lovely face;
God in his mercy send her grace,
        The Lady of Shalott.'

MAUD

(XVIII)

I HAVE led her home, my love, my only friend.
There is none like her, none.
And never yet so warmly ran my blood
And sweetly, on and on
Calming itself to the long-wish'd-for end,
Full to the banks, close on the promised good.

None like her, none.
Just now the dry-tongued laurels' pattering talk
Seem'd her light foot along the garden walk,
And shook my heart to think she comes once more;
But even then I heard her close the door,
The gates of Heaven are closed, and she is gone.

There is none like her, none.
Nor will be when our summers have deceased.
O, art thou sighing for Lebanon
In the long breeze that streams to thy delicious East,
Sighing for Lebanon,
Dark cedar, tho' thy limbs have here increased,
Upon a pastoral slope as fair,
And looking to the South, and fed
With honey'd rain and delicate air,
And haunted by the starry head
Of her whose gentle will has changed my fate,
And made my life a perfumed altar-flame;
And over whom thy darkness must have spread
With such delight as theirs of old, thy great
Forefathers of the thornless garden, there
Shadowing the snow-limb'd Eve from whom she came.

(XXII)

Come into the garden, Maud,
  For the black bat, night, has flown,
Come into the garden, Maud,

I am here at the gate alone;
And the woodbine spices are wafted abroad,
  And the musk of the rose is blown.

For a breeze of morning moves,
  And the planet of Love is on high,
Beginning to faint in the light that she loves
  On a bed of daffodil sky,
To faint in the light of the sun she loves,
  To faint in his light, and to die.

All night have the roses heard
  The flute, violin, bassoon;
All night has the casement jessamine stirr'd
  To the dancers dancing in tune;
Till a silence fell with the waking bird,
  And a hush with the setting moon.

I said to the lily, 'There is but one
  With whom she has heart to be gay.
When will the dancers leave her alone?
  She is weary of dance and play.'
Now half to the setting moon are gone,
  And half to the rising day;
Low on the sand and loud on the stone
  The last wheel echoes away.

I said to the rose, 'The brief night goes
  In babble and revel and wine.
O young lord-lover, what sighs are those,
  For one that will never be thine?
But mine, but mine,' so I sware to the rose,
  'For ever and ever, mine.'

And the soul of the rose went into my blood,
  As the music clash'd in the hall;
And long by the garden lake I stood,
  For I heard your rivulet fall
From the lake to the meadow and on to the wood,
  Our wood, that is dearer than all;

From the meadow your walks have left so sweet
    That whenever a March-wind sighs
He sets the jewel-print of your feet
    In violets blue as your eyes,
To the woody hollows in which we meet
    And the valleys of Paradise.

The slender acacia would not shake
    One long milk-bloom on the tree;
The white lake-blossom fell into the lake
    As the pimpernel dozed on the lea;
But the rose was awake all night for your sake,
    Knowing your promise to me;
The lilies and roses were all awake,
    They sigh'd for the dawn and thee.

Queen rose of the rosebud garden of girls,
    Come hither, the dances are done,
In gloss of satin and glimmer of pearls,
    Queen lily and rose in one;
Shine out, little head, sunning over with curls,
    To the flowers, and be their sun.

There has fallen a splendid tear
    From the passion-flower at the gate.
She is coming, my dove, my dear;
    She is coming, my life, my fate;
The red rose cries, 'She is near, she is near;'
    And the white rose weeps, 'She is late;'
The larkspur listens, 'I hear, I hear;'
    And the lily whispers, 'I wait.'

She is coming, my own, my sweet;
    Were it ever so airy a tread,
My heart would hear her and beat,
    Were it earth in an earthy bed;
My dust would hear her and beat,
    Had I lain for a century dead;
Would start and tremble under her feet,
    And blossom in purple and red.

BREAK, BREAK, BREAK

BREAK, break, break,
  On thy cold grey stones, O Sea!
And I would that my tongue could utter
  The thoughts that arise in me.

O well for the fisherman's boy,
  That he shouts with his sister at play!
O well for the sailor lad,
  That he sings in his boat on the bay!

And the stately ships go on
  To their haven under the hill;
But O for the touch of a vanish'd hand,
  And the sound of a voice that is still!

Break, break, break,
  At the foot of thy crags, O Sea!
But the tender grace of a day that is dead
  Will never come back to me.

IN MEMORIAM

XI

CALM is the morn without a sound,
    Calm as to suit a calmer grief,
    And only thro' the faded leaf
The chestnut pattering to the ground:

Calm and deep peace on this high wold,
    And on these dews that drench the furze,
    And all the silvery gossamers
That twinkle into green and gold:

Calm and still light on yon great plain
    That sweeps with all its autumn bowers,
    And crowded farms and lessening towers,
To mingle with the bounding main:

Calm and deep peace in this wide air,
    These leaves that redden to the fall;
    And in my heart, if calm at all,
If any calm, a calm despair:

Calm on the seas, and silver sleep,
　　And waves that sway themselves in rest,
　　And dead calm in that noble breast
Which heaves but with the heaving deep.

CVI

Ring out, wild bells, to the wild sky,
　　The flying cloud, the frosty light:
　　The year is dying in the night;
Ring out, wild bells, and let him die.

Ring out the old, ring in the new,
　　Ring, happy bells, across the snow:
　　The year is going, let him go;
Ring out the false, ring in the true.

Ring out the grief that saps the mind,
　　For those that here we see no more;
　　Ring out the feud of rich and poor,
Ring in redress to all mankind.

Ring out a slowly dying cause,
　　And ancient forms of party strife;
　　Ring in the nobler modes of life,
With sweeter manners, purer laws.

Ring out the want, the care, the sin,
　　The faithless coldness of the times;
　　Ring out, ring out my mournful rhymes,
But ring the fuller minstrel in.

Ring out false pride in place and blood,
　　The civic slander and the spite;
　　Ring in the love of truth and right,
Ring in the common love of good.

Ring out old shapes of foul disease;
　　Ring out the narrowing lust of gold;
　　Ring out the thousand wars of old,
Ring in the thousand years of peace.

THE EAGLE

HE clasps the crag with crooked hands;
Close to the sun in lonely lands,
Ring'd with the azure world, he stands.

The wrinkled sea beneath him crawls;
He watches from his mountain walls,
And like a thunderbolt he falls.

THE LOTOS-EATERS

'COURAGE!' he said, and pointed toward the land,
'This mounting wave will roll us shoreward soon.'
In the afternoon they came unto a land
In which it seemed always afternoon.
All round the coast the languid air did swoon,
Breathing like one that hath a weary dream.
Full-faced above the valley stood the moon;
And like a downward smoke, the slender stream
Along the cliff to fall and pause and fall did seem.

A land of streams! some, like a downward smoke,
Slow-dropping veils of thinnest lawn, did go;
And some thro' wavering lights and shadows broke,
Rolling a slumbrous sheet of foam below.
They saw the gleaming river seaward flow
From the inner land: far off, three mountain-tops,
Three silent pinnacles of aged snow,
Stood sunset-flush'd: and, dew'd with showery drops,
Up-clomb the shadowy pine above the woven copse.

The charmed sunset linger'd low adown
In the red West: thro' mountain clefts the dale
Was seen far inland, and the yellow down
Border'd with palm, and many a winding vale
And meadow, set with slender galingale;
A land where all things always seem'd the same!
And round about the keel with faces pale,
Dark faces pale against that rosy flame,
The mild-eyed melancholy Lotos-eaters came.

Branches they bore of that enchanted stem,
Laden with flower and fruit, whereof they gave
To each, but whoso did receive of them,
And taste, to him the gushing of the wave
Far far away did seem to mourn and rave
On alien shores; and if his fellow spake,
His voice was thin, as voices from the grave;
And deep-asleep he seem'd, yet all awake,
And music in his ears his beating heart did make.

They sat them down upon the yellow sand,
Between the sun and moon upon the shore;
And sweet it was to dream of Fatherland,
Of child, and wife, and slave; but evermore
Most weary seem'd the sea, weary the oar,
Weary the wandering fields of barren foam.
Then some one said, 'We will return no more;'
And all at once they sang, 'Our island home
Is far beyond the wave; we will no longer roam.'

CHORIC SONG

THERE is sweet music here that softer falls
Than petals from blown roses on the grass,
Or night-dews on still waters between walls
Of shadowy granite, in a gleaming pass;
Music that gentlier on the spirit lies,
Than tir'd eyelids upon tir'd eyes;
Music that brings sweet sleep down from the blissful skies.
Here are cool mosses deep,
And thro' the moss the ivies creep,
And in the stream the long-leaved flowers weep,
And from the craggy ledge the poppy hangs in sleep.

Why are we weigh'd upon with heaviness,
And utterly consumed with sharp distress,
While all things else have rest from weariness?
All things have rest: why should we toil alone,
We only toil, who are the first of things,
And make perpetual moan,
Still from one sorrow to another thrown:

Nor ever fold our wings,
And cease from wanderings,
Nor steep our brows in slumber's holy balm;
Nor hearken what the inner spirit sings,
'There is no joy but calm!'
Why should we only toil, the roof and crown of things?

Lo! in the middle of the wood,
The folded leaf is woo'd from out the bud
With winds upon the branch, and there
Grows green and broad, and takes no care,
Sun-steep'd at noon, and in the moon
Nightly dew-fed; and turning yellow
Falls, and floats adown the air.
Lo! sweeten'd with the summer light,
The full-juiced apple, waxing over-mellow,
Drops in a silent autumn night.
All its allotted length of days,
The flower ripens in its place,
Ripens and fades, and falls, and hath no toil,
Fast-rooted in the fruitful soil.

Hateful is the dark-blue sky,
Vaulted o'er the dark-blue sea.
Death is the end of life; ah, why
Should life all labour be?
Let us alone. Time driveth onward fast,
And in a little while our lips are dumb.
Let us alone. What is it that will last?
All things are taken from us, and become
Portions and parcels of the dreadful Past.
Let us alone. What pleasure can we have
To war with evil? Is there any peace
In ever climbing up the climbing wave?
All things have rest, and ripen toward the grave
In silence; ripen, fall and cease:
Give us long rest or death, dark death, or dreamful ease.

How sweet it were, hearing the downward stream,
With half-shut eyes ever to seem
Falling asleep in a half-dream!

To dream and dream, like yonder amber light,
Which will not leave the myrrh-bush on the height;
To hear each other's whisper'd speech;
Eating the Lotos day by day,
To watch the crisping ripples on the beach,
And tender curving lines of creamy spray;
To lend our hearts and spirits wholly
To the influence of mild-minded melancholy;
To muse and brood and live again in memory,
With those old faces of our infancy
Heap'd over with a mound of grass,
Two handfuls of white dust, shut in an urn of brass!

Dear is the memory of our wedded lives,
And dear the last embraces of our wives
And their warm tears: but all hath suffer'd change;
For surely now our household hearths are cold:
Our sons inherit us: our looks are strange:
And we should come like ghosts to trouble joy.
Or else the island princes over-bold
Have eat our substance, and the minstrel sings
Before them of the ten-years' war in Troy,
And our great deeds, as half-forgotten things.
Is there confusion in the little isle?
Let what is broken so remain.
The Gods are hard to reconcile:
'Tis hard to settle order once again.
There *is* confusion worse than death,
Trouble on trouble, pain on pain,
Long labour unto aged breath,
Sore task to hearts worn out by many wars
And eyes grown dim with gazing on the pilot-stars.

But, propt on beds of amaranth and moly,
How sweet (while warm airs lull us, blowing lowly)
With half-dropt eyelids still,
Beneath a heaven dark and holy,
To watch the long bright river drawing slowly
His waters from the purple hill—

To hear the dewy echoes calling
From cave to cave thro' the thick-twined vine—
To watch the emerald-colour'd water falling
Thro' many a wov'n acanthus-wreath divine!
Only to hear and see the far-off sparkling brine,
Only to hear were sweet, stretch'd out beneath the pine.

The Lotos blooms below the barren peak:
The Lotos blows by every winding creek:
All day the wind breathes low with mellower tone:
Thro' every hollow cave and alley lone
Round and round the spicy downs the yellow Lotos-dust is
    blown.
We have had enough of action, and of motion we,
Roll'd to starboard, roll'd to larboard, when the surge was
    seething free,
Where the wallowing monster spouted his foam-fountains
    in the sea.
Let us swear an oath, and keep it with an equal mind,
In the hollow Lotos-land to live and lie reclined
On the hills like Gods together, careless of mankind.
For they lie beside their nectar, and the bolts are hurl'd
Far below them in the valleys, and the clouds are lightly
    curl'd
Round their golden houses, girdled with the gleaming world:
Where they smile in secret, looking over wasted lands,
Blight and famine, plague and earthquake, roaring deeps
    and fiery sands,
Clanging fights, and flaming towns, and sinking ships, and
    praying hands.
But they smile, they find a music centred in a doleful song
Steaming up, a lamentation and an ancient tale of wrong,
Like a tale of little meaning tho' the words are strong;
Chanted from an ill-used race of men that cleave the soil,
Sow the seed, and reap the harvest with enduring toil,
Storing yearly little dues of wheat, and wine and oil;
Till they perish and they suffer—some, 'tis whisper'd—
    down in hell
Suffer endless anguish, others in Elysian valleys dwell,
Resting weary limbs at last on beds of asphodel.

Surely, surely, slumber is more sweet than toil, the shore
Than labour in the deep mid-ocean, wind and wave and
    oar;
Oh rest ye, brother mariners, we will not wander more.

TEARS, IDLE TEARS

TEARS, idle tears, I know not what they mean,
Tears from the depth of some divine despair
Rise in the heart, and gather to the eyes,
In looking on the happy Autumn-fields,
And thinking of the days that are no more.

Fresh as the first beam glittering on a sail,
That brings our friends up from the underworld,
Sad as the last which reddens over one
That sinks with all we love below the verge;
So sad, so fresh, the days that are no more.

Ah, sad and strange as in dark summer dawns
The earliest pipe of half-awaken'd birds
To dying ears, when unto dying eyes
The casement slowly grows a glimmering square;
So sad, so strange, the days that are no more.

Dear as remember'd kisses after death,
And sweet as those by hopeless fancy feign'd
On lips that are for others; deep as love,
Deep as first love, and wild with all regret;
O Death in Life, the days that are no more.

THE SPLENDOUR FALLS

THE splendour falls on castle walls
    And snowy summits old in story:
The long light shakes across the lakes,
    And the wild cataract leaps in glory.
Blow, bugle, blow, set the wild echoes flying,
Blow, bugle; answer, echoes, dying, dying, dying.

O hark, O hear! how thin and clear,
    And thinner, clearer, farther going!
O sweet and far from cliff and scar
    The horns of Elfland faintly blowing.
Blow, let us hear the purple glens replying:
Blow, bugle; answer, echoes, dying, dying, dying.

O love, they die in yon rich sky,
    They faint on hill or field or river:
Our echoes roll from soul to soul,
    And grow for ever and for ever.
Blow, bugle, blow, set the wild echoes flying,
And answer, echoes, answer, dying, dying, dying.

NOW SLEEPS THE CRIMSON PETAL

'Now sleeps the crimson petal, now the white;
Nor waves the cypress in the palace walk;
Nor winks the gold fin in the porphyry font:
The fire-fly wakens: waken thou with me.

Now droops the milkwhite peacock like a ghost,
And like a ghost she glimmers on to me.

Now lies the Earth all Danaë to the stars,
And all thy heart lies open unto me.

Now slides the silent meteor on, and leaves
A shining furrow, as thy thoughts in me.

Now folds the lily all her sweetness up,
And slips into the bosom of the lake:
So fold thyself, my dearest, thou, and slip
Into my bosom and be lost in me.'

ULYSSES

It little profits that an idle king,
By this still hearth, among these barren crags,
Match'd with an aged wife, I mete and dole
Unequal laws unto a savage race,
That hoard, and sleep, and feed, and know not me.
I cannot rest from travel: I will drink

Life to the lees: all times I have enjoy'd
Greatly, have suffer'd greatly, both with those
That loved me, and alone; on shore, and when
Thro' scudding drifts the rainy Hyades
Vext the dim sea: I am become a name;
For always roaming with a hungry heart
Much have I seen and known; cities of men
And manners, climates, councils, governments,
Myself not least, but honour'd of them all;
And drunk delight of battle with my peers,
Far on the ringing plains of windy Troy.
I am a part of all that I have met;
Yet all experience is an arch wherethro'
Gleams that untravell'd world, whose margin fades
For ever and for ever when I move.
How dull it is to pause, to make an end,
To rust unburnish'd, not to shine in use!
As tho' to breathe were life. Life piled on life
Were all too little, and of one to me
Little remains: but every hour is saved
From that eternal silence, something more,
A bringer of new things; and vile it were
For some three suns to store and hoard myself,
And this grey spirit yearning in desire
To follow knowledge, like a sinking star,
Beyond the utmost bound of human thought.

    This is my son, mine own Telemachus,
To whom I leave the sceptre and the isle—
Well-loved of me, discerning to fulfil
This labour, by slow prudence to make mild
A rugged people, and thro' soft degrees
Subdue them to the useful and the good.
Most blameless is he, centred in the sphere
Of common duties, decent not to fail
In offices of tenderness, and pay
Meet adoration to my household gods,
When I am gone. He works his work, I mine.

    There lies the port: the vessel puffs her sail:
There gloom the dark broad seas. My mariners,
Souls that have toil'd, and wrought, and thought with me—

That ever with a frolic welcome took
The thunder and the sunshine, and opposed
Free hearts, free foreheads—you and I are old;
Old age hath yet his honour and his toil;
Death closes all: but something ere the end,
Some work of noble note, may yet be done,
Not unbecoming men that strove with Gods.
The lights begin to twinkle from the rocks:
The long day wanes: the slow moon climbs: the deep
Moans round with many voices. Come, my friends,
'Tis not too late to seek a newer world.
Push off, and sitting well in order smite
The sounding furrows; for my purpose holds
To sail beyond the sunset, and the baths
Of all the western stars, until I die.
It may be that the gulfs will wash us down:
It may be we shall touch the Happy Isles,
And see the great Achilles, whom we knew.
Tho' much is taken, much abides; and tho'
We are not now that strength which in old days
Moved earth and heaven; that which we are, we are;
One equal temper of heroic hearts,
Made weak by time and fate, but strong in will
To strive, to seek, to find, and not to yield.

MORTE D'ARTHUR

So all day long the noise of battle roll'd
Among the mountains by the winter sea;
Until King Arthur's table, man by man,
Had fall'n in Lyonnesse about their Lord,
King Arthur: then, because his wound was deep,
The bold Sir Bedivere uplifted him,
Sir Bedivere, the last of all his knights,
And bore him to a chapel nigh the field,
A broken chancel with a broken cross,
That stood on a dark strait of barren land.
On one side lay the Ocean, and on one
Lay a great water, and the moon was full.
Then spake King Arthur to Sir Bedivere:

'The sequel of to-day unsolders all
The goodliest fellowship of famous knights
Whereof this world holds record. Such a sleep
They sleep—the men I loved. I think that we
Shall never more, at any future time,
Delight our souls with talk of knightly deeds,
Walking about the gardens and the halls
Of Camelot, as in the days that were.
I perish by this people which I made,—
Tho' Merlin sware that I should come again
To rule once more—but let what will be, be,
I am so deeply smitten thro' the helm
That without help I cannot last till morn.
Thou therefore take my brand Excalibur,
Which was my pride: for thou rememberest how
In those old days, one summer noon, an arm
Rose up from out the bosom of the lake,
Clothed in white samite, mystic, wonderful,
Holding the sword—and how I row'd across
And took it, and have worn it, like a king:
And, wheresoever I am sung or told
In aftertime, this also shall be known:
But now delay not: take Excalibur,
And fling him far into the middle mere:
Watch what thou seëst, and lightly bring me word.'

To him replied the bold Sir Bedivere:
'It is not meet, Sir King, to leave thee thus,
Aidless, alone, and smitten thro' the helm.
A little thing may harm a wounded man.
Yet I thy hest will all perform at full,
Watch what I see, and lightly bring thee word.'

So saying, from the ruin'd shrine he stept
And in the moon athwart the place of tombs,
Where lay the mighty bones of ancient men,
Old knights, and over them the sea-wind sang
Shrill, chill, with flakes of foam. He, stepping down
By zig-zag paths, and juts of pointed rock,
Came on the shining levels of the lake.

There drew he forth the brand Excalibur,
And o'er him, drawing it, the winter moon,

Brightening the skirts of a long cloud, ran forth
And sparkled keen with frost against the hilt:
For all the haft twinkled with diamond sparks,
Myriads of topaz-lights, and jacinth-work
Of subtlest jewellery. He gazed so long
That both his eyes were dazzled, as he stood,
This way and that dividing the swift mind,
In act to throw: but at the last it seem'd
Better to leave Excalibur conceal'd
There in the many-knotted waterflags,
That whistled stiff and dry about the marge.
So strode he back slow to the wounded King.

    Then spake King Arthur to Sir Bedivere:
'Hast thou perform'd my mission which I gave?
What is it thou hast seen? or what hast heard?'

    And answer made the bold Sir Bedivere:
'I heard the ripple washing in the reeds,
And the wild water lapping on the crag.'

    To whom replied King Arthur, faint and pale:
'Thou hast betray'd thy nature and thy name,
Not rendering true answer, as beseem'd
Thy fëalty, nor like a noble knight:
For surer sign had follow'd, either hand,
Or voice, or else a motion of the mere.
This is a shameful thing for men to lie.
Yet now, I charge thee, quickly go again
As thou art lief and dear, and do the thing
I bad thee, watch, and lightly bring me word.'

    Then went Sir Bedivere the second time
Across the ridge, and paced beside the mere,
Counting the dewy pebbles, fix'd in thought;
But when he saw the wonder of the hilt,
How curiously and strangely chased, he smote
His palms together, and he cried aloud,

    'And if indeed I cast the brand away,
Surely a precious thing, one worthy note,
Should thus be lost for ever from the earth,
Which might have pleased the eyes of many men.
What good should follow this, if this were done?
What harm, undone? deep harm to disobey,

Seeing obedience is the bond of rule.
Were it well to obey then, if a king demand
An act unprofitable, against himself?
The King is sick, and knows not what he does.
What record, or what relic of my lord
Should be to aftertime, but empty breath
And rumours of a doubt? but were this kept,
Stored in some treasure-house of mighty kings,
Some one might show it at a joust of arms,
Saying, "King Arthur's sword, Excalibur,
Wrought by the lonely maiden of the Lake.
Nine years she wrought it, sitting in the deeps
Upon the hidden bases of the hills".
So might some old man speak in the aftertime
To all the people, winning reverence.
But now much honour and much fame were lost.'
   So spake he, clouded with his own conceit,
And hid Excalibur the second time,
And so strode back slow to the wounded King.
   Then spoke King Arthur, breathing heavily:
'What is it thou hast seen? or what hast heard?'
   And answer made the bold Sir Bedivere:
'I heard the water lapping on the crag,
And the long ripple washing in the reeds.'
   To whom replied King Arthur, much in wrath:
'Ah, miserable and unkind, untrue,
Unknightly, traitor-hearted! Woe is me!
Authority forgets a dying king,
Laid widow'd of the power in his eye
That bow'd the will. I see thee what thou art,
For thou, the latest-left of all my knights,
In whom should meet the offices of all,
Thou wouldst betray me for the precious hilt;
Either from lust of gold, or like a girl
Valuing the giddy pleasure of the eyes.
Yet, for a man may fail in duty twice,
And the third time may prosper, get thee hence:
But, if thou spare to fling Excalibur,
I will arise and slay thee with my hands.'
   Then quickly rose Sir Bedivere, and ran,

And, leaping down the ridges lightly, plunged
Among the bulrush-beds, and clutch'd the sword,
And strongly wheel'd and threw it. The great brand
Made lightnings in the splendour of the moon,
And flashing round and round, and whirl'd in an arch,
Shot like a streamer of the northern morn,
Seen where the moving isles of winter shock
By night, with noises of the northern sea.
So flash'd and fell the brand Excalibur:
But ere he dipt the surface, rose an arm
Clothed in white samite, mystic, wonderful,
And caught him by the hilt, and brandish'd him
Three times, and drew him under in the mere.
And lightly went the other to the King.

Then spoke King Arthur, drawing thicker breath:
'Now see I by thine eyes that this is done.
Speak out: what is it thou hast heard, or seen?'

And answer made the bold Sir Bedivere:
'Sir King, I closed mine eyelids, lest the gems
Should blind my purpose, for I never saw,
Nor shall see, here or elsewhere, till I die,
Not tho' I live three lives of mortal men,
So great a miracle as yonder hilt.
Then with both hands I flung him, wheeling him;
But when I look'd again, behold an arm,
Clothed in white samite, mystic, wonderful,
That caught him by the hilt, and brandish'd him
Three times, and drew him under in the mere.'

And answer made King Arthur, breathing hard:
'My end draws nigh; 'tis time that I were gone.
Make broad thy shoulders to receive my weight,
And bear me to the margin; yet I fear
My wound hath taken cold, and I shall die.'

So saying, from the pavement he half rose,
Slowly, with pain, reclining on his arm,
And looking wistfully with wide blue eyes
As in a picture. Him Sir Bedivere
Remorsefully regarded thro' his tears,
And would have spoken, but he found not words,
Then took with care, and kneeling on one knee,

O'er both his shoulders drew the languid hands,
And rising bore him thro' the place of tombs.

But, as he walk'd, King Arthur panted hard,
Like one that feels a nightmare on his bed
When all the house is mute. So sigh'd the King,
Muttering and murmuring at his ear, 'Quick, quick!
I fear it is too late, and I shall die.'
But the other swiftly strode from ridge to ridge,
Clothed with his breath, and looking, as he walk'd,
Larger than human on the frozen hills.
He heard the deep behind him, and a cry
Before. His own thought drove him, like a goad.
Dry clash'd his harness in the icy caves
And barren chasms, and all to left and right
The bare black cliff clang'd round him, as he based
His feet on juts of slippery crag that rang
Sharp-smitten with the dint of armed heels—
And on a sudden, lo! the level lake,
And the long glories of the winter moon.

Then saw they how there hove a dusky barge,
Dark as a funeral scarf from stem to stern,
Beneath them; and descending they were ware
That all the decks were dense with stately forms
Black-stoled, black-hooded, like a dream—by these
Three Queens with crowns of gold—and from them rose
A cry that shiver'd to the tingling stars,
And, as it were one voice, an agony
Of lamentation, like a wind, that shrills
All night in a waste land, where no one comes,
Or hath come, since the making of the world.

Then murmur'd Arthur, 'Place me in the barge,'
And to the barge they came. There those three Queens
Put forth their hands, and took the King, and wept.
But she, that rose the tallest of them all
And fairest, laid his head upon her lap,
And loosed the shatter'd casque, and chafed his hands,
And call'd him by his name, complaining loud,
And dropping bitter tears against his brow
Striped with dark blood: for all his face was white
And colourless, and like the wither'd moon

Smote by the fresh beam of the springing east;
And all his greaves and cuisses dash'd with drops
Of onset; and the light and lustrous curls—
That made his forehead like a rising sun
High from the dais-throne—were parch'd with dust;
Or, clotted into points and hanging loose,
Mix'd with the knightly growth that fringed his lips.
So like a shatter'd column lay the King;
Not like that Arthur who, with lance in rest,
From spur to plume a star of tournament,
Shot thro' the lists at Camelot, and charged
Before the eyes of ladies and of kings.

Then loudly cried the bold Sir Bedivere,
'Ah! my Lord Arthur, whither shall I go?
Where shall I hide my forehead and my eyes?
For now I see the true old times are dead,
When every morning brought a noble chance,
And every chance brought out a noble knight.
Such times have been not since the light that led
The holy Elders with the gift of myrrh.
But now the whole ROUND TABLE is dissolved
Which was an image of the mighty world;
And I, the last, go forth companionless,
And the days darken round me, and the years,
Among new men, strange faces, other minds.'

And slowly answered Arthur from the barge:
'The old order changeth, yielding place to new,
And God fulfils Himself in many ways,
Lest one good custom should corrupt the world.
Comfort thyself: what comfort is in me?
I have lived my life, and that which I have done
May He within Himself make pure! but thou,
If thou shouldst never see my face again,
Pray for my soul. More things are wrought by prayer
Than this world dreams of. Wherefore, let thy voice
Rise like a fountain for me night and day.
For what are men better than sheep or goats
That nourish a blind life within the brain,
If, knowing God, they lift not hands of prayer
Both for themselves and those who call them friend?

416

For so the whole round earth is every way
Bound by gold chains about the feet of God.
But now farewell. I am going a long way
With these thou seëst—if indeed I go—
(For all my mind is clouded with a doubt)
To the island-valley of Avilion;
Where falls not hail, or rain, or any snow,
Nor ever wind blows loudly; but it lies
Deep-meadow'd, happy, fair with orchard-lawns
And bowery hollows crown'd with summer sea,
Where I will heal me of my grievous wound.'
  So said he, and the barge with oar and sail
Moved from the brink, like some full-breasted swan
That, fluting a wild carol ere her death,
Ruffles her pure cold plume, and takes the flood
With swarthy webs. Long stood Sir Bedivere
Revolving many memories, till the hull
Look'd one black dot against the verge of dawn,
And on the mere the wailing died away.

CROSSING THE BAR

Sunset and evening star,
    And one clear call for me!
And may there be no moaning of the bar,
    When I put out to sea,

But such a tide as moving seems asleep,
    Too full for sound and foam,
When that which drew from out the boundless deep
    Turns again home.

Twilight and evening bell,
    And after that the dark!
And may there be no sadness of farewell,
    When I embark;

For tho' from out our bourne of Time and Place
    The flood may bear me far,
I hope to see my Pilot face to face
    When I have crost the bar.

ROBERT BROWNING

ROBERT BROWNING (1812–89) was privately educated. His first poem, *Pauline*, appeared in 1833. *Paracelsus*, which attracted the friendly notice of Carlyle, Wordsworth, and other men of letters, appeared in 1835. He next published *Strafford*, a tragedy, which was played at Covent Garden in 1837. *Sordello* followed in 1840. In 1842, he published *Dramatic Lyrics*: and, in 1845, *Dramatic Romances*, as iii and vii of the series *Bells and Pomegranates*. In 1846 he married Elizabeth Barrett and lived with her mainly in Italy at Pisa, Florence, and Rome, until her death in 1861, after which Browning settled in London. In 1850 he published *Christmas Eve and Easter Day*, and in 1855 *Men and Women*. *Dramatis Personae* appeared in 1864, and in 1868–9 the long poem, *The Ring and the Book*. His last volume of poems, *Asolando*, was published on the day of his death.

BROWNING is paradoxically the most original and the most representative poet of the nineteenth century. In his struggle to find the technique which would 'all-express' him, he defied more poetic conventions and invented more new forms than did any of his contemporaries. His artistic derelictions seemed sometimes like sabotage, and the instruments he shaped looked more like industrial salvage than lutes and viols for song. Yet the strains he was contriving were more distinctively the voice of his time than were the less heterodox melodies of his fellow poets. He is the prophet of Victorian individualism. His most vivid sense of existence was an awareness of his own personality; and so his strongest conviction was a belief in the sanctity of the individual. For him, therefore, all moral experience is by its nature a striving of the individual to put himself in his right relationship with God: and truth is a record of the infinitude of ways in which man has sought God. But each man's path is his own path; and the poet, as historian of the soul's journeyings, must seize the crucial turning—points peculiar to each man's pilgrimage. The artistic susceptibilities of a poet who sees his office so are closely bound up with his moral sentiments. His literary technique is but a means to an end. He must find a mode of expression and a style of communication which will reflect the facets of experience in true focus, catching every angle and every shade in their precise relationship to the whole spiritual pattern, as he himself sees it. Hence Browning's many diversions from conventional poetic practice, his frequent hazards in metre and imagery and vocabulary; hence, too, the seeming strangeness in his choice of material.

In his early poems, *Pauline*, *Paracelsus*, and *Sordello*, Browning is wrestling uncertainly with the problem which must loom most largely in a consciousness such as his. His individualism urges him to explore avenues by which the individual life may be fulfilled, and self grow to larger selfhood. But in *Pauline* self sinks into selfishness, clinging only to a desperate hope of salvation through a woman's love. This way of finding communion, though but a communion of two, in what else is a chorus of human atoms, is broadened in *Paracelsus*. Paracelsus seeks the means to rear his own individuality into a spiritual achievement, the rightness of which the world will instinctively recognize. But the course of his own growth sets him more and more at odds with others. He fails because he lacks love—love, however, now signifying more than the love of man for woman. Still holding to his faith in individualism, Browning avoids the dilemma by finding flaws in the personality of Paracelsus. He has trusted to reason and starved emotion, followed intellect and scorned intuition. His rational powers have smothered his spontaneous sympathies, cutting him off from his fellow mortals. In *Sordello* the quest is followed farther. Selfhood is attained through service, man gains his own soul by sacrifice. Most failure is most success.

But neither morally nor artistically has Browning truly found himself in these poems. They depict the individual striving with himself in the solitude of his own conscience. But this was a distorted picture of what the real experience of living was to a man like Browning, whose intuitive impulse was to nourish his own soul in the rich environment of the world and all the world's other souls: 'how good is man's life, the mere living.' These early poems fail formally since they do not present the force of circumstance as the vital machinery which gives to souls their bent. So Browning next turned to drama: for drama presents individuals, not in isolation, but in the encounters and conflicts of corporate life. Yet despite the many dramatic qualities of his genius, Browning failed as a dramatist. Although men and women excited his imagination more urgently than did inanimate nature, and although, above all, his eye was caught by the crucial moments at which a soul is being shaped in the stress of circumstance, yet a view of life so essentially dramatic as this was frustrated by Browning's belief in the autonomy of the individual in the only realm of high, spiritual significance, the kingdom of his own conscience. His heroes are formally tragic in that they are brought to death; but, dying, they attain spiritual integrity: and the audience is left in the confusion of irreconcilable values. In the meantime, however, there are magnificent scenes— the noble wrestlings of a tormented soul, or the mood and temperament of conflicting personalities welded dynamically by the heat of strife into lifelike characterization. The Ottima-Sebald scene of *Pippa Passes* displays Browning's dramatic genius magnificently. But it reveals the limited range within which his best was possible: and two characters do not make a play.

Browning's great discovery was the dramatic lyric and monologue. It was an instrument which reflected life just as his poetic vision took it to be. It mirrored the individual finding his place in his universe. It depicted a situation in which soul was made manifest through circumstance. The volumes of 1842, 1845, 1855, and 1864 are, with *The Ring and the Book*, Browning's real legacy. He did not at first realize all the possibilities of the new form, though even in 1842 there are *My Last Duchess* and the *Soliloquy in a Spanish Cloister*. But he discovered its ampler range by experiment. The main stuff of the dramatic lyric (or monologue—the form is the same whatever the title) is the personality of the speaker and the nature of the circumstances in which he speaks. At first, there was drama enough if one of these components was arresting. Johannes Agricola is a striking figure; the incident of the French Camp is a striking situation. In *Cristina* and *Porphyria's Lover*, person and situation are held together more dramatically, the situation proceeding from character, and the action itself being the means of characterization. In *Through the Metidja*, dramatization is still more complete, situation and character in actual interplay; as he rides, the riding excites the rider to the sublimation of his character in an ecstasy of exaltation. But there is yet an apparent handicap in the dramatic lyric. It seems more apt to the portraiture of persons so individual as to be abnormal, fanatics or even madmen. Its artistic value as a mirror of more representative human experience will depend on its power to focus no less vividly persons in whom the striking traits are attributes more normal in kind, though more exquisite in quality, and not the odd derangements of curious obsessions. *My Last Duchess* is a hint of such wider adjustment. Observers seeking the readiest signs of original personality have found them most abundantly in men of artistic temperament. Vasari's *Lives of the Painters* and Cellini's *Autobiography* are prototypes of the new literary art which the Renaissance passion for personality established, the art of biography. A man of artistic sensitiveness has not only these more picturesque spiritual features: his larger resources of subconscious apprehensiveness make him potentially a vastly richer personality. So Browning the individualist was more and more drawn to the artist type for his subjects. The aesthetic sensibilities of the last duchess's duke, however, are only used objectively by the poet as the dramatic features of the poem: the artists of the later poems will be ready to take the prior's pulpit-place, interpret God to all.

The 1845 volume explores farther into the range of the

dramatic lyric. Some of its poems are hardly dramatic at
all: personal lyrics merely given locality, like *Home
Thoughts*; or pieces of vivid but hardly dramatized narrative, *How They Brought the Good News*; or flashing pictures
of a lively scenario, *The Englishman in Italy*; or a sketch for
frontispiece to a political tract for the times, *The Lost
Leader*. Others are more directly dramatic; the melodra-
matic situation of *The Confessional* or the no less melodra-
matic character of the lady in *The Laboratory*. But there are
experiments in applying the form to lighter or to more
familiar circumstance, *Garden Fancies* and *Meeting at Night*
and *Parting at Morning*. In *The Lost Mistress* the inter-
weaving of circumstance and mood is sheer dramatic
divination: the sparrows, the leaf-buds on the vine, the easy
colloquial phrase mingling with more stilted expression,
and the metrical modifications all work together to effect
dramatic characterization. Of the lost mistress herself we
learn little, yet more than we know of the mistress from
whom another of Browning's singers parted at morn. The
limelight always shines so strongly on the protagonist that
the secondary person is often left in the shadow of the background. The major pieces of the 1845 volume are *The Bishop
orders his Tomb at St. Praxed's* and *Saul*. *St. Praxed's* is of the
same genre as *My Last Duchess*, but is a more complex and
thus a more humanized representation of the Renaissance
temperament so apt to Browning's artistic purpose. *Saul*,
that is, the part of *Saul* which appeared in 1845, brings the
dramatic lyric to the technical effectiveness which qualified
it for the fuller functions it was to serve in *Men and Women*
(1855). The *Saul* of 1845 is pure drama, and nothing more.
Its interest is psychological, not spiritual. It is the dramatic
exhibition of psychiatry at work; Saul is raised from torpor
to a normal nervous awareness, and the mental suggestions
which induce his gradual recovery are provided by the
themes of David's songs. But the finished *Saul* of 1855
transfers the interest from medicine to religion.

After Browning published the 1845 poems, he married Elizabeth Barrett. It was an event which for him fulfilled in experience all the intuitive expectations which his consciousness of life had excited. It gave his imagination élan and confidence. It promised validity to his imaginative speculations. It supplied the impulse for wider ventures of imaginative exploration in search of the ultimate meaning of life itself. The first-fruits, *Christmas Eve* and *Easter Day*, suffer because the full discipline of the dramatic lyric is abandoned, and inspiration is refracted by discourse.

Men and Women shows the full power of Browning's imaginative faculty. In the dedicatory *One Word More* he offers the volume to his wife as a true measure of his genius; and in *Transcendentalism* he claims for the poet a creative function by means of which he reaches intuitively to the mind of God. All the poems in this volume are projects with this purpose, though often their immediate subject seems much more ostensibly mundane. They are poems concerned with love, with art, and with religion. But these are merely rubrics for a catalogue, describing more or less conveniently the preoccupations of the persons of the poems. They are all of them pictures of men finding in the multiplicity of their experiences the peculiar way of their own destiny, men attaining their individuality through love or art or religion. Browning's own preoccupation with these themes is characteristic. The deepest stirrings of his consciousness are sensations of personal existence; but before they have reached consciousness, they have prompted other subconscious impulses, a bent to optimism, a sense of immortality and an instinct for God. These are the mainsprings of Browning's character.

Because Browning sees living in all its manifestations as a seeking after God, his poems are love poems or art poems or religious poems. Since God is God and man is man, there is a great gulf fixed; God, being God, is not man; and man, being man, is not God. The individualist's chaos appears inescapable. There is God, and there is man, distinct and apart. But once, and only once, chaos was bridged: God gave his only Son to be a man amongst men. For Browning the Incarnation is a historic fact, the one pledge of a divine purpose which unifies the diverse elements of existence. Hence Browning's religion was indifferent to all articles of faith except the Incarnation; hence, too, of all types of religious belief, unitarianism was the one with which he had no sympathy. Like the higher criticism, attempting to rationalize faith, it stultified reason by depriving it of the aid of intuition. In none of Browning's poems does he go behind the axiom that in the beginning was God. Man, like Caliban, may be remaking God in his own image. But God *is*. The more doctrinal poems like *Cleon*, *Karshish* and *A Death in the Desert* do not speculate about the existence of God. They are dramatic projections of the modes in which man responds to the thought that the divine nature may be this or may be that, an all-knowing or all-powerful God such as Cleon's or Karshish's, or a Christian God of love.

The Incarnation is the link between man and God. But how is man to have vital apprehension of this link? Deep in human nature, there are susceptibilities which, set vibrating by this or that impact of circumstance, stir man's whole sentient being to a responsiveness in which all his apprehensive faculties are active. In moments like this, sure though seldom, his personality, white-hot with its own energies, attains a supernormal capacity of perception. The nervous constitution of the artist makes him most apt to these intenser moments. That is his value to the rest of us. In their moments of 'possession' artists see into the heart of things, and having seen, they communicate the vision in a way which excites similar stirrings in us and so makes their experience authentically ours. Lippo Lippi and Abt Vogler are God's apostles: artistic rapture is a mode of religious experience.

Moments of artistic ecstasy, however, are rare; and their efficacy requires more than normal sensitiveness in men. Art cannot be the sole way to salvation. But all men are liable to love. For Browning falling in love is the circumstance which for the million provides the transcending experience in which their whole being is strung to its highest percipience: it is their moment of vision; their attainment of a conscious participation in the mind and purpose of God. So, like his art poems, Browning's love poems are religious poems. *Saul* depicts how a love greater than the love of man for woman is, as an actual and communicable sensation, the revelation of the love of God manifested by the gift of the God-man Christ. More usually, Browning's love poems express the passion of man for woman, and in them he is notoriously more prone to reveal, not the ecstasy of perfect fulfilment, but rather the partial benefactions of unrequited devotion; benefactions at least reconciling the lover to his lot as not all loss, and sometimes as in *The Last Ride* prompting him to a mystical perception of immortal love.

The prevailing undertone, the benevolence of the broken arc, brings us to themes even more characteristic of *Dramatis Personae* (1864). In the meantime, Browning's wife had died. His creative energy is diminished, its spontaneity flags. He is less able to lift his theme to the height of direct imaginative apprehension, less able to sustain it there. There are intermittent flashes of the old clear vision—'Fear death? to feel the fog in my throat?' But in the main, the weight of dead loss is a palpable burden. It is not that Browning's optimism had hitherto blinded him to sorrow and pain and sin; but he had seen these as those stresses of circumstance by which men are moulded. Now, however, there is more insistent need for a hereafter, not, indeed, as a compensation, but as opportunity to realize the perfection adumbrated by earth's imperfection. Abt Vogler's grasp of real permanence is reached by perceptions as immediate as those of the earlier poems, but it is only maintained by the force of argumentations which incite the reason to suspect fallacy. *Rabbi ben Ezra* is more homogeneously poetic; an old man's experiences, reviewed in rumination, stir him to a mood which finds sufficient conviction in a not unreasonable faith. But in the main *Dramatis Personae* sees more of the sombreness of life than of the joys of living.

The Ring and the Book is the last of Browning's poems in which the poetic power is adequate to its purpose. In many respects it is his greatest poem. But no poem of such length is all poetry. Much of the matter of it is the serious or playful exercise of an agile and brilliant mind. When the dramatized lyric spreads to the monologue, it dulls the sense of circumstance operating dynamically; when the monologue grows to the length of a book the power of circumstance in shaping destiny becomes a matter to measure in thought rather than to experience imaginatively in act. Yet the length is not all loss: the figures of Pompilia and Caponsacchi provide ampler material for closer and more sustained contemplation in what therefore may seem a more solid substantiation of the values which Browning had hitherto attributed to life in the brighter, briefer flashes of it caught in the dramatic lyrics. Finest of all is the book of the Pope: the characterization of Antonio Pignatelli in the fullness of his nature and the circumstance of his extreme old age gives to the findings of his judgement a broader validity than cool reason ever could adduce.

There were still volumes and volumes to come from Browning; but they are the writings of a man of letters rather than the creations of a poet. They are fuller of what he thinks than of what he sees and feels. There are momentary recaptures of the first fine careless raptures; almost from his deathbed, the *Epilogue to Asolando* is the individual's triumphant reassertion of his life-long optimistic faith. But, on the grounds of his own *Transcendentalism*, most of these late volumes may be left to lovers of Browning, and not put forward to the world as revelations which all who may must read.

H. CHARLTON.

MEMORABILIA

Ah, did you once see Shelley plain,
  And did he stop and speak to you?
And did you speak to him again?
  How strange it seems, and new!

But you were living before that,
  And also you are living after,
And the memory I started at—
  My starting moves your laughter!

I crossed a moor, with a name of its own
  And a certain use in the world no doubt,
Yet a hand's-breadth of it shines alone
  'Mid the blank miles round about:

For there I picked up on the heather
  And there I put inside my breast
A moulted feather, an eagle-feather—
  Well, I forget the rest.

HOME-THOUGHTS, FROM ABROAD

Oh, to be in England
Now that April's there,
And whoever wakes in England
Sees, some morning, unaware,
That the lowest boughs and the brushwood sheaf
Round the elm-tree bole are in tiny leaf,
While the chaffinch sings on the orchard bough
In England—now!

427

And after April, when May follows,
And the whitethroat builds, and all the swallows!
Hark, where my blossomed pear-tree in the hedge
Leans to the field and scatters on the clover
Blossoms and dewdrops—at the bent spray's edge—
That's the wise thrush; he sings each song twice over,
Lest you should think he never could recapture
The first fine careless rapture!
And though the fields look rough with hoary dew,
All will be gay when noontide wakes anew
The buttercups, the little children's dower
—Far brighter than this gaudy melon-flower!

HOME-THOUGHTS, FROM THE SEA

Nobly, nobly Cape Saint Vincent to the North-west died
    away;
Sunset ran, one glorious blood-red, reeking into Cadiz Bay;
Bluish 'mid the burning water, full in face Trafalgar lay;
In the dimmest North-east distance dawned Gibraltar
    grand and gray;
'Here and here did England help me: how can I help
    England?'—say,
Whoso turns as I, this evening, turn to God to praise and
    pray,
While Jove's planet rises yonder, silent over Africa.

MEETING AT NIGHT

The grey sea and the long black land;
And the yellow half-moon large and low;
And the startled little waves that leap
In fiery ringlets from their sleep,
As I gain the cove with pushing prow,
And quench its speed i' the slushy sand.

Then a mile of warm sea-scented beach;
Three fields to cross till a farm appears;
A tap at the pane, the quick sharp scratch
And blue spurt of a lighted match,
And a voice less loud, thro' its joys and fears,
Than the two hearts beating each to each!

PARTING AT MORNING

Round the cape of a sudden came the sea,
And the sun looked over the mountain's rim:
And straight was a path of gold for him,
And the need of a world of men for me.

THE LAST RIDE TOGETHER

I said—Then, dearest, since 'tis so,
Since now at length my fate I know,
Since nothing all my love avails,
Since all, my life seemed meant for, fails,
    Since this was written and needs must be—
My whole heart rises up to bless
Your name in pride and thankfulness!
Take back the hope you gave,—I claim
Only a memory of the same,
—And this beside, if you will not blame,
    Your leave for one more last ride with me.

My mistress bent that brow of hers;
Those deep dark eyes where pride demurs
When pity would be softening through,
Fixed me a breathing-while or two
    With life or death in the balance: right!
The blood replenished me again;
My last thought was at least not vain:
I and my mistress, side by side
Shall be together, breathe and ride,
So, one day more am I deified.
    Who knows but the world may end to-night?

Hush! if you saw some western cloud
All billowy-bosomed, over-bowed
By many benedictions—sun's
And moon's and evening-star's at once—
    And so, you, looking and loving best,
Conscious grew, your passion drew
Cloud, sunset, moonrise, star-shine too,

Down on you, near and yet more near,
Till flesh must fade for heaven was here!—
Thus leant she and lingered—joy and fear!
  Thus lay she a moment on my breast.

Then we began to ride. My soul
Smoothed itself out—a long-cramped scroll
Freshening and fluttering in the wind.
Past hopes already lay behind.
  What need to strive with a life awry?
Had I said that, had I done this,
So might I gain, so might I miss.
Might she have loved me? just as well
She might have hated, who can tell!
Where had I been now if the worst befell?
  And here we are riding, she and I.

Fail I alone, in words and deeds?
Why, all men strive and who succeeds?
We rode; it seemed my spirit flew,
Saw other regions, cities new,
  As the world rushed by on either side.
I thought,—All labour, yet no less
Bear up beneath their unsuccess.
Look at the end of work, contrast
The petty done, the undone vast,
This present of theirs with the hopeful past!
  I hoped she would love me; here we ride.

What hand and brain went ever paired?
What heart alike conceived and dared?
What act proved all its thought had been?
What will but felt the fleshly screen?
  We ride and I see her bosom heave.
There's many a crown for who can reach.
Ten lines, a statesman's life in each!
The flag stuck on a heap of bones,
A soldier's doing! what atones?
They scratch his name on the Abbey-stones.
  My riding is better, by their leave.

What does it all mean, poet? well,
Your brains beat into rhythm, you tell
What we felt only; you expressed
You hold things beautiful the best,
    And pace them in rhyme so, side by side.
'Tis something, nay 'tis much: but then,
Have you yourself what's best for men?
Are you—poor, sick, old ere your time—
Nearer one whit your own sublime
Than we who never have turned a rhyme?
    Sing, riding's a joy! For me, I ride.

And you, great sculptor—so, you gave
A score of years to Art, her slave,
And that's your Venus, whence we turn
To yonder girl that fords the burn!
    You acquiesce, and shall I repine?
What, man of music, you, grown grey
With notes and nothing else to say,
Is this your sole praise from a friend,
'Greatly his opera's strains intend,
But in music we know how fashions end!'
    I gave my youth—but we ride, in fine.

Who knows what's fit for us? Had fate
Proposed bliss here should sublimate
My being—had I signed the bond—
Still one must lead some life beyond,
    —Have a bliss to die with, dim-descried.
This foot once planted on the goal,
This glory-garland round my soul,
Could I descry such? Try and test!
I sink back shuddering from the quest.
Earth being so good, would heaven seem best?
    Now, heaven and she are beyond this ride.

And yet—she has not spoke so long!
What if heaven be that, fair and strong

At life's best, with our eyes upturned
Whither life's flower is first discerned,
　　We, fixed so, ever should so abide?
What if we still ride on, we two,
With life for ever old yet new,
Changed not in kind but in degree,
The instant made eternity,—
And heaven just prove that I and she
　　Ride, ride together, for ever ride?

O LYRIC LOVE

O LYRIC Love, half angel and half bird
And all a wonder and a wild desire,—
Boldest of hearts that ever braved the sun,
Took sanctuary within the holier blue,
And sang a kindred soul out to his face,—
Yet human at the red-ripe of the heart—
When the first summons from the darkling earth
Reached thee amid thy chambers, blanched their blue,
And bared them of the glory—to drop down,
To toil for man, to suffer or to die,—
This is the same voice: can thy soul know change?
Hail then, and hearken from the realms of help!
Never may I commence my song, my due
To God who best taught song by gift of thee,
Except with bent head and beseeching hand—
That still, despite the distance and the dark,
What was, again may be; some interchange
Of grace, some splendour once thy very thought,
Some benediction anciently thy smile:
—Never conclude, but raising hand and head
Thither where eyes, that cannot reach, yet yearn
For all hope, all sustainment, all reward,
Their utmost up and on,—so blessing back
In those thy realms of help, that heaven thy home,
Some whiteness which, I judge, thy face makes proud,
Some wanness where, I think, thy foot may fall!
(From *The Ring and the Book*, Part I.)

EPILOGUE TO 'ASOLANDO'

At the midnight in the silence of the sleep-time,
    When you set your fancies free,
Will they pass to where—by death, fools think, imprisoned—
Low he lies who once so loved you, whom you loved so,
        —Pity me?

Oh to love so, be so loved, yet so mistaken!
    What had I on earth to do
With the slothful, with the mawkish, the unmanly?
Like the aimless, helpless, hopeless, did I drivel
        —Being—who?

One who never turned his back but marched breast forward,
    Never doubted clouds would break,
Never dreamed, though right were worsted, wrong would
        triumph,
Held we fall to rise, are baffled to fight better,
        Sleep to wake.

No, at noonday in the bustle of man's work-time
    Greet the unseen with a cheer!
Bid him forward, breast and back as either should be,
'Strive and thrive!' cry 'Speed,—fight on, fare ever
        There as here!'

RABBI BEN EZRA

Grow old along with me!
    The best is yet to be,
The last of life, for which the first was made:
    Our times are in His hand
    Who saith 'A whole I planned,
Youth shows but half; trust God: see all, nor be afraid!'

    Not that, amassing flowers,
    Youth sighed 'Which rose make ours,
Which lily leave and then as best recall?'
    Not that, admiring stars,
    It yearned 'Nor Jove, nor Mars;
Mine be some figured flame which blends, transcends them
    all!'

Not for such hopes and fears
  Annulling youth's brief years,
Do I remonstrate: folly wide the mark!
  Rather I prize the doubt
  Low kinds exist without,
Finished and finite clods, untroubled by a spark.

  Poor vaunt of life indeed,
  Were man but formed to feed
On joy, to solely seek and find and feast:
  Such feasting ended, then
  As sure an end to men;
Irks care the crop-full bird? Frets doubt the maw-crammed
    beast?

  Rejoice we are allied
  To That which doth provide
And not partake, effect and not receive!
  A spark disturbs our clod;
  Nearer we hold of God
Who gives, than of His tribes that take, I must believe.

  Then, welcome each rebuff
  That turns earth's smoothness rough,
Each sting that bids nor sit nor stand but go!
  Be our joys three-parts pain!
  Strive, and hold cheap the strain;
Learn, nor account the pang; dare, never grudge the throe!

  For thence,—a paradox
  Which comforts while it mocks,—
Shall life succeed in that it seems to fail:
  What I aspired to be,
  And was not, comforts me:
A brute I might have been, but would not sink i' the scale.

  What is he but a brute
  Whose flesh has soul to suit,
Whose spirit works lest arms and legs want play?
  To man, propose this test—
  Thy body at its best,
How far can that project thy soul on its lone way?

434

Yet gifts should prove their use:
  I own the Past profuse
Of power each side, perfection every turn:
  Eyes, ears took in their dole,
  Brain treasured up the whole;
Should not the heart beat once 'How good to live and learn'?

Not once beat 'Praise be Thine!
  I see the whole design,
I, who saw power, see now love perfect too:
  Perfect I call Thy plan:
  Thanks that I was a man!
Maker, remake, complete,—I trust what Thou shalt do!'

For pleasant is this flesh;
  Our soul, in its rose-mesh
Pulled ever to the earth, still yearns for rest;
  Would we some prize might hold
  To match those manifold
Possessions of the brute,—gain most, as we did best!

Let us not always say
  'Spite of this flesh to-day
I strove, made head, gained ground upon the whole!'
  As the bird wings and sings,
  Let us cry 'All good things
Are ours, nor soul helps flesh more, now, than flesh helps
     soul!'

Therefore I summon age
  To grant youth's heritage,
Life's struggle having so far reached its term:
  Thence shall I pass, approved
  A man, for aye removed
From the developed brute; a god though in the germ.

And I shall thereupon
  Take rest, ere I be gone
Once more on my adventure brave and new:
  Fearless and unperplexed,
  When I wage battle next,
What weapons to select, what armour to indue.

435

Youth ended, I shall try
My gain or loss thereby;
Be the fire ashes, what survives is gold:
And I shall weigh the same,
Give life its praise or blame:
Young, all lay in dispute; I shall know, being old.

For note, when evening shuts,
A certain moment cuts
The deed off, calls the glory from the grey:
A whisper from the west
Shoots—'Add this to the rest,
Take it and try its worth: here dies another day.'

So, still within this life,
Though lifted o'er its strife,
Let me discern, compare, pronounce at last,
'This rage was right i' the main,
That acquiescence vain:
The Future I may face now I have proved the Past.'

For more is not reserved
To man, with soul just nerved
To act to-morrow what he learns to-day:
Here, work enough to watch
The Master work, and catch
Hints of the proper craft, tricks of the tool's true play.

As it was better, youth
Should strive, through acts uncouth,
Toward making, than repose on aught found made;
So, better, age, exempt
From strife, should know, than tempt
Further. Thou waitedst age; wait death nor be afraid!

Enough now, if the Right
And Good and Infinite
Be named here, as thou callest thy hand thine own,
With knowledge absolute,
Subject to no dispute
From fools that crowded youth, nor let thee feel alone.

Be there, for once and all,
　Severed great minds from small,
Announced to each his station in the Past!
　Was I, the world arraigned,
　Were they, my soul disdained,
Right? Let age speak the truth and give us peace at last!

Now, who shall arbitrate?
　Ten men love what I hate,
Shun what I follow, slight what I receive;
　Ten, who in ears and eyes
　Match me: we all surmise,
They this thing, and I that: whom shall my soul believe?

Not on the vulgar mass
　Called 'work' must sentence pass,
Things done, that took the eye and had the price;
　O'er which, from level stand,
　The low world laid its hand,
Found straightway to its mind, could value in a trice:

But all, the world's coarse thumb
　And finger failed to plumb,
So passed in making up the main account;
　All instincts immature,
　All purposes unsure,
That weighed not as his work, yet swelled the man's amount:

Thoughts hardly to be packed
　Into a narrow act,
Fancies that broke through language and escaped;
　All I could never be,
　All, men ignored in me,
This, I was worth to God, whose wheel the pitcher shaped.

Ay, note that Potter's wheel,
　That metaphor! and feel
Why time spins fast, why passive lies our clay,—
　Thou, to whom fools propound,
　When the wine makes its round,
'Since life fleets, all is change; the Past gone, seize to-day!'

Fool! All that is, at all,
　　Lasts ever, past recall;
Earth changes, but thy soul and God stand sure:
　　What entered into thee,
　　　That was, is, and shall be:
Time's wheel runs back or stops: Potter and clay endure.

He fixed thee mid this dance
　　Of plastic circumstance,
This Present, thou, forsooth, wouldst fain arrest:
　　Machinery just meant
　　To give thy soul its bent,
Try thee and turn thee forth, sufficiently impressed.

What though the earlier grooves
　　Which ran the laughing loves
Around thy base, no longer pause and press?
　　What though, about thy rim,
　　Scull-things in order grim
Grow out, in graver mood, obey the sterner stress?

Look not thou down but up!
　　To uses of a cup,
The festal board, lamp's flash and trumpet's peal,
　　The new wine's foaming flow,
　　The Master's lips a-glow!
Thou, heaven's consummate cup, what need'st thou with
　　earth's wheel?

But I need, now as then,
　　Thee, God, who mouldest men;
And since, not even while the whirl was worst,
　　Did I—to the wheel of life
　　With shapes and colours rife,
Bound dizzily,—mistake my end, to slake Thy thirst:

So, take and use Thy work:
　　Amend what flaws may lurk,
What strain o' the stuff, what warpings past the aim!
　　My times be in Thy hand!
　　Perfect the cup as planned!
Let age approve of youth, and death complete the same!

THE BISHOP ORDERS HIS TOMB AT SAINT PRAXED'S CHURCH

ROME, 15—.

VANITY, saith the preacher, vanity!
Draw round my bed: is Anselm keeping back?
Nephews—sons mine . . . ah God, I know not! Well—
She, men would have to be your mother once,
Old Gandolf envied me, so fair she was!
What's done is done, and she is dead beside,
Dead long ago, and I am Bishop since,
And as she died so must we die ourselves,
And thence ye may perceive the world's a dream.
Life, how and what is it? As here I lie
In this state-chamber, dying by degrees,
Hours and long hours in the dead night, I ask
'Do I live, am I dead?' Peace, peace seems all.
Saint Praxed's ever was the church for peace;
And so, about this tomb of mine. I fought
With tooth and nail to save my niche, ye know:
—Old Gandolf cozened me, despite my care;
Shrewd was that snatch from out the corner South
He graced his carrion with, God curse the same!
Yet still my niche is not so cramped but thence
One sees the pulpit o' the epistle-side,
And somewhat of the choir, those silent seats,
And up into the aery dome where live
The angels, and a sunbeam's sure to lurk:
And I shall fill my slab of basalt there,
And 'neath my tabernacle take my rest,
With those nine columns round me, two and two,
The odd one at my feet where Anselm stands:
Peach-blossom marble all, the rare, the ripe
As fresh-poured red wine of a mighty pulse.
—Old Gandolf with his paltry onion-stone,
Put me where I may look at him! True peach,
Rosy and flawless: how I earned the prize!
Draw close: that conflagration of my church
—What then? So much was saved if aught were missed!
My sons, ye would not be my death? Go dig

The white-grape vineyard where the oil-press stood,
Drop water gently till the surface sink,
And if ye find . . . Ah God, I know not, I! . . .
Bedded in store of rotten fig-leaves soft,
And corded up in a tight olive-frail,
Some lump, ah God, of *lapis lazuli*,
Big as a Jew's head cut off at the nape,
Blue as a vein o'er the Madonna's breast . . .
Sons, all have I bequeathed you, villas, all,
That brave Frascati villa with its bath,
So, let the blue lump poise between my knees,
Like God the Father's globe on both his hands
Ye worship in the Jesu Church so gay,
For Gandolf shall not choose but see and burst!
Swift as a weaver's shuttle fleet our years:
Man goeth to the grave, and where is he?
Did I say basalt for my slab, sons? Black—
'Twas ever antique-black I meant! How else
Shall ye contrast my frieze to come beneath?
The bas-relief in bronze ye promised me,
Those Pans and Nymphs ye wot of, and perchance
Some tripod, thyrsus, with a vase or so,
The Saviour at his sermon on the mount,
Saint Praxed in a glory, and one Pan
Ready to twitch the Nymph's last garment off,
And Moses with the tables . . . but I know
Ye mark me not! What do they whisper thee,
Child of my bowels, Anselm? Ah, ye hope
To revel down my villas while I gasp
Bricked o'er with beggar's mouldy travertine
Which Gandolf from his tomb-top chuckles at!
Nay, boys, ye love me—all of jasper, then!
'Tis jasper ye stand pledged to, lest I grieve.
My bath must needs be left behind, alas!
One block, pure green as a pistachio-nut,
There's plenty jasper somewhere in the world—
And have I not Saint Praxed's ear to pray
Horses for ye, and brown Greek manuscripts,
And mistresses with great smooth marbly limbs?
—That's if ye carve my epitaph aright,

Choice Latin, picked phrase, Tully's every word,
No gaudy ware like Gandolf's second line—
Tully, my masters? Ulpian serves his need!
And then how I shall lie through centuries,
And hear the blessed mutter of the mass,
And see God made and eaten all day long,
And feel the steady candle-flame, and taste
Good strong thick stupefying incense-smoke!
For as I lie here, hours of the dead night,
Dying in state and by such slow degrees,
I fold my arms as if they clasped a crook,
And stretch my feet forth straight as stone can point,
And let the bedclothes, for a mortcloth, drop
Into great laps and folds of sculptor's-work:
And as yon tapers dwindle, and strange thoughts
Grow, with a certain humming in my ears,
About the life before I lived this life,
And this life too, popes, cardinals and priests,
Saint Praxed at his sermon on the mount,
Your tall pale mother with her talking eyes,
And new-found agate urns as fresh as day,
And marble's language, Latin pure, discreet,
—Aha, ELUCESCEBAT quoth our friend?
No Tully, said I, Ulpian at the best!
Evil and brief hath been my pilgrimage.
All *lapis*, all, sons! Else I give the Pope
My villas! Will ye ever eat my heart?
Ever your eyes were as a lizard's quick,
They glitter like your mother's for my soul,
Or ye would heighten my impoverished frieze,
Piece out its starved design, and fill my vase
With grapes, and add a vizor and a Term,
And to the tripod ye would tie a lynx
That in his struggle throws the thyrsus down,
To comfort me on my entablature
Whereon I am to lie till I must ask
'Do I live, am I dead?' There, leave me, there!
For ye have stabbed me with ingratitude
To death—ye wish it—God, ye wish it! Stone—
Gritstone, a-crumble! Clammy squares which sweat

As if the corpse they keep were oozing through—
And no more *lapis* to delight the world!
Well, go! I bless ye. Fewer tapers there,
But in a row: and, going, turn your backs
—Ay, like departing altar-ministrants,
And leave me in my church, the church for peace,
That I may watch at leisure if he leers—
Old Gandolf, at me, from his onion-stone,
As still he envied me, so fair she was!

PROSPICE

Fear death?—to feel the fog in my throat,
  The mist in my face,
When the snows begin, and the blasts denote
  I am nearing the place,
The power of the night, the press of the storm,
  The post of the foe;
Where he stands, the Arch Fear in a visible form,
  Yet the strong man must go:
For the journey is done and the summit attained,
  And the barriers fall,
Though a battle's to fight ere the guerdon be gained,
  The reward of it all.
I was ever a fighter, so—one fight more,
  The best and the last!
I would hate that death bandaged my eyes, and forbore,
  And bade me creep past.
No! let me taste the whole of it, fare like my peers
  The heroes of old,
Bear the brunt, in a minute pay glad life's arrears
  Of pain, darkness and cold.
For sudden the worst turns the best to the brave,
  The black minute's at end,
And the elements' rage, the fiend-voices that rave,
  Shall dwindle, shall blend,
Shall change, shall become first a peace out of pain,
  Then a light, then thy breast,
O thou soul of my soul! I shall clasp thee again,
  And with God be the rest!

THE LOST MISTRESS

ALL's over, then: does truth sound bitter
   As one at first believes?
Hark, 'tis the sparrows' good-night twitter
   About your cottage eaves!

And the leaf-buds on the vine are woolly,
   I noticed that, to-day;
One day more bursts them open fully
   —You know the red turns grey.

To-morrow we meet the same then, dearest?
   May I take your hand in mine?
Mere friends are we,—well, friends the merest
   Keep much that I resign:

For each glance of the eye so bright and black,
   Though I keep with heart's endeavour,—
Your voice, when you wish the snowdrops back,
   Though it stay in my soul for ever!—

Yet I will but say what mere friends say,
   Or only a thought stronger;
I will hold your hand but as long as all may,
   Or so very little longer!

MY LAST DUCHESS

FERRARA

THAT's my last Duchess painted on the wall,
Looking as if she were alive. I call
That piece a wonder, now: Frà Pandolf's hands
Worked busily a day, and there she stands.
Will't please you sit and look at her? I said
'Frà Pandolf' by design, for never read
Strangers like you that pictured countenance,
The depth and passion of its earnest glance,
But to myself they turned (since none puts by
The curtain I have drawn for you, but I)
And seemed as they would ask me, if they durst,

443

How such a glance came there; so, not the first
Are you to turn and ask thus. Sir, 't was not
Her husband's presence only, called that spot
Of joy into the Duchess' cheek: perhaps
Frà Pandolf chanced to say 'Her mantle laps
Over my Lady's wrist too much,' or 'Paint
Must never hope to reproduce the faint
Half-flush that dies along her throat:' such stuff
Was courtesy, she thought, and cause enough
For calling up that spot of joy. She had
A heart . . . how shall I say? . . . too soon made glad,
Too easily impressed; she liked whate'er
She looked on, and her looks went everywhere.
Sir, 't was all one! My favour at her breast,
The dropping of the daylight in the West,
The bough of cherries some officious fool
Broke in the orchard for her, the white mule
She rode with round the terrace—all and each
Would draw from her alike the approving speech,
Or blush, at least. She thanked men—good! but thanked
Somehow—I know not how—as if she ranked
My gift of a nine-hundred-years-old name
With anybody's gift. Who'd stoop to blame
This sort of trifling? Even had you skill
In speech—(which I have not)—to make your will
Quite clear to such an one, and say 'Just this
Or that in you disgusts me; here you miss,
Or there exceed the mark'—and if she let
Herself be lessoned so, nor plainly set
Her wits to yours, forsooth, and made excuse,
—E'en then would be some stooping, and I choose
Never to stoop. Oh sir, she smiled, no doubt,
Whene'er I passed her; but who passed without
Much the same smile? This grew; I gave commands;
Then all smiles stopped together. There she stands
As if alive. Will't please you rise? We'll meet
The company below, then. I repeat,
The Count your master's known munificence
Is ample warrant that no just pretence
Of mine for dowry will be disallowed;

Though his fair daughter's self, as I avowed
At starting, is my object. Nay, we'll go
Together down, Sir. Notice Neptune, though,
Taming a sea-horse, thought a rarity,
Which Claus of Innsbruck cast in bronze for me.

From SAUL

.   .   .   .

THEN I tuned my harp,—took off the lilies we twine round
    its chords
Lest they snap 'neath the stress of the noontide—those sun-
    beams like swords!
And I first played the tune all our sheep know, as, one after
    one,
So docile they come to the pen-door, till folding be done.
They are white and untorn by the bushes, for lo, they have
    fed
Where the long grasses stifle the water within the stream's
    bed;
And now one after one seeks its lodging, as star follows star
Into eve and the blue far above us,—so blue and so far!

—Then the tune, for which quails on the cornland will each
    leave his mate
To fly after the player; then, what makes the crickets elate
Till for boldness they fight one another: and then, what has
    weight
To set the quick jerboa a-musing outside his sand house—
There are none such as he for a wonder, half bird and half
    mouse!
God made all the creatures and gave them our love and our
    fear,
To give sign, we and they are His children, one family here.

Then I played the help-tune of our reapers, their wine-
    song, when hand
Grasps at hand, eye lights eye in good friendship, and great
    hearts expand

And grow one in the sense of this world's life.—And then,
the last song
When the dead man is praised on his journey—'Bear, bear
him along
With his few faults shut up like dead flowerets! are balm-
seeds not here
To console us? The land has none left such as he on the
bier.
Oh, would we might keep thee, my brother!'—And then,
the glad chaunt
Of the marriage,—first go the young maidens, next, she
whom we vaunt
As the beauty, the pride of our dwelling.—And then, the
great march
Wherein man runs to man to assist him and buttress an arch
Nought can break; who shall harm them, our friends?—
Then, the chorus intoned
As the Levites go up to the altar in glory enthroned.
But I stopped here: for here in the darkness Saul groaned.

And I paused, held my breath in such silence, and listened
apart;
And the tent shook, for mighty Saul shuddered—and
sparkles 'gan dart
From the jewels that woke in his turban, at once with a
start,
All its lordly male-sapphires, and rubies courageous at
heart.
So the head: but the body still moved not, still hung there
erect.
And I bent once again to my playing, pursued it unchecked,
As I sang,—

'Oh, our manhood's prime vigour! No spirit feels waste,
Not a muscle is stopped in its playing nor sinew unbraced.
Oh, the wild joys of living! the leaping from rock up to
rock,
The strong rending of boughs from the fir-tree,—the cool
silver shock
Of the plunge in a pool's living water, the hunt of the bear,
And the sultriness showing the lion is couched in his lair.

And the meal, the rich dates yellowed over with gold dust
    divine,
And the locust-flesh steeped in the pitcher, the full draught
    of wine,
And the sleep in the dried river-channel where bulrushes
    tell
That the water was wont to go warbling so softly and well.
How good is man's life, the mere living! how fit to employ
All the heart and the soul and the senses for ever in joy!
Hast thou loved the white locks of thy father, whose sword
    thou didst guard
When he trusted thee forth with the armies, for glorious
    reward?
Didst thou see the thin hands of thy mother, held up as men
    sung
The low song of the nearly-departed, and heard her faint
    tongue
Joining in while it could to the witness, 'Let one more attest,
I have lived, seen God's hand thro' a lifetime, and all was
    for best?'
Then they sung thro' their tears in strong triumph, not
    much, but the rest.
And thy brothers, the help and the contest, the working
    whence grew
Such result as, from seething grape-bundles, the spirit
    strained true:
And the friends of thy boyhood—that boyhood of wonder
    and hope,
Present promise, and wealth of the future beyond the eye's
    scope,—
Till lo, thou art grown to a monarch; a people is thine;
And all gifts, which the world offers singly, on one head
    combine!
On one head, all the beauty and strength, love and rage
    (like the throe
That, a-work in the rock, helps its labour and lets the gold
    go)
High ambition and deeds which surpass it, fame crowning
    them,—all
Brought to blaze on the head of one creature—King Saul!'

ONE WORD MORE[1]

TO E. B. B.

London, September 1855

THERE they are, my fifty men and women
Naming me the fifty poems finished!
Take them, Love, the book and me together:
Where the heart lies, let the brain lie also.

Rafael made a century of sonnets,
Made and wrote them in a certain volume
Dinted with the silver-pointed pencil
Else he only used to draw Madonnas:
These, the world might view—but one, the volume.
Who that one, you ask? Your heart instructs you.
Did she live and love it all her lifetime?
Did she drop, his lady of the sonnets,
Die, and let it drop beside her pillow
Where it lay in place of Rafael's glory,
Rafael's cheek so duteous and so loving—
Cheek, the world was wont to hail a painter's,
Rafael's cheek, her love had turned a poet's?

You and I would rather read that volume,
(Taken to his beating bosom by it)
Lean and list the bosom-beats of Rafael,
Would we not? than wonder at Madonnas—
Her, San Sisto names, and Her, Foligno,
Her, that visits Florence in a vision,
Her, that's left with lilies in the Louvre—
Seen by us and all the world in circle.

You and I will never read that volume.
Guido Reni, like his own eye's apple
Guarded long the treasure-book and loved it.
Guido Reni dying, all Bologna
Cried, and the world cried too, 'Ours, the treasure!'
Suddenly, as rare things will, it vanished.

[1] Originally appended to the collection of poems called *Men and Women*.

Dante once prepared to paint an angel:
Whom to please? You whisper 'Beatrice'.
While he mused and traced it and retraced it,
(Peradventure with a pen corroded
Still by drops of that hot ink he dipped for,
When, his left-hand i' the hair o' the wicked,
Back he held the brow and pricked its stigma,
Bit into the live man's flesh for parchment,
Loosed him, laughed to see the writing rankle,
Let the wretch go festering through Florence)—
Dante, who loved well because he hated,
Hated wickedness that hinders loving,
Dante standing, studying his angel,—
In there broke the folk of his Inferno.
Says he—'Certain people of importance'
(Such he gave his daily dreadful line to)
'Entered and would seize, forsooth, the poet.'
Says the poet—'Then I stopped my painting.'

You and I would rather see that angel,
Painted by the tenderness of Dante,
Would we not?—than read a fresh Inferno.

You and I will never see that picture.
While he mused on love and Beatrice,
While he softened o'er his outlined angel,
In they broke, those 'people of importance':
We and Bice bear the loss for ever.

What of Rafael's sonnets, Dante's picture?
This: no artist lives and loves, that longs not
Once, and only once, and for one only,
(Ah, the prize!) to find his love a language
Fit and fair and simple and sufficient—
Using nature that's an art to others,
Not, this one time, art that's turned his nature.
Ay, of all the artists living, loving,
None but would forego his proper dowry,—
Does he paint? he fain would write a poem,—
Does he write? he fain would paint a picture,
Put to proof art alien to the artist's,

Once, and only once, and for one only,
So to be the man and leave the artist,
Gain the man's joy, miss the artist's sorrow.

Wherefore? Heaven's gift takes earth's abatement!
He who smites the rock and spreads the water,
Bidding drink and live a crowd beneath him,
Even he, the minute makes immortal,
Proves, perchance, but mortal in the minute,
Desecrates, belike, the deed in doing.
While he smites, how can he but remember,
So he smote before, in such a peril,
When they stood and mocked—'Shall smiting help us?'
When they drank and sneered—'A stroke is easy!'
When they wiped their mouths and went their journey,
Throwing him for thanks—'But drought was pleasant.'
Thus old memories mar the actual triumph;
Thus the doing savours of disrelish;
Thus achievement lacks a gracious somewhat;
O'er-importuned brows becloud the mandate,
Carelessness or consciousness—the gesture.
For he bears an ancient wrong about him,
Sees and knows again those phalanxed faces,
Hears, yet one time more, the 'customed prelude—
'How shouldst thou, of all men, smite, and save us?'
Guesses what is like to prove the sequel—
'Egypt's flesh-pots—nay, the drought was better.'

Oh, the crowd must have emphatic warrant!
Theirs, the Sinai-forehead's cloven brilliance,
Right-arm's rod-sweep, tongue's imperial fiat.
Never dares the man put off the prophet.

Did he love one face from out the thousands,
(Were she Jethro's daughter, white and wifely,
Were she but the Æthiopian bondslave,)
He would envy yon dumb patient camel,
Keeping a reserve of scanty water
Meant to save his own life in the desert;
Ready in the desert to deliver
(Kneeling down to let his breast be opened)
Hoard and life together for his mistress.

450

I shall never, in the years remaining,
Paint you pictures, no, nor carve you statues,
Make you music that should all-express me;
So it seems: I stand on my attainment.
This of verse alone, one life allows me;
Verse and nothing else have I to give you.
Other heights in other lives, God willing:
All the gifts from all the heights, your own, Love!

Yet a semblance of resource avails us—
Shade so finely touched, love's sense must seize it.
Take these lines, look lovingly and nearly,
Lines I write the first time and the last time.
He who works in fresco, steals a hair-brush,
Curbs the liberal hand, subservient proudly,
Cramps his spirit, crowds its all in little,
Makes a strange art of an art familiar,
Fills his lady's missal-marge with flowerets.
He who blows thro' bronze, may breathe thro' silver,
Fitly serenade a slumbrous princess.
He who writes, may write for once as I do.

Love, you saw me gather men and women,
Live or dead or fashioned by my fancy,
Enter each and all, and use their service,
Speak from every mouth,—the speech, a poem.
Hardly shall I tell my joys and sorrows,
Hopes and fears, belief and disbelieving:
I am mine and yours—the rest be all men's,
Karshish, Cleon, Norbert and the fifty.
Let me speak this once in my true person,
Not as Lippo, Roland or Andrea,
Though the fruit of speech be just this sentence:
Pray you, look on these my men and women,
Take and keep my fifty poems finished;
Where my heart lies, let my brain lie also!
Poor the speech; be how I speak, for all things.

Not but that you know me! Lo, the moon's self!
Here in London, yonder late in Florence,
Still we find her face, the thrice-transfigured.

451

Curving on a sky imbrued with colour,
Drifted over Fiesole by twilight,
Came she, our new crescent of a hair's-breadth.
Full she flared it, lamping Samminiato,
Rounder 'twixt the cypresses and rounder,
Perfect till the nightingales applauded.
Now, a piece of her old self, impoverished,
Hard to greet, she traverses the house-roofs,
Hurries with unhandsome thrift of silver,
Goes dispiritedly, glad to finish.

What, there's nothing in the moon noteworthy?
Nay: for if that moon could love a mortal,
Use, to charm him (so to fit a fancy),
All her magic ('tis the old sweet mythos),
She would turn a new side to her mortal,
Side unseen of herdsman, huntsman, steersman—
Blank to Zoroaster on his terrace,
Blind to Galileo on his turret,
Dumb to Homer, dumb to Keats—him, even!
Think, the wonder of the moonstruck mortal—
When she turns round, comes again in heaven,
Opens out anew for worse or better!
Proves she like some portent of an iceberg
Swimming full upon the ship it founders,
Hungry with huge teeth of splintered crystals?
Proves she as the paved work of a sapphire
Seen by Moses when he climbed the mountain?
Moses, Aaron, Nadab and Abihu
Climbed and saw the very God, the Highest,
Stand upon the paved work of a sapphire.
Like the bodied heaven in his clearness
Shone the stone, the sapphire of that paved work,
When they ate and drank and saw God also!

What were seen? None knows, none ever shall know.
Only this is sure—the sight were other,
Not the moon's same side, born late in Florence,
Dying now impoverished here in London.
God be thanked, the meanest of his creatures

Boasts two soul-sides, one to face the world with,
One to show a woman when he loves her!

This I say of me, but think of you, Love!
This to you—yourself my moon of poets!
Ah, but that's the world's side, there's the wonder,
Thus they see you, praise you, think they know you!
There, in turn I stand with them and praise you
Out of my own self, I dare to phrase it.
But the best is when I glide from out them,
Cross a step or two of dubious twilight,
Come out on the other side, the novel
Silent silver lights and darks undreamed of,
Where I hush and bless myself with silence.

Oh, their Rafael of the dear Madonnas,
Oh, their Dante of the dread Inferno,
Wrote one song—and in my brain I sing it,
Drew one angel—borne, see, on my bosom!

MATTHEW ARNOLD

MATTHEW ARNOLD (1822–88), son of T. Arnold, the great headmaster of Rugby, became fellow of Oriel College, Oxford, and an inspector of schools, and was professor of poetry at Oxford (1857–67). His first volume of poems (1849) contained *The Forsaken Merman* and the sonnet on Shakespeare. In 1853 appeared a volume of *Poems* containing extracts from the earlier book, and, in addition, *Sohrab and Rustum* and *The Scholar Gipsy; Poems, Second Series*, including *Balder Dead*, appeared in 1855; *Merope, a Tragedy* in 1858; and *New Poems*, including *Thyrsis, Rugby Chapel*, and other well-known pieces, in 1867. The later part of his life was devoted to prose writings of literary criticism, and essays on religion, philosophy, and questions of social policy.

MATTHEW ARNOLD'S imagination was haunted by the idea of the Great Poem. What the Great Poem was he supposed to be most easily divined from the study of Greek antiquity. The Great Poem is essentially a poem of action. All the other kinds—those not excepted in which Matthew Arnold's own power finds its best expression, the elegiac and lyric—are subordinate, are less interesting and vital. 'What', he writes, 'are the eternal objects of Poetry, among all nations and at all times? They are actions; human actions.' In the poetry of human actions, his single success is *Sohrab and Rustum*. In this poem alone, he fulfilled the desire of his heart: *Sohrab and Rustum* shines in solitary starlike splendour. It is easy to accuse its rather *studied* beauty; and permissible, perhaps, in connexion with Matthew Arnold's poetry generally, to wonder whether the beautiful is quite as hard as he found it, or quite so dependent as he supposed on the elements of harmony and proportion. Yet here, in *Sohrab and Rustum*, are the cognizable lineaments of the Great Poem. No other poem of the age, perhaps no other poem from any age of our poetry, has the same serenity and severity of beauty; for a composition equally pure and noble in all its parts we must go, where Matthew Arnold went, to the Greeks.

The volume which contained *Sohrab and Rustum* contained

also *The Scholar Gipsy*. But for *The Scholar Gipsy* Matthew
Arnold had no use. 'What does it *do* for you?', he asks
Clough, impatiently. 'Sohrab and Rustum *animates*—the
Gipsy Scholar at best awakens a pleasing melancholy. But
this is not what we want.' I do not think the world will
willingly let die *Sohrab and Rustum*. But whatever dies, it
will save *The Scholar Gipsy*, with its companion-poem *Thyrsis*;
and if it saves *Sohrab and Rustum*, it will save it, perhaps, for
a quality which does not belong to the Great Poem. In
Sohrab and Rustum Matthew Arnold supposed himself to have
'imitated Homer'. In trying to be like Homer, he certainly
succeeded in being like Virgil—the same is true of Virgil
himself. 'Over the whole of the great poem of Virgil',
Matthew Arnold writes, 'there broods an ineffable melancholy . . . a sweet touching sadness'; the poem expresses,
not action, but 'the haunting, the irresistible self-dissatis-
faction of Virgil's heart'—the epic he designed had turned
to elegy. *Sohrab and Rustum* is so far like the *Aeneid* that it
wears the beauty of elegy. It is less like the Great Poem
than Matthew Arnold supposed; and more like himself.

Sohrab and Rustum was published in 1853. Matthew
Arnold essayed the Great Poem again in 1855, with *Balder
Dead*, and in 1858, with *Merope*. But it was not given to him
to be great in this kind twice; and in any lesser greatness he
was unwilling to interest himself. Men demand, he says,
something more from poetry than that it should 'add zest
to their melancholy or grace to their dreams'; and 'a feeling
of this kind', he adds, 'is the basis of my nature—and of my
poetics'. After *Merope*, accordingly, he wrote very little
poetry. Most of the so-called *New Poems* of 1867 are not
new at all: except for *Thyrsis*, written in 1864–5, the book
contains almost nothing to which a date later than 1858
can be certainly assigned. The Great Poem, or nothing—
it had come to that! That he should fall from action to
reflection, that his best in poetry should express only a
miscellany of lovely melancholies, the heart's obscure and

abiding self-dissatisfactions,—this was hardly to be borne. Of no poet, who did not die young, is the poetry so short-lived; and the explanation must be fetched, I fancy, from his preoccupation with the Great Poem. The *Poems* of 1849 had been preceded, in 1849 by *The Strayed Reveller*, and in 1852 by *Empedocles on Etna*. But Matthew Arnold had printed the *Reveller* and *Empedocles*, it would seem, only for the pleasure of withdrawing them from the press imme-diately—*an ideo tantum veneras ut exires?* He had no wish to be great in that department of poetry in which he is, in truth, the greatest of our poets, the department of elegy and reflection.

Of the Great Poem, *Sohrab and Rustum* is at least the im-pressive shadow. About Matthew Arnold's greatness in elegy and the reflective lyric there is nothing shadowy at all. Those twin perfections, *The Scholar Gipsy* and *Thyrsis*, sweet Hesper-Phosphor of elegy, shine unsetting, with *Lycidas* and *Adonais*, in a firmament where any neighbouring star is of secondary magnitude. Matthew Arnold confessed a debt here to Theocritus; so unwilling was he to be like himself. But if in these two poems he is debtor to any one, it is to Keats. The form of his stanza is certainly modelled on Keats; and both poems wear just that 'perfection of loveli-ness' which only the great Odes of Keats have. When he printed *The Scholar Gipsy*—though hardly when he wrote it—he was (his letters show) temporarily out of love with Keats—hence that fretful 'What does it *do* for you?' *What does it do for you!* It does only what only the great Odes of Keats do in the same degree; it exercises that sway over mind and heart which belongs to mere 'perfection of loveliness'.

These two poems are perhaps not especially individual. Matthew Arnold uses for them a manner richer and more ornate than he affects elsewhere. Disciplined in the Great Poem—of which he conceived expression and ornament to be 'subordinate characters' only—he affected, when he

456

passed from this to other kinds, a manner the barest imaginable. I have placed in this Selection the poem entitled *Growing Old*; not because Matthew Arnold did not write many greater lyrics, but because he wrote none more individual. He had it in mind, I must think, when he wrote it, to see just how bare poetry could be without becoming prose. 'Plainness and clearness without shadow of stain', bareness wintry beyond Wordsworth—all these are here; but the thing is still a poem, a poem with its own music and emotion. In truth, it is a test poem—if you do not like it, you will not like Matthew Arnold, and you will be in some danger of liking prettiness, caprice, rhodomontade.

Growing Old was first printed in 1867; but it would not surprise me to be told that it was written three years earlier. Just three years earlier, Browning had given to the world *Rabbi Ben Ezra*. In 1853 Matthew Arnold had deliberately challenged the *Morte d'Arthur* with *Sohrab and Rustum*. But if he hated prettiness, he hated quite as much caprice and rhodomontade. 'Grow old along with me, the best is yet to be'—'What *is* it to grow old?' It is difficult not to see in *Growing Old* a deliberate challenge to *Rabbi Ben Ezra*. He owed Browning, perhaps, a better return; for if Browning had admired less generously the long soliloquy in the first part of *Empedocles on Etna*, *Rabbi Ben Ezra* might never have been written. Tennyson and Browning, of course, had the world with them. Against the world Matthew Arnold had with him the integrity of his own conscience—and Swinburne. Reviewing the volume of 1867, 'The majesty and composure of thought and verse', Swinburne writes, 'the perfect clearness and competence of words, distinguish this from other poetry of the intellect now more approved and applauded'—in the last clause, he is plainly glancing at Browning and Tennyson. Defining more closely Matthew Arnold's competence of words, 'He has matched', he says, 'against the Attic of the Gods this Hyperborean dialect of ours, and has not earned the doom of Marsyas. Here is indeed the triumph of the lyre; and he has had to refashion it for himself among a nation and in an age of flute-players and horn-blowers.' Among the flute-players was Tennyson, and first of the horn-blowers Browning. Other phrases of the same essay hit off finely some of Matthew Arnold's characteristic excellences: 'chastity of colour and noble justice of composition, the faithful and fruitful touches of landscape incident'; 'music and colour and bright sadness as of a rainy sunset or sundawn'.

Swinburne's later and more corrupt judgements on Matthew Arnold are—with their ignoble causes—best forgotten. But in 1867 he knew, he only, who was the greatest of the Victorian poets.

H. W. GARROD.

THE FORSAKEN MERMAN

COME, dear children, let us away;
Down and away below!
Now my brothers call from the bay,
Now the great winds shorewards blow,
Now the salt tides seawards flow;
Now the wild white horses play,
Champ and chafe and toss in the spray.
Children dear, let us away!
This way, this way!

Call her once before you go—
Call once yet!
In a voice that she will know:
'Margaret! Margaret!'
Children's voices should be dear
(Call once more) to a mother's ear;
Children's voices, wild with pain—
Surely she will come again!
Call her once and come away;
This way, this way!
'Mother dear, we cannot stay!
The wild white horses foam and fret.'
Margaret! Margaret!

458

Come, dear children, come away down;
Call no more!
One last look at the white-wall'd town,
And the little grey church on the windy shore,
Then come down!
She will not come though you call all day;
Come away, come away!

Children dear, was it yesterday
We heard the sweet bells over the bay?
In the caverns where we lay,
Through the surf and through the swell,
The far-off sound of a silver bell?
Sand-strewn caverns, cool and deep,
Where the winds are all asleep;
Where the spent lights quiver and gleam,
Where the salt weed sways in the stream,
Where the sea-beasts, ranged all round,
Feed in the ooze of their pasture-ground;
Where the sea-snakes coil and twine,
Dry their mail and bask in the brine;
Where great whales come sailing by,
Sail and sail, with unshut eye,
Round the world for ever and aye?
When did music come this way?
Children dear, was it yesterday?

Children dear, was it yesterday
(Call yet once) that she went away?
Once she sate with you and me,
On a red gold throne in the heart of the sea,
And the youngest sate on her knee.
She comb'd its bright hair, and she tended it well,
When down swung the sound of a far-off bell.
She sigh'd, she look'd up through the clear green sea;
She said; 'I must go, for my kinsfolk pray
In the little grey church on the shore to-day.
'Twill be Easter-time in the world—ah me!
And I lose my poor soul, Merman! here with thee.'

I said: 'Go up, dear heart, through the waves;
Say thy prayer, and come back to the kind sea-caves!'
She smiled, she went up through the surf in the bay.
Children dear, was it yesterday?

Children dear, were we long alone?
'The sea grows stormy, the little ones moan;
Long prayers,' I said, 'in the world they say;
Come!' I said, and we rose through the surf in the bay.
We went up the beach, by the sandy down
Where the sea-stocks bloom, to the white-wall'd town;
Through the narrow paved streets, where all was still,
To the little grey church on the windy hill.
From the church came a murmur of folk at their prayers,
But we stood without in the cold blowing airs.
We climb'd on the graves, on the stones worn with rains,
And we gaz'd up the aisle through the small leaded panes.
She sate by the pillar; we saw her clear:
'Margaret, hist! come quick, we are here!
Dear heart', I said, 'we are long alone;
The sea grows stormy, the little ones moan.'
But, ah, she gave me never a look,
For her eyes were seal'd to the holy book!
Loud prays the priest; shut stands the door.
Come away, children, call no more!
Come away, come down, call no more!

Down, down, down!
Down to the depths of the sea!
She sits at her wheel in the humming town,
Singing most joyfully.
Hark what she sings: 'O joy, O joy,
For the humming street, and the child with its toy!
For the priest, and the bell, and the holy well;
For the wheel where I spun,
And the blessed light of the sun!'
And so she sings her fill,
Singing most joyfully,
Till the spindle drops from her hand,

And the whizzing wheel stands still.
She steals to the window, and looks at the sand,
And over the sand at the sea;
And her eyes are set in a stare;
And anon there breaks a sigh,
And anon there drops a tear,
From a sorrow-clouded eye,
And a heart sorrow-laden,
A long, long sigh;
For the cold strange eyes of a little Mermaiden
And the gleam of her golden hair.

Come away, away children;
Come children, come down!
The hoarse wind blows coldly;
Lights shine in the town.
She will start from her slumber
When gusts shake the door;
She will hear the winds howling,
Will hear the waves roar.
We shall see, while above us
The waves roar and whirl,
A ceiling of amber,
A pavement of pearl.
Singing: 'Here came a mortal,
But faithless was she!
And alone dwell for ever
The kings of the sea.'

But, children, at midnight,
When soft the winds blow,
When clear falls the moonlight,
When spring-tides are low;
When sweet airs come seaward
From heaths starr'd with broom,
And high rocks throw mildly
On the blanch'd sands a gloom;
Up the still, glistening beaches,
Up the creeks we will hie,
Over banks of bright seaweed

461

The ebb-tide leaves dry.
We will gaze, from the sand-hills,
At the white, sleeping town;
At the church on the hill-side—
And then come back down.
Singing: 'There dwells a loved one,
But cruel is she!
She left lonely for ever
The kings of the sea.'

SHAKESPEARE

OTHERS abide our question. Thou art free.
We ask and ask—Thou smilest and art still,
Out-topping knowledge. For the loftiest hill
Who to the stars uncrowns his majesty,
Planting his steadfast footsteps in the sea,
Making the heaven of heavens his dwelling-place,
Spares but the cloudy border of his base
To the foil'd searching of mortality:
And thou, who didst the stars and sunbeams know,
Self-school'd, self-scann'd, self-honour'd, self-secure,
Didst tread on earth unguess'd at.—Better so!
All pains the immortal spirit must endure,
All weakness which impairs, all griefs which bow,
Find their sole speech in that victorious brow.

MEMORIAL VERSES

APRIL, 1850

GOETHE in Weimar sleeps, and Greece,
Long since, saw Byron's struggle cease.
But one such death remain'd to come.
The last poetic voice is dumb—
We stand today by Wordsworth's tomb.

When Byron's eyes were shut in death,
We bow'd our head and held our breath.
He taught us little; but our soul
Had *felt* him like the thunder's roll.

462

With shivering heart the strife we saw
Of passion with eternal law;
And yet with reverential awe
We watch'd the fount of fiery life
Which served for that Titanic strife.

When Goethe's death was told, we said:
Sunk, then, is Europe's sagest head.
Physician of the iron age,
Goethe has done his pilgrimage.
He took the suffering human race,
He read each wound, each weakness clear;
And struck his finger on the place,
And said: *Thou ailest here, and here!*
He look'd on Europe's dying hour
Of fitful dream and feverish power;
His eye plung'd down the weltering strife,
The turmoil of expiring life—
He said: *The end is everywhere,*
Art still has truth, take refuge there!
And he was happy, if to know
Causes of things, and far below
His feet to see the lurid flow
Of terror, and insane distress,
And headlong fate, be happiness.

And Wordsworth!—Ah, pale ghosts, rejoice!
For never has such soothing voice
Been to your shadowy world convey'd,
Since erst, at morn, some wandering shade
Heard the clear song of Orpheus come
Through Hades, and the mournful gloom.
Wordsworth has gone from us—and ye,
Ah, may ye feel his voice as we.
He too upon a wintry clime
Had fallen—on this iron time
Of doubts, disputes, distractions, fears.
He found us when the age had bound
Our souls in its benumbing round;
He spoke, and loosed our heart in tears.

463

He laid us as we lay at birth
On the cool flowery lap of earth,
Smiles broke from us and we had ease;
The hills were round us, and the breeze
Went o'er the sun-lit fields again;
Our foreheads felt the wind and rain.
Our youth return'd: for there was shed
On spirits that had long been dead,
Spirits dried up and closely furl'd,
The freshness of the early world.

Ah, since dark days still bring to light
Man's prudence and man's fiery might,
Time may restore us in his course
Goethe's sage mind and Byron's force;
But where will Europe's latter hour
Again find Wordsworth's healing power?
Others will teach us how to dare,
And against fear our breast to steel;
Others will strengthen us to bear—
But who, ah! who, will make us feel?
The cloud of mortal destiny,
Others will front it fearlessly—
But who, like him, will put it by?

Keep fresh the grass upon his grave
O Rotha, with thy living wave!
Sing him thy best! for few or none
Hears thy voice right, now he is gone.

TO MARGUERITE

Yes! in the sea of life enisled,
With echoing straits between us thrown,
Dotting the shoreless watery wild,
We mortal millions live *alone*.
The islands feel the enclasping flow,
And then their endless bounds they know.

But when the moon their hollows lights,
And they are swept by balms of spring,
And in their glens, on starry nights,
The nightingales divinely sing;
And lovely notes, from shore to shore,
Across the sounds and channels pour—

Oh! then a longing like despair
Is to their farthest caverns sent;
For surely once, they feel, we were
Parts of a single continent!
Now round us spreads the watery plain—
Oh might our marges meet again!

Who order'd, that their longing's fire
Should be, as soon as kindled, cool'd?
Who renders vain their deep desire?—
A God, a God their severance ruled;
And bade betwixt their shores to be
The unplumb'd, salt, estranging sea.

THE SONG OF CALLICLES

Far, far from here,
The Adriatic breaks in a warm bay
Among the green Illyrian hills; and there
The sunshine in the happy glens is fair,
And by the sea, and in the brakes.
The grass is cool, the sea-side air
Buoyant and fresh, the mountain flowers
More virginal and sweet than ours.
And there, they say, two bright and agèd snakes,
Who once were Cadmus and Harmonia,
Bask in the glens or on the warm sea-shore,
In breathless quiet, after all their ills;
Nor do they see their country, nor the place
Where the Sphinx lived among the frowning hills,
Nor the unhappy palace of their race,
Nor Thebes, nor the Ismenus, any more.

There those two live, far in the Illyrian brakes!
They had stay'd long enough to see,
In Thebes, the billow of calamity
Over their own dear children roll'd,
Curse upon curse, pang upon pang,
For years, they sitting helpless in their home,
A grey old man and woman; yet of old
The Gods had to their marriage come,
And at the banquet all the Muses sang.

Therefore they did not end their days
In sight of blood; but were rapt, far away,
To where the west-wind plays,
And murmurs of the Adriatic come
To those untrodden mountain-lawns; and there
Placed safely in changed forms, the pair
Wholly forget their first sad life, and home,
And all that Theban woe, and stray
For ever through the glens, placid and dumb.

(Empedocles on Etna, Act i, Scene 2.)

LIFE AND THOUGHT

But mind, but thought—
If these have been the master part of us—
Where will *they* find their parent element?
What will receive *them*, who will call *them* home?
But we shall still be in them, and they in us,
And we shall be the strangers of the world,
And they will be our lords, as they are now;
And keep us prisoners of our consciousness,
And never let us clasp and feel the All
But through their forms, and modes, and stifling veils.
And we shall be unsatisfied as now,
And we shall feel the agony of thirst,
The ineffable longing for the life of life
Baffled for ever; and still thought and mind
Will hurry us with them on their homeless march,
Over the unallied unopening earth,
Over the unrecognising sea; while air
Will blow us fiercely back to sea and earth,

466

And fire repel us from its living waves.
And then we shall unwillingly return
Back to this meadow of calamity,
This uncongenial place, this human life;
And in our individual human state
Go through the sad probation all again,
To see if we will poise our life at last,
To see if we will now at last be true
To our own only true, deep-buried selves,
Being one with which we are one with the whole world;
Or whether we will once more fall away
Into some bondage of the flesh or mind,
Some slough of sense, or some fantastic maze
Forged by the imperious lonely thinking-power.
And each succeeding age in which we are born
Will have more peril for us than the last;
Will goad our senses with a sharper spur,
Will fret our minds to an intenser play,
Will make ourselves harder to be discern'd.
And we shall struggle awhile, gasp and rebel—
And we shall fly for refuge to past times,
Their soul of unworn youth, their breath of greatness;
And the reality will pluck us back,
Knead us in its hot hand, and change our nature
And we shall feel our powers of effort flag,
And rally them for one last fight—and fail;
And we shall sink in the impossible strife,
And be astray for ever.

(Empedocles on Etna, Act ii.)

SONG FOR APOLLO

THROUGH the black, rushing smoke-bursts,
Thick breaks the red flame;
All Etna heaves fiercely
Her forest-clothed frame.

Not here, O Apollo!
Are haunts meet for thee.
But, where Helicon breaks down
In cliff to the sea,

Where the moon-silver'd inlets
Send far their light voice
Up the still vale of Thisbe,
O speed, and rejoice!

On the sward at the cliff-top
Lie strewn the white flocks,
On the cliff-side the pigeons
Roost deep in the rocks.

In the moonlight the shepherds,
Soft lull'd by the rills,
Lie wrapt in their blankets
Asleep on the hills.

—What forms are these coming
So white through the gloom?
What garments out-glistening
The gold-flower'd broom?

What sweet-breathing presence
Out-perfumes the thyme?
What voices enrapture
The night's balmy prime?—

'Tis Apollo comes leading
His choir, the Nine.
—The leader is fairest,
But all are divine.

They are lost in the hollows!
They stream up again!
What seeks on this mountain
The glorified train?—

They bathe on this mountain,
In the spring by their road;
Then on to Olympus,
Their endless abode.

—Whose praise do they mention?
Of what is it told?—
What will be for ever;
What was from of old.

First hymn they the Father
Of all things; and then
The rest of immortals,
The action of men.

The day in his hotness,
The strife with the palm;
The night in her silence,
The stars in their calm.

(*Empedocles on Etna*, Act ii.)

REQUIESCAT

Strew on her roses, roses,
  And never a spray of yew!
In quiet she reposes;
  Ah, would that I did too.

Her mirth the world required;
  She bathed it in smiles of glee.
But her heart was tired, tired,
  And now they let her be.

Her life was turning, turning,
  In mazes of heat and sound.
But for peace her soul was yearning,
  And now peace laps her round.

Her cabin'd, ample spirit,
  It flutter'd and fail'd for breath.
To-night it doth inherit
  The vasty hall of death.

THE SCHOLAR GIPSY

Go, for they call you, shepherd, from the hill;
  Go, shepherd, and untie the wattled cotes:
  No longer leave thy wistful flock unfed,
Nor let thy bawling fellows rack their throats,
  Nor the cropp'd herbage shoot another head.
    But when the fields are still,

469

And the tired men and dogs all gone to rest,
    And only the white sheep are sometimes seen
      Cross and recross the strips of moon-blanch'd green;
Come, Shepherd, and again renew the quest.

Here, where the reaper was at work of late—
    In this high field's dark corner, where he leaves
      His coat, his basket, and his earthen cruse,
    And in the sun all morning binds the sheaves,
      Then here, at noon, comes back his stores to use—
        Here will I sit and wait,
    While to my ear from uplands far away
      The bleating of the folded flocks is borne,
      With distant cries of reapers in the corn—
All the live murmur of a summer's day.

Screen'd is this nook o'er the high, half-reap'd field,
    And here till sun-down, shepherd! will I be.
      Through the thick corn the scarlet poppies peep,
    And round green roots and yellowing stalks I see
      Pale pink convolvulus in tendrils creep;
        And air-swept lindens yield
    Their scent, and rustle down their perfum'd showers
      Of bloom on the bent grass where I am laid,
      And bower me from the August sun with shade;
And the eye travels down to Oxford's towers.

And near me on the grass lies Glanvil's book—
    Come, let me read the oft-read tale again!
      The story of the Oxford scholar poor,
    Of pregnant parts and quick inventive brain,
      Who, tired of knocking at preferment's door,
        One summer-morn forsook
    His friends, and went to learn the gipsy lore,
      And roam'd the world with that wild brotherhood,
      And came, as most men deem'd, to little good,
But came to Oxford and his friends no more.

But once, years after, in the country-lanes,
    Two scholars, whom at college erst he knew,
      Met him, and of his way of life enquired;

Whereat he answer'd, that the gipsy-crew,
    His mates, had arts to rule as they desired
        The workings of men's brains,
And they can bind them to what thoughts they will.
    'And I,' he said, 'the secret of their art,
        When fully learn'd, will to the world impart;
But it needs heaven-sent moments for this skill.'

This said, he left them, and return'd no more.—
    But rumours hung about the country-side,
        That the lost Scholar long was seen to stray,
    Seen by rare glimpses, pensive and tongue-tied,
        In hat of antique shape, and cloak of grey,
            The same the gipsies wore.
    Shepherds had met him on the Hurst in spring;
        At some lone alehouse in the Berkshire moors,
        On the warm ingle-bench, the smock-frock'd boors
    Had found him seated at their entering,

But, 'mid their drink and clatter, he would fly.
    And I myself seem half to know thy looks,
        And put the shepherds, wanderer! on thy trace;
    And boys who in lone wheatfields scare the rooks
        I ask if thou hast pass'd their quiet place;
            Or in my boat I lie
    Moor'd to the cool bank in the summer-heats,
        'Mid wide grass meadows which the sunshine fills,
        And watch the warm, green-muffled Cumner hills,
    And wonder if thou haunt'st their shy retreats.

For most, I know, thou lov'st retired ground!
    Thee at the ferry Oxford riders blithe,
        Returning home on summer-nights, have met
    Crossing the stripling Thames at Bab-lock-hithe,
        Trailing in the cool stream thy fingers wet,
            As the punt's rope chops round:
    And leaning backward in a pensive dream,
        And fostering in thy lap a heap of flowers
        Pluck'd in shy fields and distant Wychwood bowers,
    And thine eyes resting on the moonlit stream.

And then they land, and thou art seen no more!—
 Maidens who from the distant hamlets come
  To dance around the Fyfield elm in May,
 Oft through the darkening fields have seen thee roam,
  Or cross a stile into the public way.
   Oft thou hast given them store
 Of flowers—the frail-leaf'd, white anemony—
  Dark bluebells drench'd with dews of summer eves,
  And purple orchises with spotted leaves—
 But none hath words she can report of thee.

And, above Godstow Bridge, when hay-time's here
 In June, and many a scythe in sunshine flames,
  Men who through those wide fields of breezy grass
 Where black-wing'd swallows haunt the glittering Thames,
  To bathe in the abandoned lasher pass,
   Have often pass'd thee near
 Sitting upon the river bank o'ergrown;
  Mark'd thine outlandish garb, thy figure spare,
  Thy dark vague eyes, and soft abstracted air—
 But, when they came from bathing, thou wast gone!

At some lone homestead in the Cumner hills,
 Where at her open door the housewife darns,
  Thou hast been seen, or hanging on a gate
 To watch the threshers in the mossy barns.
  Children, who early range these slopes and late
   For cresses from the rills,
 Have known thee eying, all an April-day,
  The springing pastures and the feeding kine;
  And mark'd thee, when the stars come out and shine,
 Through the long dewy grass move slow away.

In autumn, on the skirts of Bagley Wood,
 Where most the gipsies by the turf-edged way
  Pitch their smoked tents, and every bush you see
 With scarlet patches tagg'd and shreds of grey,
  Above the forest-ground called Thessaly—
   The blackbird, picking food,

Sees thee, nor stops his meal, nor fears at all;
  So often has he known thee past him stray,
  Rapt, twirling in thy hand a wither'd spray,
And waiting for the spark from Heaven to fall.

And once, in winter, on the causeway chill
  Where home through flooded fields foot-travellers go,
  Have I not pass'd thee on the wooden bridge,
Wrapt in thy cloak and battling with the snow,
  Thy face tow'rd Hinksey and its wintry ridge?
    And thou hast climb'd the hill,
And gain'd the white brow of the Cumner range,
  Turn'd once to watch, while thick the snowflakes fall,
  The line of festal light in Christ-Church hall—
Then sought thy straw in some sequester'd grange.

But what—I dream! Two hundred years are flown
  Since first thy story ran through Oxford halls,
  And the grave Glanvil did the tale inscribe
That thou wert wander'd from the studious walls
  To learn strange arts, and join a gipsy-tribe;
    And thou from earth art gone
Long since, and in some quiet churchyard laid—
  Some country-nook, where o'er thy unknown grave
  Tall grasses and white flowering nettles wave,
Under a dark, red-fruited yew-tree's shade.

—No, no, thou hast not felt the lapse of hours!
  For what wears out the life of mortal men?
  'Tis that from change to change their being rolls;
'Tis that repeated shocks, again, again,
  Exhaust the energy of strongest souls
    And numb the elastic powers.
Till having used our nerves with bliss and teen,
  And tired upon a thousand schemes our wit,
  To the just-pausing Genius we remit
Our worn-out life, and are—what we have been.

Thou hast not lived, why should'st thou perish, so?
  Thou hadst *one* aim, *one* business, *one* desire;
    Else wert thou long since number'd with the dead!

Else hadst thou spent, like other men, thy fire!
The generations of thy peers are fled,
    And we ourselves shall go;
But thou possessest an immortal lot,
    And we imagine thee exempt from age
    And living as thou liv'st on Glanvil's page,
Because thou hadst—what we, alas! have not.

For early didst thou leave the world, with powers
Fresh, undiverted to the world without,
    Firm to their mark, not spent on other things;
Free from the sick fatigue, the languid doubt,
    Which much to have tried, in much been baffled,
        brings.
        O life unlike to ours!
Who fluctuate idly without term or scope,
    Of whom each strives, nor knows for what he strives,
    And each half lives a hundred different lives;
Who wait like thee, but not, like thee, in hope.

Thou waitest for the spark from heaven! and we,
Vague half-believers of our casual creeds,
    Who never deeply felt, nor clearly will'd,
Whose insight never has borne fruit in deeds,
    Whose weak resolves never have been fulfill'd;
        For whom each year we see
Breeds new beginnings, disappointments new;
    Who hesitate and falter life away,
    And lose to-morrow the ground won to-day—
Ah! do not we, wanderer! await it too?

Yes, we await it! but it still delays,
And then we suffer! and amongst us one,
    Who most has suffer'd, takes dejectedly
His seat upon the intellectual throne;
    And all his store of sad experience he
        Lays bare of wretched days;
Tells us his misery's birth and growth and signs,
    And how the dying spark of hope was fed,
    And how the breast was soothed, and how the head,
And all his hourly varied anodynes.

This for our wisest! and we others pine,
   And wish the long unhappy dream would end,
      And waive all claim to bliss, and try to bear;
   With close-lipp'd patience for our only friend,
      Sad patience, too near neighbour to despair—
         But none has hope like thine!
Thou through the fields and through the woods dost
      stray,
   Roaming the country-side, a truant boy,
   Nursing thy project in unclouded joy,
And every doubt long blown by time away.

O born in days when wits were fresh and clear,
   And life ran gaily as the sparkling Thames;
      Before this strange disease of modern life,
   With its sick hurry, its divided aims,
      Its heads o'ertax'd, its palsied hearts, was rife—
         Fly hence, our contact fear!
Still fly, plunge deeper in the bowering wood!
   Averse, as Dido did with gesture stern
   From her false friend's approach in Hades turn,
Wave us away, and keep thy solitude!

Still nursing the unconquerable hope,
   Still clutching the inviolable shade,
      With a free, onward impulse brushing through,
   By night, the silver'd branches of the glade—
      Far on the forest-skirts, where none pursue,
         On some mild pastoral slope
Emerge, and resting on the moonlit pales
   Freshen thy flowers as in former years
   With dew, or listen with enchanted ears,
From the dark dingles, to the nightingales.

But fly our paths, our feverish contact fly!
   For strong the infection of our mental strife,
      Which, though it gives no bliss, yet spoils for rest;
   And we should win thee from thy own fair life,
      Like us distracted, and like us unblest.
         Soon, soon thy cheer would die,

Thy hopes grow timorous, and unfix'd thy powers,
   And thy clear aims be cross and shifting made;
   And then thy glad perennial youth would fade,
Fade, and grow old at last, and die like ours.

Then fly our greetings, fly our speech and smiles!
   —As some grave Tyrian trader, from the sea,
   Descried at sunrise an emerging prow
Lifting the cool-hair'd creepers stealthily,
   The fringes of a southward-facing brow
      Among the Aegean isles;
And saw the merry Grecian coaster come,
   Freighted with amber grapes, and Chian wine,
   Green, bursting figs, and tunnies steep'd in brine—
And knew the intruders on his ancient home,

The young light-hearted masters of the waves—
   And snatch'd his rudder, and shook out more sail;
   And day and night held on indignantly
O'er the blue Midland waters with the gale,
   Betwixt the Syrtes and soft Sicily,
      To where the Atlantic raves
Outside the western straits, and unbent sails
   There, where down cloudy cliffs, through sheets of foam,
   Shy traffickers, the dark Iberians come;
And on the beach undid his corded bales.

THYRSIS

A MONODY, *to commemorate the author's friend*, ARTHUR HUGH
CLOUGH, *who died at Florence*, 1861

> Thus yesterday, to-day, to-morrow come,
> They hustle one another and they pass;
> But all our hustling morrows only make
> The smooth to-day of God.
>
> *From* LUCRETIUS, *an unpublished Tragedy.*

How changed is here each spot man makes or fills!
   In the two Hinkseys nothing keeps the same;
      The village street its haunted mansion lacks,

And from the sign is gone Sibylla's name,
    And from the roofs the twisted chimney-stacks—
      Are ye too changed, ye hills?
See, 'tis no foot of unfamiliar men
    To-night from Oxford up your pathway strays!
    Here came I often, often, in old days—
Thyrsis and I; we still had Thyrsis then.

Runs it not here, the track by Childsworth Farm,
    Past the high wood, to where the elm-tree crowns
      The hill behind whose ridge the sunset flames?
The signal-elm, that looks on Ilsley Downs,
    The Vale, the three lone weirs, the youthful Thames?—
      This winter-eve is warm,
Humid the air! leafless, yet soft as spring,
    The tender purple spray on copse and briers!
    And that sweet city with her dreaming spires,
She needs not June for beauty's heightening,

Lovely all times she lies, lovely to-night!—
    Only, methinks, some loss of habit's power
      Befalls me wandering through this upland dim.
Once pass'd I blindfold here, at any hour,
    Now seldom come I, since I came with him.
      That single elm-tree bright
Against the west—I miss it! is it gone?
    We prized it dearly; while it stood, we said,
    Our friend, the Gipsy-Scholar, was not dead;
While the tree lived, he in these fields lived on.

Too rare, too rare, grow now my visits here,
    But once I knew each field, each flower, each stick;
      And with the country-folk acquaintance made
By barn in threshing-time, by new-built rick.
    Here, too, our shepherd-pipes we first assay'd.
      Ah me! this many a year
My pipe is lost, my shepherd's holiday!
    Needs must I lose them, needs with heavy heart
    Into the world and wave of men depart;
But Thyrsis of his own will went away.

It irk'd him to be here, he could not rest.
　He loved each simple joy the country yields,
　　He loved his mates; but yet he could not keep,
For that a shadow lour'd on the fields,
　　Here with the shepherds and the silly sheep.
　　　Some life of men unblest
He knew, which made him droop, and fill'd his head.
　He went; his piping took a troubled sound
　Of storms that rage outside our happy ground;
He could not wait their passing, he is dead!

So, some tempestuous morn in early June,
　When the year's primal burst of bloom is o'er,
　　Before the roses and the longest day—
When garden-walks and all the grassy floor
　　With blossoms red and white of fallen May
　　　And chestnut-flowers are strewn—
So have I heard the cuckoo's parting cry,
　From the wet field, through the vext garden-trees,
　Come with the volleying rain and tossing breeze:
The bloom is gone, and with the bloom go I.

Too quick despairer, wherefore wilt thou go?
　Soon will the high Midsummer pomps come on,
　　Soon will the musk carnations break and swell,
Soon shall we have gold-dusted snapdragon,
　　Sweet-William with his homely cottage-smell,
　　　And stocks in fragrant blow;
Roses that down the alleys shine afar,
　And open, jasmine-muffled lattices,
　And groups under the dreaming garden-trees,
And the full moon, and the white evening-star.

He hearkens not! light comer, he is flown!
　What matters it? next year he will return,
　　And we shall have him in the sweet spring-days,
With whitening hedges, and uncrumpling fern,
　　And blue-bells trembling by the forest-ways,
　　　And scent of hay new-mown.

478

But Thyrsis never more we swains shall see;
 See him come back, and cut a smoother reed,
 And blow a strain the world at last shall heed—
For Time, not Corydon, hath conquer'd thee.

Alack, for Corydon no rival now!—
 But when Sicilian shepherds lost a mate,
  Some good survivor with his flute would go,
 Piping a ditty sad for Bion's fate,
  And cross the unpermitted ferry's flow,
   And relax Pluto's brow,
 And make leap up with joy the beauteous head
  Of Proserpine, among whose crownèd hair
  Are flowers first open'd on Sicilian air,
 And flute his friend, like Orpheus, from the dead.

O easy access to the hearer's grace
 When Dorian shepherds sang to Proserpine!
  For she herself had trod Sicilian fields,
 She knew the Dorian water's gush divine,
  She knew each lily white which Enna yields,
   Each rose with blushing face;
 She loved the Dorian pipe, the Dorian strain.
  But ah, of our poor Thames she never heard!
  Her foot the Cumner cowslips never stirr'd;
 And we should tease her with our plaint in vain!

Well! wind-dispersed and vain the words will be,
 Yet, Thyrsis, let me give my grief its hour
  In the old haunt, and find our tree-topp'd hill!
 Who, if not I, for questing here hath power?
  I know the wood which hides the daffodil,
   I know the Fyfield tree,
 I know what white, what purple fritillaries
  The grassy harvest of the river-fields,
  Above by Ensham, down by Sandford, yields,
 And what sedged brooks are Thames's tributaries;

I know these slopes; who knows them if not I?—
 But many a dingle on the loved hill-side,
  With thorns once studded, old, white-blossom'd trees,

Where thick the cowslips grew, and far descried
  High tower'd the spikes of purple orchises,
    Hath since our day put by
The coronals of that forgotten time;
    Down each green bank hath gone the ploughboy's
      team,
    And only in the hidden brookside gleam
Primroses, orphans of the flowery prime.

Where is the girl, who by the boatman's door,
  Above the locks, above the boating throng,
    Unmoor'd our skiff when through the Wytham flats,
Red loosestrife and blond meadow-sweet among
    And darting swallows and light water-gnats,
      We track'd the shy Thames shore?
Where are the mowers, who, as the tiny swell
  Of our boat passing heaved the river-grass,
  Stood with suspended scythe to see us pass?—
They all are gone, and thou art gone as well!

Yes, thou art gone! and round me too the night
  In ever-nearing circle weaves her shade.
    I see her veil draw soft across the day,
I feel her slowly chilling breath invade
    The cheek grown thin, the brown hair sprent with grey;
      I feel her finger light
Laid pausefully upon life's headlong train;—
  The foot less prompt to meet the morning dew,
  The heart less bounding at emotion new,
And hope, once crush'd, less quick to spring again.

And long the way appears, which seem'd so short
  To the less practised eye of sanguine youth;
    And high the mountain-tops, in cloudy air,
The mountain-tops where is the throne of Truth,
    Tops in life's morning-sun so bright and bare!
      Unbreachable the fort
Of the long-batter'd world uplifts its wall;
  And strange and vain the earthly turmoil grows,
  And near and real the charm of thy repose,
And night as welcome as a friend would fall.

But hush! the upland hath a sudden loss
  Of quiet!—Look, adown the dusk hill-side,
    A troop of Oxford hunters going home,
  As in old days, jovial and talking, ride!
    From hunting with the Berkshire hounds they come.
      Quick! let me fly, and cross
  Into yon farther field!—'Tis done; and see,
    Back'd by the sunset, which doth glorify
    The orange and pale violet evening-sky,
  Bare on its lonely ridge, the Tree! the Tree!

I take the omen! Eve lets down her veil,
  The white fog creeps from bush to bush about,
    The west unflushes, the high stars grow bright,
  And in the scatter'd farms the lights come out.
    I cannot reach the signal-tree to-night,
      Yet, happy omen, hail!
  Hear it from thy broad lucent Arno-vale
    (For there thine earth-forgetting eyelids keep
    The morningless and unawakening sleep
  Under the flowery oleanders pale),

Hear it, O Thyrsis, still our tree is there!—
  Ah, vain! These English fields, this upland dim,
    These brambles pale with mist engarlanded,
  That lone, sky-pointing tree, are not for him.
    To a boon southern country he is fled,
      And now in happier air,
  Wandering with the great Mother's train divine
    (And purer or more subtle soul than thee,
    I trow, the mighty Mother doth not see)
  Within a folding of the Apennine,

Thou hearest the immortal chants of old!—
  Putting his sickle to the perilous grain
    In the hot cornfield of the Phrygian king,
  For thee the Lityerses-song again
    Young Daphnis with his silver voice doth sing;
      Sings his Sicilian fold,

His sheep, his hapless love, his blinded eyes—
  And how a call celestial round him rang,
  And heavenward from the fountain-brink he sprang,
And all the marvel of the golden skies.

There thou art gone, and me thou leavest here
  Sole in these fields! yet will I not despair.
    Despair I will not, while I yet descry
  'Neath the mild canopy of English air
    That lonely tree against the western sky.
      Still, still these slopes, 'tis clear,
  Our Gipsy-Scholar haunts, outliving thee!
    Fields where soft sheep from cages pull the hay,
    Woods with anemonies in flower till May,
  Know him a wanderer still; then why not me?

A fugitive and gracious light he seeks,
  Shy to illumine; and I seek it too.
    This does not come with houses or with gold,
  With place, with honour, and a flattering crew;
    'Tis not in the world's market bought and sold—
      But the smooth-slipping weeks
  Drop by, and leave its seeker still untired;
    Out of the heed of mortals he is gone,
    He wends unfollow'd, he must house alone;
  Yet on he fares, by his own heart inspired.

Thou too, O Thyrsis, on like quest wast bound;
  Thou wanderedst with me for a little hour!
    Men gave thee nothing, but this happy quest,
  If men esteem'd thee feeble, gave thee power,
    If men procured thee trouble, gave thee rest.
      And this rude Cumner ground,
  Its fir-topped Hurst, its farms, its quiet fields,
    Here cam'st thou in thy jocund youthful time,
    Here was thine height of strength, thy golden prime!
  And still the haunt beloved a virtue yields.

What though the music of thy rustic flute
  Kept not for long its happy, country tone;
    Lost it too soon and learnt a stormy note

Of men contention-tost, of men who groan,
  Which task'd thy pipe too sore, and tired thy throat—
    It fail'd, and thou wast mute!
Yet hadst thou alway visions of our light,
  And long with men of care thou couldst not stay,
  And soon thy foot resumed its wandering way,
Left human haunt, and on alone till night.

Too rare, too rare, grow now my visits here!
  'Mid city-noise, not, as with thee of yore,
    Thyrsis! in reach of sheep-bells is my home.
Then through the great town's harsh, heart-wearying
      roar,
    Let in thy voice a whisper often come,
      To chase fatigue and fear:
Why faintest thou? I wander'd till I died.
Roam on! the light we sought is shining still.
Dost thou ask proof? Our tree yet crowns the hill,
Our Scholar travels yet the loved hill-side.

DOVER BEACH

The sea is calm to-night.
The tide is full, the moon lies fair
Upon the straits;—on the French coast the light
Gleams and is gone; the cliffs of England stand,
Glimmering and vast, out in the tranquil bay.
Come to the window, sweet is the night-air!
Only, from the long line of spray
Where the sea meets the moon-blanch'd land,
Listen! you hear the grating roar
Of pebbles which the waves draw back, and fling,
At their return, up the high strand,
Begin, and cease, and then again begin,
With tremulous cadence slow, and bring
The eternal note of sadness in.

Sophocles long ago
Heard it on the Ægæan, and it brought
Into his mind the turbid ebb and flow

Of human misery; we
Find also in the sound a thought,
Hearing it by this distant northern sea.

The Sea of Faith
Was once, too, at the full, and round earth's shore
Lay like the folds of a bright girdle furl'd;
But now I only hear
Its melancholy, long, withdrawing roar,
Retreating, to the breath
Of the night-wind, down the vast edges drear
And naked shingles of the world.

Ah, love, let us be true
To one another! for the world, which seems
To lie before us like a land of dreams,
So various, so beautiful, so new,
Hath really neither joy, nor love, nor light,
Nor certitude, nor peace, nor help for pain;
And we are here as on a darkling plain
Swept with confused alarms of struggle and flight,
Where ignorant armies clash by night.

THE DEATH OF SOHRAB

He spoke; and Sohrab smiled on him, and took
The spear, and drew it from his side, and eased
His wound's imperious anguish; but the blood
Came welling from the open gash, and life
Flow'd with the stream; all down his cold white side
The crimson torrent ran, dim now and soil'd,
Like the soil'd tissue of white violets
Left, freshly gather'd, on their native bank,
By children, whom their nurses call with haste
Indoors from the sun's eye; his head droop'd low,
His limbs grew slack; motionless, white, he lay—
White, with eyes closed; only when heavy gasps,
Deep heavy gasps quivering through all his frame,
Convuls'd him back to life, he open'd them,
And fix'd them feebly on his father's face;
Till now all strength was ebb'd, and from his limbs

Unwillingly the spirit fled away,
Regretting the warm mansion which it left,
And youth, and bloom, and this delightful world.

  So, on the bloody sand, Sohrab lay dead;
And the great Rustum drew his horseman's cloak
Down o'er his face, and sate by his dead son.
As those black granite pillars, once high-rear'd
By Jemshid in Persepolis, to bear
His house, now 'mid their broken flights of steps
Lie prone, enormous, down the mountain side—
So in the sand lay Rustum by his son.

  And night came down over the solemn waste,
And the two gazing hosts, and that sole pair,
And darken'd all; and a cold fog, with night,
Crept from the Oxus. Soon a hum arose,
As of a great assembly loosed, and fires
Began to twinkle through the fog; for now
Both armies moved to camp, and took their meal;
The Persians took it on the open sands
Southward, the Tartars by the river marge;
And Rustum and his son were left alone.

  But the majestic river floated on,
Out of the mist and hum of that low land,
Into the frosty starlight, and there moved,
Rejoicing, through the hush'd Chorasmian waste,
Under the solitary moon;—he flow'd
Right for the polar star, past Orgunjè,
Brimming, and bright, and large; then sands begin
To hem his watery march, and dam his streams,
And split his currents; that for many a league
The shorn and parcell'd Oxus strains along
Through beds of sand and matted rushy isles—
Oxus, forgetting the bright speed he had
In his high mountain-cradle in Pamere,
A foil'd circuitous wanderer—till at last
The long'd-for dash of waves is heard, and wide
His luminous home of waters opens, bright
And tranquil, from whose floor the new-bathed stars
Emerge, and shine upon the Aral Sea.

                                    (*Sohrab and Rustum.*)

THE SECOND ASGARD

FAR to the south, beyond the blue, there spreads
Another Heaven, the boundless—no one yet
Hath reach'd it; there hereafter shall arise
The second Asgard, with another name.
Thither, when o'er this present earth and Heavens
The tempest of the latter days hath swept,
And they from sight have disappear'd, and sunk,
Shall a small remnant of the Gods repair;
Hoder and I shall join them from the grave.
There re-assembling we shall see emerge
From the bright Ocean at our feet an earth
More fresh, more verdant than the last, with fruits
Self-springing, and a seed of man preserved,
Who then shall live in peace, as now in war.
But we in Heaven shall find again with joy
The ruin'd palaces of Odin, seats
Familiar, halls where we have supp'd of old;
Re-enter them with wonder, never fill
Our eyes with gazing, and rebuild with tears.
And we shall tread once more the well-known plain
Of Ida, and among the grass shall find
The golden dice wherewith we play'd of yore;
And that will bring to mind the former life
And pastime of the Gods, the wise discourse
Of Odin, the delights of other days.
O Hermod, pray that thou mayst join us then!
Such for the future is my hope; meanwhile,
I rest the thrall of Hela, and endure
Death, and the gloom which round me even now
Thickens, and to its inner gulph recalls.

(Balder Dead.)

IMMORTALITY

FOIL'D by our fellow-men, depress'd, outworn,
We leave the brutal world to take its way,
And, *Patience! in another life*, we say,
The world shall be thrust down, and we up-borne!

And will not, then, the immortal armies scorn
The world's poor, routed leavings? or will they,
Who fail'd under the heat of this life's day,
Support the fervours of the heavenly morn?

No, no! the energy of life may be
Kept on after the grave, but not begun;
And he who flagg'd not in the earthly strife,

From strength to strength advancing—only he,
His soul well-knit, and all his battles won,
Mounts, and that hardly, to eternal life.

GROWING OLD

What is it to grow old?
Is it to lose the glory of the form,
The lustre of the eye?
Is it for beauty to forgo her wreath?
—Yes, but not this alone.

Is it to feel our strength—
Not our bloom only, but our strength—decay?
Is it to feel each limb
Grow stiffer, every function less exact,
Each nerve more loosely strung?

Yes, this, and more; but not,
Ah, 'tis not what in youth we dream'd 'twould be!
'Tis not to have our life
Mellow'd and soften'd as with sunset glow,
A golden day's decline.

'Tis not to see the world
As from a height, with rapt prophetic eyes,
And heart profoundly stirr'd;
And weep, and feel the fulness of the past,
The years that are no more!

It is to spend long days
And not once feel that we were ever young;
It is to add, immured
In the hot prison of the present, month
To month with weary pain.

It is to suffer this,
And feel but half, and feebly, what we feel.
Deep in our hidden heart
Festers the dull remembrance of a change,
But no emotion—none.

It is—last stage of all—
When we are frozen up within, and quite
The phantom of ourselves,
To hear the world applaud the hollow ghost
Which blamed the living man.

THE LAST WORD

CREEP into thy narrow bed,
Creep, and let no more be said!
Vain thy onset! all stands fast.
Thou thyself must break at last.

Let the long contention cease!
Geese are swans, and swans are geese.
Let them have it how they will!
Thou art tired; best be still.

They out-talk'd thee, hiss'd thee, tore thee!
Better men fared thus before thee;
Fired their ringing shot and pass'd,
Hotly charged—and sank at last.

Charge once more, then, and be dumb!
Let the victors, when they come,
When the forts of folly fall,
Find thy body by the wall!

GLOSSARY OF NAMES

Abbethdin. Heb. = chief justice.

Abiram. Abiram, son of Eliab, together with Korah and Dathan, rebelled against Moses in the wilderness, and was swallowed up in the ground.

Absolon. Absalom, son of David.

Achille. Achilles.

Achitophel. 2 Sam. xv. and xvii. Used by Dryden for Anthony Ashley, Earl of Shaftesbury (1621–83), who encouraged Monmouth (Absalom) in his pretensions.

Acidalian brook. A stream near Orchomenos in Bœotia, where Venus bathed with the Graces.

Adonais. Shelley seems to have invented this name, under which he mourns the death of Keats.

Adriane. Ariadne, d. of Minos, King of Crete. She helped Theseus to kill the Minotaur and to escape from Crete, but he deserted her on the island of Naxos.

Æson. Father of Jason. His youth was restored by the enchantress Medea.

Ajax. Ajax, son of Telamon, a gigantic but stupid Greek leader in the Trojan war.

Alastor. Shelley apparently invented this name, which is from a Greek word signifying 'avenger'.

Albyn. Scotland.

Alceste. Alcestis, wife of Admetus who voluntarily died in order to lengthen the life of her husband.

Alcion. Alcyone or Halkyone. See *Ceys.* [Hercules.

Alcmena. The mother, by Zeus, of

Aleian Field. A region of Cilicia, where Bellerophon was supposed to have fallen from Pegasus.

Algarsife. One of the two sons of Cambuscan, in Chaucer's unfinished Squire's Tale.

Alphaeus. Alpheus, a river of Arcadia, which sinks underground and was supposed to come up again in Sicily.

Amaryllis. The name of a shepherdess in Virgil's Eclogues.

Amazons. A legendary race of women warriors, supposed to have lived near the Euxine.

Amram's son. Moses.

Anacreon. Greek lyric poet of the 6th century B.C. Spent most of his life at the court of Polycrates, tyrant of Samos.

Anna. Queen Anne (1702–14).

Anson. George Anson, Lord Anson (1697–1762), admiral.

Anubis. The jackal or dog-headed Egyptian god, identified by the Greeks with Hermes.

Aonian Mount. Aonia was a name of Bœotia; and the Aonian Mount is Mt. Helicon, the abode of Apollo and the Muses.

Apicius. Quintus Gavius Apicius, a gourmet of the reign of Tiberius.

Apollo. The Greek and Roman sun-god Phœbus Apollo, also god of music and leader of the Muses.

Araby. Arabia.

Arachne. A woman of Lydia, turned into a spider by Pallas Athene, whom she had challenged to a weaving contest.

Aral Sea. A brackish inland sea in Asiatic Russia.

Arbuthnot. John Arbuthnot (1667–1735), scholar and physician.

Arcadia. A mountainous region of the Peloponnese, having many

489

GLOSSARY OF NAMES

associations with Greek mythology. Hermes and Pan were
both originally Arcadian deities.

Arethuse. Arethusa, a fountain in
Sicily, used by Milton as a
symbol of pastoral poetry from
its association with Theocritus.

Argo. The ship in which Jason
and the other Argonauts went
to Colchis to fetch away the
Golden Fleece.

Argus (1) The hundred-eyed guar-
dian of Io, slain by Hermes. (2)
The builder of the ship Argo. (3)
The dog of Odysseus.

Arno vale. The Valdarno, in which
Florence lies. Clough was buried
there.

Artemis. The Greek moon-goddess,
sister of Apollo, identified with
the Roman Diana.

Asgard. In Scandinavian mythology the region in the centre of
the earth inhabited by the gods.

Ashtaroth. Astarte or Ishtar, the
Phœnician moon-goddess, identified by the Greeks and Romans
with Aphrodite or Venus.

Attic boy. Cephalus, the husband
of Procris, loved by Aurora, the
Dawn.

Atticus. Titus Pomponius Atticus
(109–32 B.C.), friend and corre-
spondent of Cicero. The name
was used by Pope to designate
Addison.

Ausonia. A poetic name for Italy,
from Ausones, an ancient name
for the inhabitants of southern
Italy.

Avicen. Avicenna or Ibn Sina, 980–
1037, Arabian Aristotelian, physician, and philosopher.

Avilion or *Avallon*, the Celtic Elysium, to which Arthur was carried after his death.

Baalim. The collective title for
all the rebel angels; from the
Palestinian gods who were

named after the chief Semitic
god Belu or Baal ('Lord').

Babilan. Babylonian.

Bab-lock-hythe. Bablockhythe, a
hamlet on the Thames not far
from Cumnor; there is still a
ferry across the river there.

Bacchus. The Roman god of wine,
identified with the Greek
Dionysos.

Bagley Wood. A large wood above
the Hinkseys, a few miles SW.
of Oxford.

Baiae's Bay. Baiae was a town
near Naples, used as a pleasure
resort by the Romans, but now
covered by the sea.

Balder. The Scandinavian sun-
god, son of Odin, killed through
the malice of Loki.

Bayana's hold. See Namancos.

Bellerus. A name for a legendary
giant coined by Milton from
Bellerium, Land's End.

Bentley, slashing. Richard Bentley
(1662–1742), scholar and writer,
Master of Trinity, Cambs.

Bion. Greek poet (*c.* 100 B.C.)
an imitator of Theocritus.

Blind Fury. Milton so names
Atropos, one of the Fates.

Bonnivard. François Bonnivard,
Swiss patriot, imprisoned in
the castle of Chillon 1530–6.

Brixseyde. Briseis, a slave-girl be-
longing to Achilles, taken from
him by Agamemnon. This
occurrence was the cause of
Achilles retiring from the war.

Brunswick's fated chieftain. Frede-
rick William, Duke of Brunswick, killed at Quatre-Bras,
1815. His father was driven
from his duchy by Napoleon
after Jena (1806) and died a
few weeks later.

Burdeux town. Bordeaux.

Burnet. Gilbert Burnet, Bishop of
Salisbury (1643–1715), Whig
historian.

Busiris. A legendary king of Egypt, supposed to have been slain by Hercules. Milton identifies him with the Pharaoh of the Exodus.

Cadmus. Greek mythological king, said to have civilized the Bœotians and taught them the use of letters.

Calypso. An enchantress living on the island of Ogygia, who by her spells kept Odysseus there for seven years.

Cambuscan and Cambell, Algarsife, Canace. Characters in Chaucer's unfinished Squire's Tale.

Camelot. In Arthurian legend, the place where Arthur held his court. Malory identifies it with Winchester.

Camilla. A maiden warrior, ally of Turnus, in the Æneid. She was so swift-footed that she could run over a field of corn without bending the blades.

Campbell. Thomas Campbell (1777–1804), poet.

Camus. The river Cam.

Canace. d. of Æolus, beloved by Macareus.

Canacee. d. of King Cambuscan in Chaucer's Squire's Tale. Chaucer left the tale unfinished. Spenser wrote a continuation of it in *The Faerie Queene.*

Caphtor, sons of. Philistines.

Castlereagh. Robert Stewart, Viscount Castlereagh (1769–1822), statesman.

Cato. Marcus Porcius Cato (95–46 B.C.) grandson of Cato the Censor, chief political antagonist of Caesar, subject of Addison's tragedy *Cato.*

Cecilia. St. Cecilia, patron saint of music.

Celeno. One of the Harpies.

Cerberus. The three-headed dog that guarded the entrance to Hades.

Ceys. Ceyx, son of the morning star, and lover of Alcyone or Halkyone; when he was drowned the gods took pity on her grief and changed them into a pair of kingfishers, during whose nesting season the seas were said always to be calm (halcyon weather).

Chaos. The primordial god in Hesiod's theogony.

Chapman. George Chapman (1559?–1634?). His translation of the Iliad was published in 1611, of the Odyssey in 1614–15.

Chepe. Cheapside.

Chersonese. The promontory of Thrace that runs along the West side of the Hellespont, the modern Gallipoli.

Childsworth Farm. A farm, now Chilswell, on the hill behind Hinksey, past which runs one of several tracks leading up Cumnor Hurst.

Chillon. A castle on the Lake of Geneva, the prison of Bonnivard, q.v.

Chorasmian waste. Chorasmia was another name for the districts of Orgunje and Khiva in central Asia.

Christ-Church hall. The hall of Christ Church. The view of it from the Cumnor range is now somewhat obscured by gasometers.

Cimmerian desert. The land of the Cimmerii, according to Homer, was on the limits of the world, where the sun never shone.

Cinthia. Cynthia, a name given to Artemis (Diana) from Mt. Cynthus in Delos, her birthplace.

Cleopatre. Cleopatra, Queen of Egypt.

Cliveden. Buckingham's house on the banks of the Thames.

Cobb. A character in Ben Jonson's play *Every Man in his Humour*.

Congreve. William Congreve (1670–1729), dramatist.

Cooke. Thomas Cooke (1703–56), translator of Hesiod, and Whig pamphleteer.

Corneille. Pierre Corneille (1608–84), French dramatist.

Cortez. Hernando Cortez (1485–1547). Spanish conqueror of Mexico. Keats mistakenly makes him the first European to gaze on the Pacific; it was actually one of his companions, Balboa, who did so.

Corydon. The name of a shepherd in pastoral poetry (e.g. in Theocritus and Virgil).

Crabbe. George Crabbe (1754–1832), poet.

Cressid. Cressida d. of Calchas, loved by Troilus, whom she later forsook for Diomede.

Creusa. d. of Creon, married by Jason after he had deserted Medea.

Crisippus. Chrysippus of Soli, a Stoic philosopher (*c.* 280–204 B.C.).

Cumner. Cumnor, a village a few miles west of Oxford.

Cupid. Roman god of love, son of Venus, often represented as a blind child.

Cyclads. The Cyclades, a group of islands in the southern Ægean.

Cyllene. A mountain in Arcadia, the birth-place of Hermes.

Cytherea. Aphrodite, called Cytherean because she landed at Cythera after her birth from the sea.

Damœtas. The name of an old Shepherd in Eclogues by Theocritus and Virgil. Milton, in

Lycidas, possibly alludes, under this name, to William Chappel, Fellow of Christ's and tutor to Milton and King.

Dante. Dante Alighieri (1265–1321), Florentine poet. He gave an account of his love for Beatrice in his *Vita Nuova,* whence Browning took the episode of his drawing.

Daphne. A girl loved by Apollo, and changed into a tree.

Darien. The Isthmus of Panama.

Darius. King of Persia (521–486 B.C.)

Delos. One of the Ægean islands, the birth-place of Artemis and Apollo.

Delphos, steep of. Delphos was the son of Poseidon and Melantho. He founded Delphi, the seat of a famous oracle. The Delphic Oracle was consulted as late as the 4th century of the Christian era.

Demetrius. Demetrius Poliorcetes, King of Macedon at the end of the 4th century. B.C.

Demophoon. In Greek legend betrothed to Phillis. When he failed to appear on their wedding day, she hanged herself, and was turned into an almond tree.

Denham. Sir John Denham (1615–69), poet.

Dennis. John Dennis (1657–1734), critic.

Deva. The river Dee.

Diana. The Roman moon-goddess identified with Greek Artemis.

Dianire. Deianeira, the wife of Hercules, who caused his death unknowingly by giving him the shirt of Nessus, and afterwards killed herself for grief.

Dido. Elissa, Queen of Carthage, loved but abandoned by Æneas, after whose departure she killed herself. In the sixth Book of the Æneid, Æneas recognizes her

GLOSSARY OF NAMES

in Hades, but she will not speak
to him.

Doeg. 1 Sam. xxi. and xxii. Used
by Dryden for Elkanah Settle.

Doric lay. Pastoral poetry. Theocritus and Moschus, who wrote
pastoral elegies on Daphnis and
Bion respectively, both came
from the Dorian settlement of
Syracuse.

Doric mothers. i.e. Spartan; Lace-
daemonia was settled by Dorians
who came from Epirus, the
modern Albania.

Dryads. Nymphs of trees.

Ector. Hector, son of Priam, the
best and bravest of the Tro-
jans.

Eleyne. Helen, d. of Zeus and Leda,
wife of Menelaus; carried off to
Troy by Paris, and so the cause
of the Trojan war.

Elysian. Of Elysium, the islands of
the blest; in Greek mythology
the place where the favourites
of the gods enjoy life after death.

Endymion. A shepherd of Mt.
Latmos, loved by Artemis, the
moon.

Enee. Æneas, the hero of Virgil's
Æneid, which tells how he
escaped from Troy after its
destruction, and eventually
reached and settled in Italy.

Eneydos. The Æneid of Virgil.

Enna. Enna in Sicily, where Persephone was gathering flowers
when she was carried off by Dis.

Ensham. Eynsham (locally pronounced Ensham), a small town
on the Thames above Oxford.

Erin. Poetical name for Ireland.

Erro. Hero; see Leander.

Erymanth. Erymanthos, a mountain in Arcadia and also a river
which rises on it and flows into
the Alphaeus.

Ester. Esther, the Jewess who became queen of Ahasuerus.

Etherege. Sir George Etherege
(1634?–1691?), dramatist.

Ethiop queen. Cassiopeia, wife of
Cepheus, King of Ethiopia, and
mother of Andromeda, who
boasted her beauty above that
of the Nereids. She was changed
into the constellation Cassiopeia,
hence the epithet 'starred'.

Etna. A volcano in Sicily.

Ettrick. River in Selkirkshire.

Ettrick Shepherd. James Hogg
(1770–1805), Scottish shepherd
and poet.

Eumaeus. The swineherd of Odysseus.

Euphrosyne. The name of one of the
three Graces. The name signifies *mirth, merriment.*

Euxine. The Black Sea.

Excalibur. The magic sword o
King Arthur.

Fabius. Quintus Fabius Maximus,
surnamed Cunctator, five times
consul. Fought against Hannibal in Italy.

Fanny, gentle. John Hervey, Lord
Hervey (1696–1743), pamphleteer and memoir-writer.

Fesole. Now Fiesole, a hill near
Florence.

Fish-strete. A street in London.

Flecknoe. Richard Flecknoe (d.
1678), Irish writer, lampooned
by Marvell.

Fletcher. John Fletcher (1579–
1625), dramatist.

Flora. The Roman goddess of
vegetation.

Foligno. A town near Perugia.
Raphael's Madonna de Foligno
is now in the Vatican.

Franks. The common name given
by Turks and other Levantines
to members of the Western
European nations.

Fyfield elm. Fyfield is a village
between Cumnor and Faring-

493

don; the remains of the ancient elm-tree still stand.

Garth, well-natured. Dr. Samuel Garth (1661–1719), an early friend and patron of Pope, d. 1718.

Gaufred. Geoffrey of Vinesaub, in his *Nova Poetria*, gives as an example of the plaintive style, a complaint against Friday, the day on which Richard I died.

Gildon. Charles Gildon (1665–1724).

Glanvil's book. 'The Vanity of Dogmatizing' 1661, by Joseph Glanvill (1636–80).

Godstow Bridge. Over the Thames about two miles north of Oxford, close to the remains of Godstow Abbey.

Goethe. Johann Wolfgang von Goethe (1749–1832), German poet and philosopher.

Goshen, sojourners of. The Israelites, who inhabited that part of Egypt called Goshen, before the Exodus.

Gower. John Gower (1330?–1408), poet and friend of Chaucer.

Granville the polite. George Granville, 1st Lord Lansdowne (1667–1735).

Great Johnson. Ben Jonson (1572–1637), dramatist.

Hammon, or *Ammon*, an Egyptian god, identified by the Romans with Jupiter, as Jupiter Ammon.

Harmonia. d. of Ares and Aphrodite; wife of Cadmus. They were turned into serpents in their old age, after many misfortunes.

Hasdrubale. Hasdrubal, brother of Hannibal, a Carthaginian general, killed in Italy, B.C. 207.

Hayles. Hailes Abbey in Gloucestershire.

Hebrus. A river of Thrace, down which the head of Orpheus floated after his death.

Hecate. Goddess of the underworld in Greek mythology, protectress of enchanters and witches.

Hela. Scandinavian goddess of death.

Helicon. A range of mountains in Boeotia, sacred to Apollo and the Muses, whence spring Aganippe and Hippocrene, the fountains of the Muses.

Hellas. The Greek name for Greece, the country of the Hellenes.

Helowys. Heloïse (1101–64), the pupil and mistress of Abelard, later a nun.

Heracleidan blood. The Kings of Sparta derived their descent from Hercules (Gr. Heracles).

Hermes. In Greek mythology the messenger of the gods, identified with the Roman Mercury.

Hermes, thrice-great. Hermes Trismegistus, the name given by neo-Platonists to the Egyptian god Thoth. Later various books on alchemy and allied subjects were attributed to Hermes Trismegistus.

Hermion. Hermione, d. of Helen and Menelaus, betrothed to Neoptolemus, who was killed by Orestes.

Hermod. One of the sons of Odin, who went down to the kingdom of the dead to recover the dead god Balder.

Herodes. Herod Antipas, who had St. John the Baptist executed at the request of Salome.

Herro. Hero, the beloved of Leander.

Heywood, Thomas (d. 1650?), dramatist.

Hinksey. There are two villages of this name, South Hinksey, and North or Ferry Hinksey, beneath the ridge of high ground leading to Cumnor.

Hippocrene. A fountain on Mount Helicon, sacred to the Muses.

Hippotades. Aeolus, god of the winds, son of Hippotes.

Hoder. In Scandinavian mythology the blind god Hodur, who was induced by Loki to kill Balder.

Hurst, the. Cumnor Hurst, a hill near Oxford.

Hyades. A constellation, whose rising with the sun was supposed to portend rain. The Greek name Hyades signifies 'the raining ones'.

Hyperion. One of the Titans. Father of Helios, or Apollo, the sun, who dethroned him.

Iberians. The early inhabitants of what are now Spain and Portugal.

Ida. A range of mountains in Phrygia, from the summit of which Zeus watched the Trojan war.

Ierne. A poetical name for Ireland, 'The sweetest lyrist of her saddest wrong' is Thomas Moore, author of Irish Melodies.

Ilioun. Ilion, or Troy.

Ilsley Downs. Part of the Berkshire Downs near Ilsley.

Islands of the Blest. See Elysian.

Isiphilee. Hypsipyle of Lemnos. When the Argonauts spent a year in Lemnos, she bore twin sons to Jason, who then left her.

Isis. An Egyptian goddess, sister and wife of Osiris and mother of Horus, worshipped in the form of a cow.

Ismenus. A river of Boeotia near Thebes.

Isoude. Isolde, the heroine of the romance of Tristan.

Ixion. A Thessalian who attempted to win the love of Hera, wife of Zeus. He was punished by being bound to an ever-turning wheel in Hades.

Jakke Straw. Jack Straw led riots against the Flemings in East Anglia in 1381.

Janus. An ancient Roman god, the custodian of the universe, the opener and shutter of gates, represented with two faces, looking before and after. The doors of his temple in Rome were closed in times of peace and opened in times of war.

Jasoun. Jason.

Jason. Son of Aeson and leader of the Argonauts to Colchis to carry off the Golden Fleece.

Jemshid. A legendary Persian king, celebrated in the *Shah-Nameh* of Firdausi.

Jeremye. The prophet Jeremiah.

Jethro's daughter. Zipporah, wife of Moses.

Jonathas. Jonathan, son of Saul and friend of David.

Jove. See Jupiter.

Jupiter (from Jovis-pater), or *Jove*, chief of the Roman gods and ruler of heaven. Identified with the Greek Zeus.

Juno. In Roman religion the wife of Jupiter, identified with the Greek Hera.

Kempenfelt. Richard Kempenfelt (1718–82), rear-admiral, went down with the *Royal George*.

Kubla Khan. A.D. 1216–94. Founder of the Mongol dynasty in China. His court is described by Marco Polo.

Lacidomie. Lacedaemon or Sparta.

Ladomëa: Laodamia, wife of Protesilaus, who was the first Greek to be killed in the Trojan war. Laodamia killed herself for grief.

Ladon. A river of Arcadia, a tributary of the Alphaeus.

Laian. Of Laius, King of Thebes. He was father of Œdipus, who killed him, as foretold by Apollo.

Lamb, the frolic and the gentle. Charles Lamb (1775–1834), essayist.

Lamedon. Laomedon, an early King of Troy, who tried to cheat the gods after they had helped him build the city.

Lamuel. The king mentioned in Prov. xxxi. 1.

Lars. The Lares, spirits worshipped by the Romans, who had special care of the house and household.

Latmian Shepherd. Endymion, a shepherd on Mt. Latmos when first seen and loved by the Moon.

Laudomia. Laodamia, wife of Protesilaus.

Lavyne. Lavinia, d. of Latinus, King of Latium, married Æneas.

Leander. A youth of Abydos, drowned when swimming the Hellespont to visit his love, the priestess Hero. Hero then drowned herself.

Lemures or *Larvae.* In Roman religion the spirits of the dead.

Lepe, near Cadiz.

Lethe. One of the rivers of Hades. Its waters induced oblivion, and were drunk by souls about to be reincarnated, so that they forgot their previous existence.

Libyc. Libyan, often used as a synonym for Egyptian.

Lityerses song. Lityerses, son of Midas, King of Phrygia, made all comers help in the harvest, until Heracles came and killed him. A harvest song was associated with his name.

Lochiel. The Laird of Lochiel is the chief of the Clan Cameron.

Longinus. The name given to the author of a Greek work 'On the Sublime', of the 1st or 2nd century A.D.

Loth. Lot, who escaped from Sodom with his two daughters.

Louvre. The Palace of the Louvre in Paris, now the national art gallery.

Lucifer. The morning star.

Lucresse. Lucretia, wife of Tarquinius Collatinus, who killed herself after being raped by Sextus Tarquinius.

Lycaeus. A mountain in Arcadia, on which there was a sanctuary to Pan.

Lycidas. The name of a shepherd in Theocritus, Bion, and Virgil. Used by Milton for his friend Edward King, drowned in the Irish Sea.

Lydian airs. One of the 4 modes of Greek music, that expressing tender and sorrowful feelings, which Plato banned from the Republic.

Lyonnesse. In the Arthurian legends the land of Tristram's birth. Supposed to be the submerged region between Cornwall and the Scillies.

Maenad. A female votary of Dionysus, the Greek god of wine.

Maenalus. A mountain in Arcadia, sacred to Pan.

Maeonides. Homer, so named from Maeonia, an ancient name of Lydia, one of the districts which claimed to be his birth-place.

Maevius. A poetaster attacked in Virgil's 3rd Eclogue and Horace's 10th Epode.

Marathon. A plain near Athens where the Athenians, under Miltiades, defeated the Persians in 490 B.C.

Marcellus. Marcus Claudius Marcellus, nephew and adopted son of Augustus, who died at the age of 20, and is celebrated by Virgil at the end of the 6th book of the Æneid. Dryden calls Oldham 'Marcellus of our tongue' on account of his comparatively early death.

Marcia Catoun. Marcia, d. of M. Cato Uticensis.

Margaret Queen. Keats probably alludes to Margaret of Anjou, the fierce queen of Henry VI.

Mars. Roman god of war, lover of Venus, identified with Greek Ares.

Mart. Mars, the God of War.

Medea. d. of Aëtes of Colchis, an enchantress. For the sake of Jason she left her house and murdered her brother and his uncle. When Jason cast her off to marry the d. of Creon, King of Corinth, she killed the King and his daughter, and then her own two children by Jason.

Memnon's sister. Memnon, a beautiful but black Egyptian prince slain by Achilles (*Odyssey*, xi. 522). His sister's name was Hemera.

Memphian. Of Memphis, the ancient capital of Egypt and centre of the worship of the gods.

Merlin. The enchanter who looked after Arthur in his infancy and aided him after he became king.

Miltiades. Miltiades the younger, tyrant of the Chersonese, who commanded the Athenian forces at Marathon.

Mincius. The river Mincio, a tributary of the Po, which it joins near Mantua. As Virgil dwelt on its banks, Milton uses it to typify Roman poetry.

Moloch. A god of the Phoenicians, whose rites included the sacrifice of children.

Mona. The Isle of Man.

Moore. Thomas Moore (1779–1852), Irish poet.

Morpheus. The Greek god of dreams.

Mount Abora. Coleridge was perhaps thinking of Milton's Mount Amara (Amhara in Johnson's *Rasselas*), a district of Abyssinia.

Musaeus. A legendary Greek poet, said to have been a pupil of Orpheus.

Naiads. Nymphs of the springs, rivers, and lakes.

Namancos. A place near Finisterre in Galicia, marked on Mercator's map, near the castle of Bayona.

Neaera. The name of a shepherdess in Virgil's Eclogues.

Nero. Roman Emperor A.D. 54–68.

Nisus. (1) Friend of Euryalus. They both take part in the boat-race in the 5th book of the Æneid. (2) King of Megara. See Scylla (2).

Odin. The chief Scandinavian deity, the father of the gods.

Odysseus. King of Ithaca, hero of the *Odyssey*, which recounts the story of his return home, after 10 years of wanderings, from the Trojan war.

Og. Deut. iii. 2. Used by Dryden for Thomas Shadwell.

Oldham. John Oldham (1653–83), poet.

Oldmixon. John Oldmixon (1673–1742).

Olympia. Olympias, the mother of Alexander.

Olympus. A mountain overlooking the vale of Tempe. In Greek mythology, its summit was regarded as the dwelling-place of the gods.

Omer. Homer.

Oreb. Mt. Horeb, part of the

Sinai range, on which Moses received the law.

Orgunje. In central Asia. The Oxus, after flowing west for much of its course, here turns NW. towards the Aral Sea.

Orion. The constellation of that name. Virgil and Milton call it armed, because of the Belt and Sword.

Orpheus. A legendary Greek poet, son of Calliope, one of the Muses, said to play on the lyre so that all who heard were spellbound. Went down to Hades, and by his playing induced Persephone and Pluto to restore his dead wife Eurydice. He broke the condition that he should not look at her until they reached the upper air and she vanished for ever. Orpheus was later torn to pieces by Thracian Maenads, and his head floated down the river Hebrus still speaking.

Orus. The Egyptian god Horus, son of Isis and Osiris, worshipped in the form of a hawk.

Osiris. Egyptian god, brother and husband of Isis, worshipped in the form of the sacred bull Apis.

Otter. A character in Ben Jonson's play *Epicoene.*

Otway. Thomas Otway (1652–85), dramatist.

Ovyde. Publius Ovidius Naso, 43 B.C.–A.D. 17. Roman poet.

Oxus. Now the Amu Daria or Jihun, the principal river of central Asia. It rises near Pamir on the frontiers of Eastern Turkestan and empties itself into the Aral Sea.

Ozymandias. The tomb of Rameses II at Thebes is called by Diodorus Siculus, the tomb of Ozymandias.

Palestine, twice-battered god of.

Dagon, the half-human, half-fish god worshipped by the Philistines.

Pamere. Pamir on the borders of eastern Turkestan, where the Oxus rises.

Pan. Originally an Arcadian deity, the god of flocks and inventor of the shepherd's pipe, represented as a man with goat's horns and legs.

Pardlike Spirit. Shelley himself.

Parga. A city on the Albanian coast. The inhabitants made an heroic resistance to the Turks, and in 1819 destroyed their city and migrated rather than submit.

Parnasse. Parnassus, a mountain near Delphi, sacred to Apollo and the Muses.

Parthes. Parthia, a country in Western Asia, east of Media and south of Hyrcania.

Pegasean. Of Pegasus, the winged horse of the Muses.

Pelops line. Pelops was the father of Atreus, and grandfather of Agamemnon, Menelaus, and Aegisthus, great-grandfather of Orestes, Iphigenia, and Electra. The history of the Atrides was the subject of many Greek tragedies, e.g. the *Oresteia*, a trilogy by Æschylus, the *Electra*, *Orestes*, *Iphigenia* of Euripides, the *Electra* of Sophocles.

Penelopee. Penelope, wife of Odysseus, the type of the faithful wife.

Peneus. The principal river of Thessaly, which flows through the vale of Tempe.

Peor. A name of Baal.

Persepolis. Ancient Persian capital, destroyed by Alexander.

Phebus. Phœbus Apollo, the sun-god.

Philip's warlike son. Alexander the Great.

Phillis. See *Demophoon.*

Philomel. The nightingale. Philomela, sister of Procne, was outraged by her brother-in-law, who cut out her tongue so that she should not tell. She was turned into a nightingale and Procne into a swallow.

Phineus. A legendary King of Salmydessus, blinded, and tormented by Harpies, according to one account because of his misuse of the gift of prophecy.

Phyllis. The name of a shepherdess in one of Virgil's Eclogues.

Pierides. An epithet of the Muses, the original seat of their worship having been at Pieria on the slopes of Mt. Olympus.

Pilgrim of Eternity. Byron.

Pilot of the Galilaean lake. St. Peter.

Pirrus. Pyrrhus or Neoptolemus, son of Achilles; killed Priam at the sack of Troy.

Pluto. Roman god of the underworld.

Polixene. Polyxena, d. of Priam, sacrificed on the tomb of Achilles.

Polycrates. Tyrant of Samos in the 2nd half of the 6th century B.C.

Pouke. Puck.

Prince of the Brazils. The Prince Regent of Portugal, who removed his government to Brazil during the Napoleonic occupation of Portugal.

Priamus. Priam, King of Troy.

Prior, Mat. Matthew Prior (1664–1721), poet.

Prometheus. The son of the Titan Iapetus. According to a Greek myth, he made mankind out of clay, and stole fire from heaven to give them. To punish him for his rebellious conduct, Zeus chained him to a rock in the Caucasus, where an eagle daily fed on his liver, which was restored in the night.

Proserpine. Greek Persephone, the daughter of Zeus and Demeter, carried off by Hades and made his queen in the lower world. Her mother sought her through the earth. Zeus finally arranged that Persephone should spend half the year in Hades and half on earth.

Proteus. An 'old man of the sea' in Greek mythology, with the power of changing his shape as often as he wished.

Psyche. A girl loved by Cupid, who visited her only in the dark. When out of curiosity she lit a lamp to look at him, he left her, and she was set many tasks by Venus (who was jealous of her) before being reunited to her lover.

Pyrrhic dance. The Spartan mimic war-dance. The origin of the name is unknown.

Pyrrhic phalanx. The phalanx was the Macedonian military formation consisting of sixteen ranks of foot soldiers armed with long spears. Pyrrhus, King of Epirus, was a cousin of Alexander the Great.

Racine. Jean Racine (1639–99), French dramatic poet.

Rafael, Raphael. Raffaello Sanzio (1483–1520), the famous Italian painter.

Reni, Guido. (1575–1642) Italian painter.

Rhodope. A mountain range in Thrace.

Rochel. La Rochelle, French port on the Bay of Biscay.

Rochester, mitred. Francis Atterbury, Bishop of Rochester (1662–1732).

Rogers. Samuel Rogers (1763–1855), poet.

Romano. Giulio Romano (1492–1546), pupil of Raphael. Dryden mistakenly thought of him as the master of Raphael.

Rotha. The stream which flows past the churchyard at Grasmere, where Wordsworth is buried.

Ruth. The principal character in the O.T. Book of Ruth. She gleaned in the fields of Boaz, who married her, and was the ancestor of David.

St. Agnes. The patron saint of virgins. Girls used to perform various rites on the eve of her festival, in order to dream of their future husbands.

St. John. Henry St. John, Viscount Bolingbroke (1678–1751).

Salamis. The Greeks, in 480 B.C., defeated the fleet of Xerxes, King of Persia, off Salamis, an island near Athens.

Samian wine. From Samos, an island off the coast of Asia Minor.

San Sisto. Raphael's Sistine Madonna is now at Dresden.

Sandford. A village on the Thames some five miles below Oxford.

Sappho. Lesbian woman poet, 7th century B.C.

Saturn. Roman god of agriculture identified with Greek Cronos, the father of Zeus. The period of his rule was the Golden Age on earth.

Saul. The first King of Israel. When he was mad he was soothed by the harp-playing of the shepherd boy David.

Scian Muse. Homer. Scio, the ancient Chios, was one of the places which claimed to have given him birth.

Scipio. Publius Cornelius Scipio Africanus Major, 236–183 B.C. Commanded Roman forces in Spain at the age of 25, and on his return was made consul though under the legal age. He was opposed by the aged Fabius.

Scylla. (1) Daughter of Phorcys and Hecate, loved by Poseidon, and turned, by her rival Amphitrite, into a monster which seized and devoured sailors near her cave, which was situated on the Straits of Messina opposite the whirlpool Charybdis.
(2) Daughter of Nisus, King of Megara, for love of Minos betrayed her father who was safe so long as a purple lock among his white hair was intact. She was turned into a sea-gull forever pursued by her father, who was turned into a sea-eagle.

Senek. Lucius Annaeus Seneca, *c.* 4 B.C.–A.D. 65. Roman stoic philosopher.

Shadwell, Thomas (1642?–92), dramatist and poet, an enemy and butt of Dryden, whom he succeeded as poet laureate.

Sheffield. John Sheffield, 3rd Earl of Mulgrave and 1st Duke of Buckingham (1648–1721).

Shirley, James (1596–1666), a prolific dramatist.

Shrewsbury, wanton. Countess of Shrewsbury, mistress of 2nd Duke of Buckingham, who killed the Earl of Shrewsbury in a duel.

Sicilian Muse. Pastoral poetry, in allusion to the Sicilian poet Theocritus.

Sinai. The mountain on which Moses received the law.

Somers. John, Lord Somers (1651–1716).

Southern. Thomas Southern (1659–1746), dramatist.

Sphinx. A monster, who propounded riddles and destroyed those who could not answer them. Œdipus succeeded in answering her riddle, whereupon she killed herself.

Stace. Statius, the Latin poet.

Stilbon. The story is told in the Polycraticus of John of Salisbury, the name there being given as Chilon, one of the seven Sages.

Strode. Ralph Strode (fl. 1350–1400), scholastic philosopher and logician.

Stygian. Of the Styx, the principal river of the underworld.

Suli's rock. A mountain in Southern Albania, a district which was never wholly subdued by the Turks.

Sunium. The southernmost point of Attica. A temple of Athene stood on the headland.

Swift. Jonathan Swift (1667–1745), satirist.

Sylvan. Silvanus, Roman god of the woods.

Syrinx. A nymph loved by Pan, who fled him and was turned into a reed.

Syrtes. Gulfs of the coasts of Tripoli and Tunis.

Talbot, courtly. Charles Talbot, 12th Earl and only Duke of Shrewsbury (1660–1718).

Tanaquil. The wife of Tarquinius Priscus, the first King of Rome. Spenser uses the name to signify Queen Elizabeth.

Tate. Nahum Tate (1652–1715), poetaster and dramatist.

Teian muse. Anacreon, the Greek lyric poet, born at Teos in Ionia.

Telemachus. The son of Odysseus and Penelope.

Tellus. In Roman mythology the Earth, the equivalent of the Greek Ge, wife of Uranus and mother of the Titans.

Tempe. A valley in Thessaly, through which the river Peneus flows; celebrated for its beauty.

Tertulan. Tertullian, *De Exhortatione Castitatis.*

Tewnes. Tunis.

Thais. A famous Athenian courtesan. Athenaeus states that she was kept by Alexander, and that it was after drinking with her that he destroyed Persepolis.

Thamuz. The Syrian Adonis, whose death and resurrection were annually celebrated by women.

Thamyris. A Thracian poet who challenged the Muses to a trial of skill and was by them deprived of sight and of the power of song.

Thebes. The capital of Boeotia, and the scene of Aeschylus' *Seven against Thebes;* of the *Œdipus Tyrannus* and *Antigone* of Sophocles, and the *Bacchae* of Euripides.

Theofraste. Theophrastus; a fragment of his *de Nuptiis* was preserved in St. Jerome's treatise against Jovinian.

Thermopylae. A narrow pass on the boundary of Thessaly, the eastern gate of Greece, held against the Persians for 2 days by a small force of Greeks. The final stand was made by 300 Spartans who were all killed, together with their king Leonidas.

Thessaly, forest ground called. On the outskirts of Bagley Wood.

Thestylis. The name of a girl in one of the Eclogues of Theocritus.

Thisbe. A town in Boeotia, abounding in doves.

Thomas, St. Thomas Becket, Archbishop of Canterbury, 1118–1170. 'Watering of seint Thomas', a stream crossed by the Canterbury Road near Southwark.

Thracian Bard. Orpheus.

Thyrsis. The name of a shepherd in Virgil's Eclogues. Arnold uses the name to designate his friend Arthur Hugh Clough (1819–61).

Tibbald, piddling. Lewis Theobald (1688–1744), editor of Shakespeare.

Timon. 5th c. B.C. Athenian misanthrope.

Timotheus. Athenaeus gives this as the name of a flute-player at Alexander's wedding, and Suidas says he could move Alexander as he would by his music. Dryden may have confused him with the great musician of the same name who d. B.C. 357.

Tiresias. Teiresias, a blind Theban soothsayer.

Tirynthian groom. Hercules, son of Zeus and Alcmena; his labours were performed for Eurystheus at Tiryns.

Tisbee. Thisbe, a maiden of Babylon, loved by Pyramus. She killed herself on his sword when she found him dying.

Titans. In Greek mythology the children of Uranus and Ge, who were defeated by the younger Olympian gods, led by Zeus.

Tom the First. Thomas Rhymer, historiographer royal, an office in which he was succeeded by Shadwell.

Tom the Second. Thomas Shadwell.

Triton. In Greek mythology a merman, son of Poseidon, commonly represented blowing a conch.

Troilus. A younger son of Priam, whose love for the false Cressida was a favourite subject of medieval romance.

Trotula. Not identified.

Tuscan artist. Galileo (1564–1642), who made various astronomical discoveries with the aid of the telescope. He spent his later years at Florence.

Typhon. A monster with a hundred serpents' heads, slain by Zeus; identified by the Greeks with the Egyptian god Set, brother of Osiris.

Tyro Apollonius. A Greek novel, surviving only in a later translation; the ultimate source of Shakespeare's Pericles.

Ulysses. Latin name of Odysseus, q.v.

Urania. The Muse of Astronomy. But Milton uses the name for a personification of divine inspiration, in which he was followed by Shelley.

Utopia. The name was invented by Sir Thomas More for his book of that name, published 1516, describing an imaginary island, with a perfect social and political system. It is from Greek *ou*, not, and *topos*, place. William Morris, therefore, calls his English Utopia, Nowhere.

Valdarno. The valley of the Arno, in which Florence is situated.

Valerie. Walter Map's *Epistola Valerii ad Rufinum de non ducenda uxore.*

Vallombrosa. A shady valley about 18 miles from Florence.

Venus. In Roman religion the goddess of love, identified with the Greek Aphrodite.

Vesta. Roman goddess of the hearth, identified with Greek Hestia, d. and wife of Cronos (= Roman Saturn).

Villiers. George Villiers, 2nd Duke of Buckingham (1627–87), d. at Helmsley in Yorkshire.

Vision of the guarded mount. St. Michael, said to have been seen sitting on St. Michael's Mount looking out to sea.

Vitruvius (*c.* 50–26 B.C.) author of a treatise *De Architectura.*

Waller. Edmund Waller (1606–87), poet.

Walsh, knowing. William Walsh (1663–1708), critic and man of fashion, an early patron of Pope.

Western Straits. The Straits of Gibraltar.

Winander. Windermere, earlier Winandermere.

Wycherly. William Wycherly (1640–1716), dramatist.

Wychwood. Wychwood forest, some miles north-west of Oxford.

Wytham. A small village near the Thames above Oxford.

Xanadu. Coleridge got this name from *Purchas, his Pilgrimage* (1619): 'in Xanadu did Cublai Can build a stately palace'.

Yarrow. The River Yarrow, which joins the Ettrick near Selkirk.

Ynd. India.

Ypermistra. Hypermnestra, one of the Danaides, the fifty daughters of Danaus who married their cousins, the sons of Aegyptus. Hypermnestra alone disobeyed the order of Danaus that they should kill their husbands on the marriage night.

Ysiphile: see Isiphilee.

Zephirus. Zephyrus, the west wind.

Zoroaster. The Greek form of Zarathrustra, the name of the founder of the Persian religion of sun worship.

PRINTED IN
GREAT BRITAIN
AT THE
UNIVERSITY PRESS
OXFORD
BY
JOHN JOHNSON
PRINTER
TO THE
UNIVERSITY

In time   World dead

In time to come when the moon
O three times thrice infinity
And the sun shines but at
And glittering stars put

The Undertow

Time is an
        abstract
    rope weaver